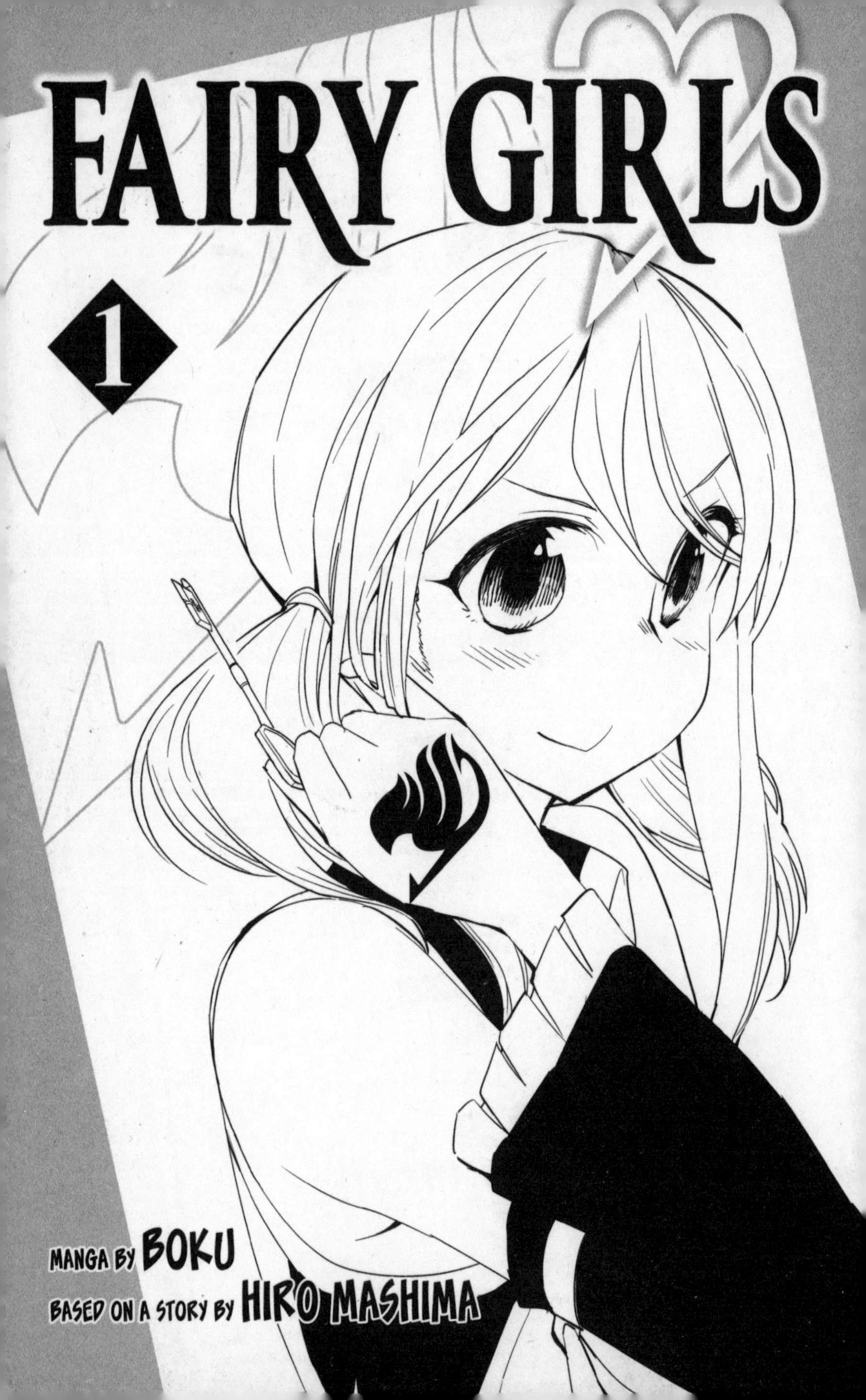
FAIRY GIRLS
1
MANGA BY BOKU
BASED ON A STORY BY HIRO MASHIMA

CONTENTS

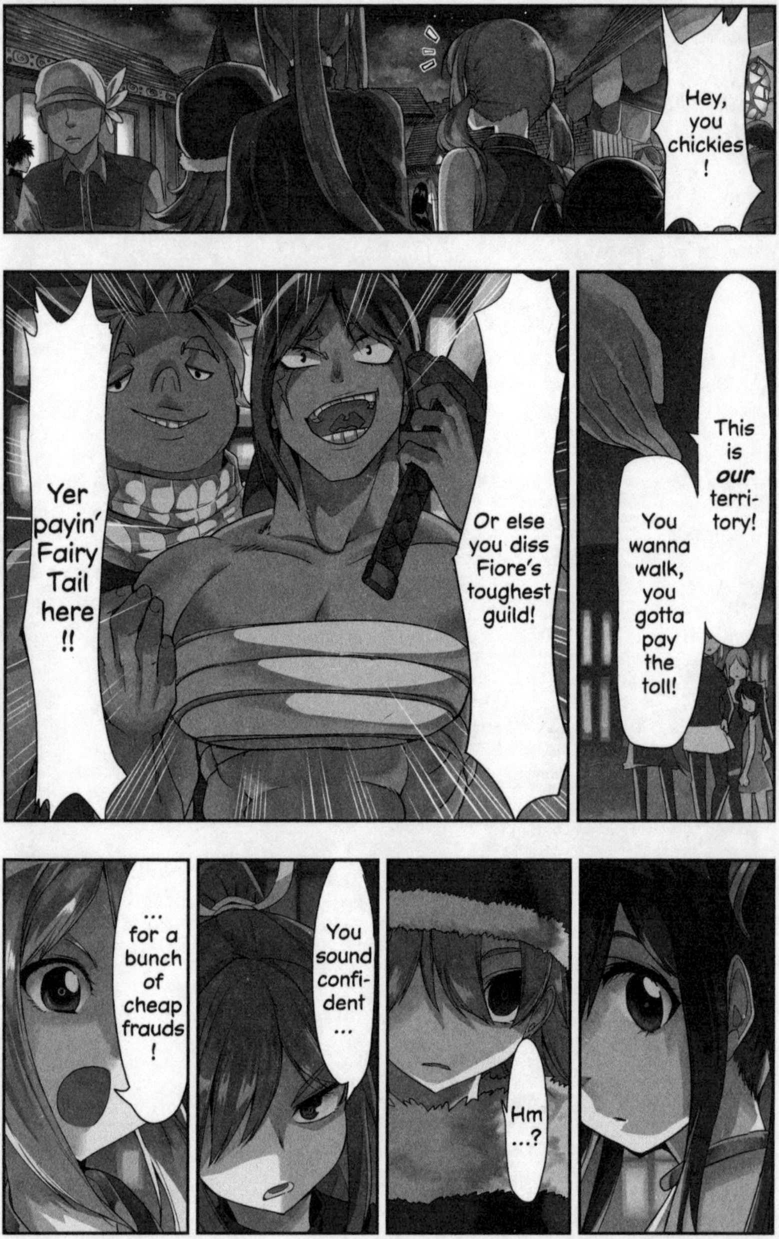
Hey, you chickies!
This is *our* territory!
You wanna walk, you gotta pay the toll!
Or else you diss Fiore's toughest guild!
Yer payin' Fairy Tail here!!
Hm...?
You sound confident...
...for a bunch of cheap frauds!

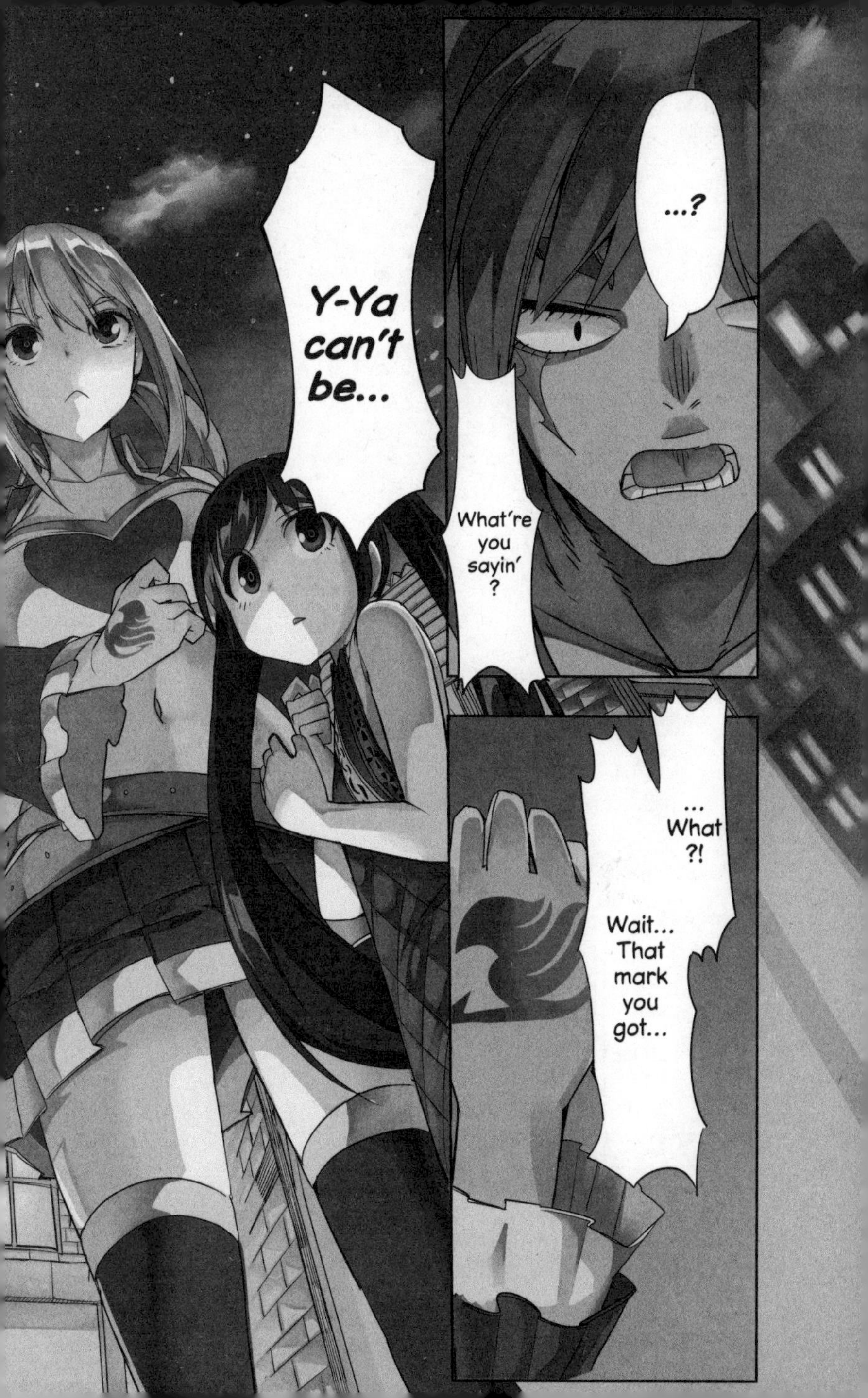
...?
What're you sayin' ?
... What ?!
Wait... That mark you got...
Y-Ya can't be...

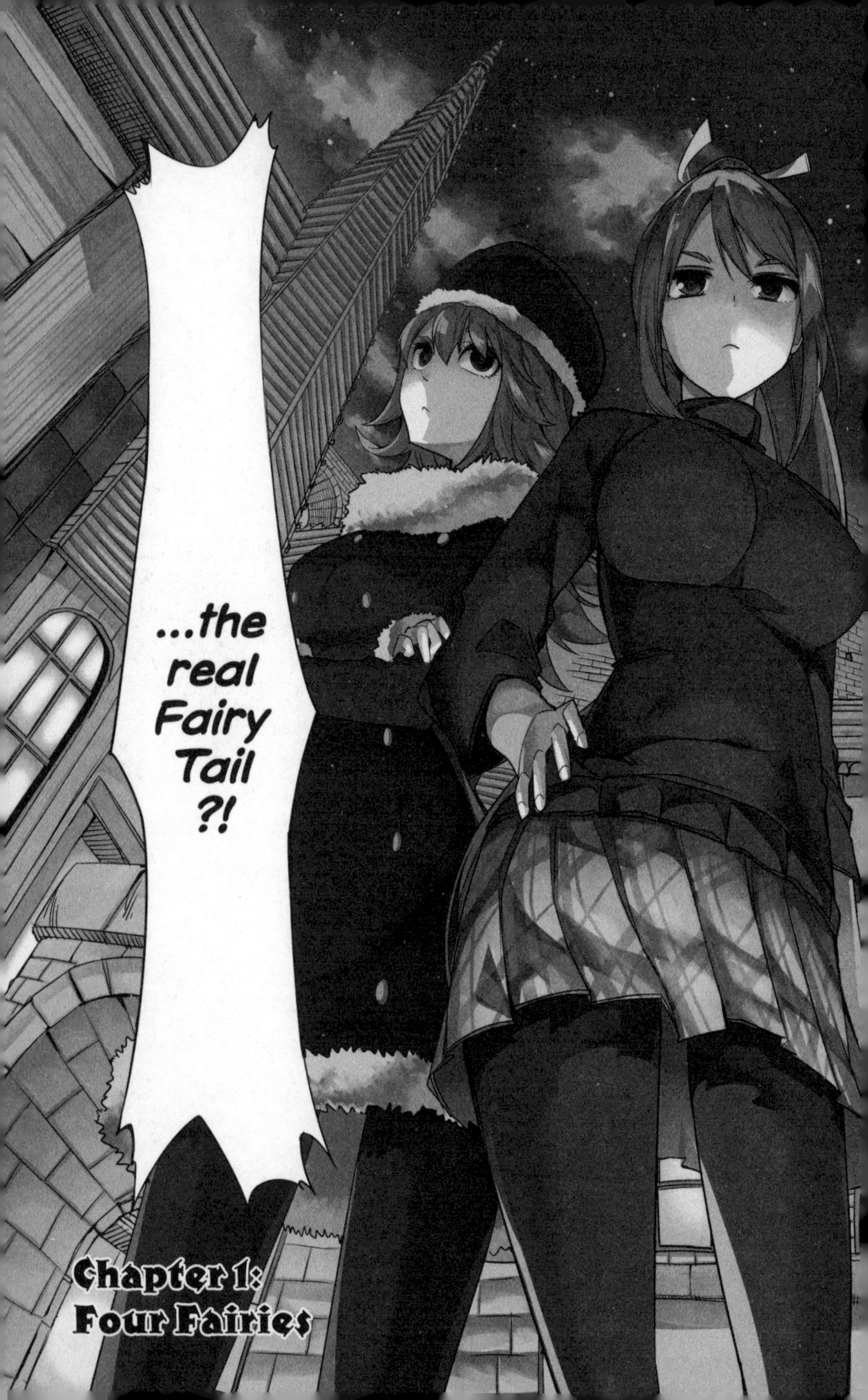
...the real Fairy Tail ?!
Chapter 1: Four Fairies

FAIRY GIRLS

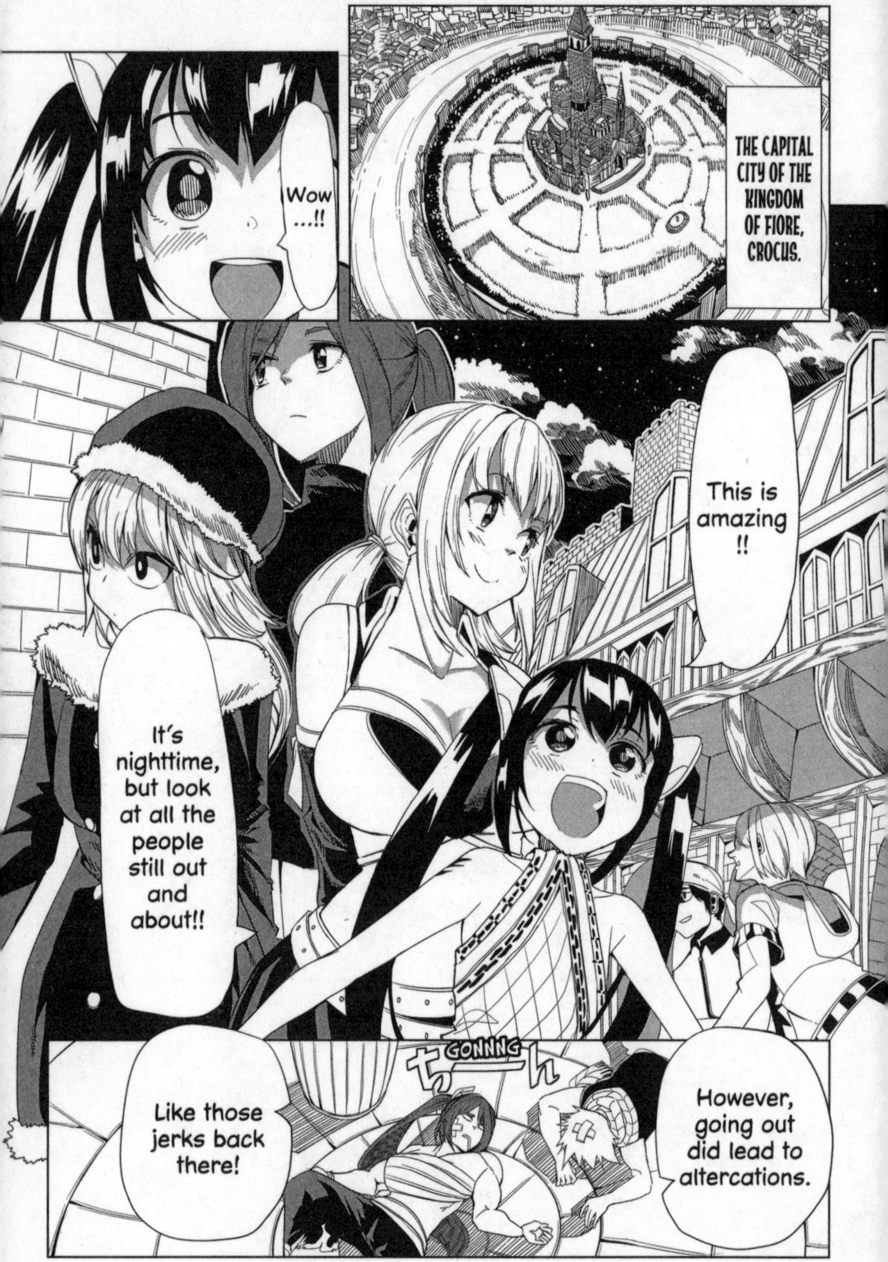
THE CAPITAL CITY OF THE KINGDOM OF FIORE, CROCUS.
Wow ...!!
This is amazing !!
It's nighttime, but look at all the people still out and about!!
However, going out did lead to altercations.
GONNNG
Like those jerks back there!

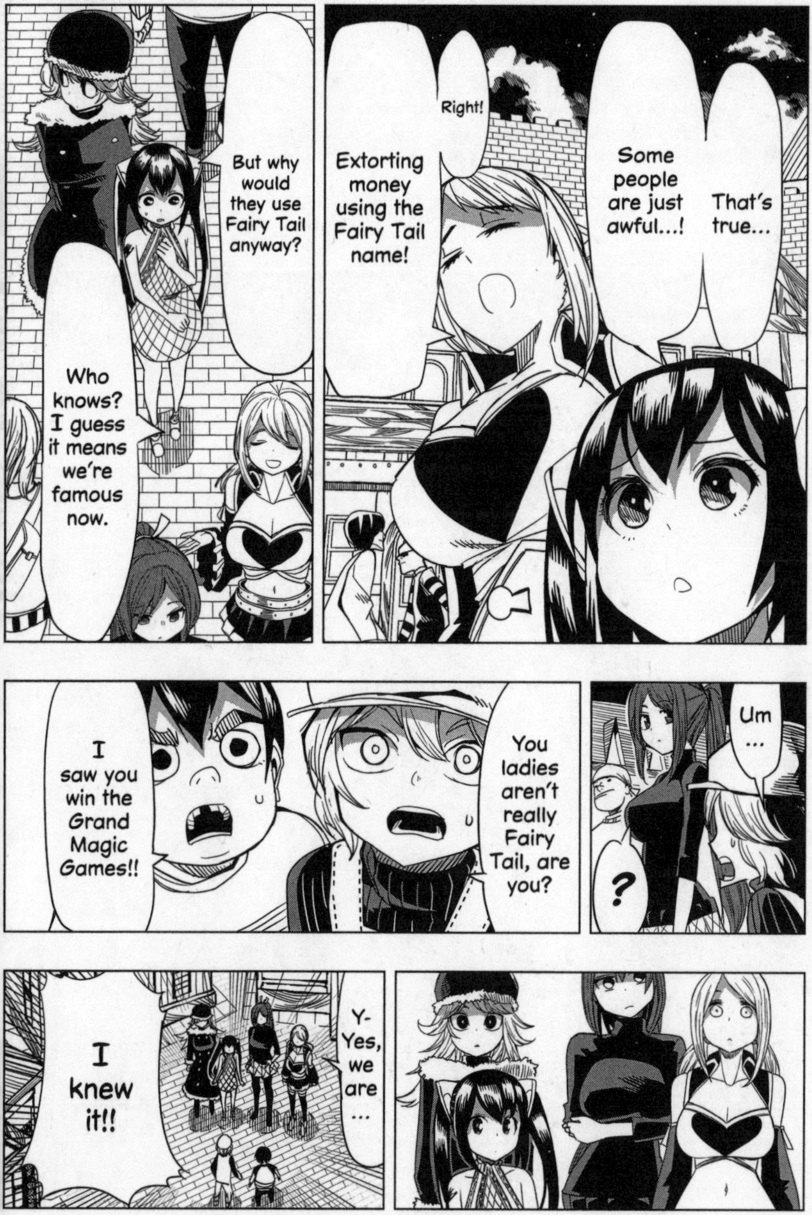
That's true...
Some people are just awful...!
Right!
Extorting money using the Fairy Tail name!
But why would they use Fairy Tail anyway?
Who knows? I guess it means we're famous now.
Um ...
?
You ladies aren't really Fairy Tail, are you?
I saw you win the Grand Magic Games!!
Y-Yes, we are ...
I knew it!!

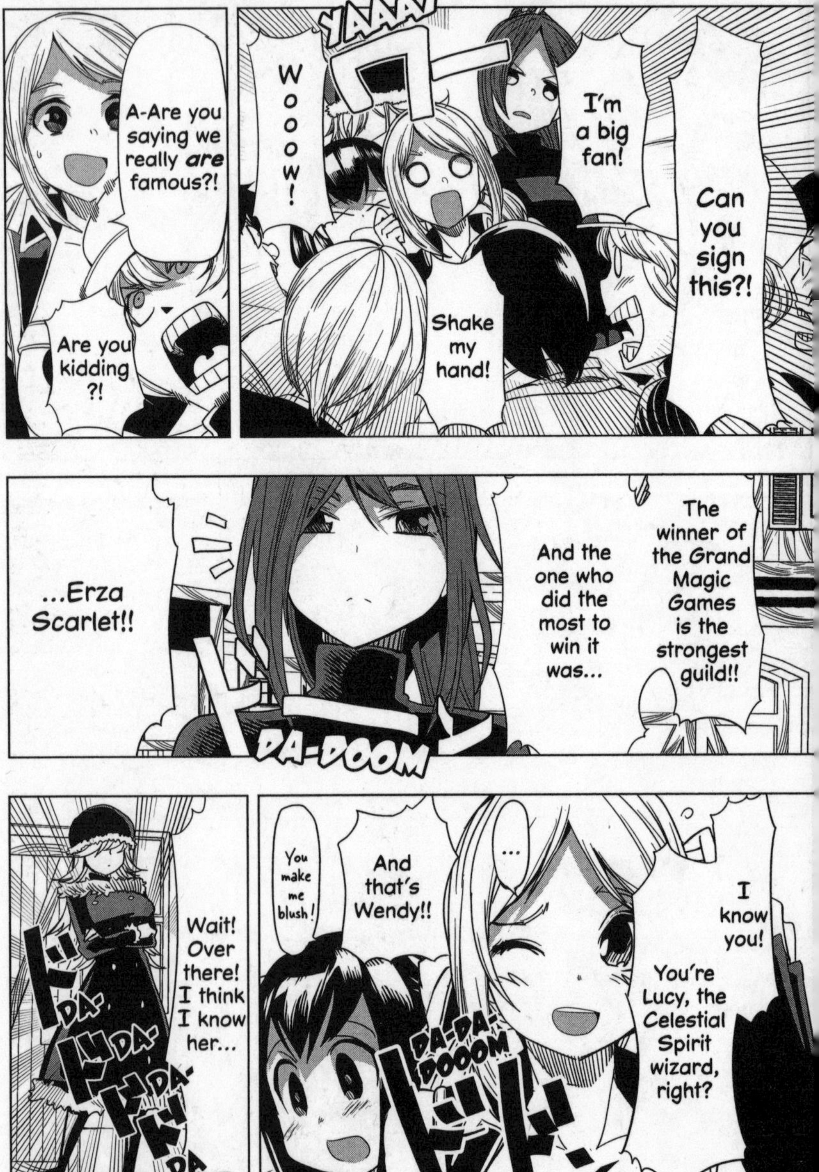
Can you sign this?!
I'm a big fan!
YAAAY
Woooow!
Shake my hand!
A-Are you saying we really *are* famous?!
Are you kidding?!
The winner of the Grand Magic Games is the strongest guild!!
And the one who did the most to win it was...
...Erza Scarlet!!
DA-DOOM
I know you!
You're Lucy, the Celestial Spirit wizard, right?
...
And that's Wendy!!
You make me blush!
DA-DA-DOOOM
Wait! Over there! I think I know her...
DA-DA-DA-DA

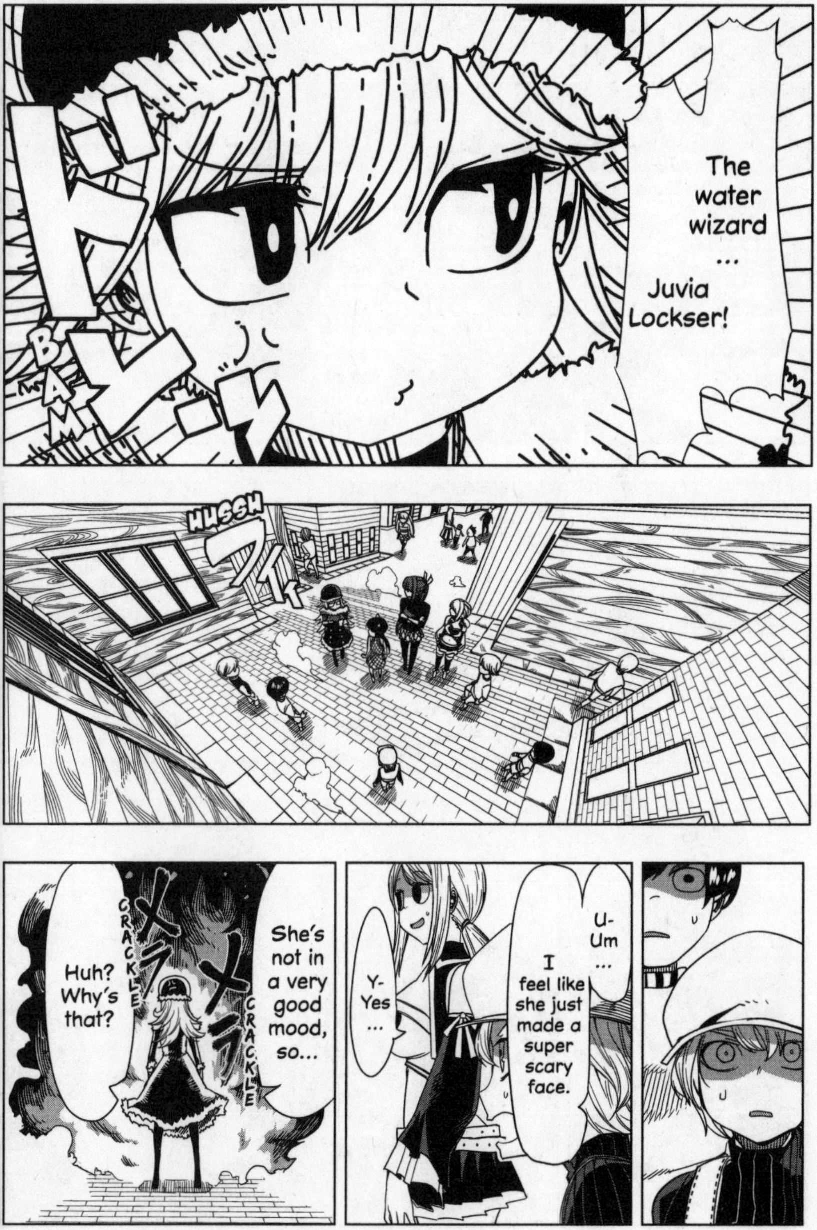
The water wizard ... Juvia Lockser!
BAM
HUSSH
U-Um ...
I feel like she just made a super scary face.
Y-Yes ...
She's not in a very good mood, so...
CRACKLE
CRACKLE
Huh? Why's that?

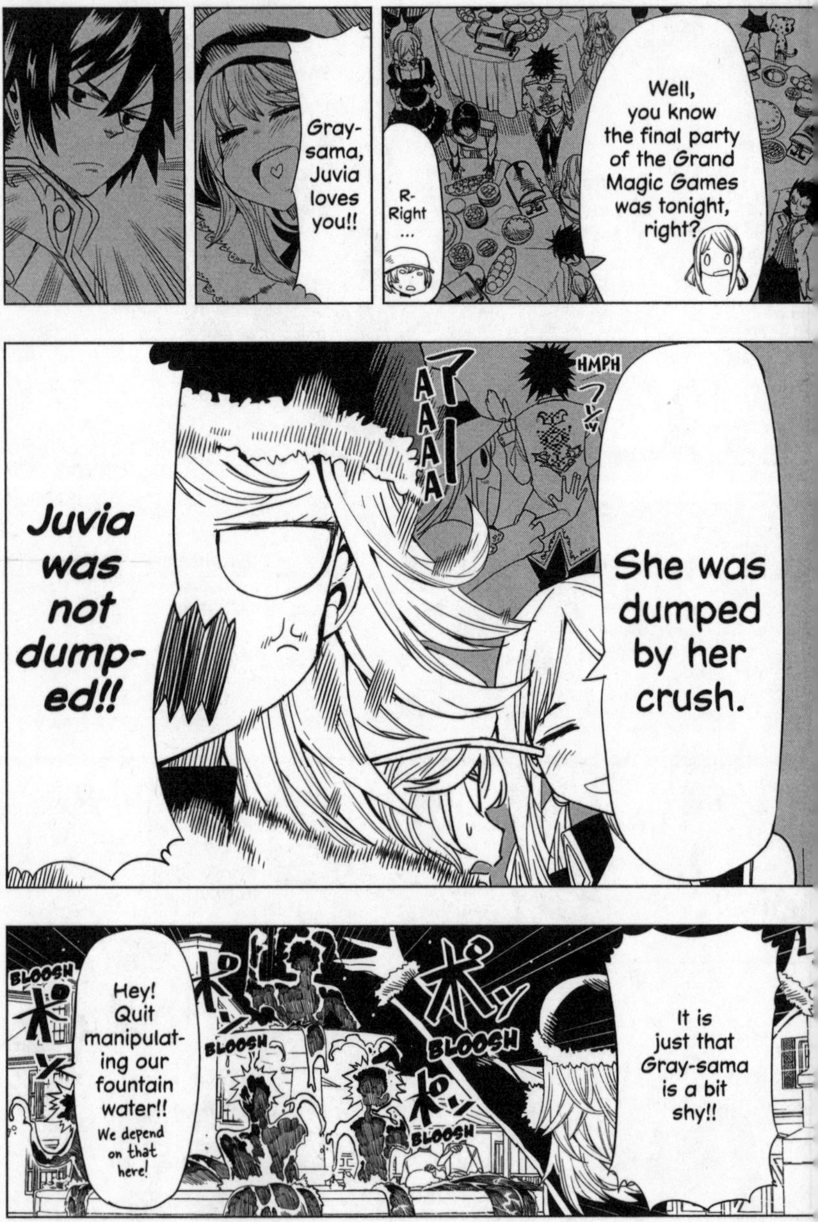
Well, you know the final party of the Grand Magic Games was tonight, right?
R-Right ...
Gray-sama, Juvia loves you!!
She was dumped by her crush.
HMPH
AAAAA
Juvia was not dump-ed!!
It is just that Gray-sama is a bit shy!!
BLOOSH
BLOOSH
BLOOSH
BLOOSH
Hey! Quit manipulat-ing our fountain water!!
We depend on that here!

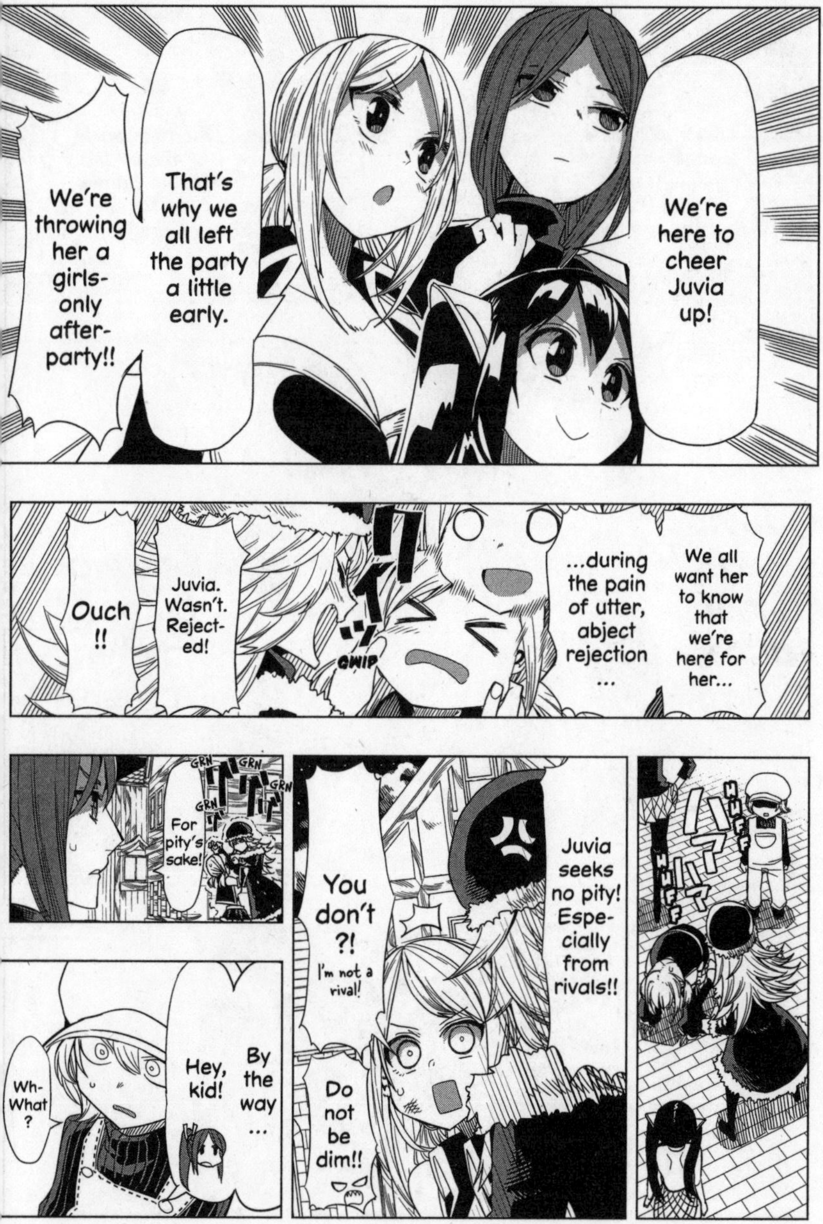
We're here to cheer Juvia up!
That's why we all left the party a little early.
We're throwing her a girls-only after-party!!
We all want her to know that we're here for her...
...during the pain of utter, abject rejection...
GWIP
Juvia. Wasn't. Reject-ed!
Ouch!!
HUFF
HUFF
Juvia seeks no pity! Especially from rivals!!
You don't?!
I'm not a rival!
Do not be dim!!
GRN GRN GRN GRN
For pity's sake!
By the way...
Hey, kid!
Wh- What?

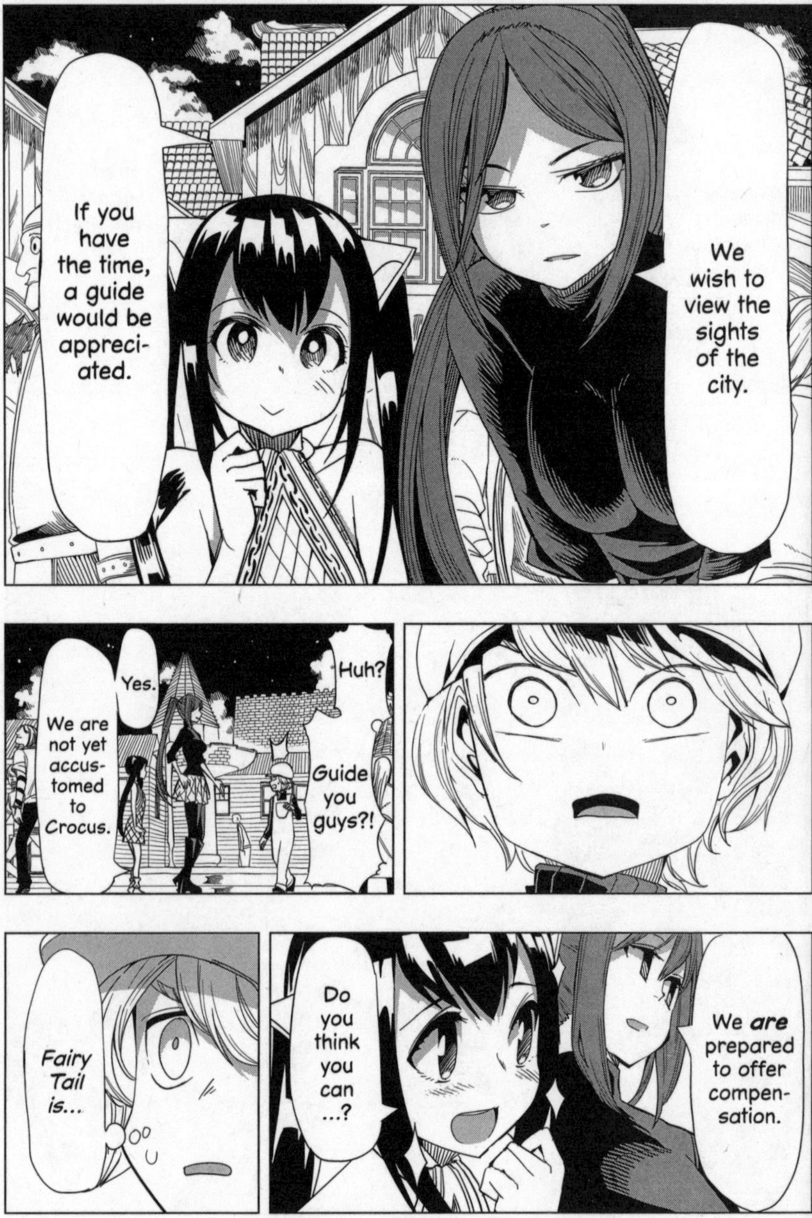
We wish to view the sights of the city.
If you have the time, a guide would be appreciated.
Huh?
Guide you guys?!
Yes.
We are not yet accustomed to Crocus.
We ***are*** prepared to offer compensation.
Do you think you can ...?
Fairy Tail is...

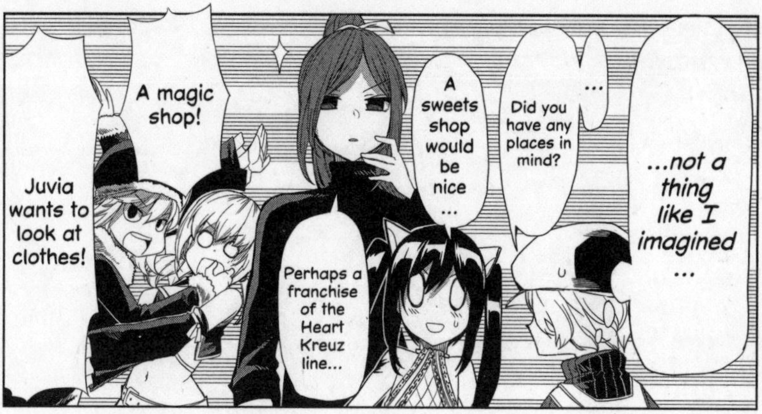
...not a thing like I imagined ...
...
Did you have any places in mind?
A sweets shop would be nice ...
Perhaps a franchise of the Heart Kreuz line...
A magic shop!
Juvia wants to look at clothes!

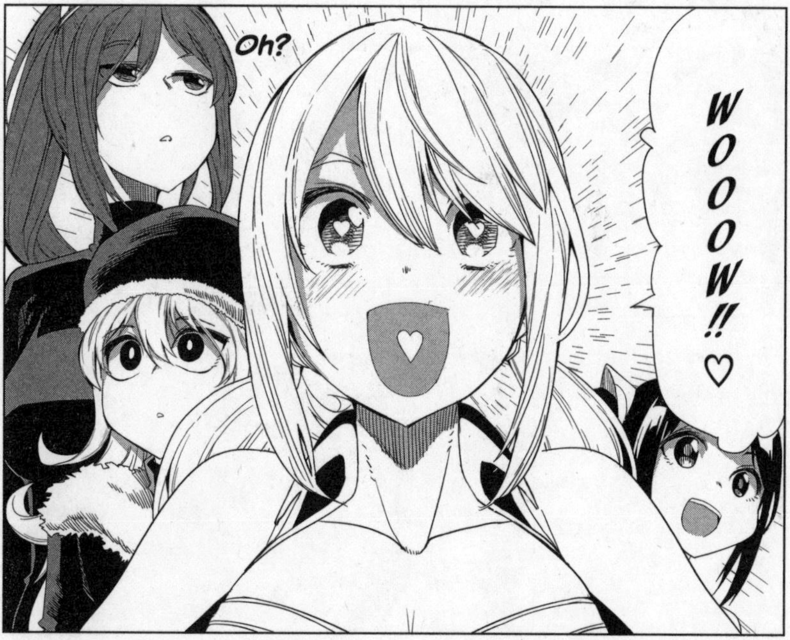
WOOOOW!! ♡
Oh?

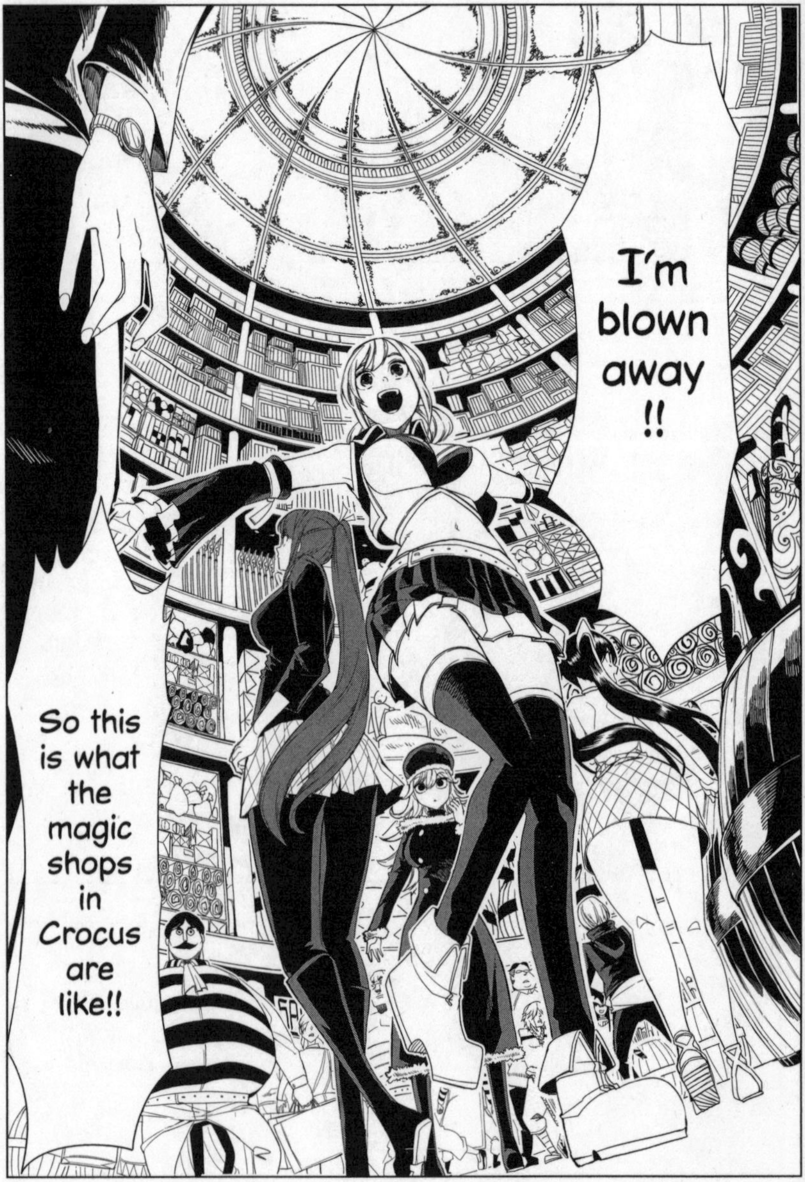
I'm blown away!!
So this is what the magic shops in Crocus are like!!

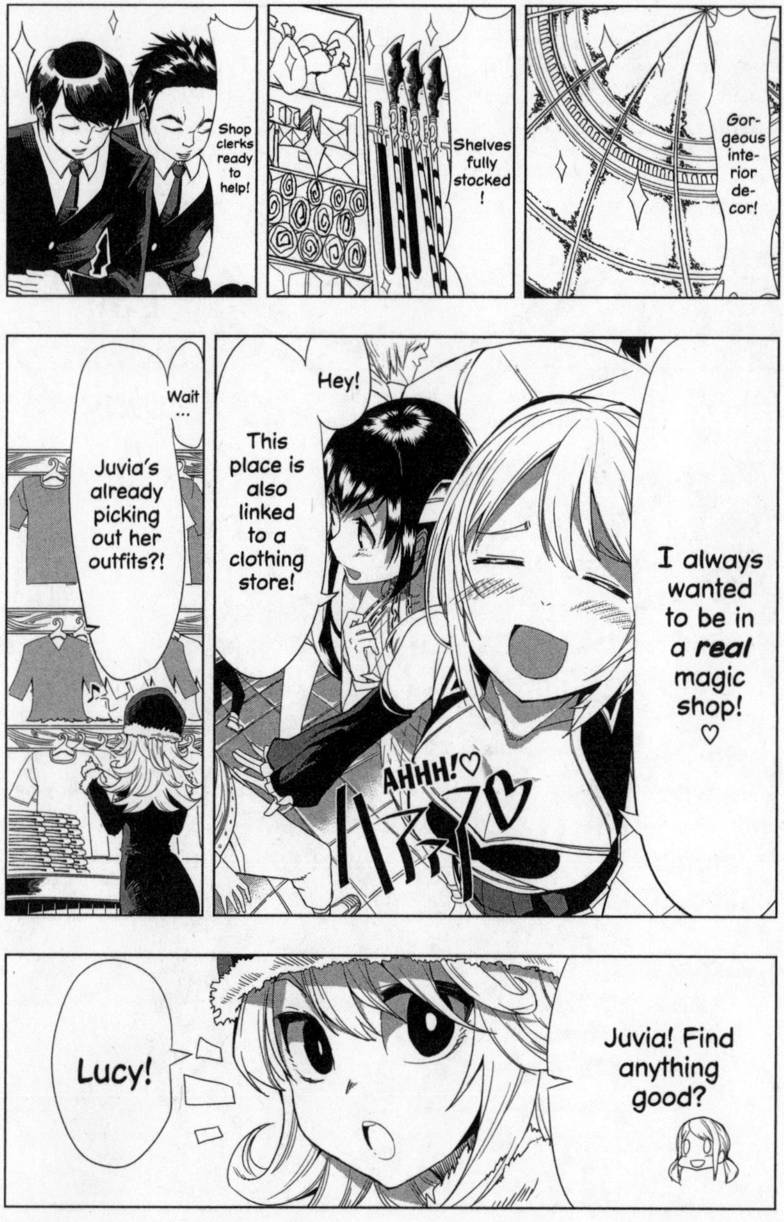
Gor-geous inte-rior de-cor!
Shelves fully stocked!
Shop clerks ready to help!
I always wanted to be in a *real* magic shop! ♡
AHHH!♡
Hey!
This place is also linked to a clothing store!
Wait ...
Juvia's already picking out her outfits?!
Juvia! Find anything good?
Lucy!

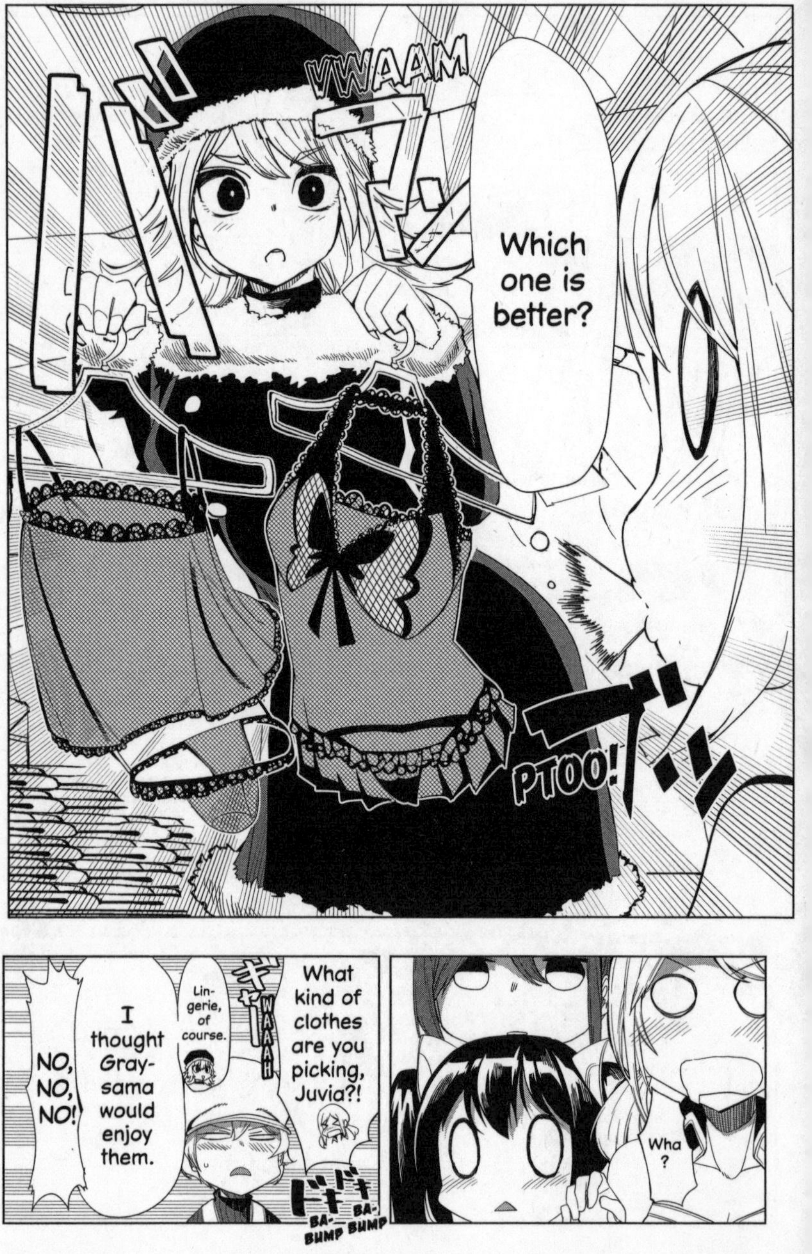
VWAAM
Which one is better?
PTOO!
Wha?
What kind of clothes are you picking, Juvia?!
WAAAH
Lin-gerie, of course.
I thought Gray-sama would enjoy them.
NO, NO, NO!
BA-BUMP BA-BUMP

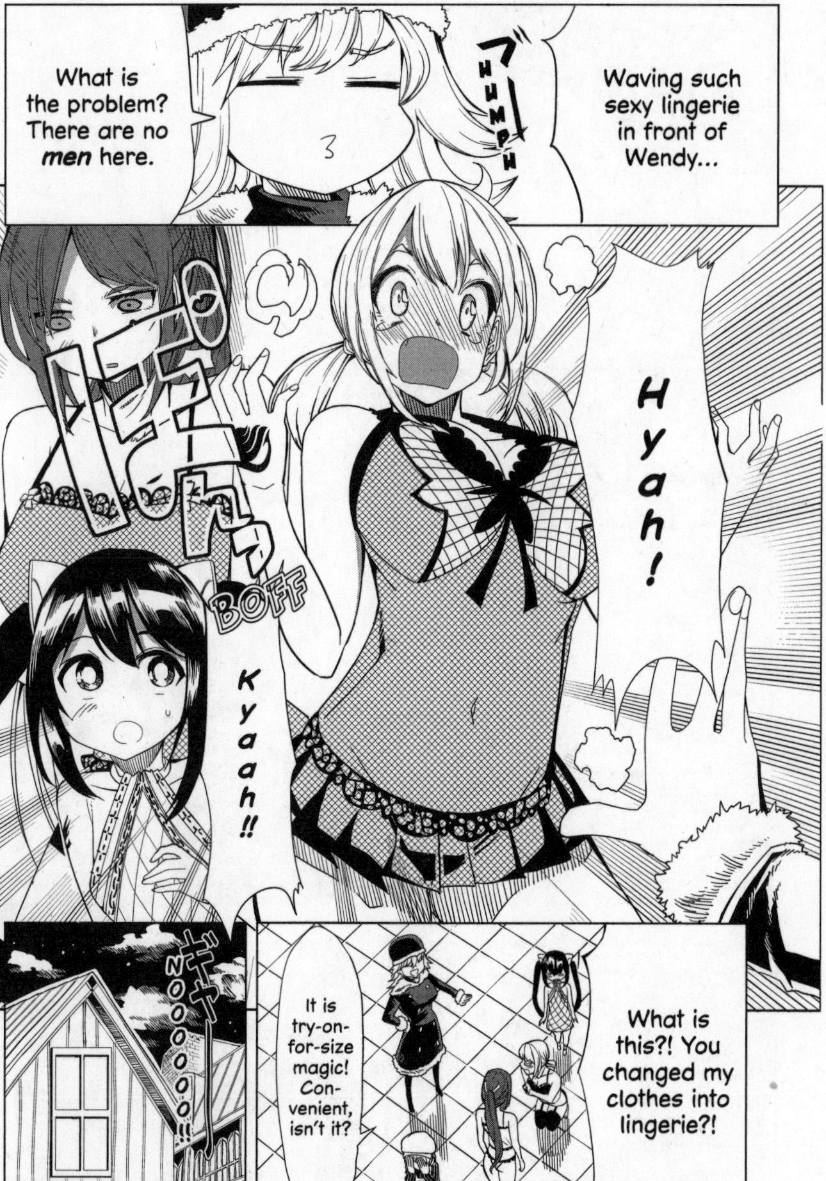
Waving such sexy lingerie in front of Wendy...
HUMPH
What is the problem? There are no men here.
Hyah!
BOFF
Kyaah!!
What is this?! You changed my clothes into lingerie?!
It is try-on-for-size magic! Convenient, isn't it?
NOOOOOOOO!!

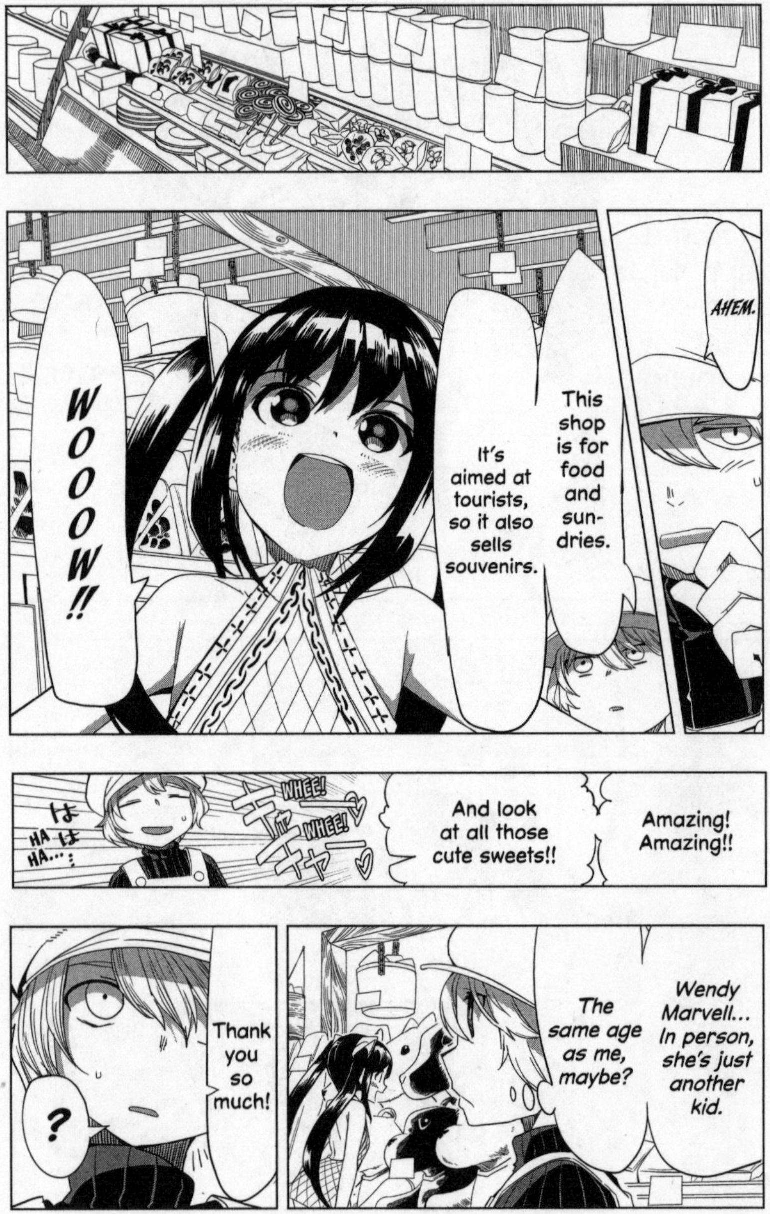
AHEM.
This shop is for food and sundries.
It's aimed at tourists, so it also sells souvenirs.
WOOOOW!!
Amazing! Amazing!!
And look at all those cute sweets!!
キャー WHEE!
キャー WHEE!
はは HA
はは HA...
Wendy Marvell... In person, she's just another kid.
The same age as me, maybe?
Thank you so much!
?

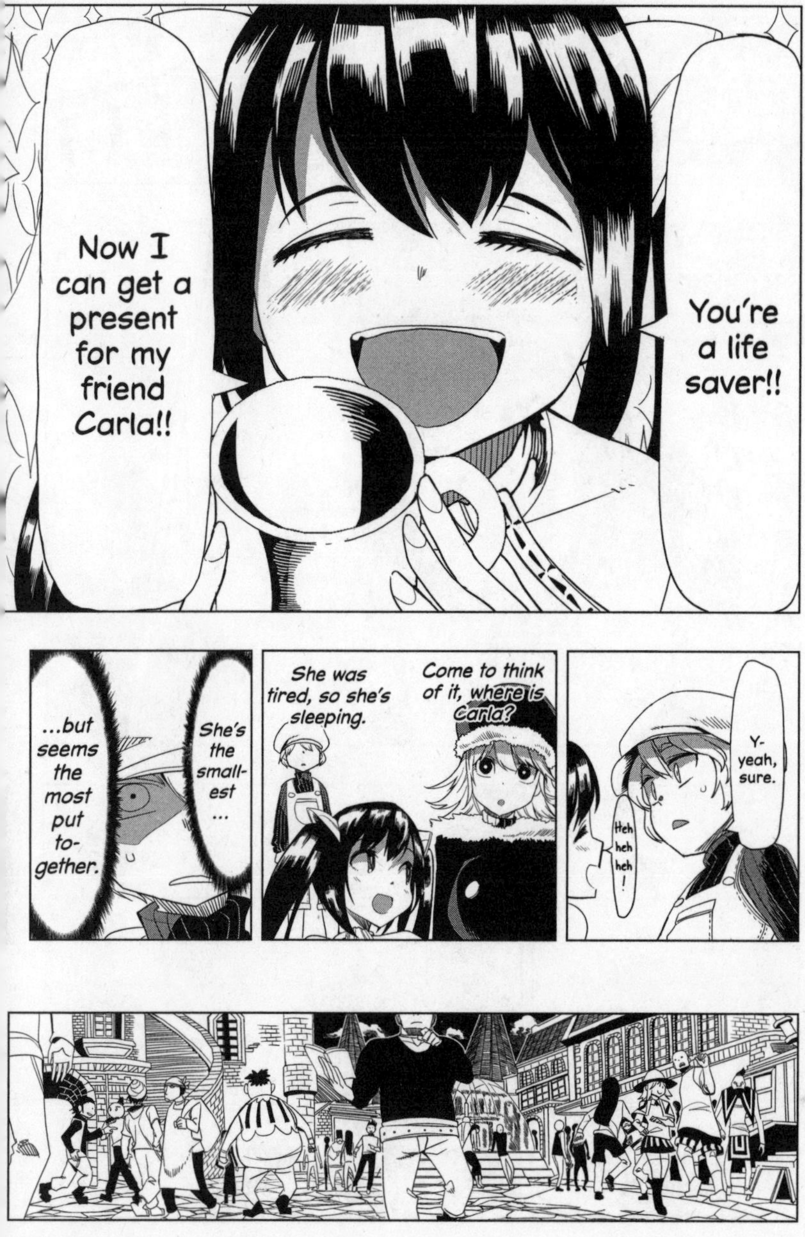
You're a life saver!!
Now I can get a present for my friend Carla!!
Y- yeah, sure.
Heh heh heh!
Come to think of it, where is Carla?
She was tired, so she's sleeping.
She's the small- est ...
...but seems the most put to- gether.

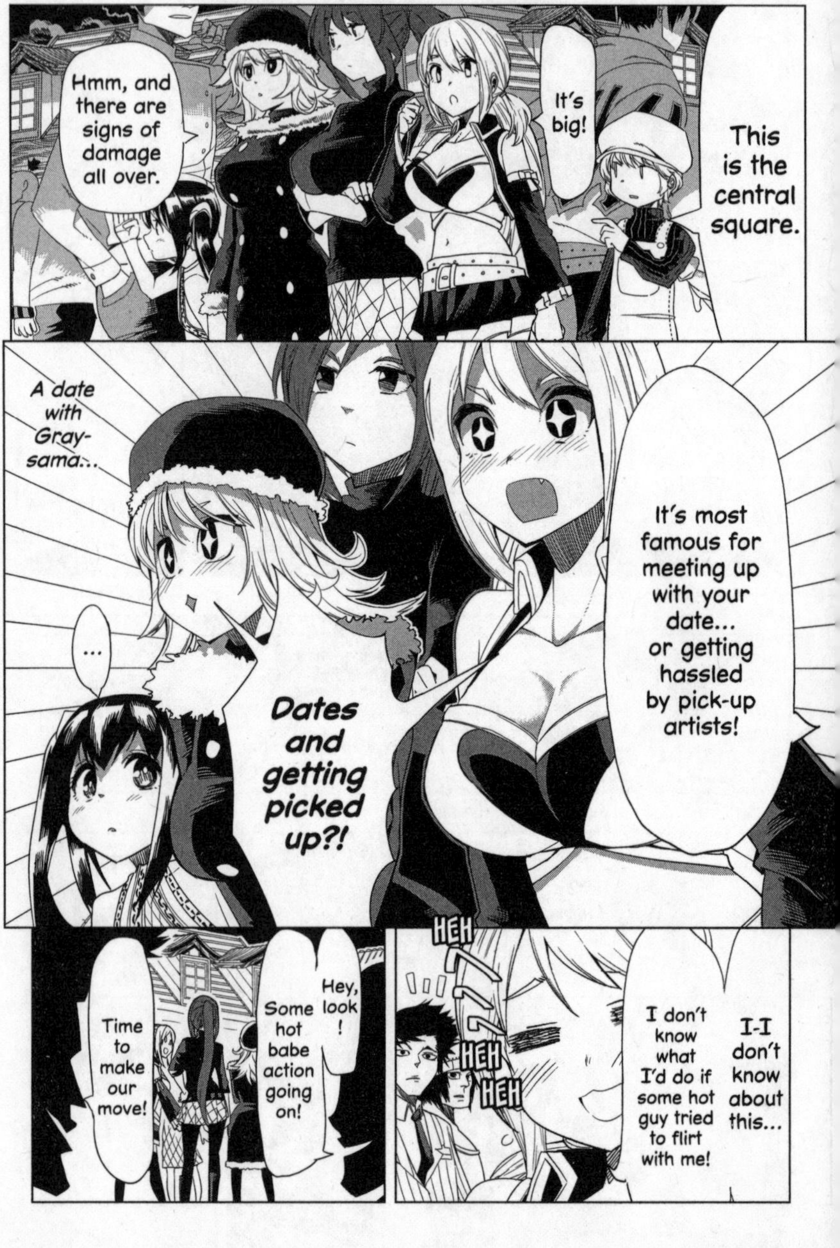
This is the central square.
It's big!
Hmm, and there are signs of damage all over.
It's most famous for meeting up with your date... or getting hassled by pick-up artists!
Dates and getting picked up?!
A date with Gray-sama...
...
I-I don't know about this...
I don't know what I'd do if some hot guy tried to flirt with me!
HEH HEH HEH
Hey, look!
Some hot babe action going on!
Time to make our move!

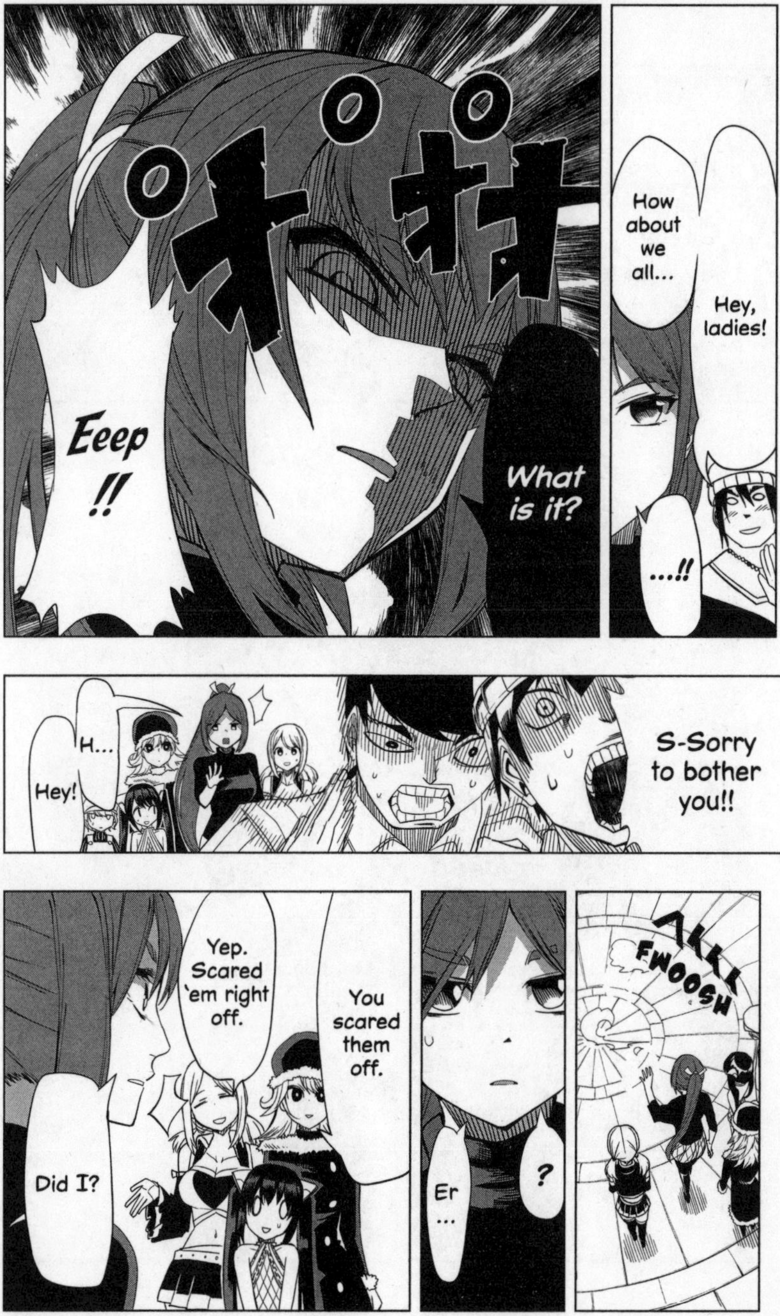
Hey, ladies!
How about we all...
...!!
What is it?
Eeep !!
S-Sorry to bother you!!
H...
Hey!
FWOOSH
?
Er ...
You scared them off.
Yep. Scared 'em right off.
Did I?

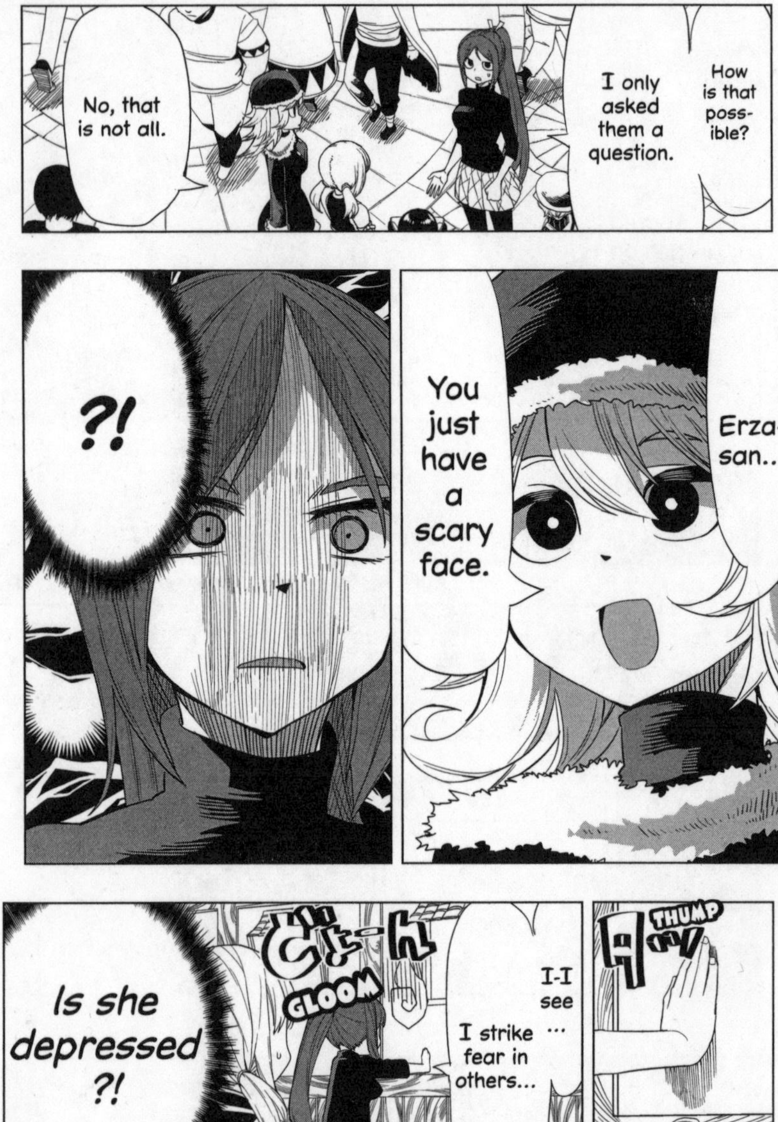
How is that possible?
I only asked them a question.
No, that is not all.
Erza-san...
You just have a scary face.
?!
THUMP
I-I see...
I strike fear in others...
GLOOM
Is she depressed?!

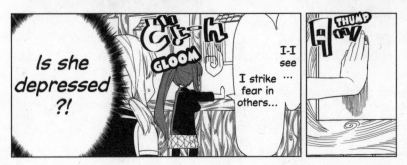

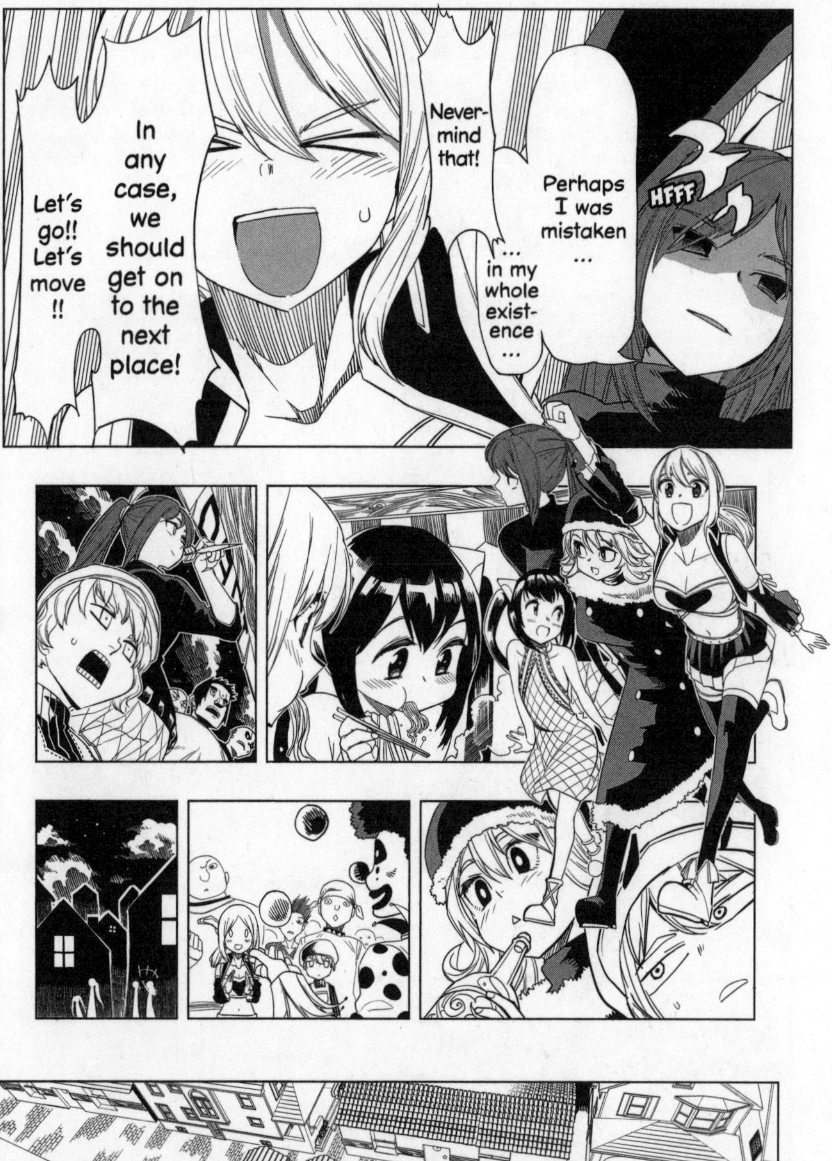
Perhaps I was mistaken ...
HFFF
... in my whole exist-ence ...
Never-mind that!
In any case, we should get on to the next place!
Let's go!! Let's move !!

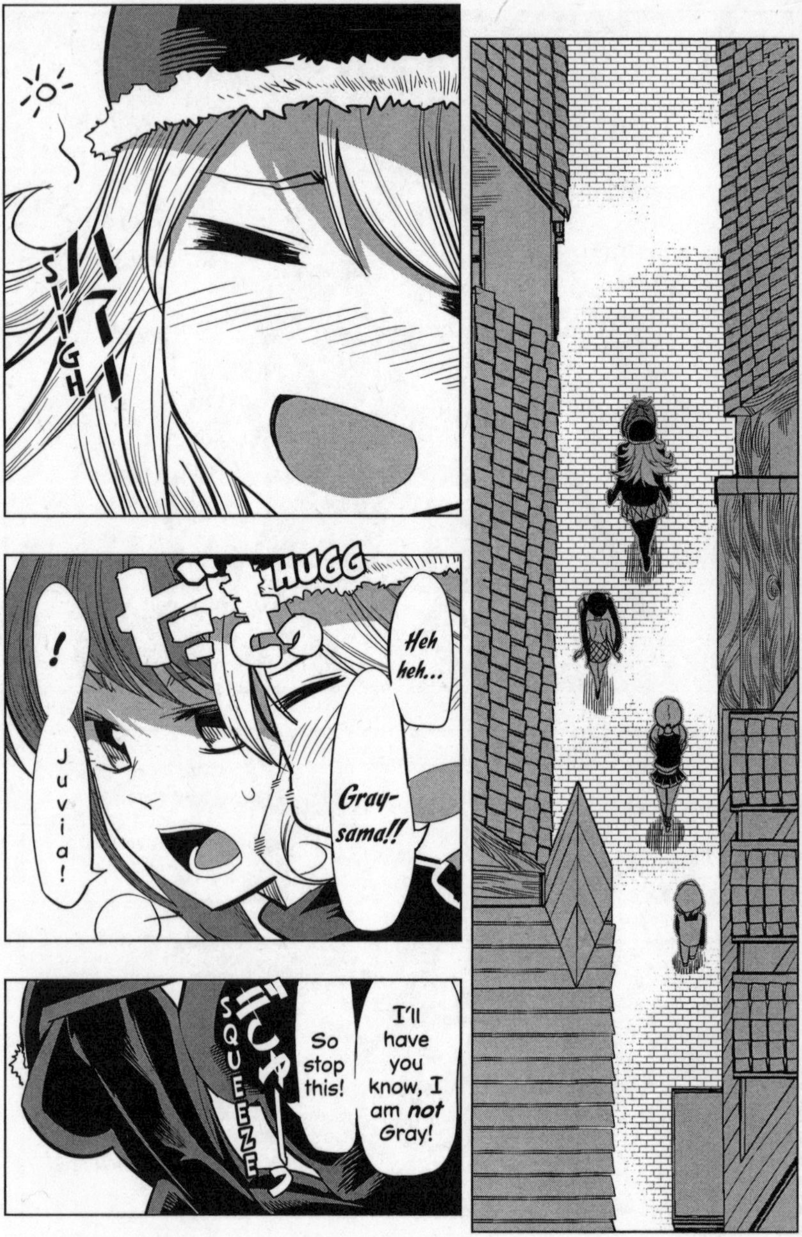
SIGH
HUGG
Heh heh...
Gray-sama!!
!
Juvia!
I'll have you know, I am *not* Gray!
So stop this!
SQUEEZE

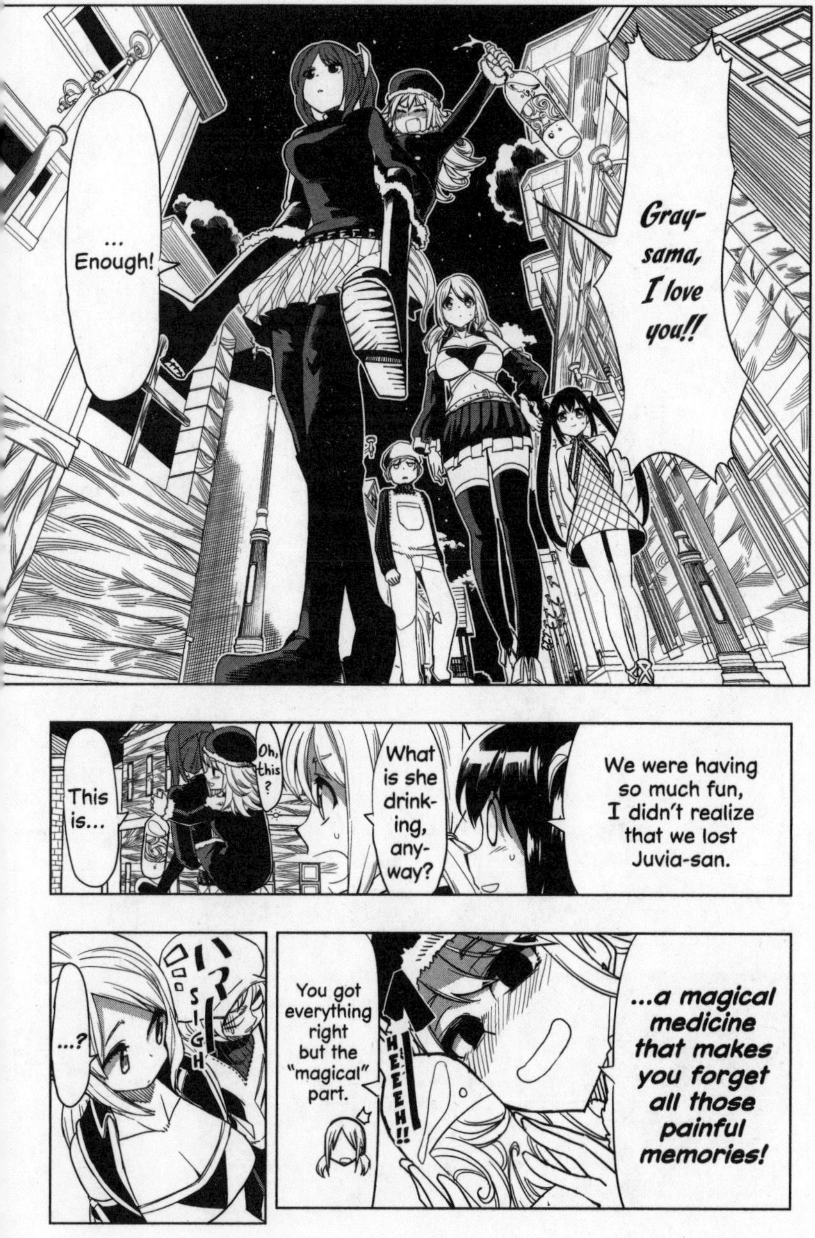
Gray-sama, I love you!!
... Enough!
We were having so much fun, I didn't realize that we lost Juvia-san.
What is she drinking, anyway?
Oh, this?
This is...
...a magical medicine that makes you forget all those painful memories!
HEEEEH!!
You got everything right but the "magical" part.
SIGH
...?

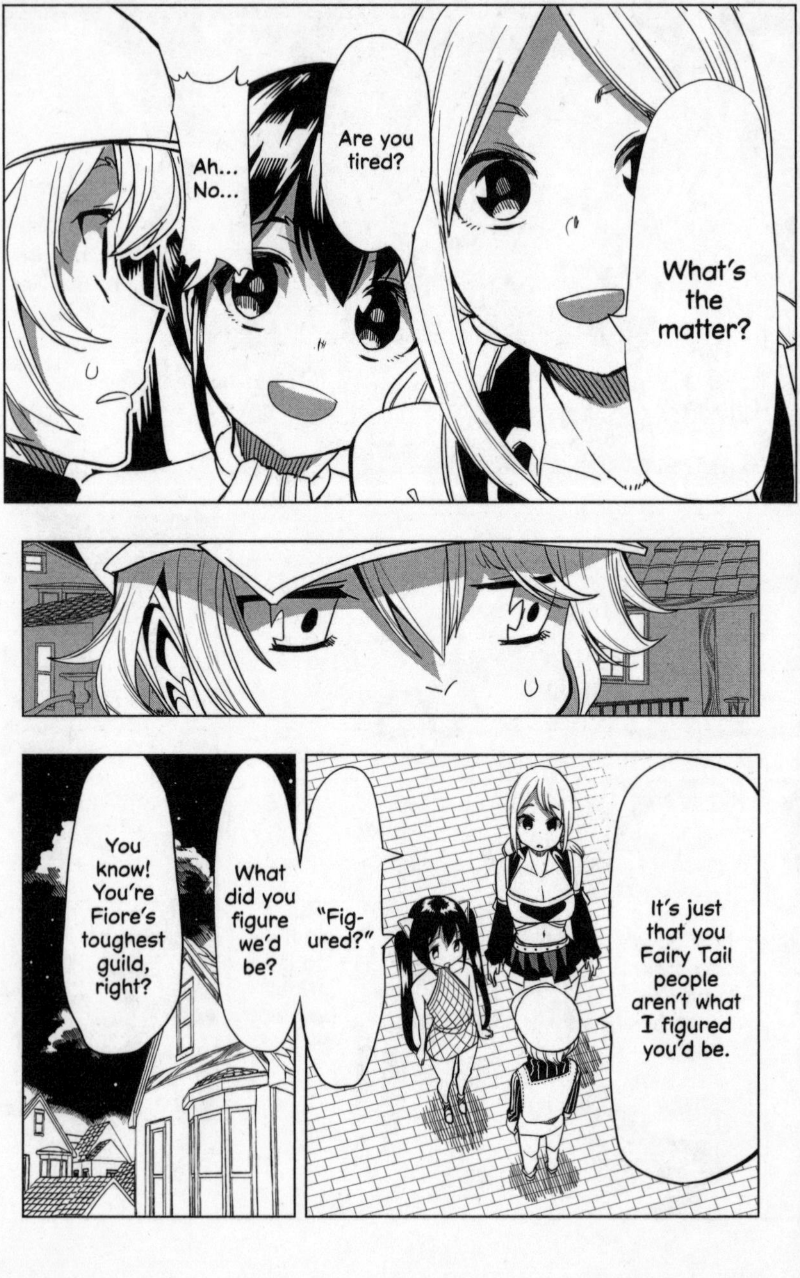
What's the matter?
Are you tired?
Ah... No...
It's just that you Fairy Tail people aren't what I figured you'd be.
"Fig-ured?"
What did you figure we'd be?
You know! You're Fiore's toughest guild, right?

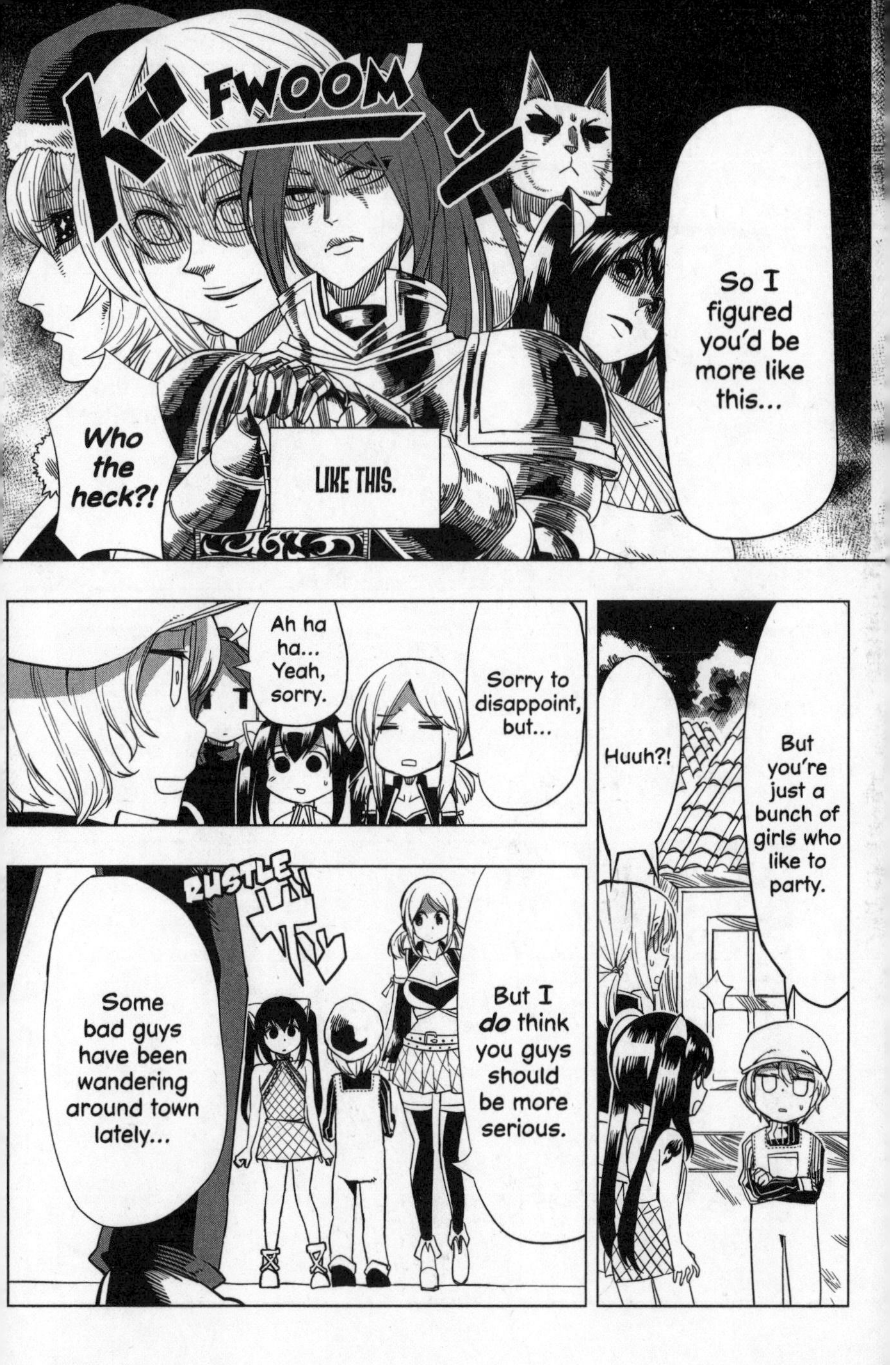

So I figured you'd be more like this...
FWOOM
LIKE THIS.
Who the heck?!
But you're just a bunch of girls who like to party.
Huuh?!
Sorry to disappoint, but...
Ah ha ha... Yeah, sorry.
But I *do* think you guys should be more serious.
RUSTLE
Some bad guys have been wandering around town lately...

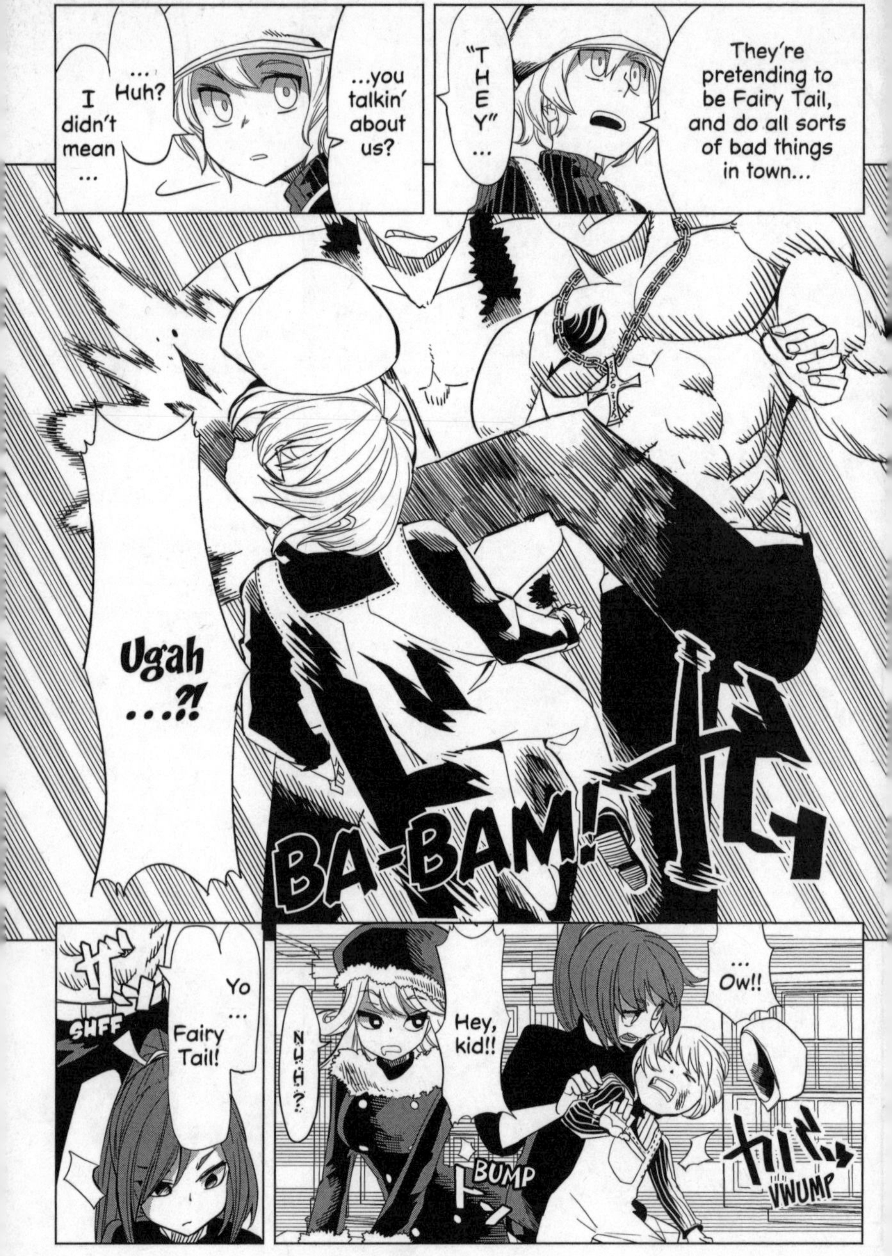
They're pretending to be Fairy Tail, and do all sorts of bad things in town...
"THEY" ...
...you talkin' about us?
... Huh?
I didn't mean ...
Ugah ...?!
BA-BAM!
... Ow!!
Hey, kid!!
NUH?
BUMP
VWUMP
Yo ... Fairy Tail!
SHFF

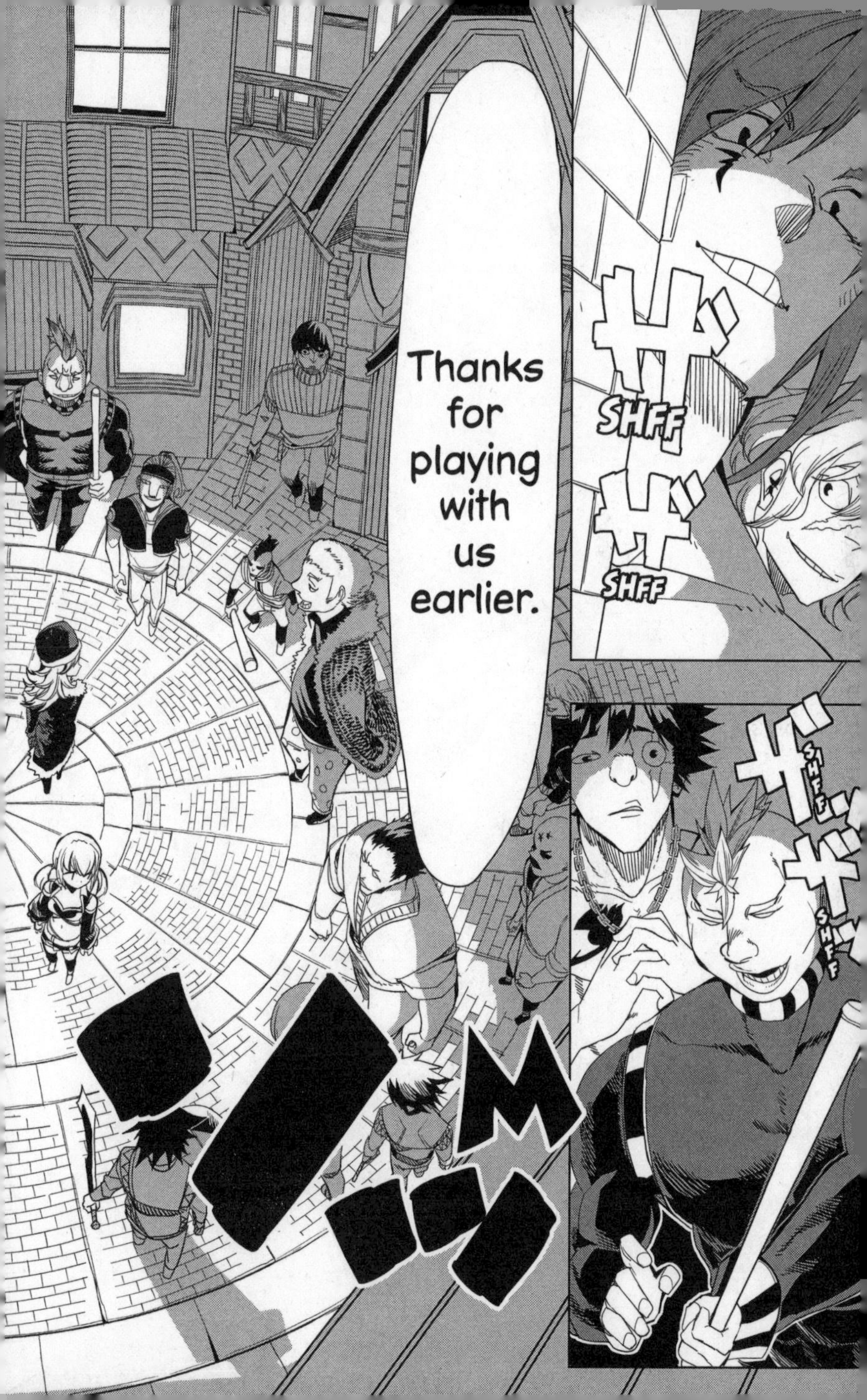
SHFF
SHFF
SHFF
SHFF
Thanks for playing with us earlier.

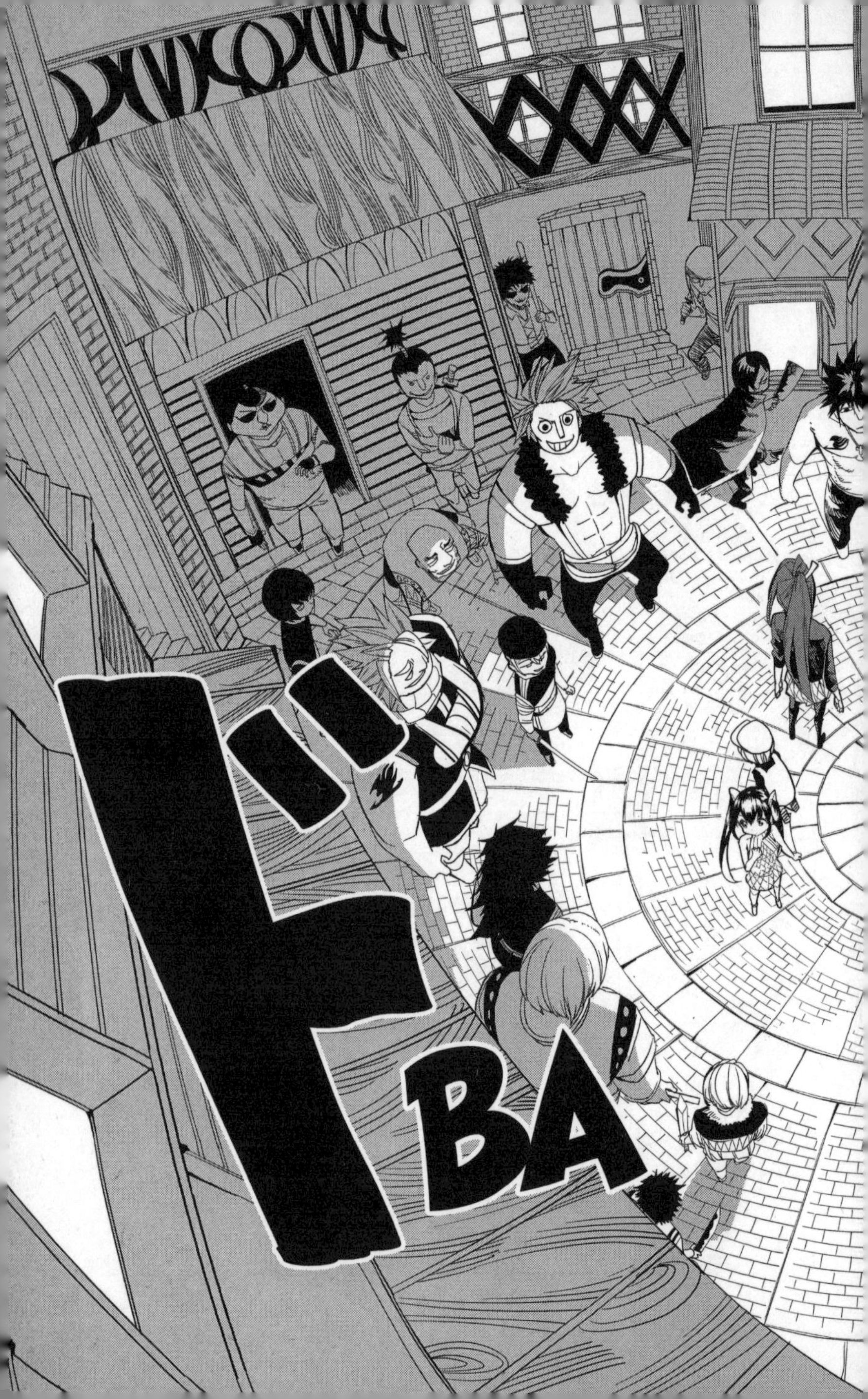
BA

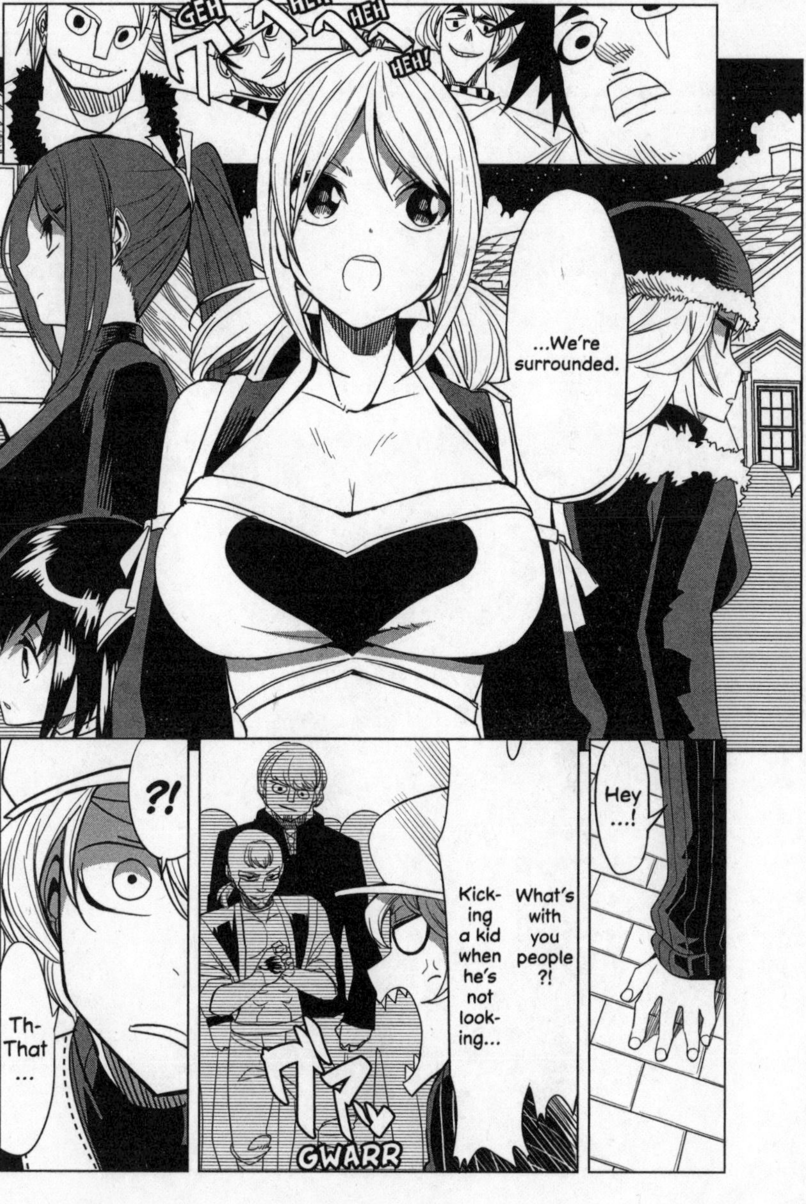
GEH HEH HEH HEH!
...We're surrounded.
Hey ...!
What's with you people ?!
Kick-ing a kid when he's not look-ing...
GWARR
?!
Th- That ...

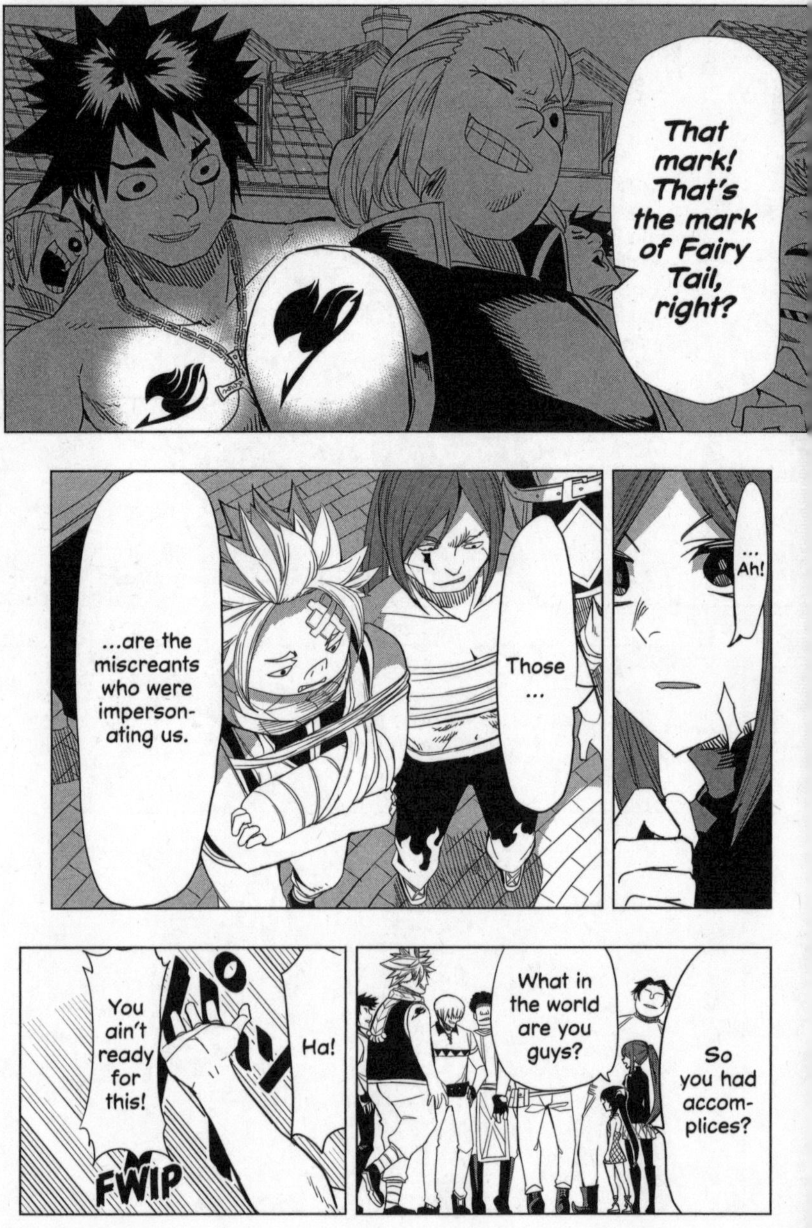
That mark! That's the mark of Fairy Tail, right?
... Ah!
Those ...
...are the miscreants who were imperson-ating us.
So you had accom-plices?
What in the world are you guys?
Ha!
You ain't ready for this!
FWIP

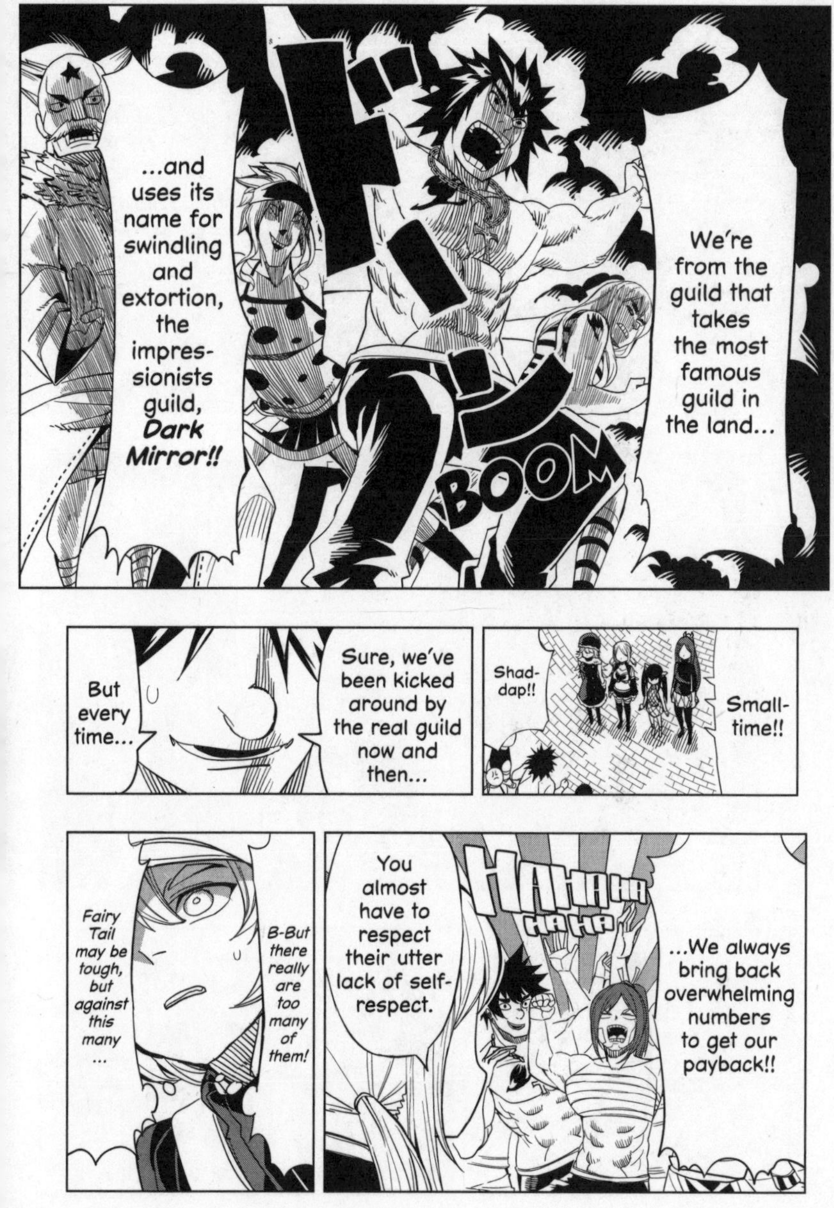
We're from the guild that takes the most famous guild in the land...
...and uses its name for swindling and extortion, the impressionists guild, **Dark Mirror!!**
BOOM
Small-time!!
Shad-dap!!
Sure, we've been kicked around by the real guild now and then...
But every time...
...We always bring back overwhelming numbers to get our payback!!
HAHAHA HAHA
You almost have to respect their utter lack of self-respect.
B-But there really are too many of them!
Fairy Tail may be tough, but against this many ...

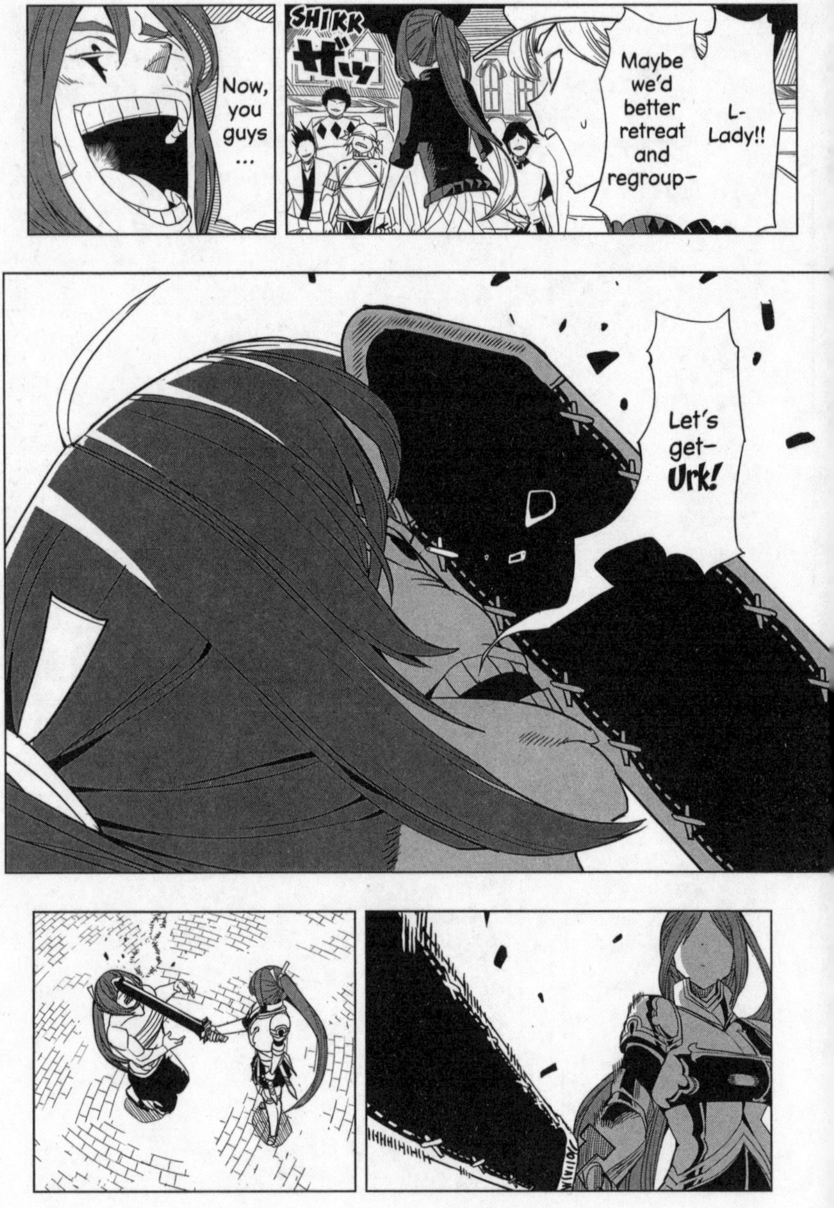
L-Lady!!
Maybe we'd better retreat and regroup–
SHIKK
ザッ
Now, you guys ...
Let's get–Urk!

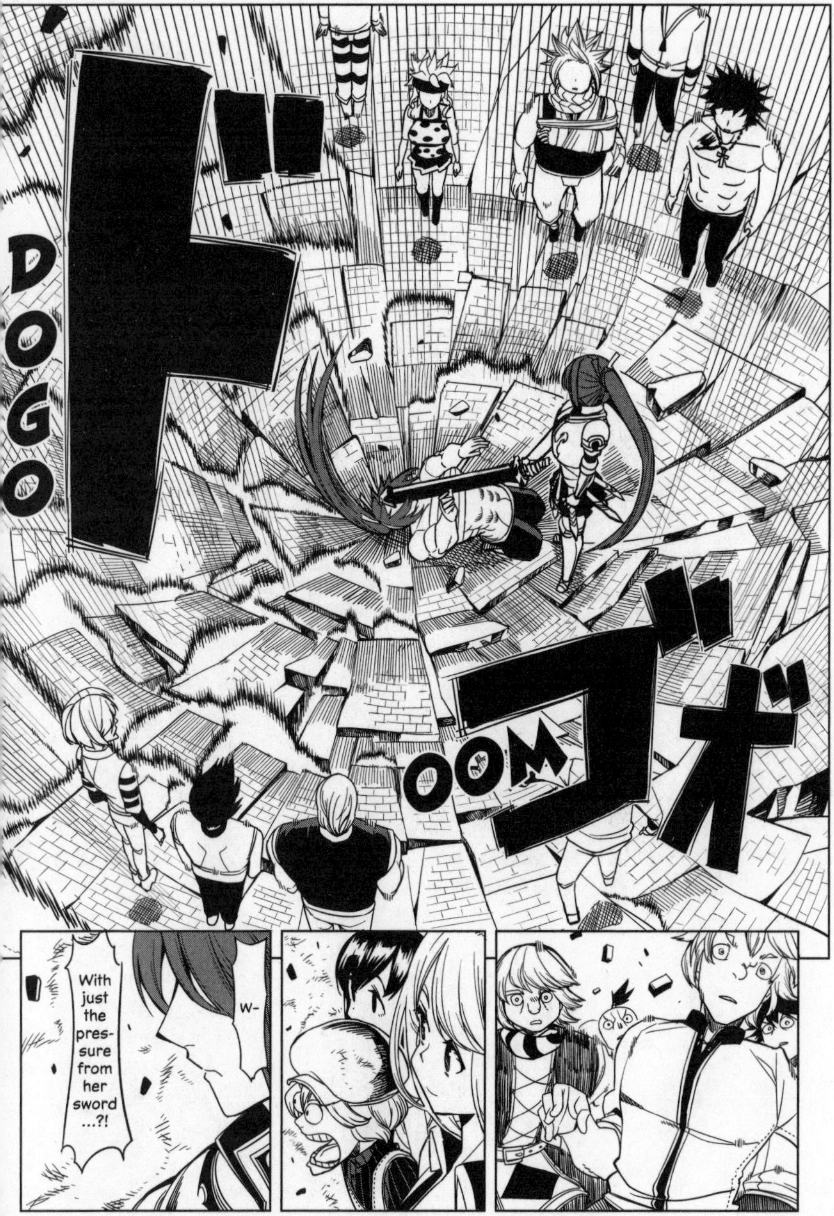
ド
DOGO
ゴオ
OOM
W-
With just the pres-sure from her sword ...?!

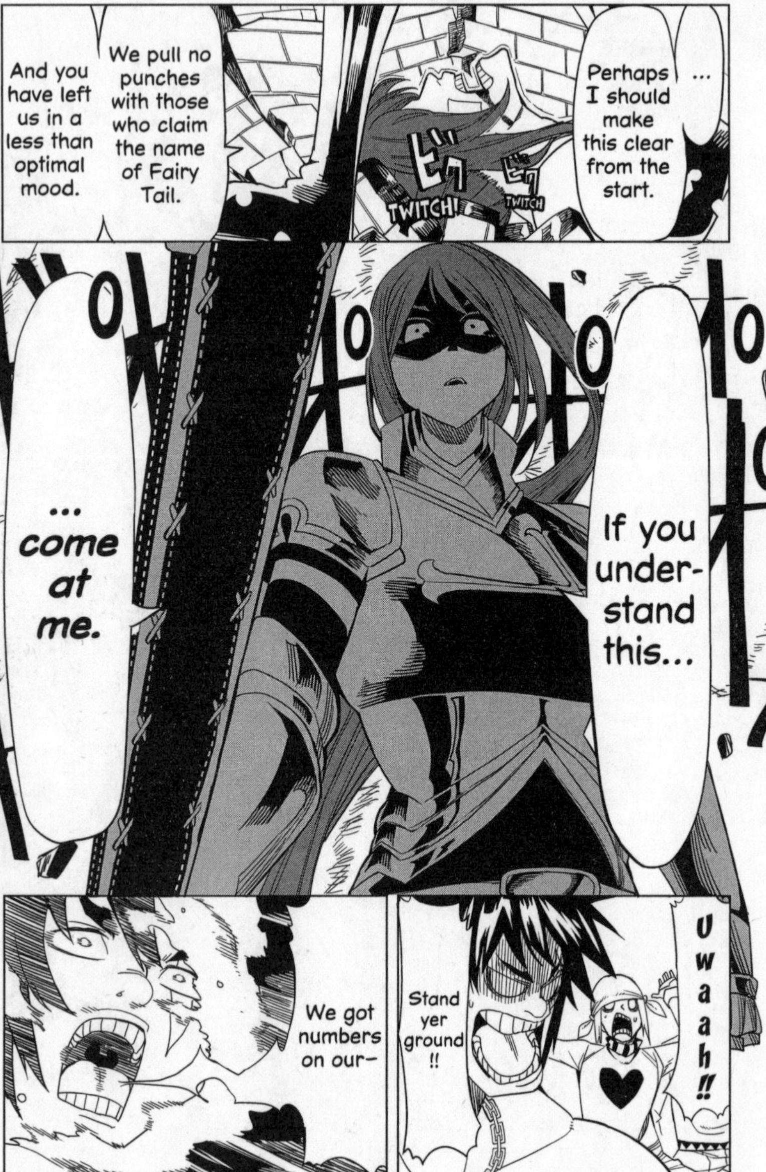
...
Perhaps I should make this clear from the start.
TWITCH! TWITCH
We pull no punches with those who claim the name of Fairy Tail.
And you have left us in a less than optimal mood.
If you understand this...
... come at me.
Uwaah!!
Stand yer ground !!
We got numbers on our-

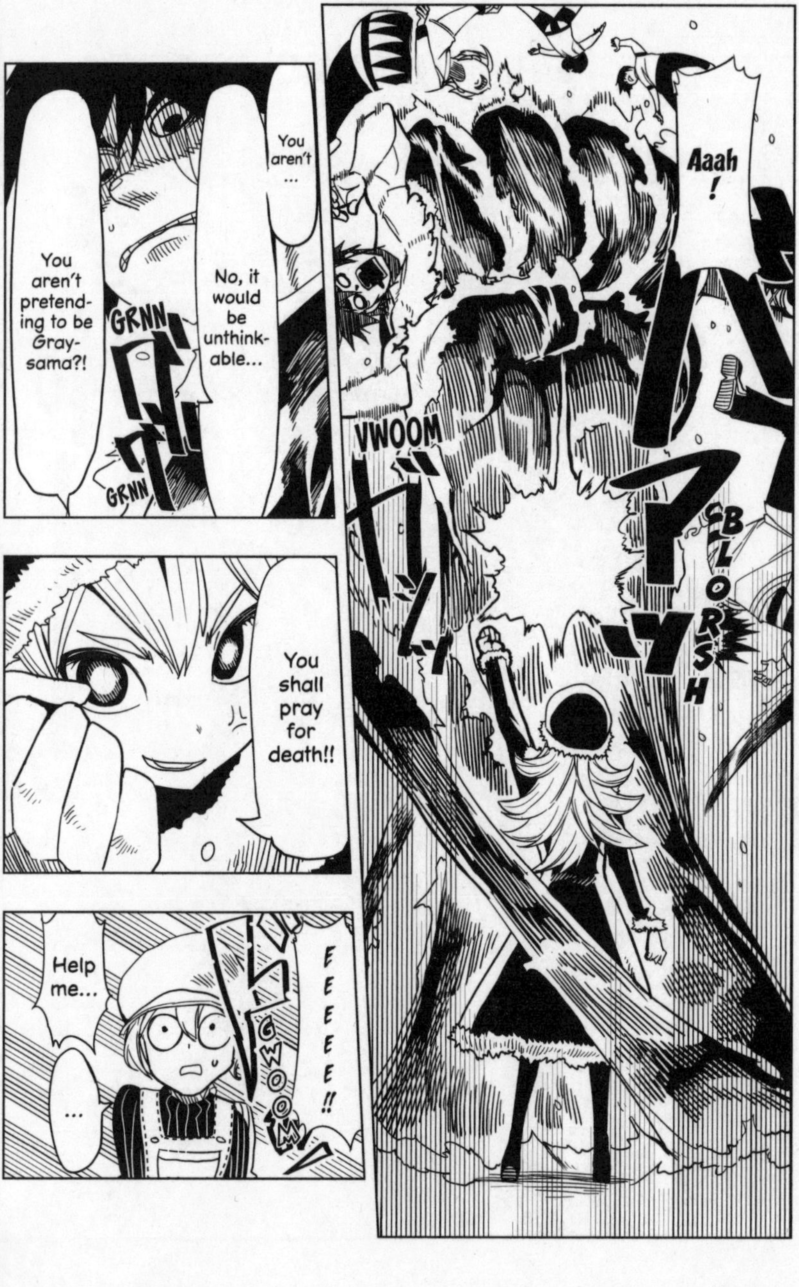
Aaah!
VWOOM
BLORSH
You aren't ...
No, it would be unthinkable...
You aren't pretending to be Gray-sama?!
GRNN
GRNN
You shall pray for death!!
EEEEEE!!
GWOOOM
Help me...
...

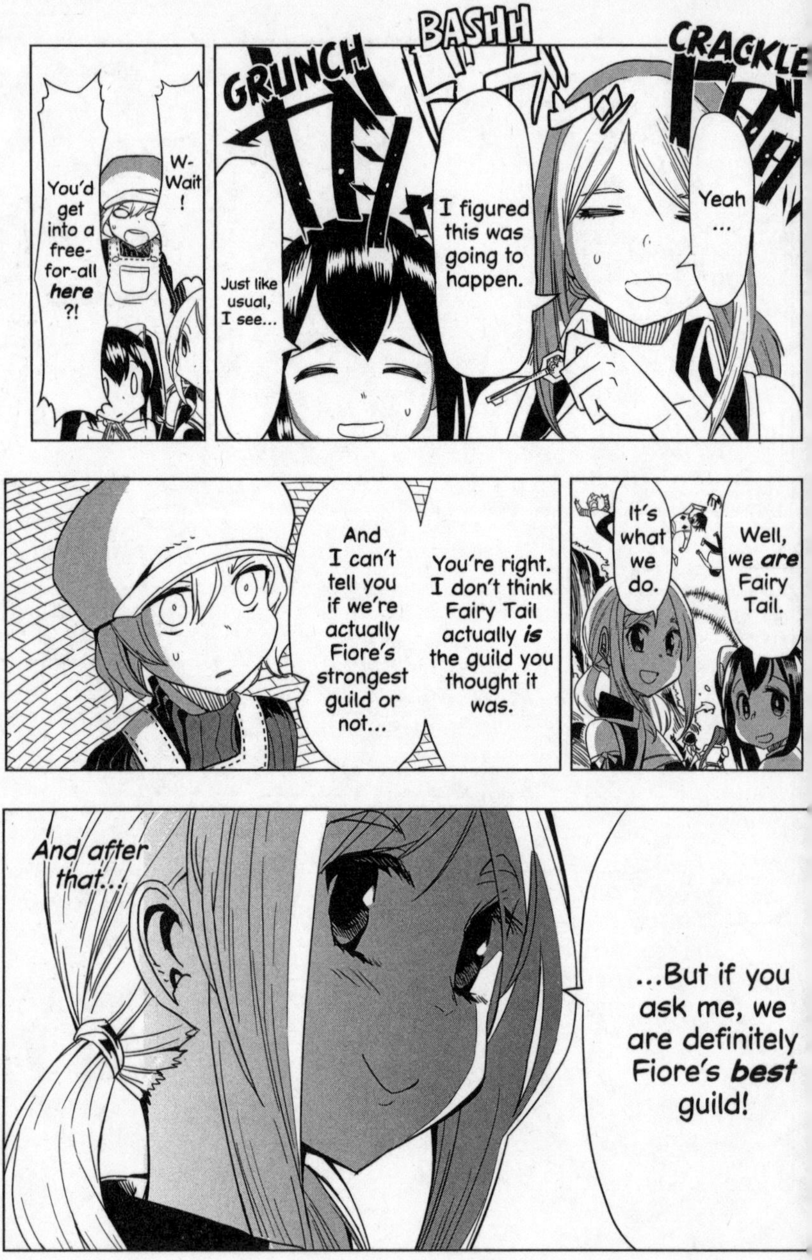
CRACKLE
Yeah...
BASHH
I figured this was going to happen.
GRUNCH
Just like usual, I see...
W-Wait!
You'd get into a free-for-all *here*?!
Well, we *are* Fairy Tail.
It's what we do.
You're right. I don't think Fairy Tail actually *is* the guild you thought it was.
And I can't tell you if we're actually Fiore's strongest guild or not...
...But if you ask me, we are definitely Fiore's **best** guild!
And after that...

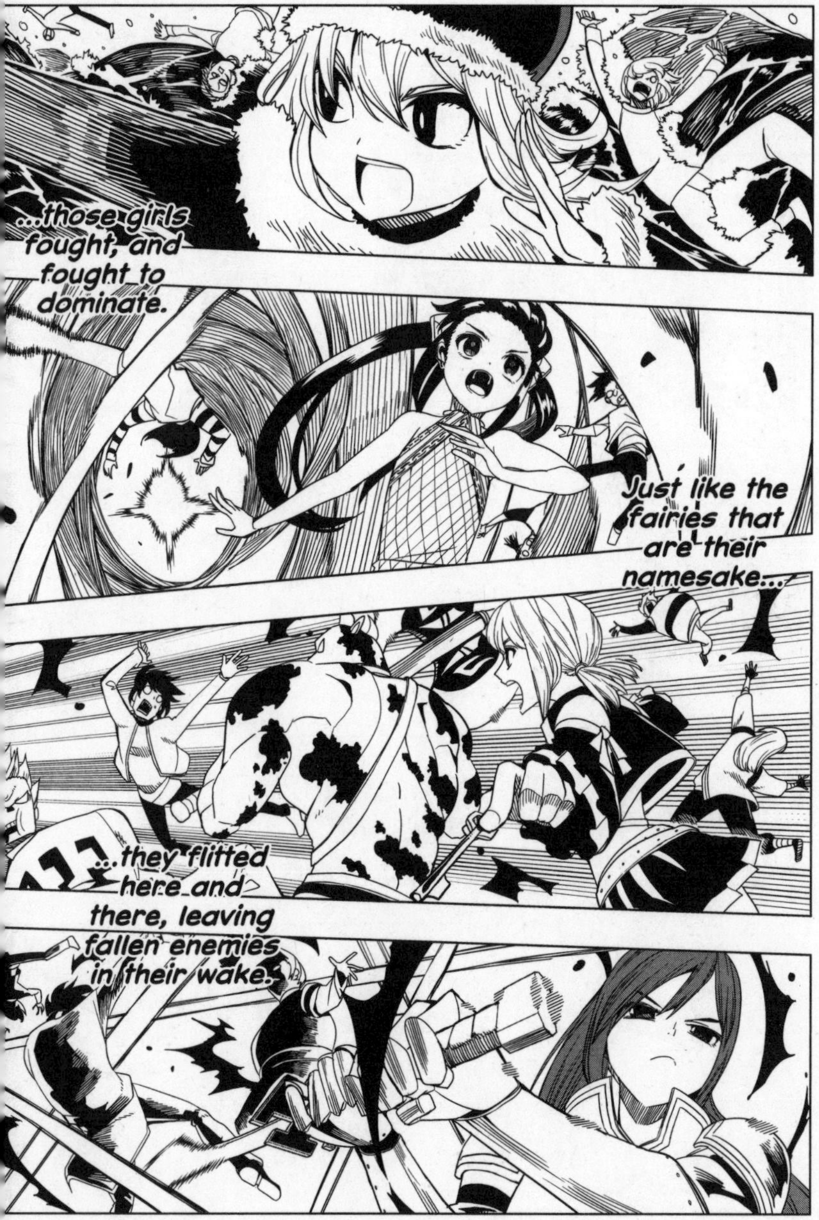
...those girls fought, and fought to dominate.
Just like the fairies that are their namesake...
...they flitted here and there, leaving fallen enemies in their wake.

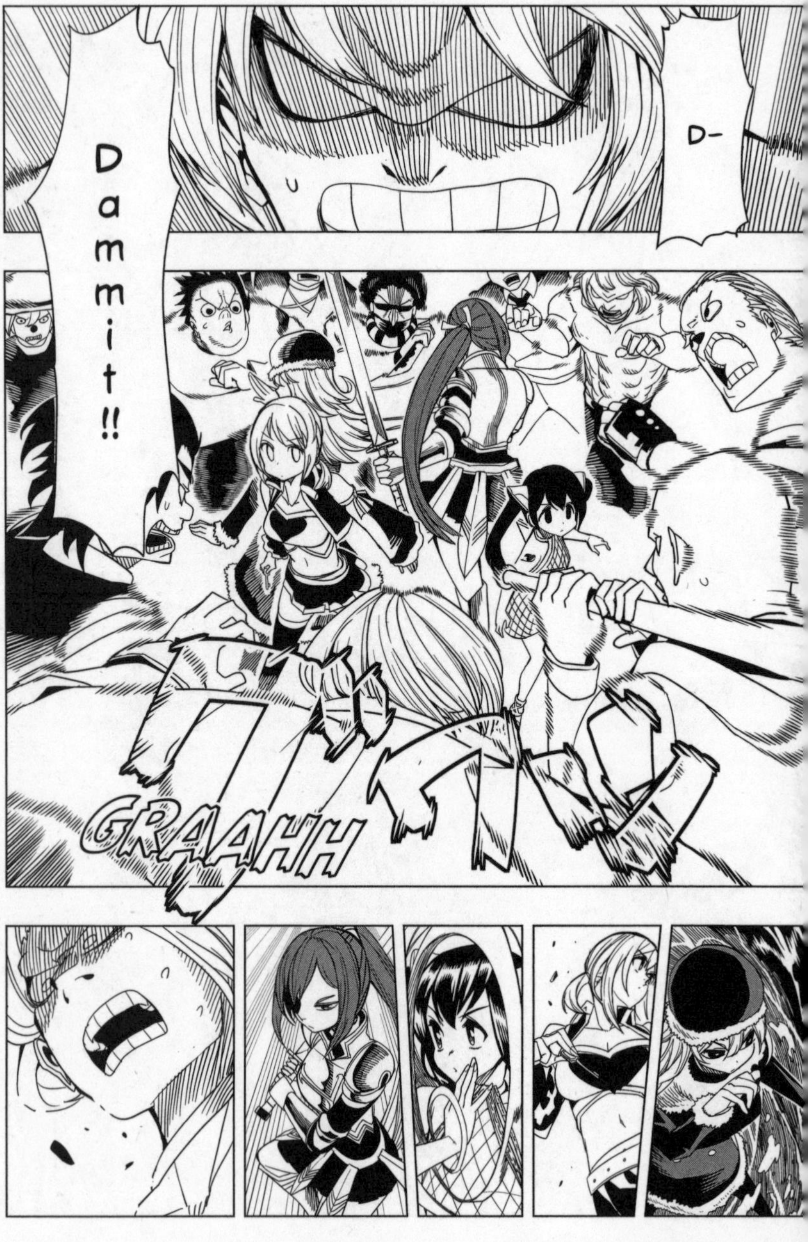
D-
Dammit!!
GRAAHH

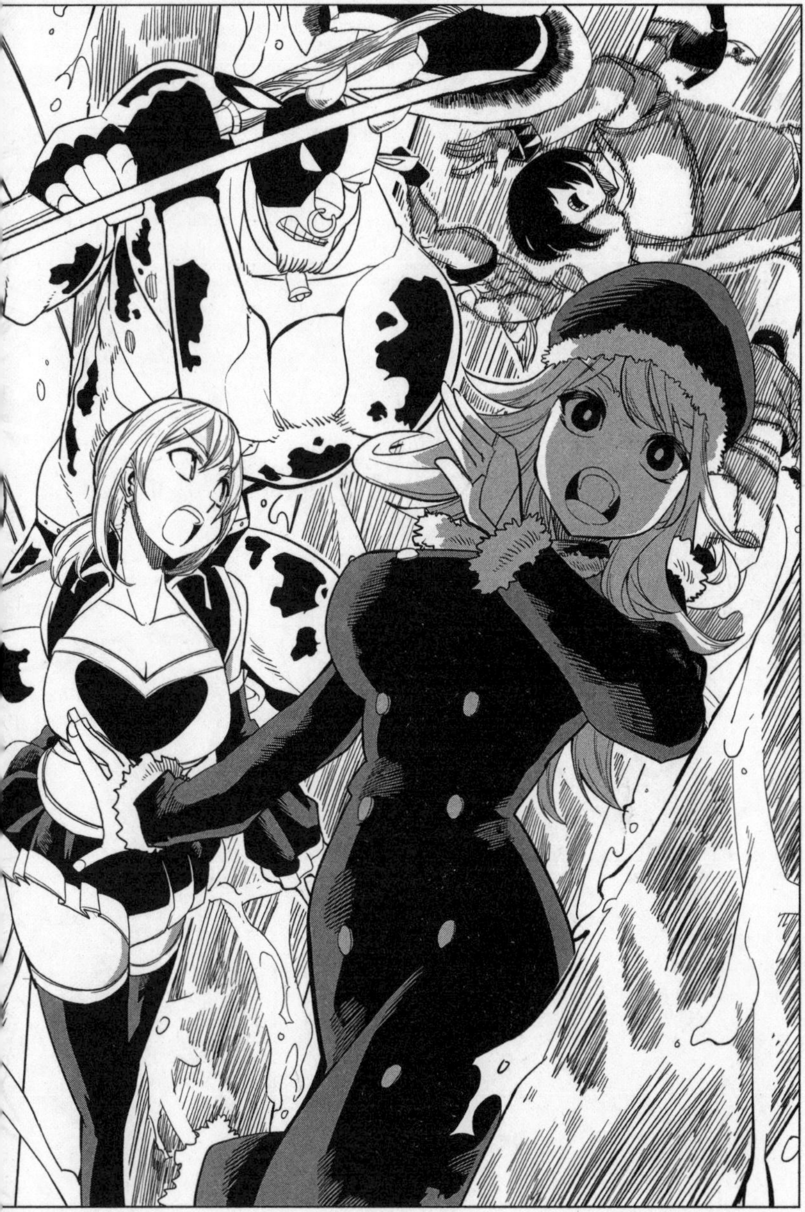

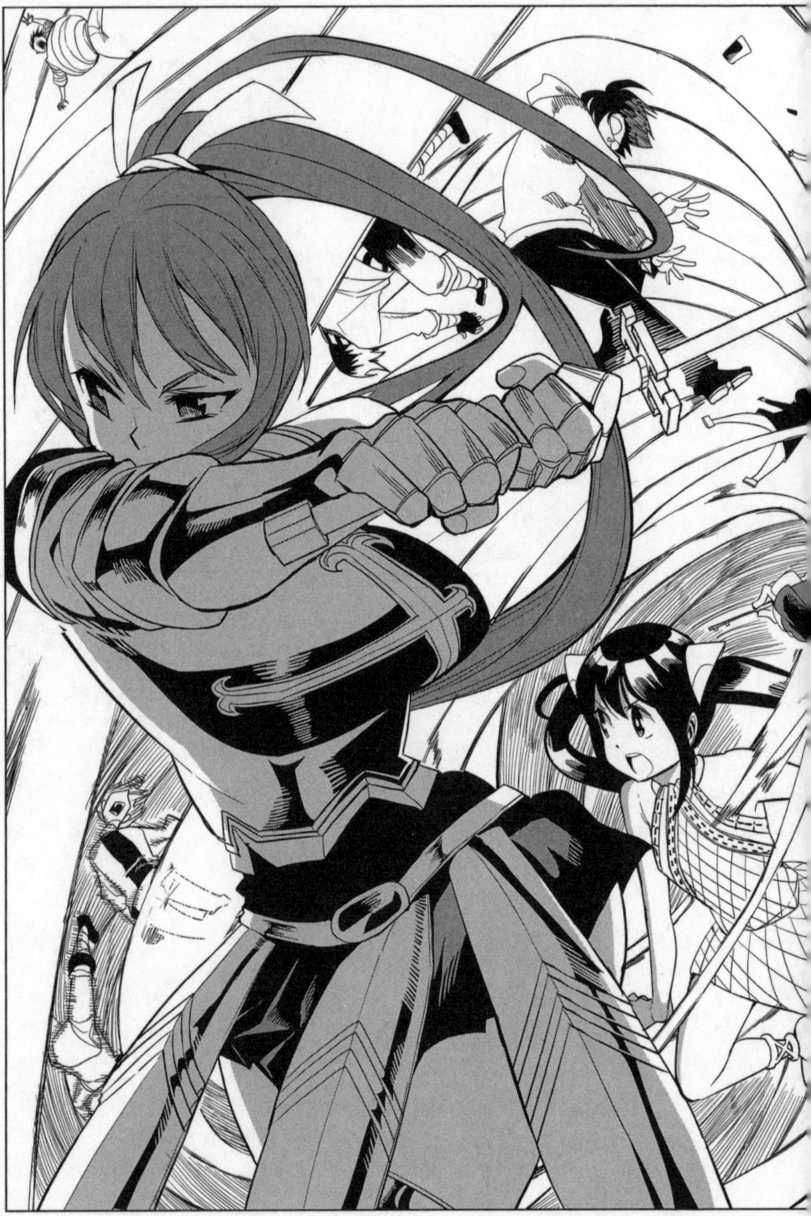

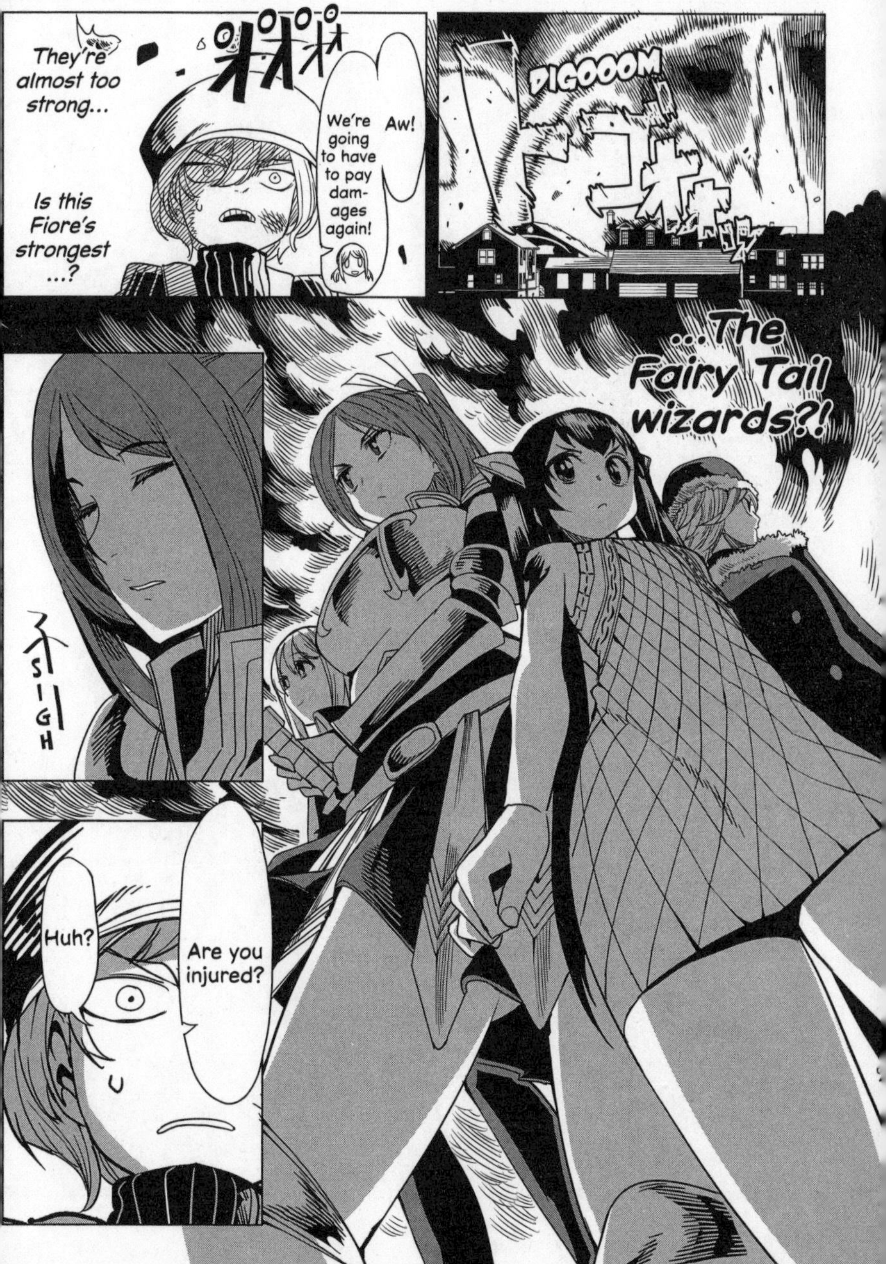
DIGOOOM
O-O-O-O
We're going to have to pay damages again!
Aw!
They're almost too strong...
Is this Fiore's strongest ...?
...The Fairy Tail wizards?!
SIGH
Are you injured?
Huh?

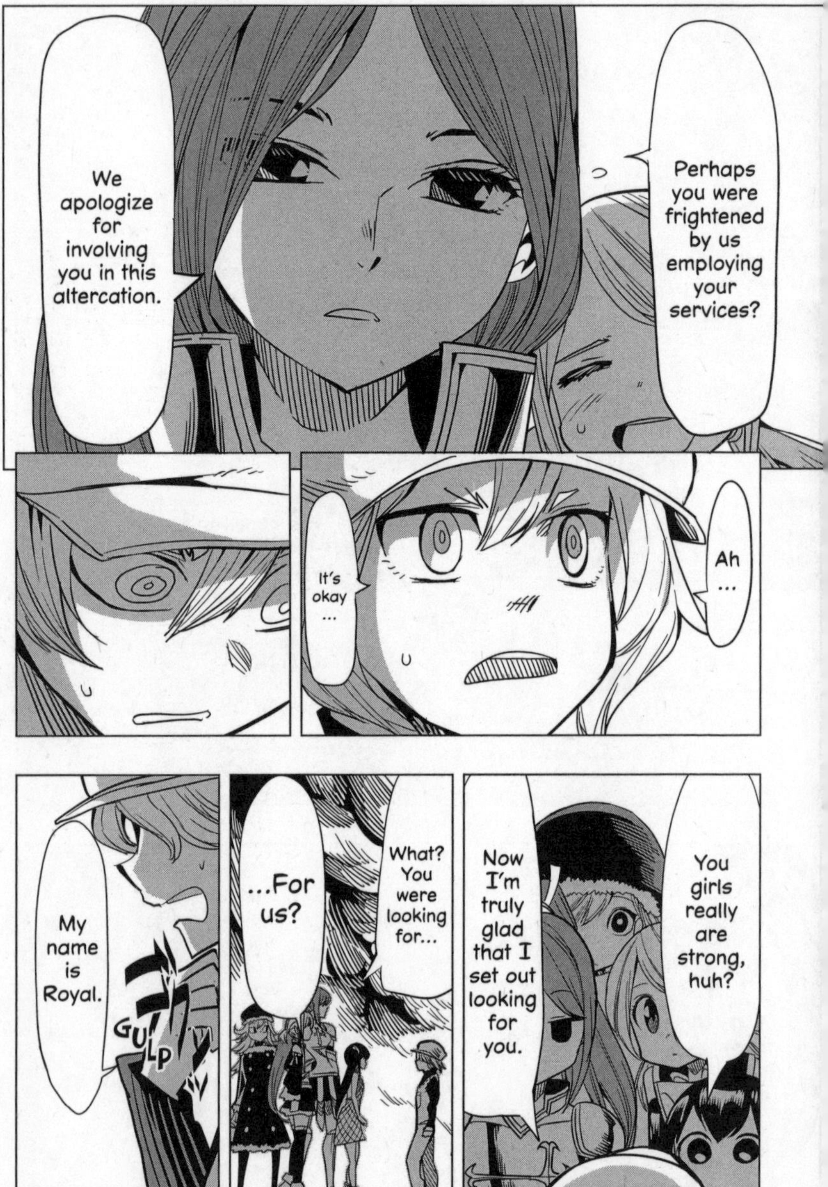
Perhaps you were frightened by us employing your services?
We apologize for involving you in this altercation.
Ah...
It's okay...
You girls really are strong, huh?
Now I'm truly glad that I set out looking for you.
What? You were looking for...
...For us?
My name is Royal.
GULP

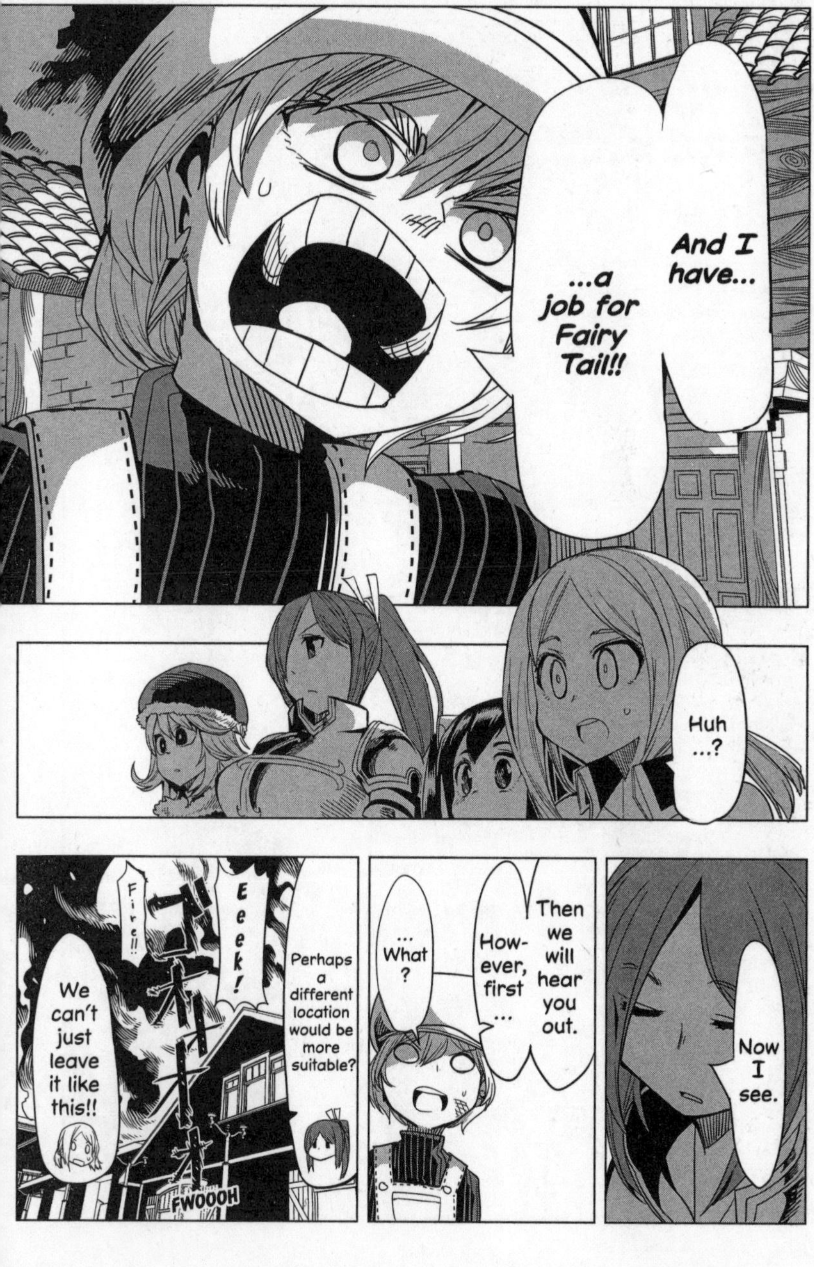
And I have...
...a job for Fairy Tail!!
Huh ...?
Now I see.
Then we will hear you out.
How-ever, first ...
... What ?
Perhaps a different location would be more suitable?
Eeek!
Fire!!
We can't just leave it like this!!
FWOOOH

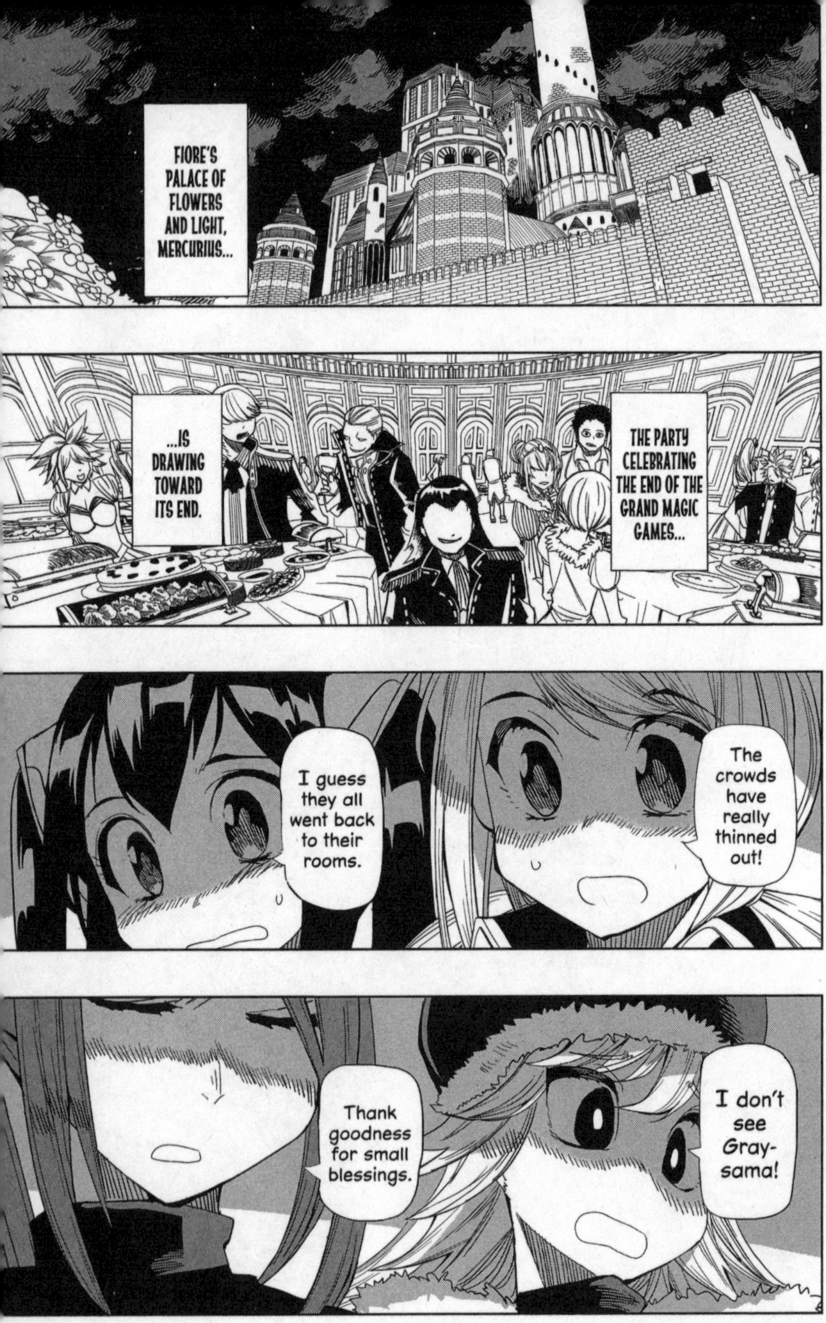
FIORE'S PALACE OF FLOWERS AND LIGHT, MERCURIUS...
THE PARTY CELEBRATING THE END OF THE GRAND MAGIC GAMES...
...IS DRAWING TOWARD ITS END.
The crowds have really thinned out!
I guess they all went back to their rooms.
I don't see Gray-sama!
Thank goodness for small blessings.

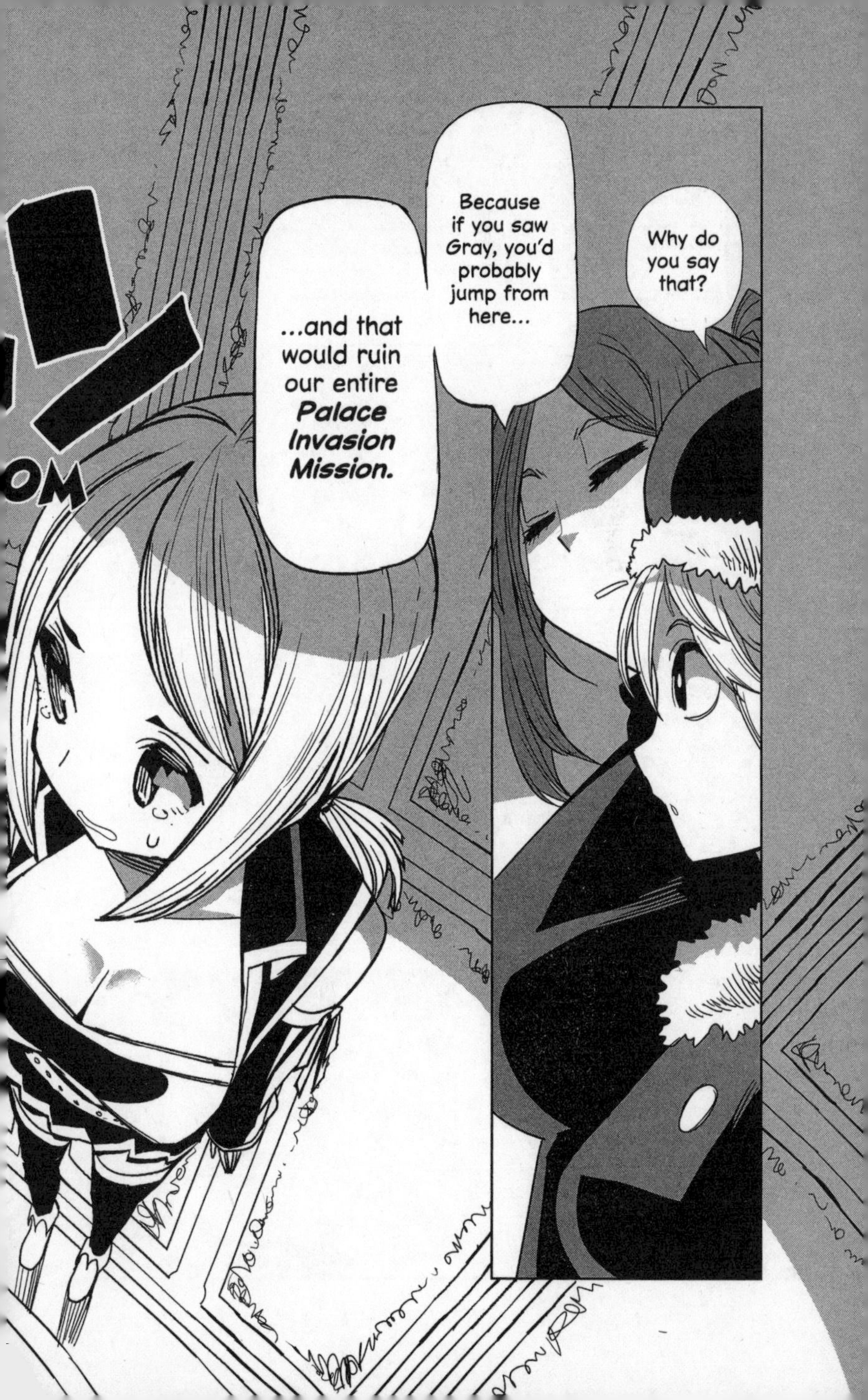
Why do you say that?
Because if you saw Gray, you'd probably jump from here...
...and that would ruin our entire ***Palace Invasion Mission.***

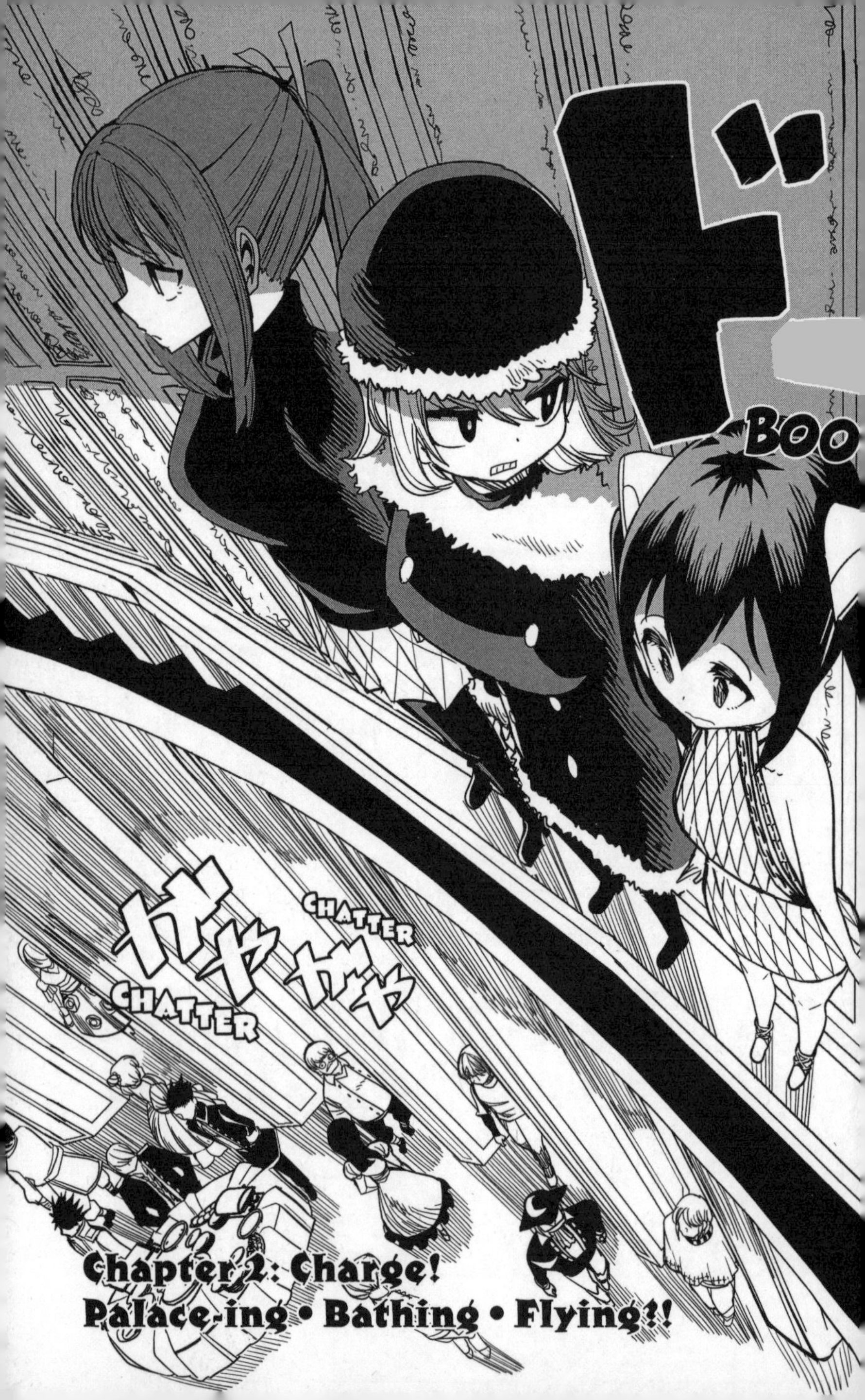
BOO
CHATTER
CHATTER

Chapter 2: Charge! Palace-ing • Bathing • Flying?!

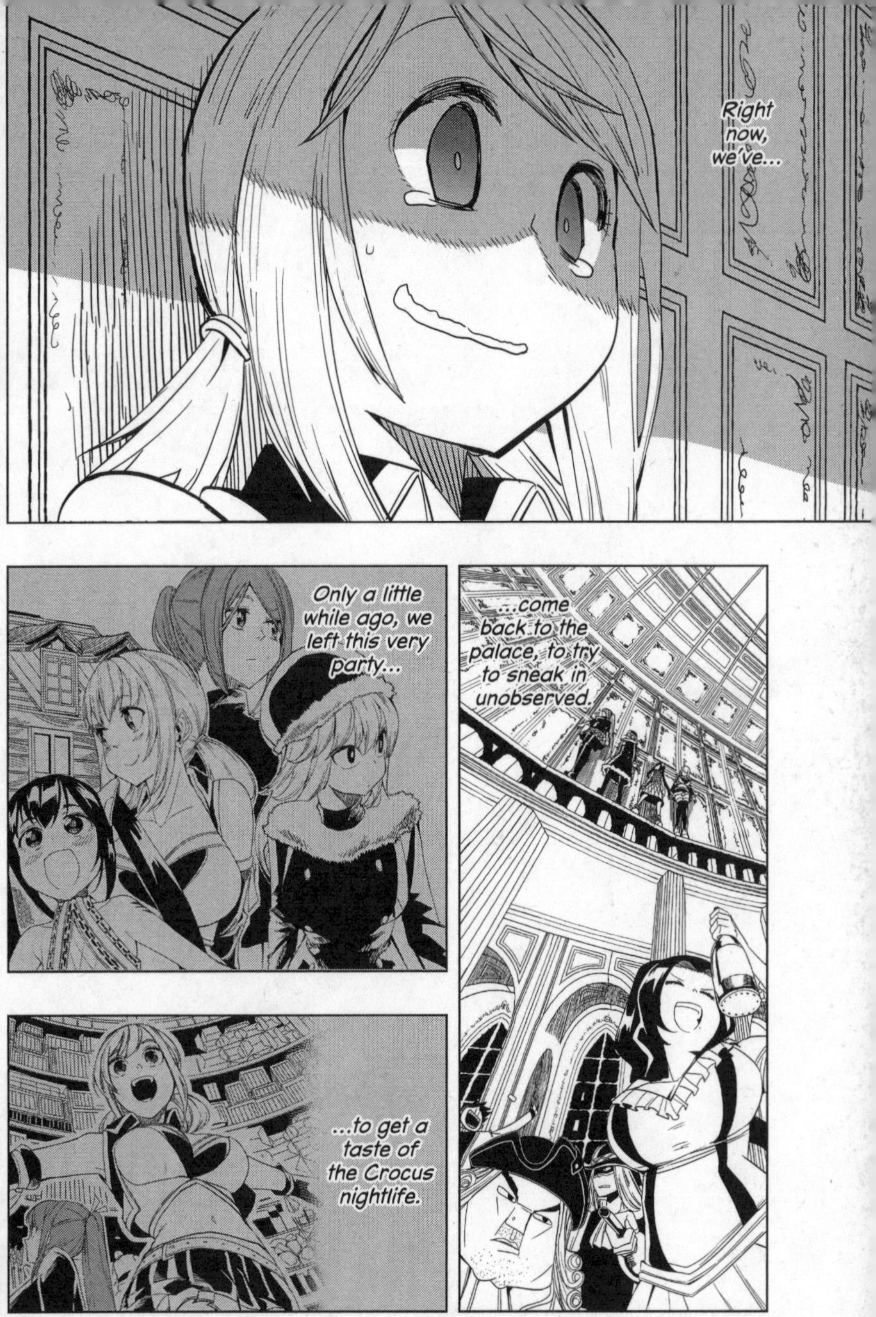
Right now, we've...
...come back to the palace, to try to sneak in unobserved.
Only a little while ago, we left this very party...
...to get a taste of the Crocus nightlife.

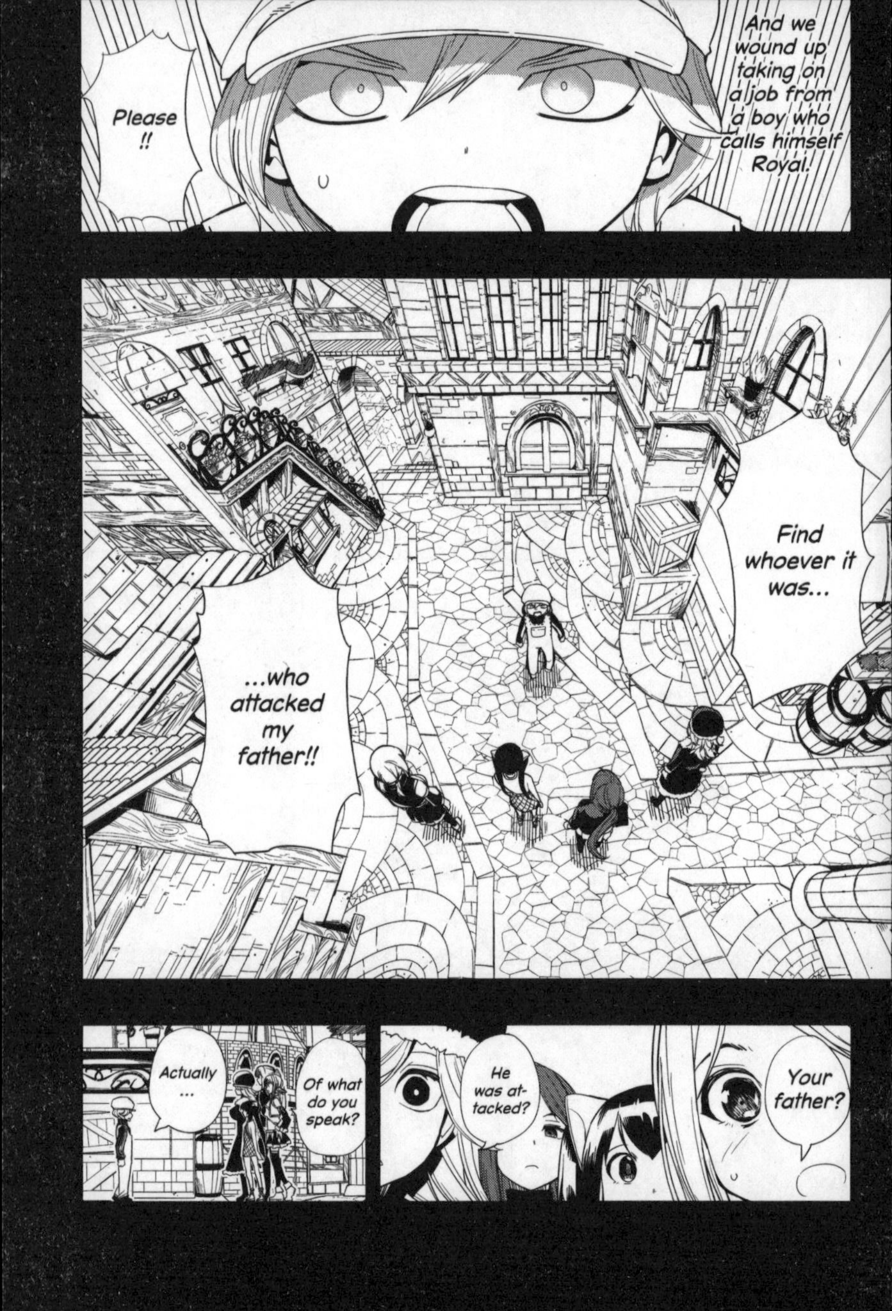
And we wound up taking on a job from a boy who calls himself Royal!
Please !!
Find whoever it was...
...who attacked my father!!
Your father?
He was at-tacked?
Of what do you speak?
Actually ...

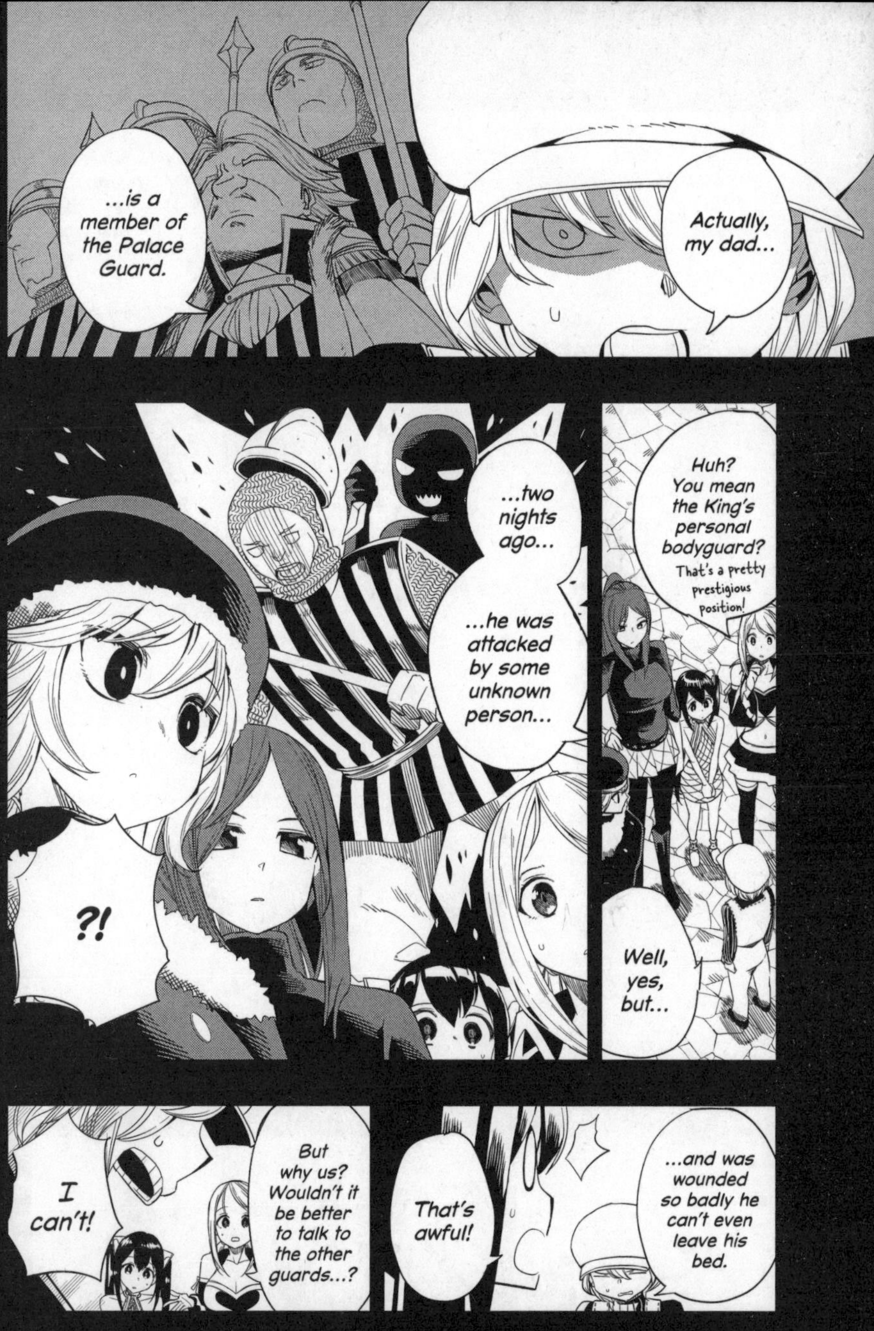

Actually, my dad...
...is a member of the Palace Guard.
Huh? You mean the King's personal bodyguard?
That's a pretty prestigious position!
Well, yes, but...
...two nights ago...
...he was attacked by some unknown person...
?!
...and was wounded so badly he can't even leave his bed.
That's awful!
But why us? Wouldn't it be better to talk to the other guards...?
I can't!

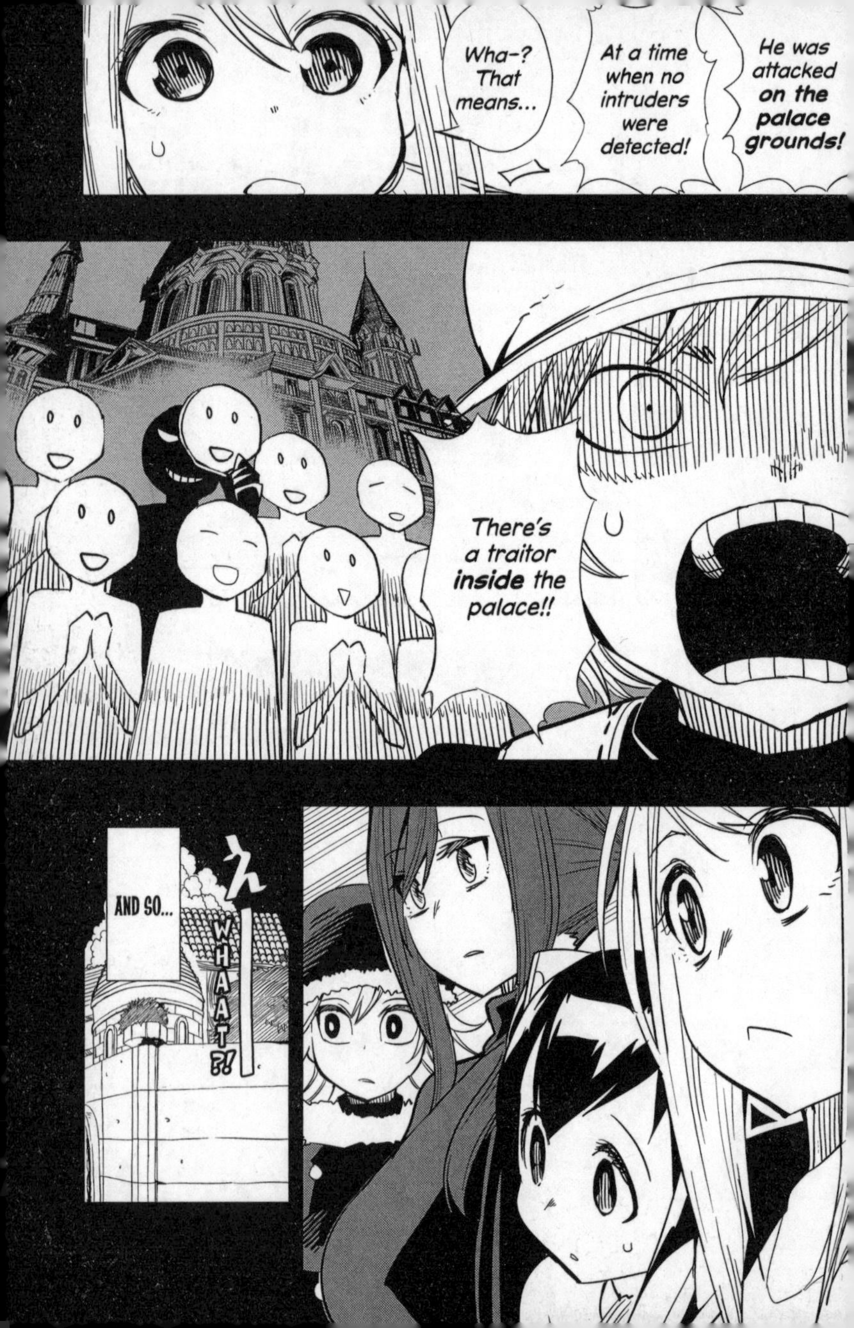
He was attacked on the palace grounds!
At a time when no intruders were detected!
Wha-? That means...
There's a traitor inside the palace!!
WHAAAT?!
AND SO...

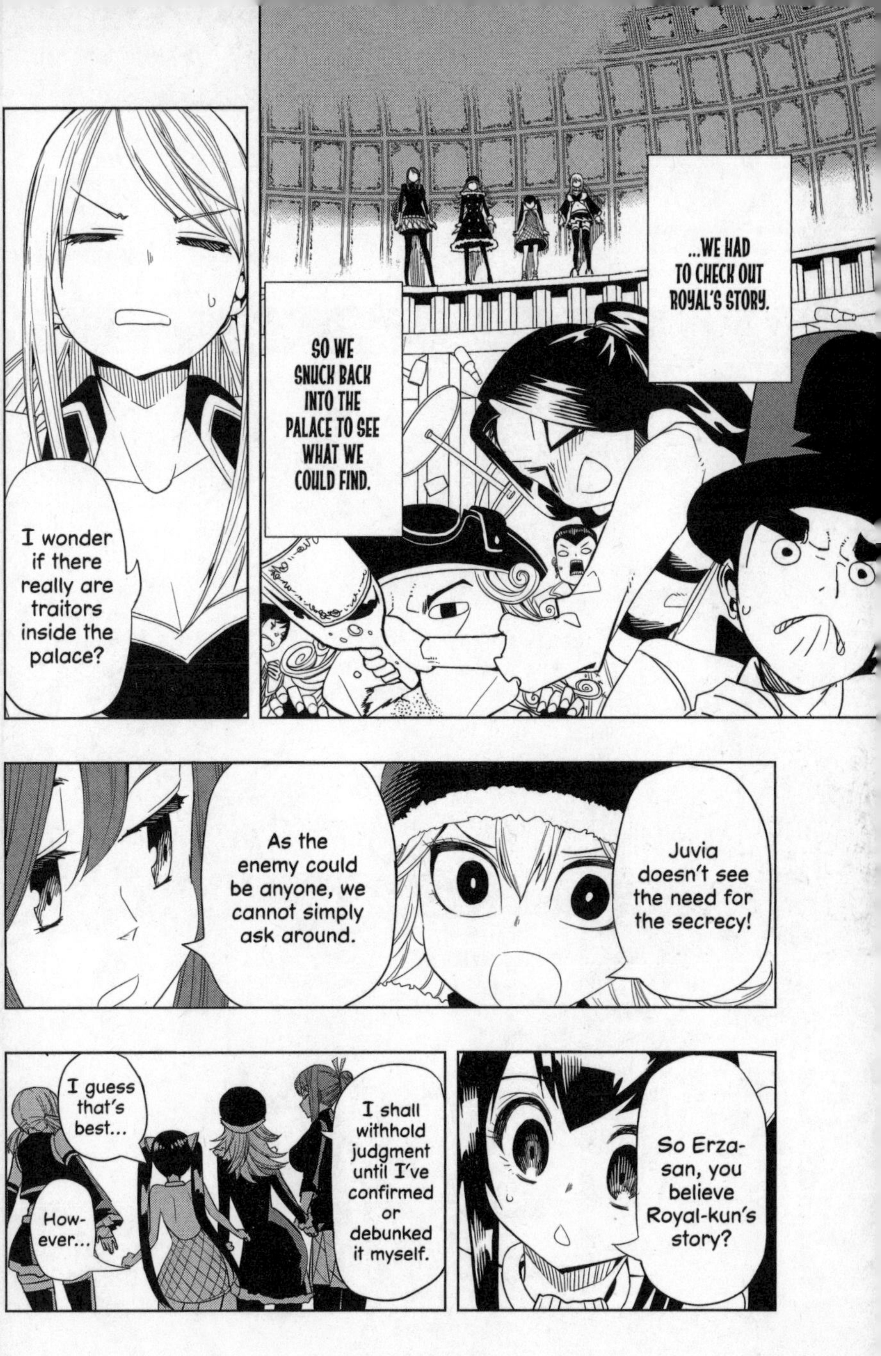
...WE HAD TO CHECK OUT ROYAL'S STORY.
SO WE SNUCK BACK INTO THE PALACE TO SEE WHAT WE COULD FIND.
I wonder if there really are traitors inside the palace?
Juvia doesn't see the need for the secrecy!
As the enemy could be anyone, we cannot simply ask around.
So Erza-san, you believe Royal-kun's story?
I shall withhold judgment until I've confirmed or debunked it myself.
I guess that's best...
How-ever...

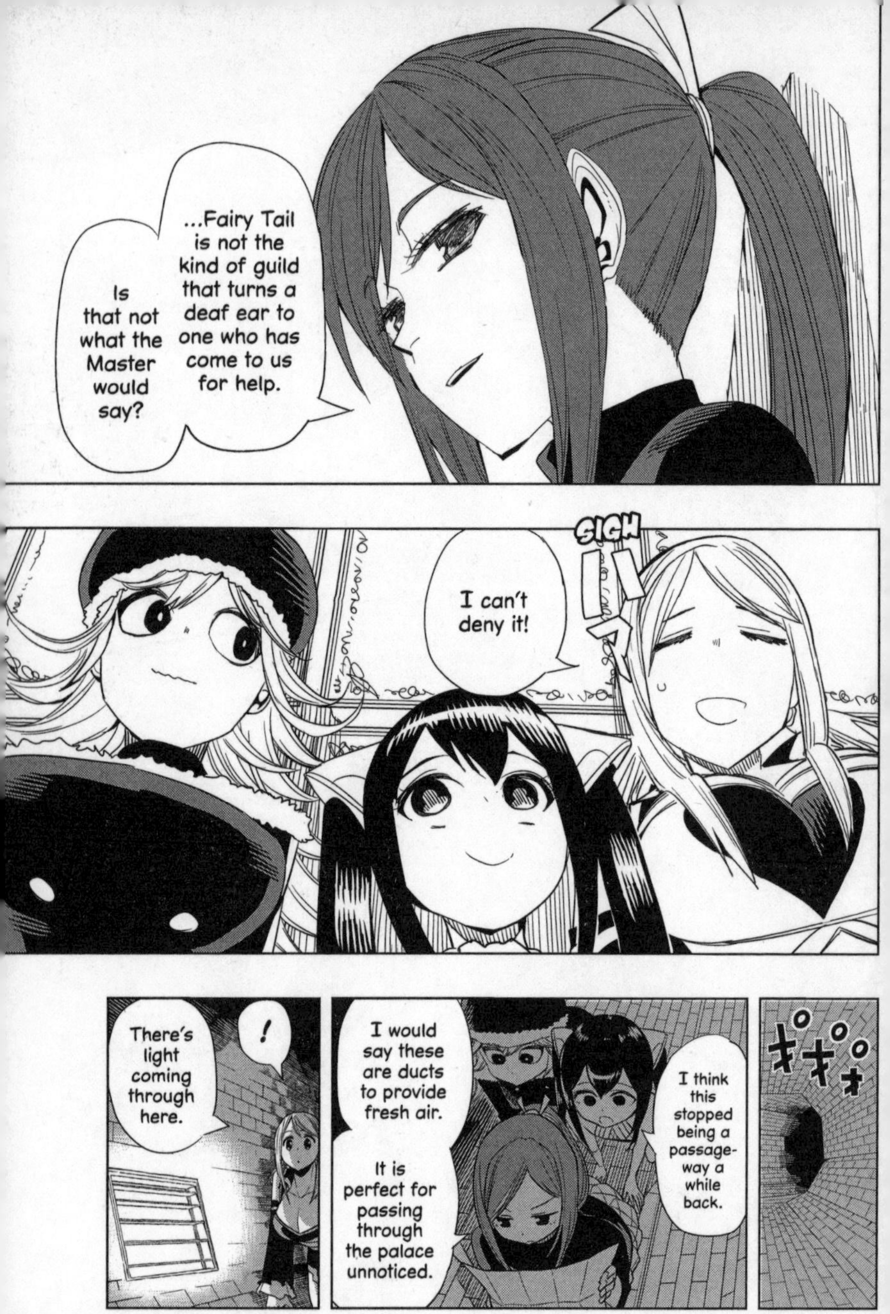
...Fairy Tail is not the kind of guild that turns a deaf ear to one who has come to us for help.
Is that not what the Master would say?
SIGH
I can't deny it!
I think this stopped being a passage-way a while back.
I would say these are ducts to provide fresh air.
It is perfect for passing through the palace unnoticed.
!
There's light coming through here.

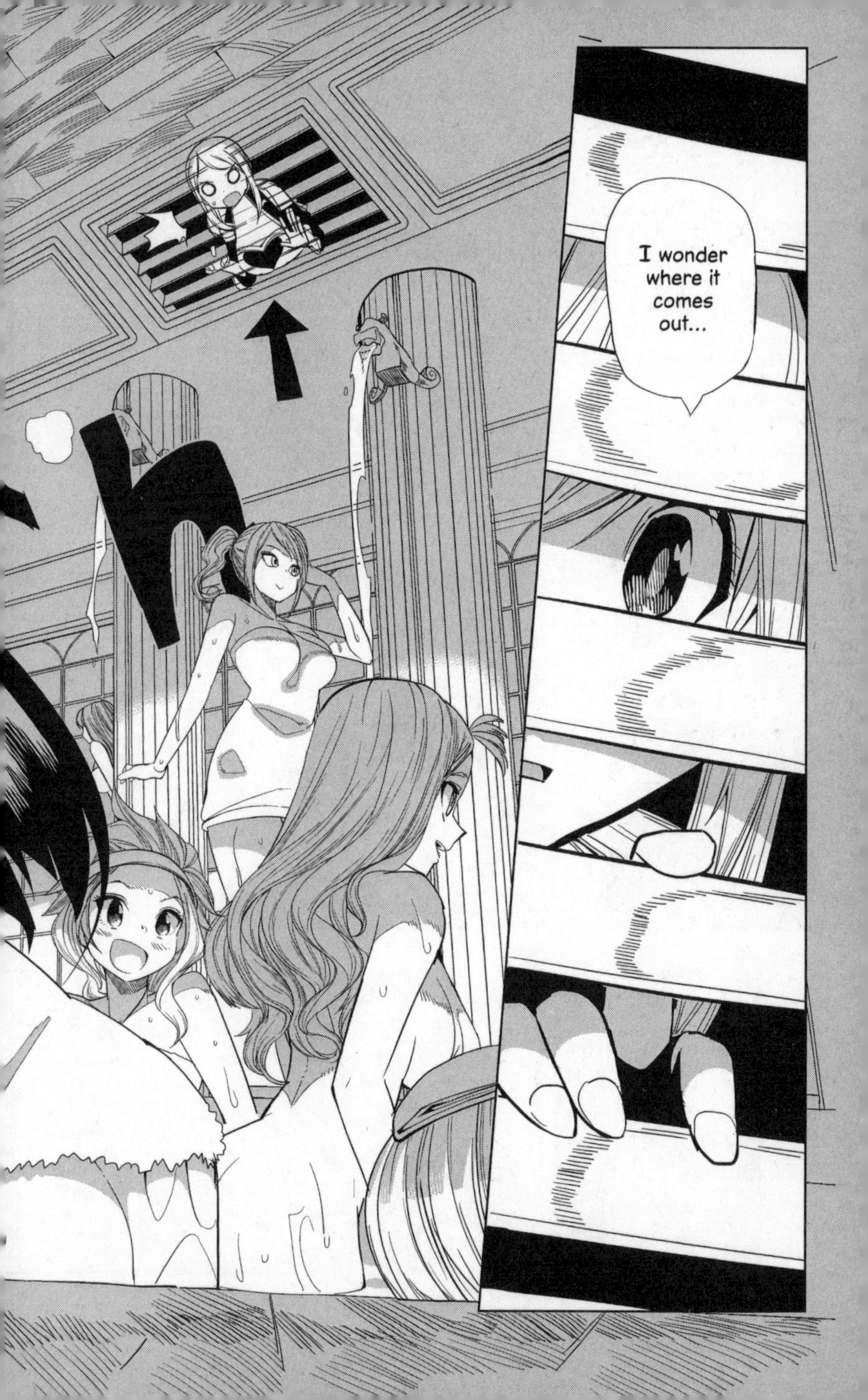
I wonder where it comes out...

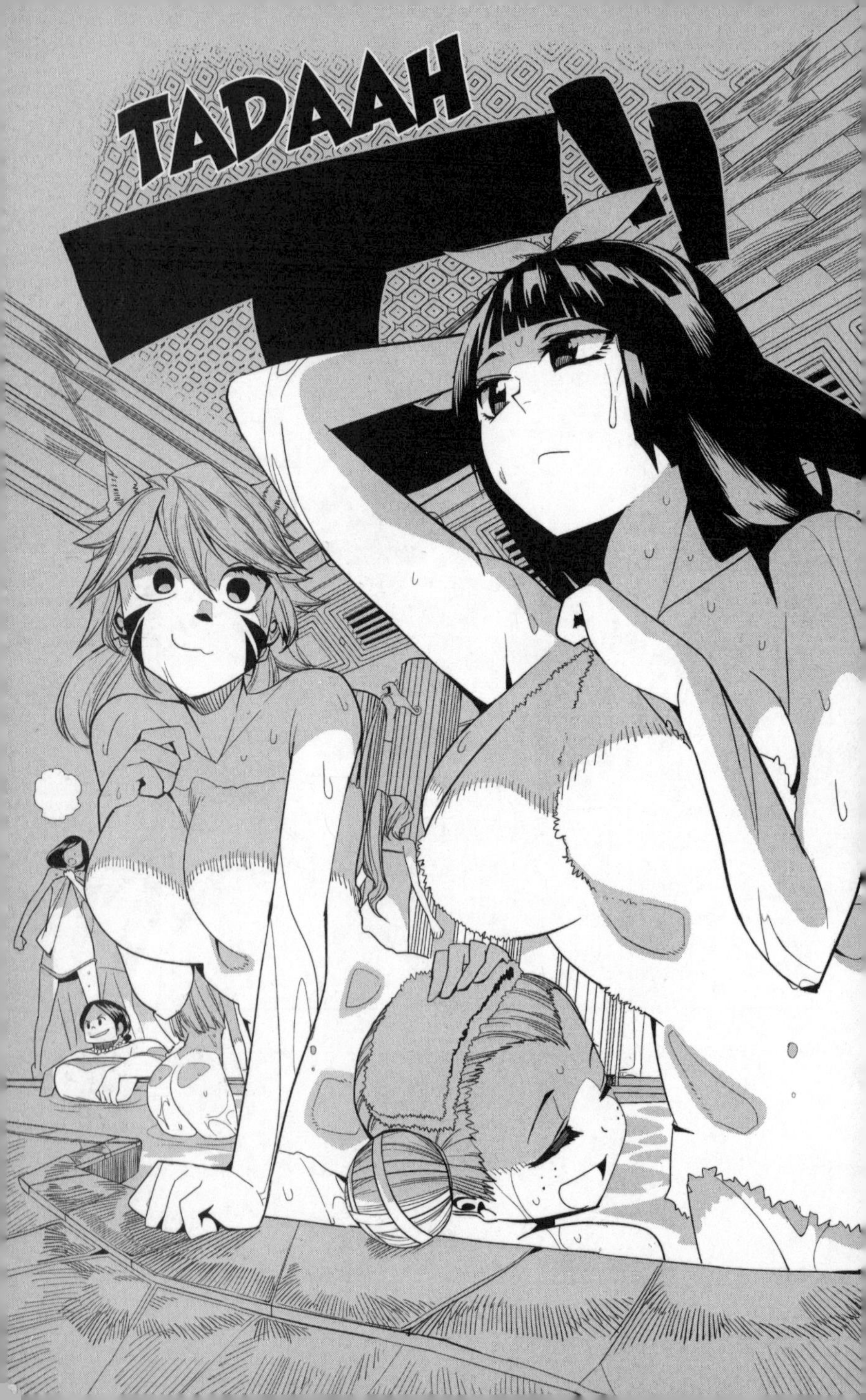
TADAAH

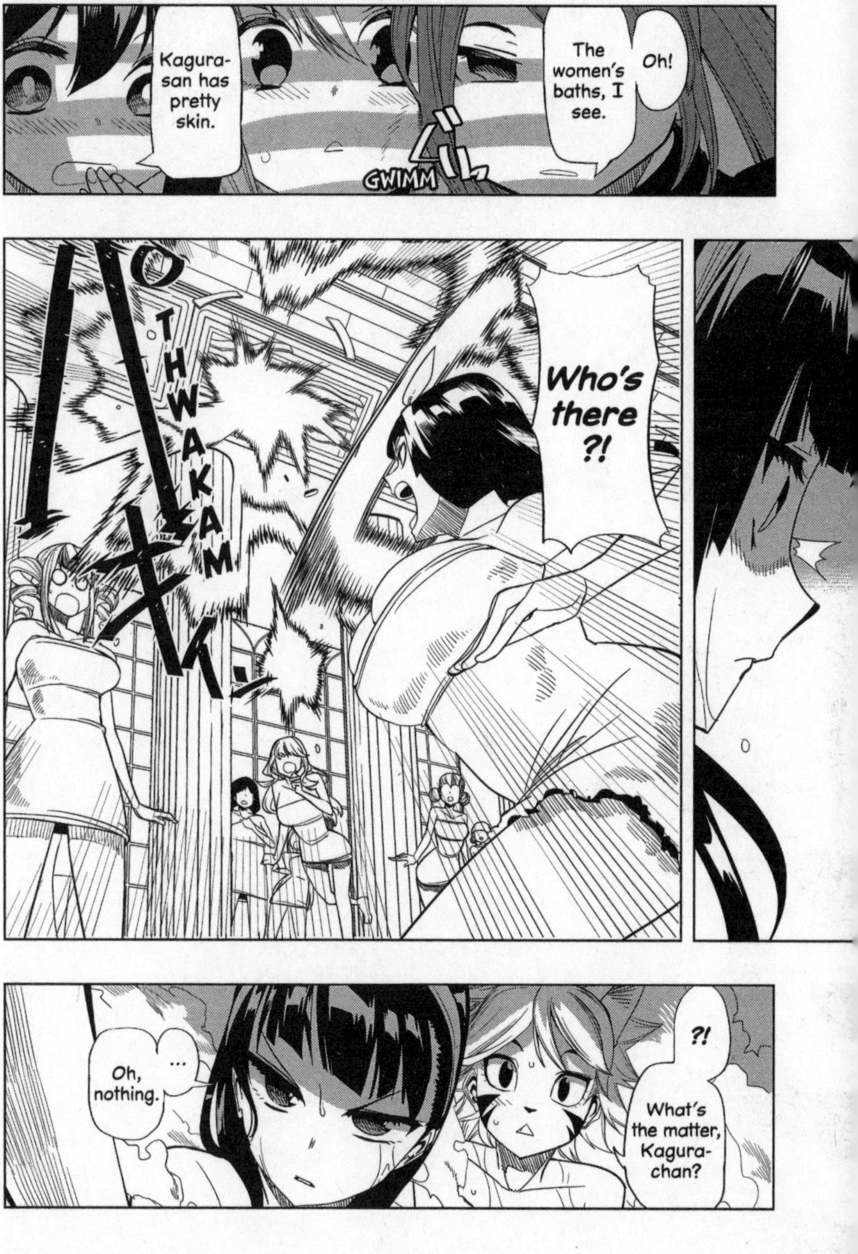
Oh!
The women's baths, I see.
GWIMM
Kagura-san has pretty skin.
Who's there ?!
THWAKAM
?!
What's the matter, Kagura-chan?
...
Oh, nothing.

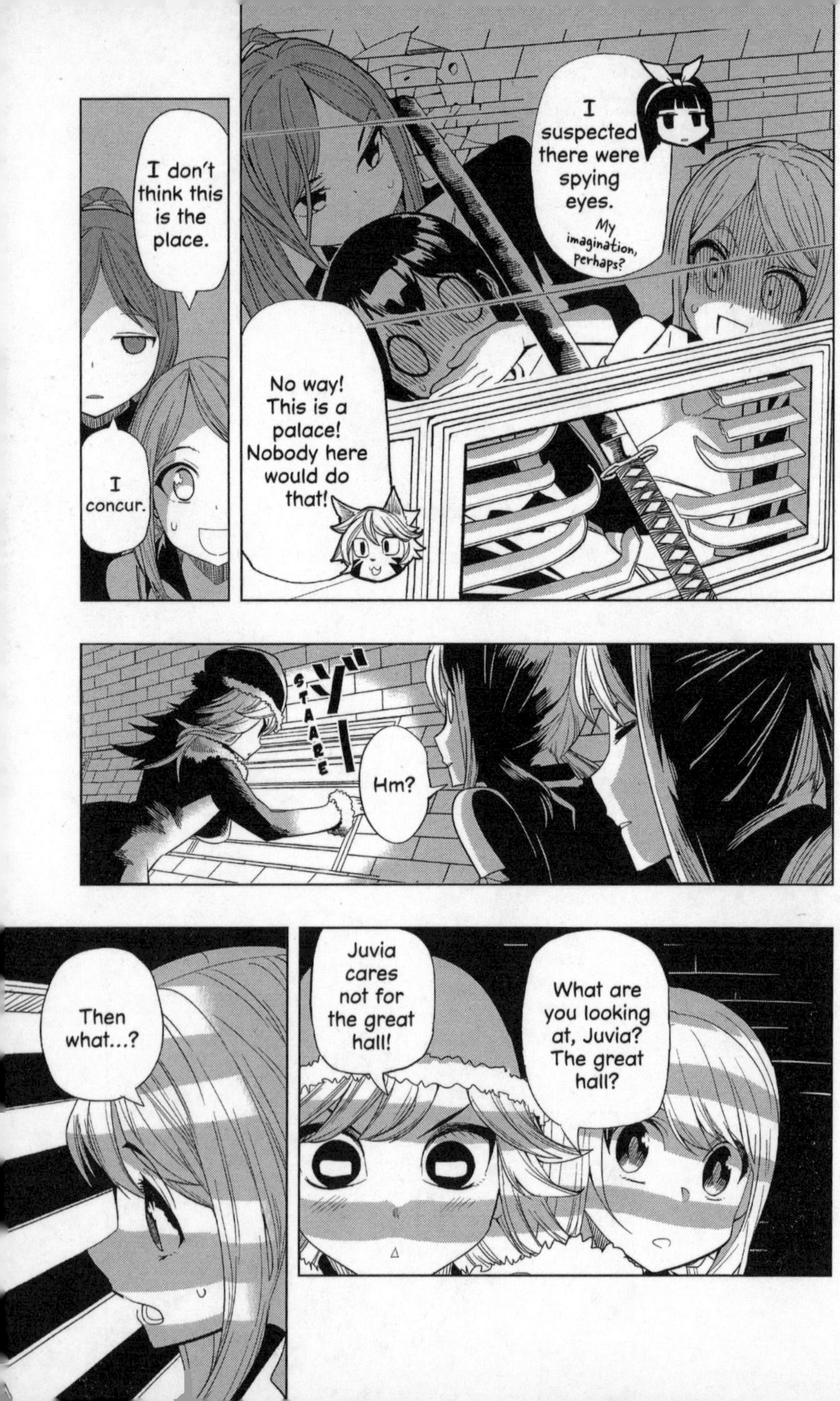
I suspected there were spying eyes.
My imagination, perhaps?
No way! This is a palace! Nobody here would do that!
I don't think this is the place.
I concur.
STAARE
Hm?
What are you looking at, Juvia? The great hall?
Juvia cares not for the great hall!
Then what...?

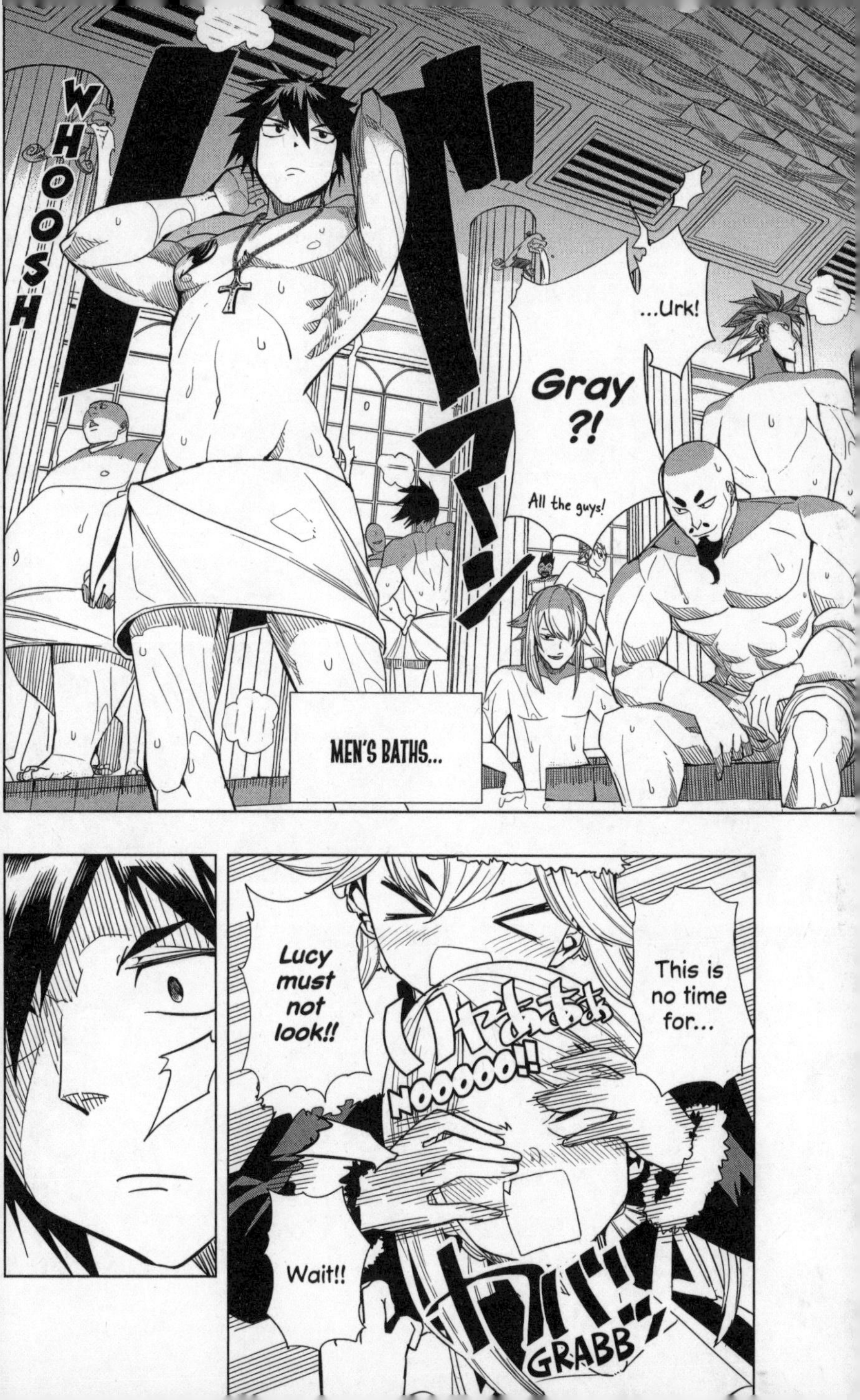
...Urk!
Gray ?!
All the guys!
WHOOSH
MEN'S BATHS...
This is no time for...
Lucy must not look!!
NOOOOO!!
Wait!!
GRABB

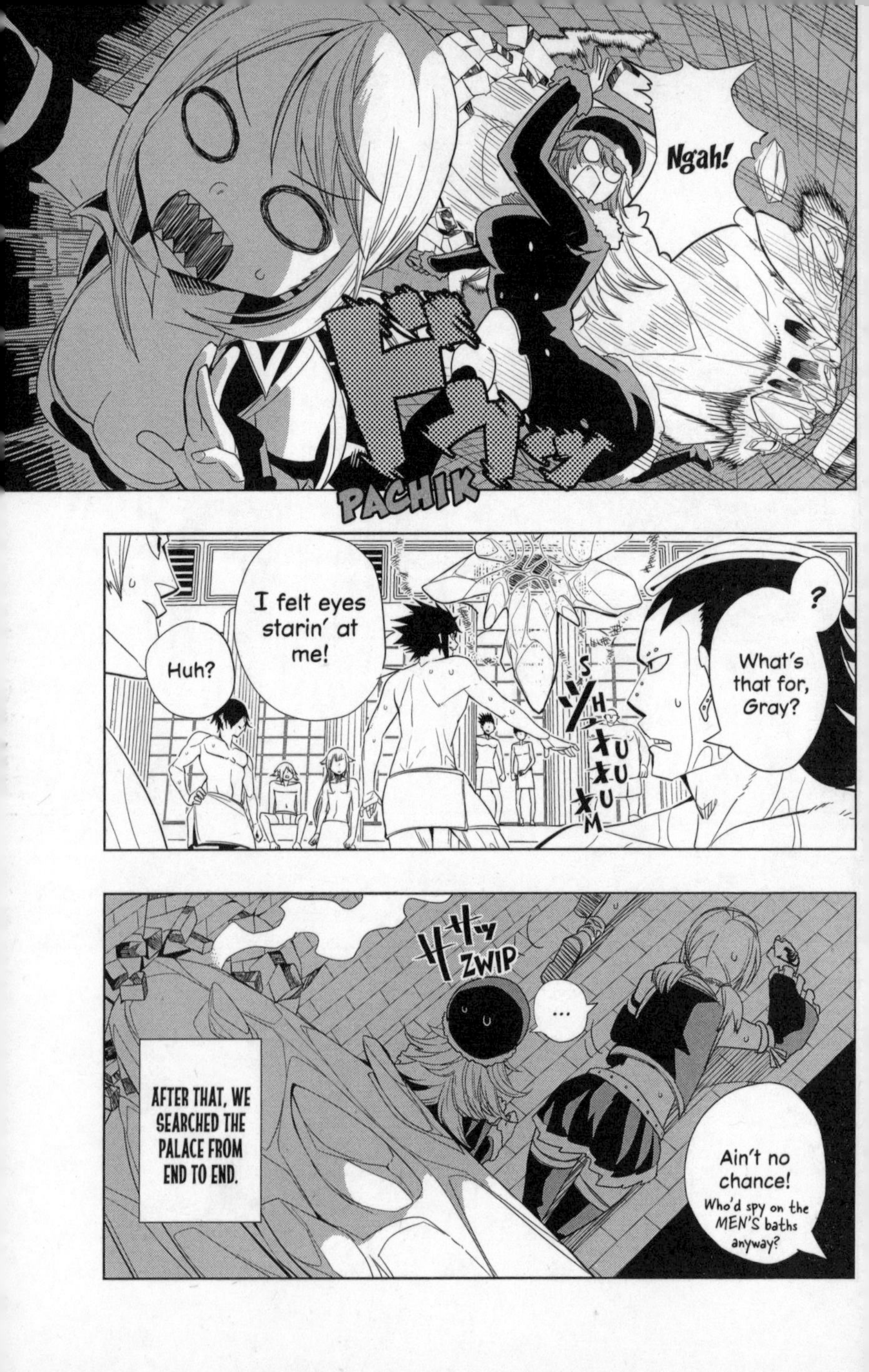
Ngah!
PACHIK
?
What's that for, Gray?
SHUUUM
I felt eyes starin' at me!
Huh?
Ain't no chance!
Who'd spy on the MEN'S baths anyway?
...
ZWIP
AFTER THAT, WE SEARCHED THE PALACE FROM END TO END.

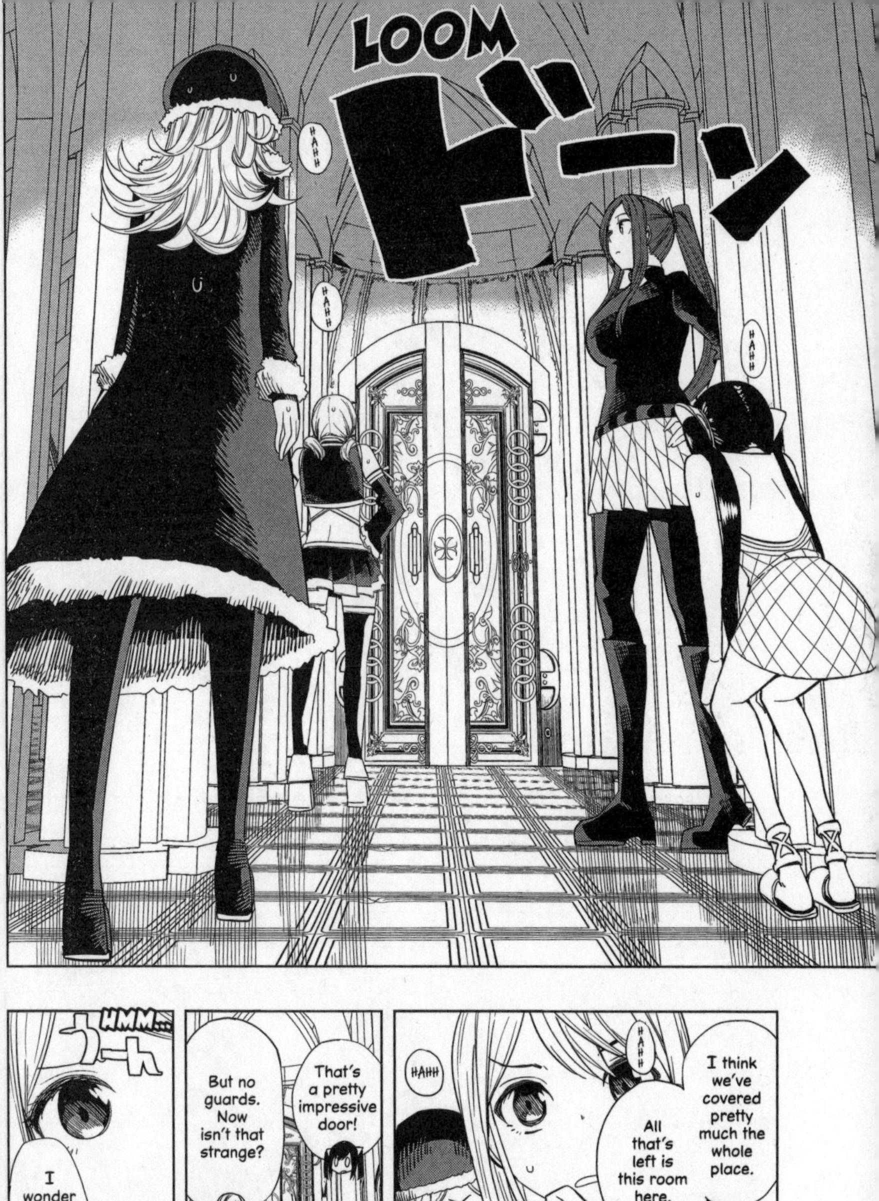
LOOM
ドーン
HAHH
HAHH
HAHH
HAHH
I think we've covered pretty much the whole place.
All that's left is this room here.
HAHH
HAHH
That's a pretty impressive door!
But no guards. Now isn't that strange?
HMM...
うーん
I wonder where this door leads...

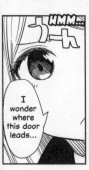

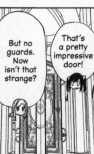

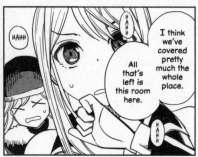

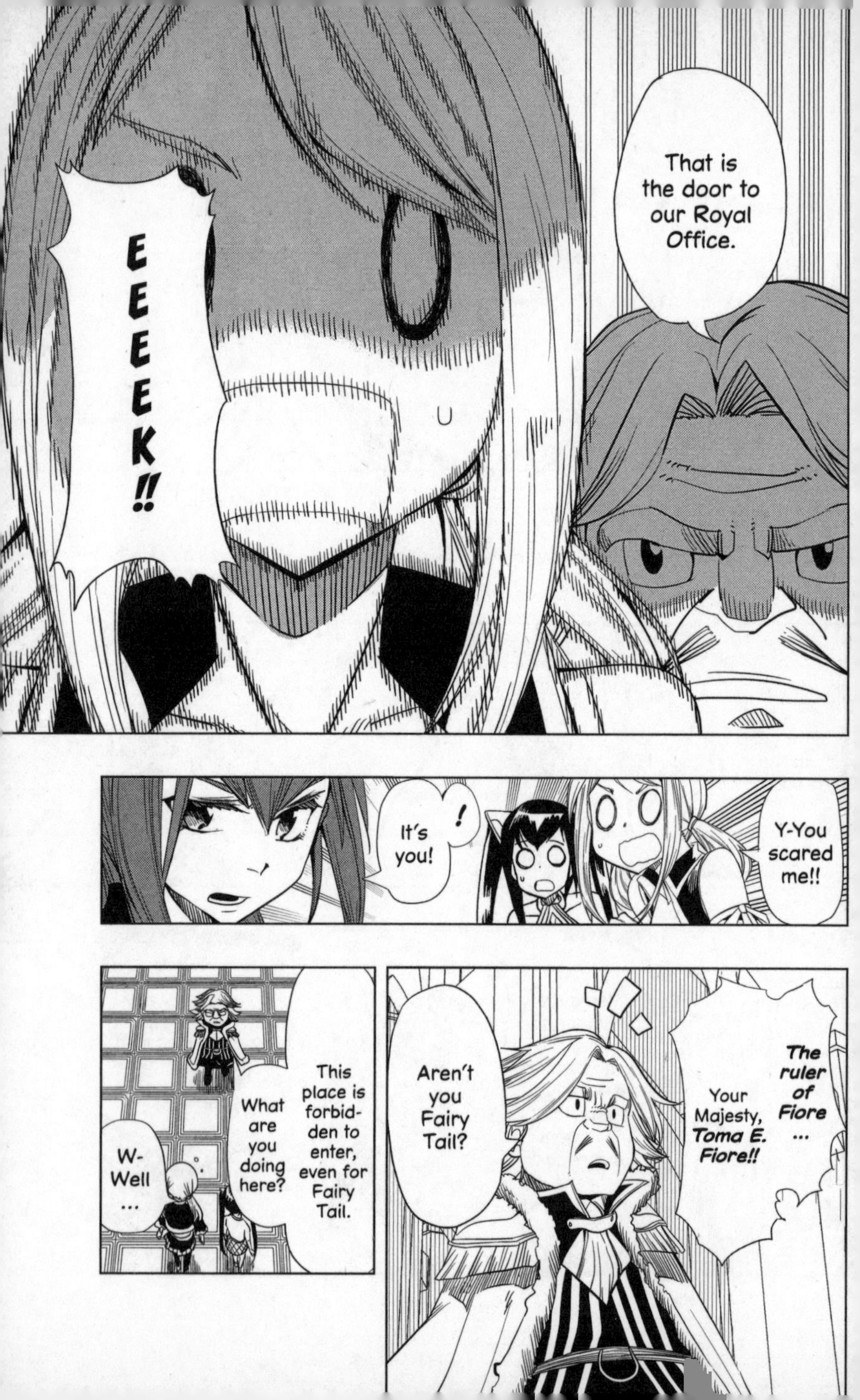
That is the door to our Royal Office.
EEEEK!!
Y-You scared me!!
!
It's you!
The ruler of Fiore ...
Your Majesty, *Toma E. Fiore!!*
Aren't you Fairy Tail?
This place is forbid-den to enter, even for Fairy Tail.
What are you doing here?
W-Well ...

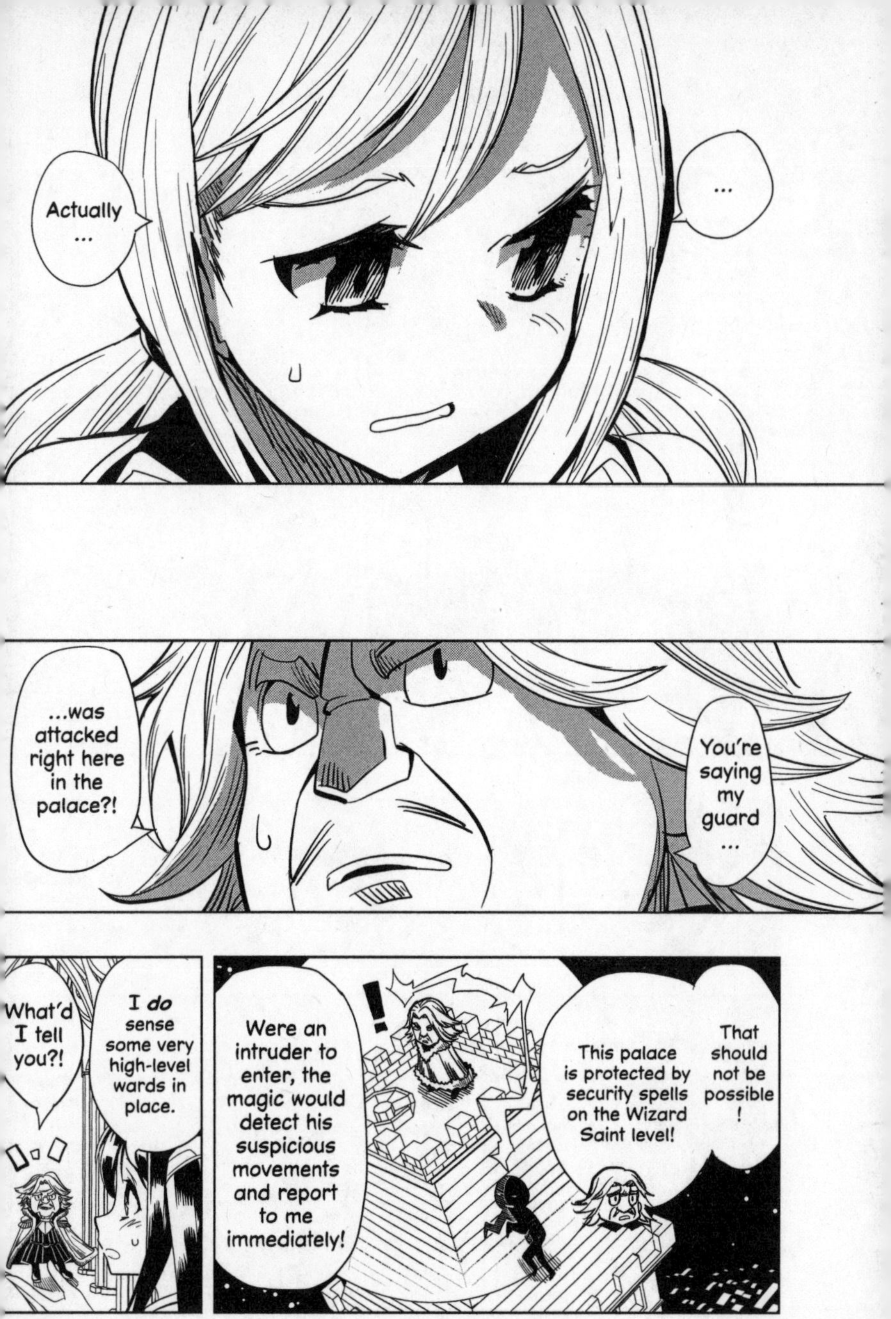
...
Actually ...
You're saying my guard ...
...was attacked right here in the palace?!
That should not be possible!
This palace is protected by security spells on the Wizard Saint level!
Were an intruder to enter, the magic would detect his suspicious movements and report to me immediately!
I *do* sense some very high-level wards in place.
What'd I tell you?!

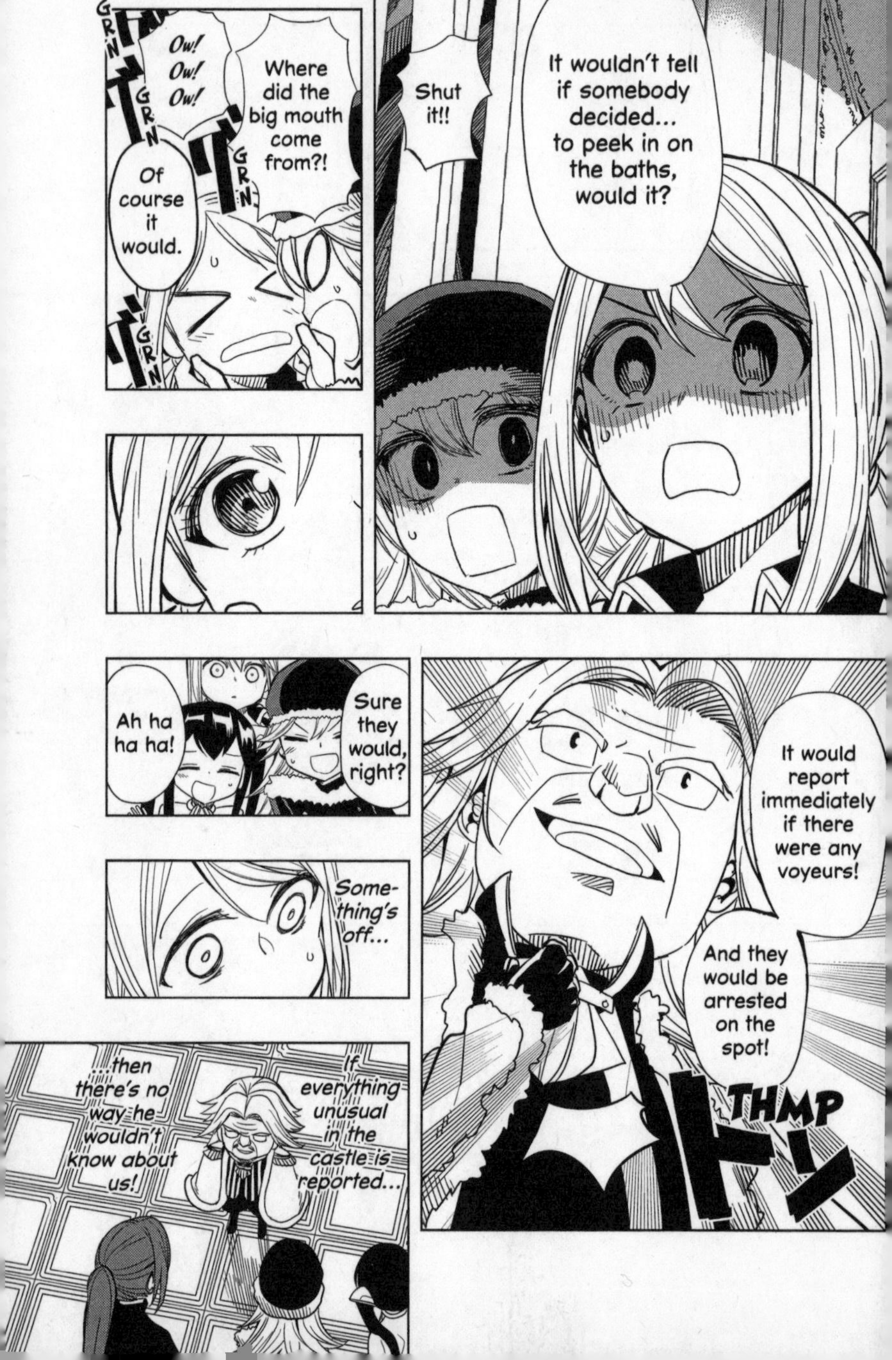
It wouldn't tell if somebody decided... to peek in on the baths, would it?
Shut it!!
Where did the big mouth come from?!
Ow! Ow! Ow!
GRN GRN GRN GRN
Of course it would.
It would report immediately if there were any voyeurs!
And they would be arrested on the spot!
THMP
Sure they would, right?
Ah ha ha ha!
Something's off...
If everything unusual in the castle is reported...
...then there's no way he wouldn't know about us!

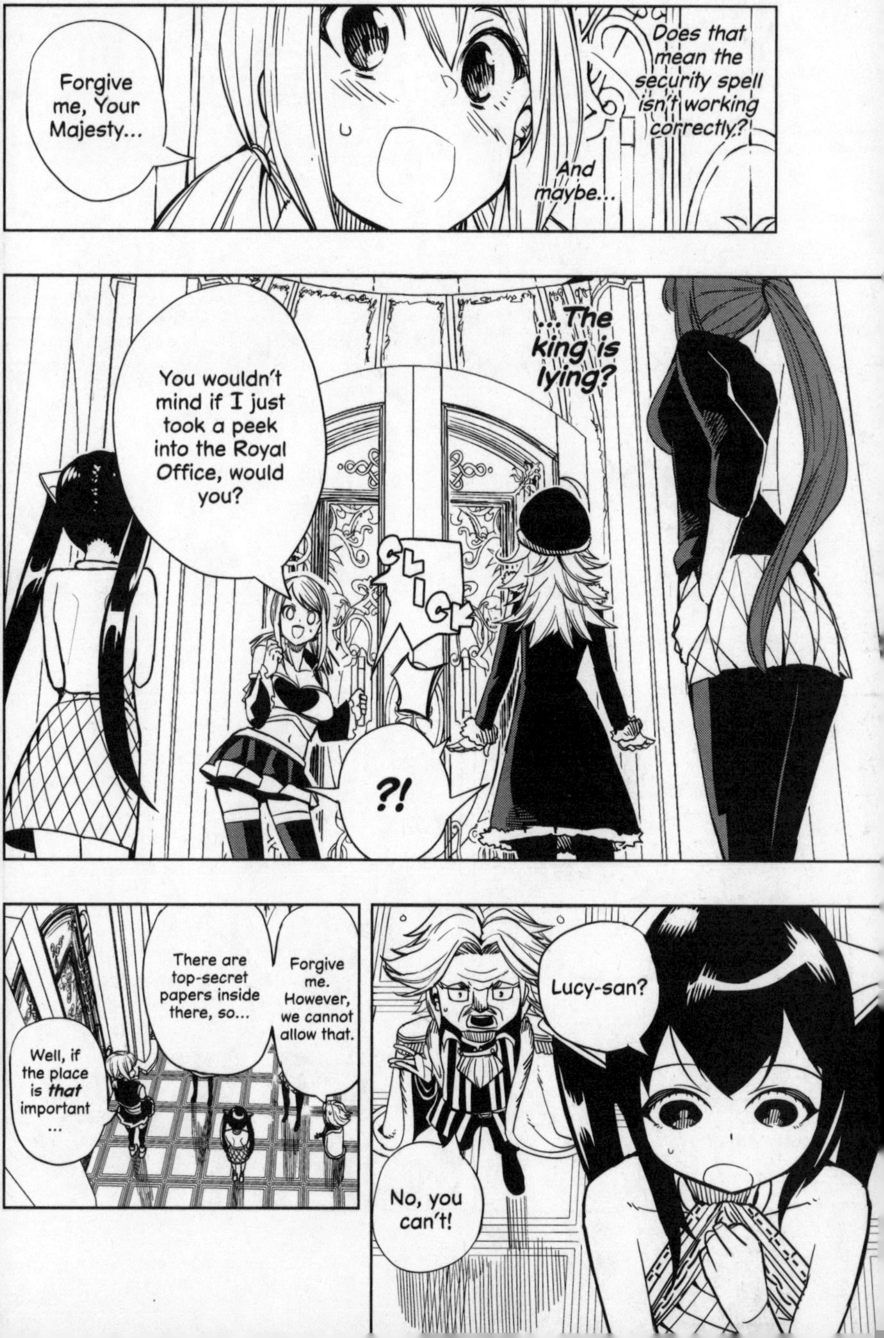

Does that mean the security spell isn't working correctly?
And maybe...
Forgive me, Your Majesty...
...The king is lying?
You wouldn't mind if I just took a peek into the Royal Office, would you?
CLICK
?!
Lucy-san?
No, you can't!
Forgive me. However, we cannot allow that.
There are top-secret papers inside there, so...
Well, if the place is *that* important ...

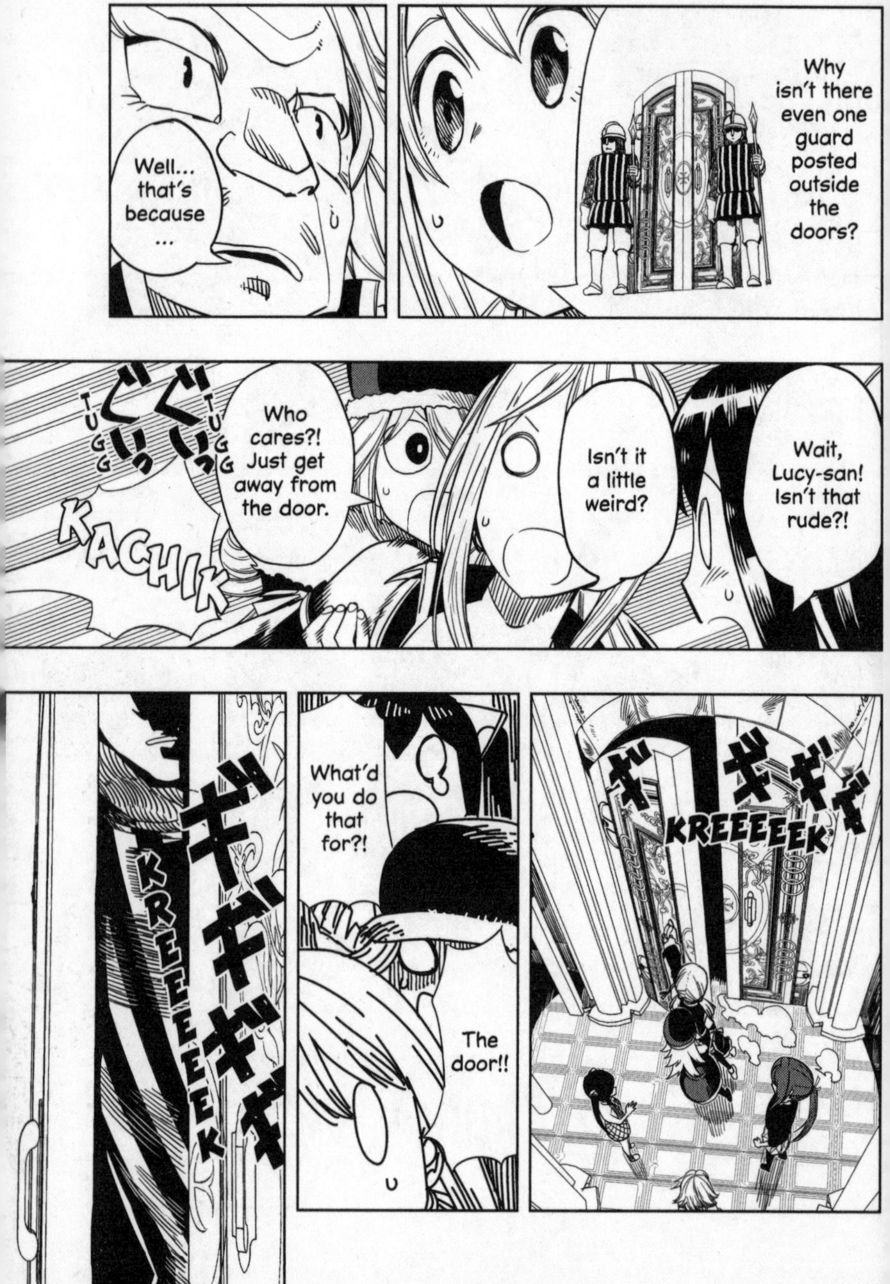
Why isn't there even one guard posted outside the doors?
Well... that's because ...
Wait, Lucy-san! Isn't that rude?!
Isn't it a little weird?
Who cares?! Just get away from the door.
TUGG
TUGG
KACHIK
KREEEEEK
What'd you do that for?!
The door!!
KREEEEEEK

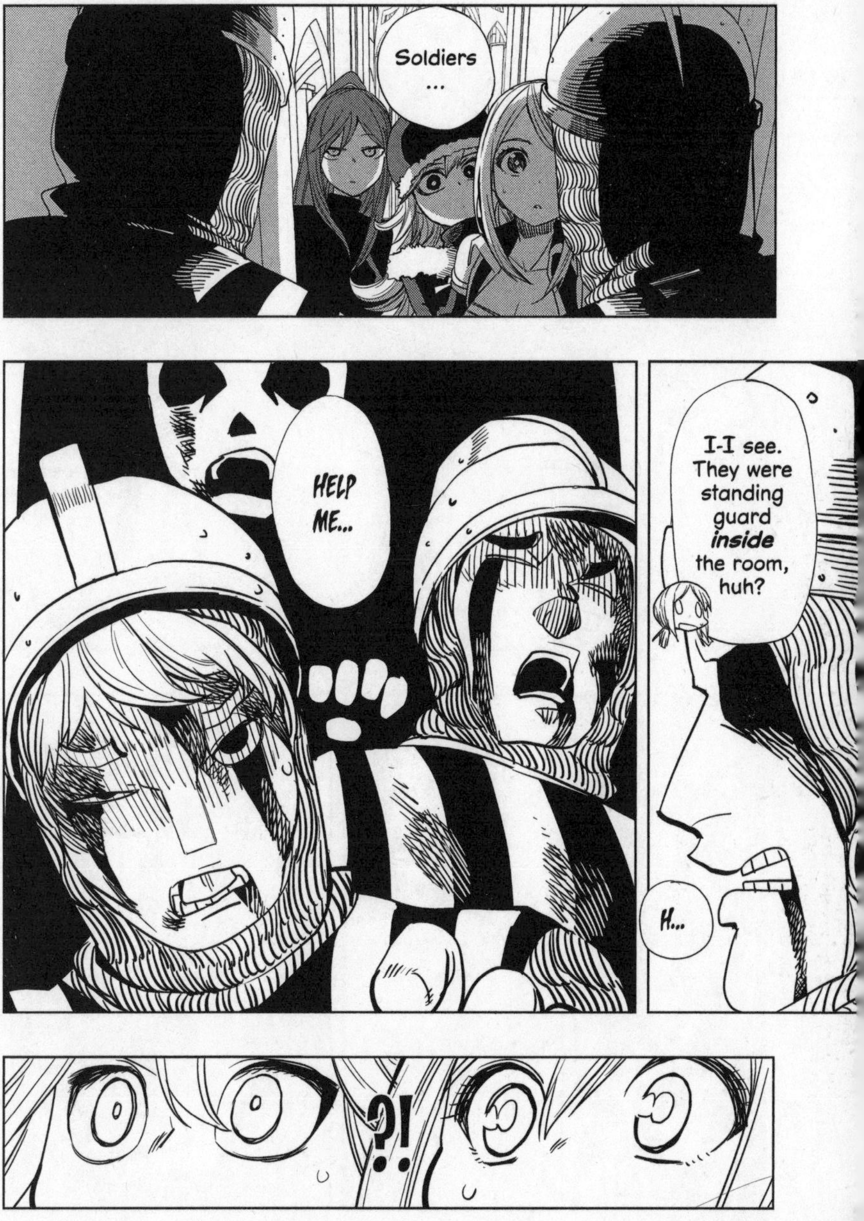
Soldiers ...
I-I see. They were standing guard *inside* the room, huh?
H...
HELP ME...
?!

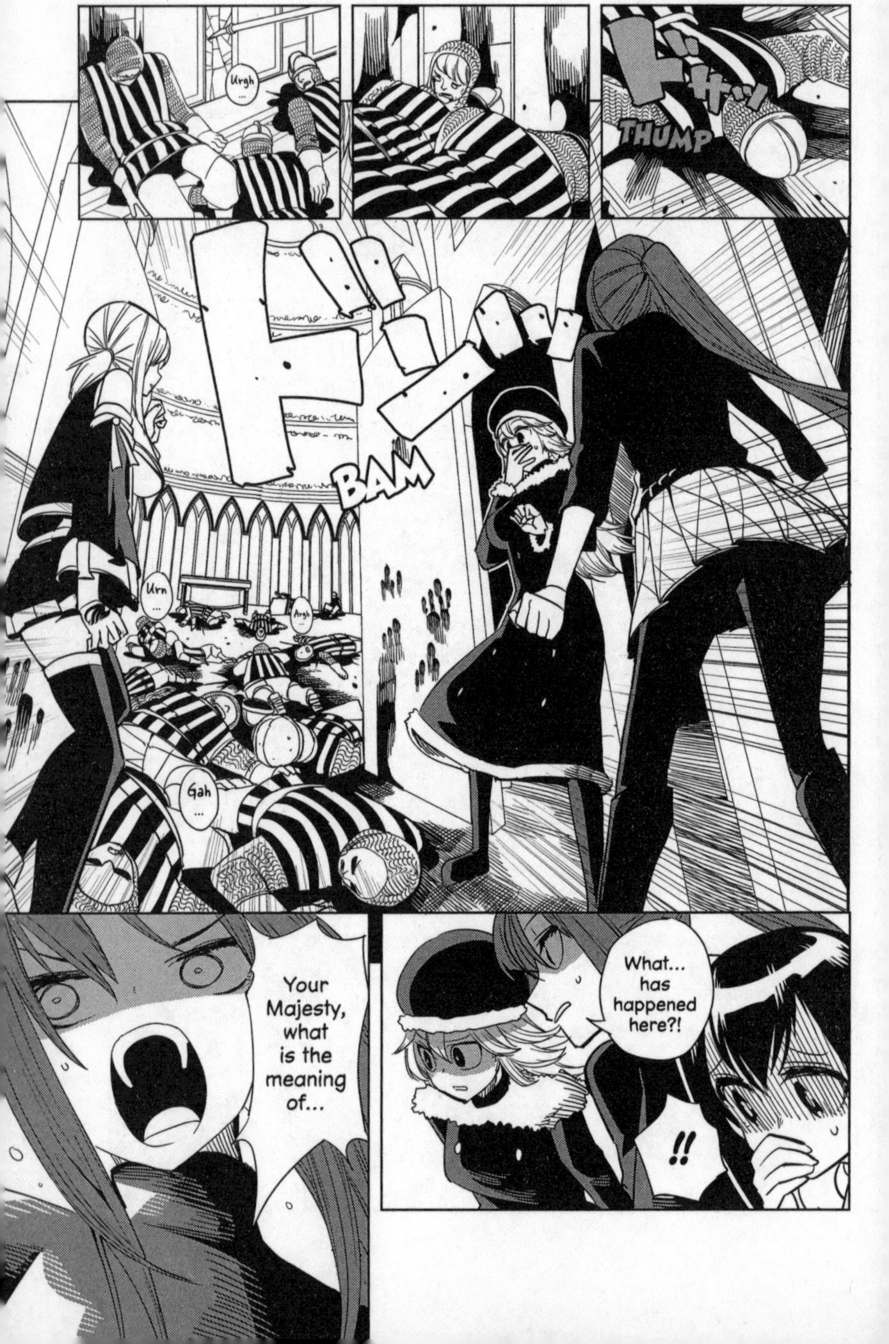
THUMP
Urgh...
BAM
Urn...
Argh...
Gah...
What... has happened here?!
!!
Your Majesty, what is the meaning of...

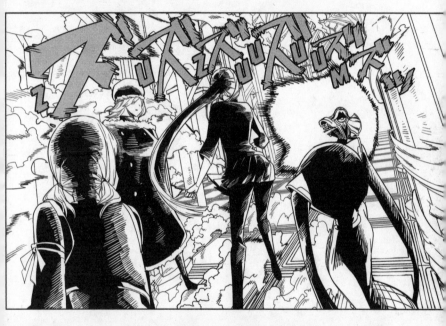

Figured me out, huh?

Heh!

What...?

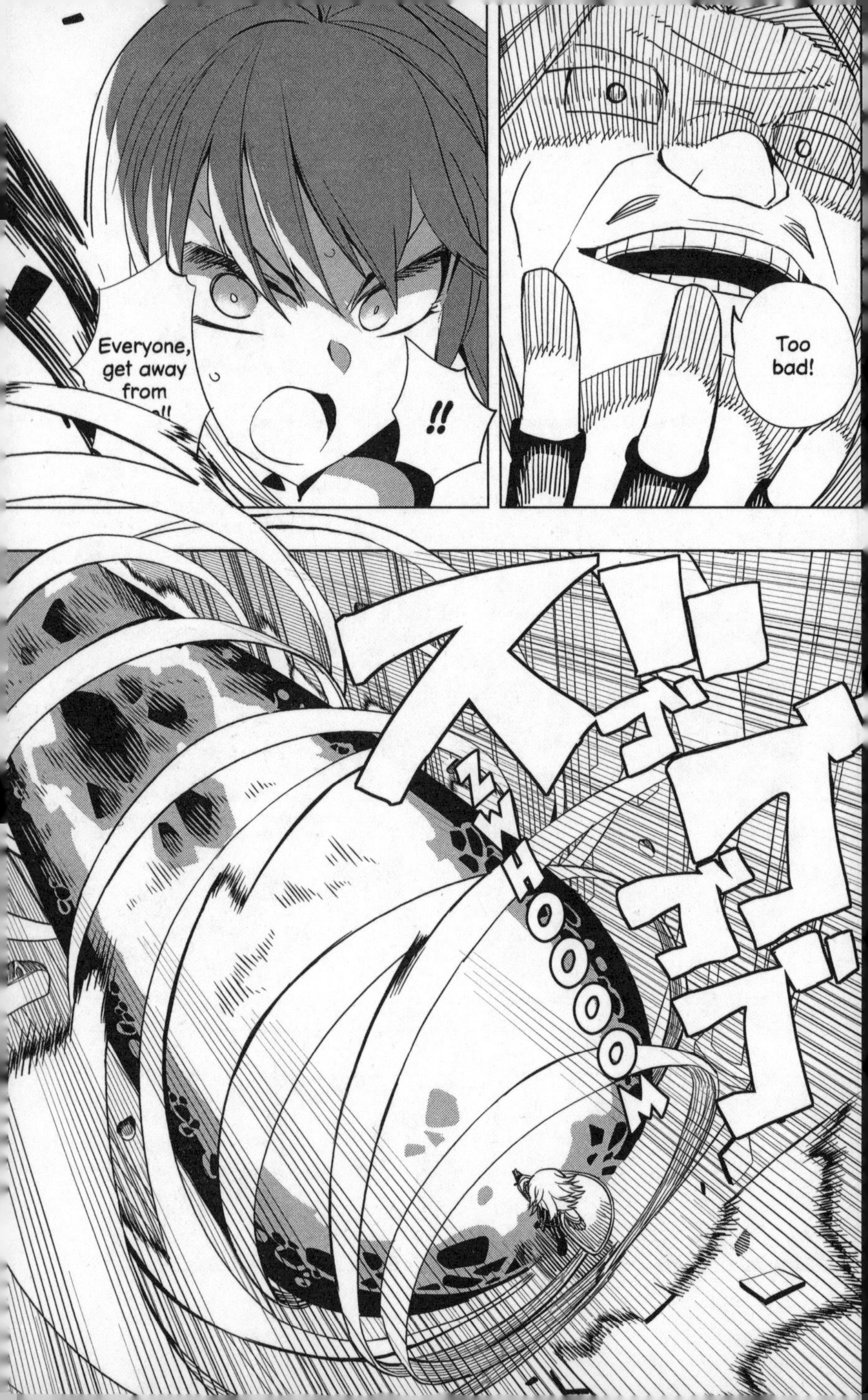
Too bad!
Everyone, get away from
!!
ZWHOOOOOM

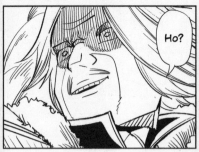

Ho?
You'd even protect the guards?
But in exchange, it's left Juvia in tatters...
HAHH
We were careless!
HAHH

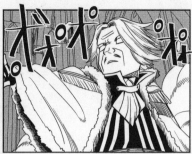

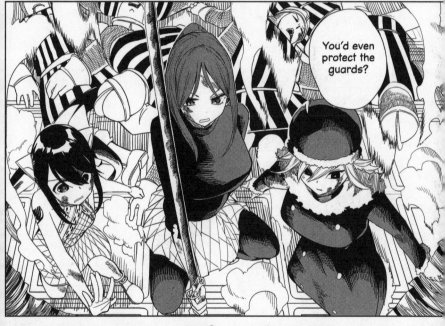

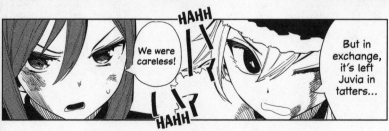

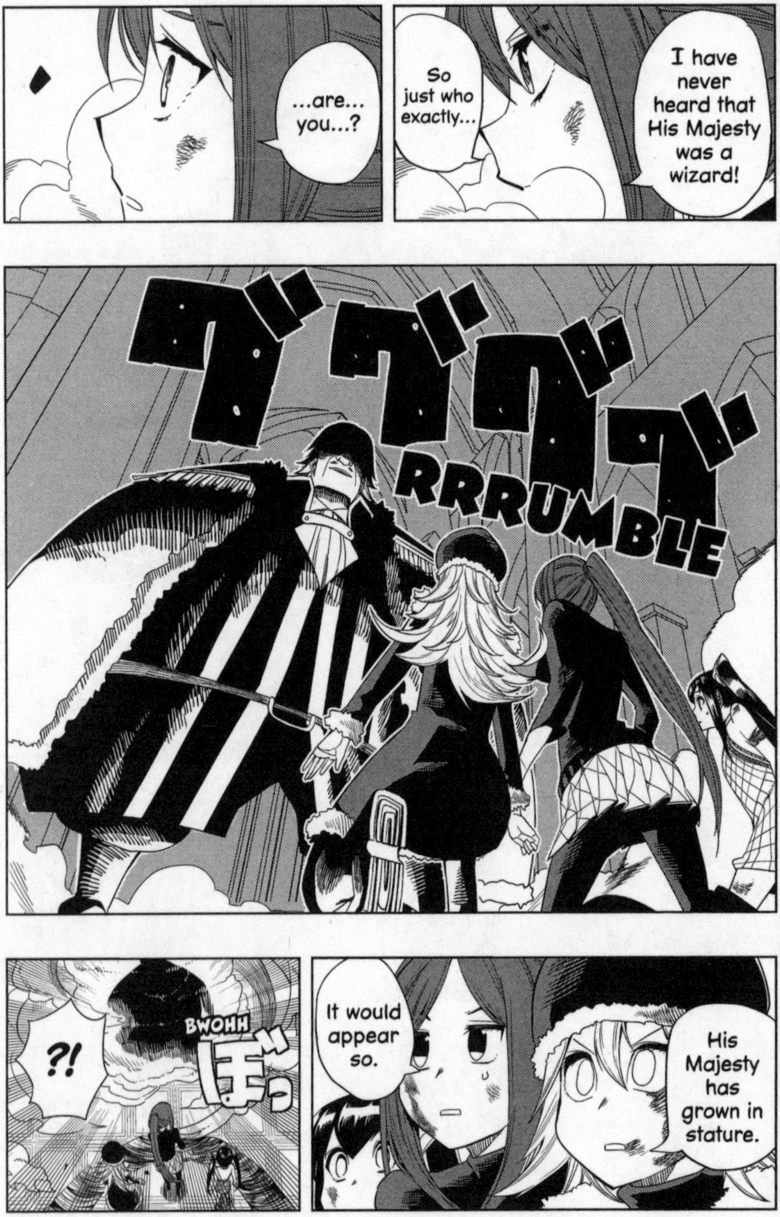
I have never heard that His Majesty was a wizard!
So just who exactly...
...are... you...?
ゴゴゴゴ
RRRUMBLE
His Majesty has grown in stature.
It would appear so.
BWOHH
ぼっ
?!

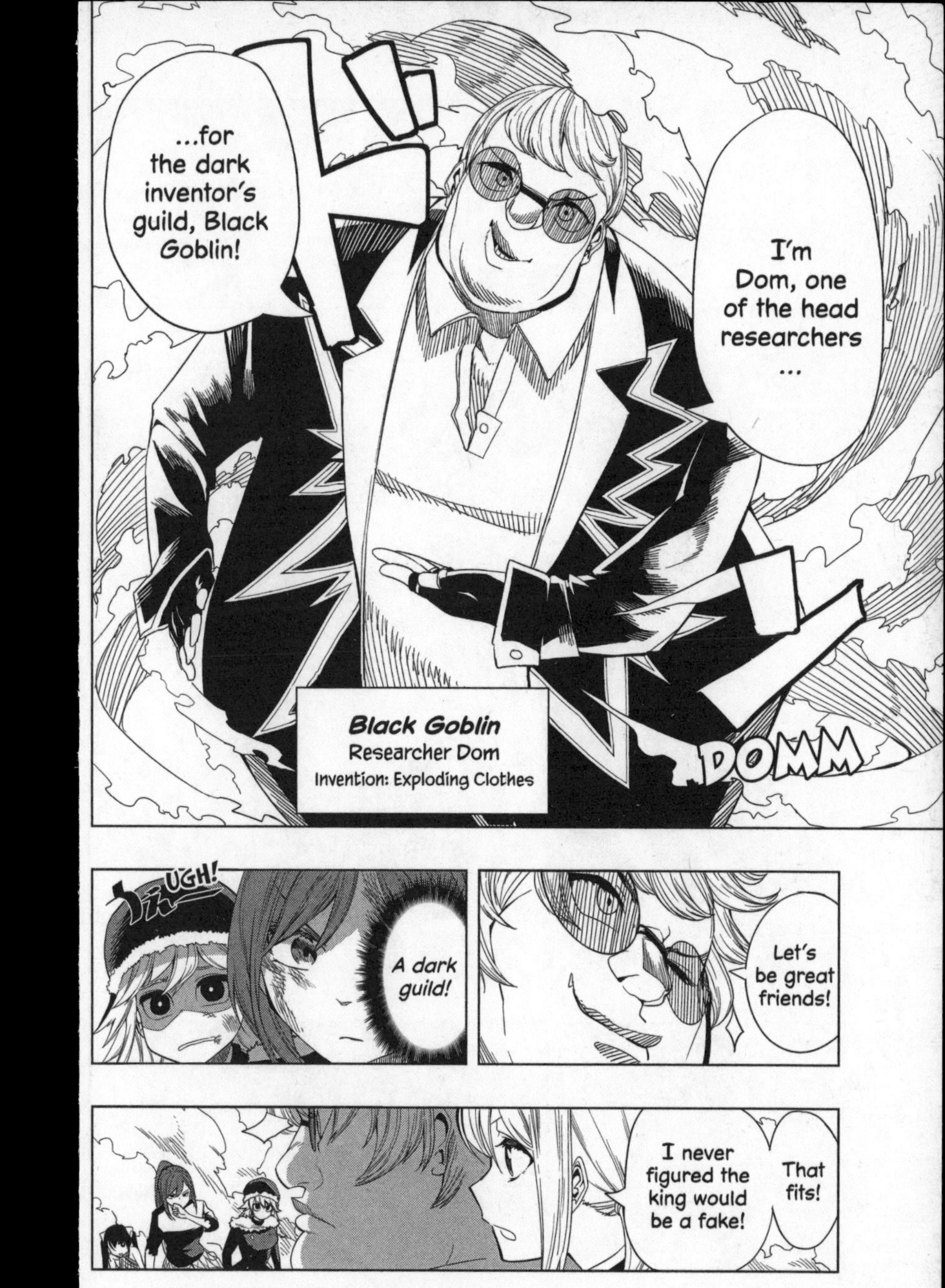
I'm Dom, one of the head researchers ...
...for the dark inventor's guild, Black Goblin!
Black Goblin
Researcher Dom
Invention: Exploding Clothes
DOMM
Let's be great friends!
UGH!
A dark guild!
That fits!
I never figured the king would be a fake!

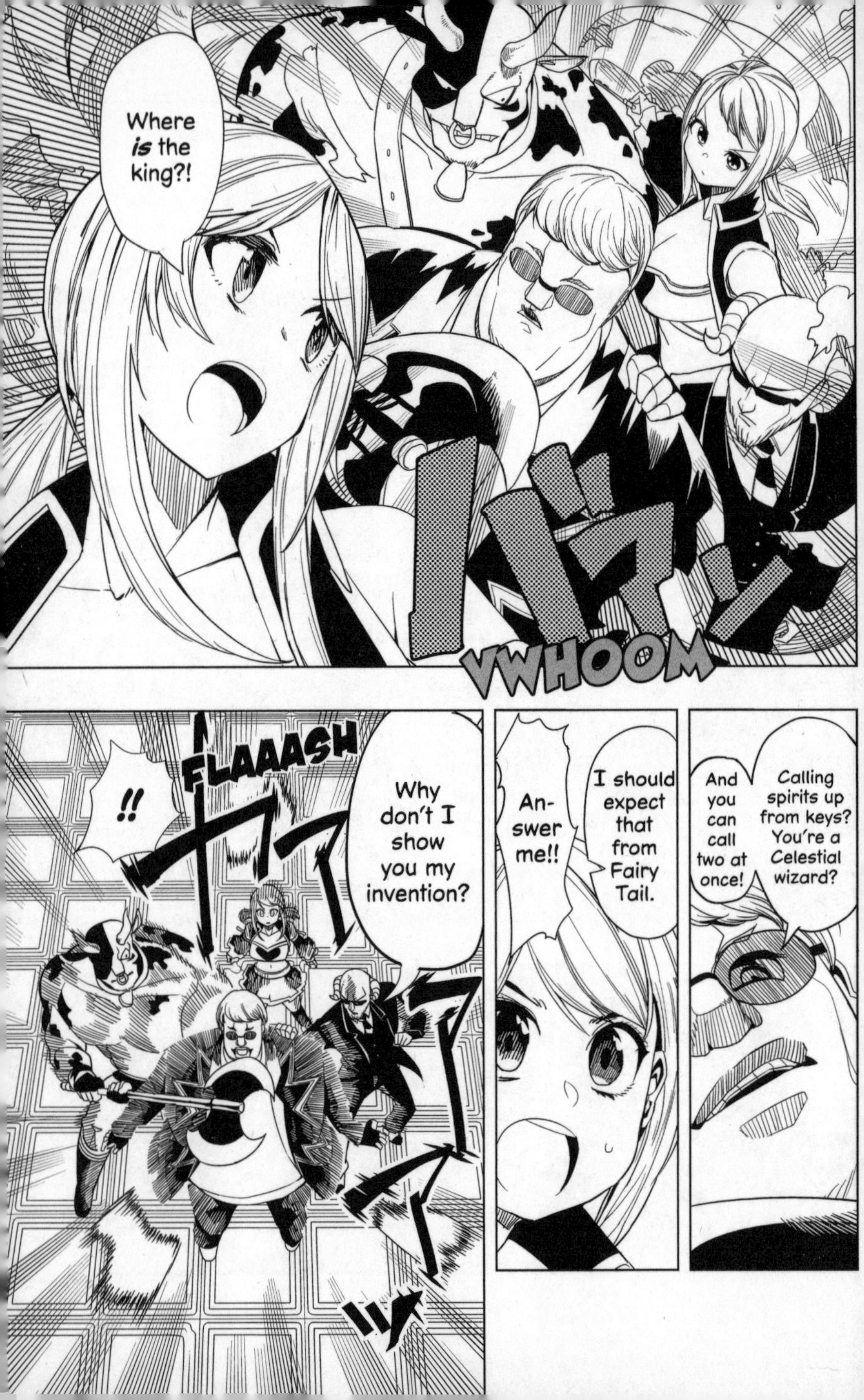
Where *is* the king?!
ドバッ
VWHOOM
Calling spirits up from keys? You're a Celestial wizard?
And you can call two at once!
I should expect that from Fairy Tail.
An-swer me!!
Why don't I show you my invention?
!!
FLAAASH

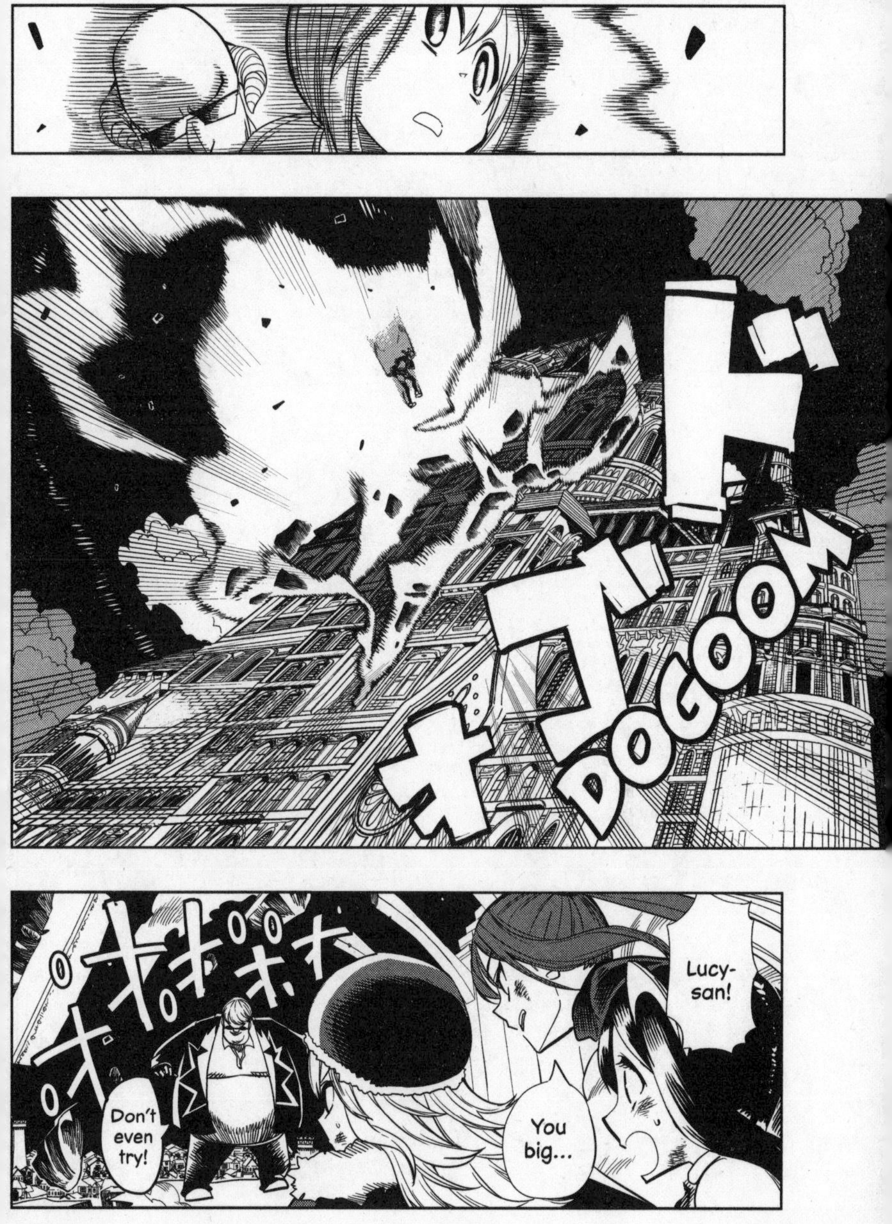
DOGOOM
Lucy-san!
You big...
Don't even try!

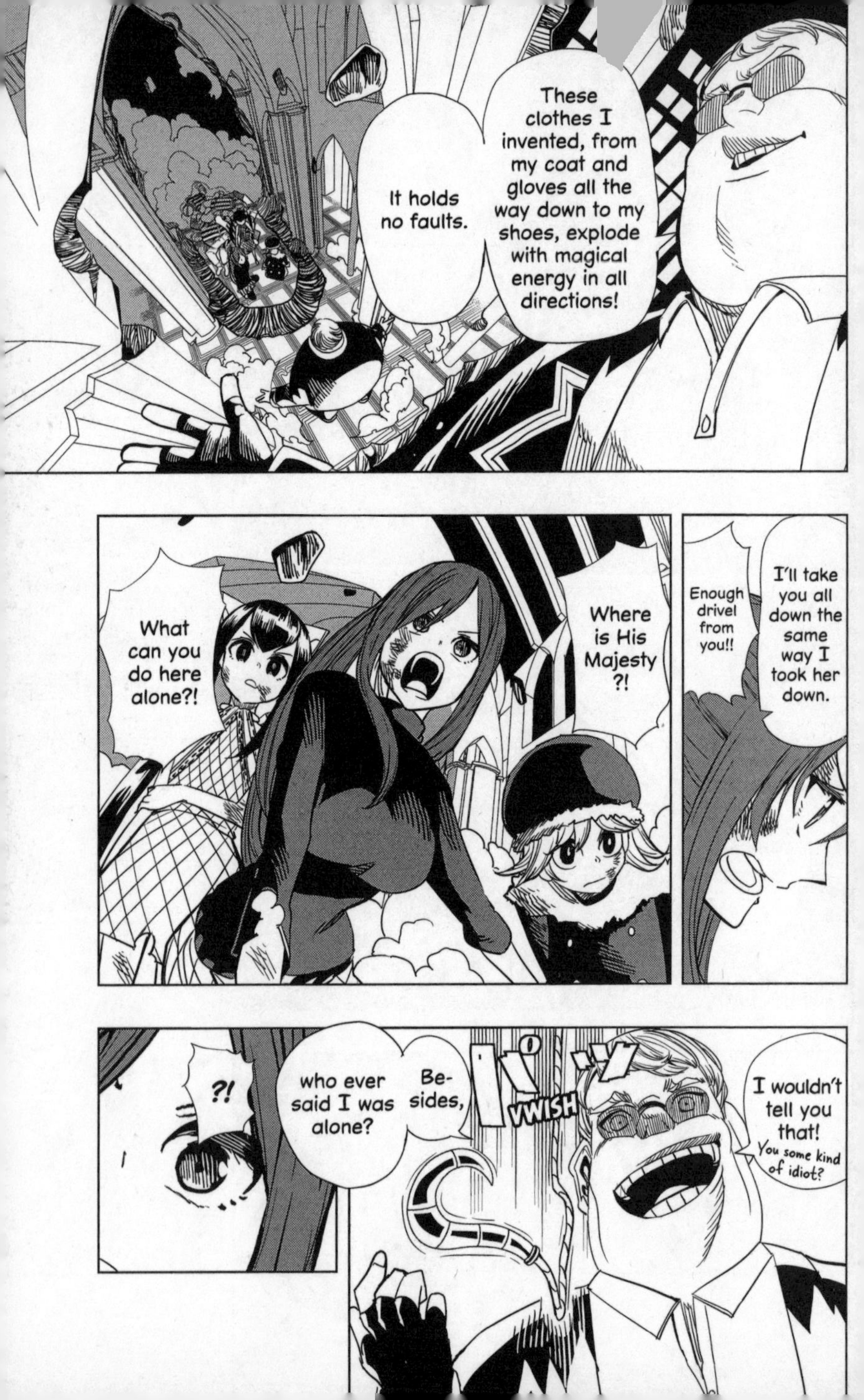

These clothes I invented, from my coat and gloves all the way down to my shoes, explode with magical energy in all directions!
It holds no faults.
I'll take you all down the same way I took her down.
Enough drivel from you!!
Where is His Majesty?!
What can you do here alone?!
I wouldn't tell you that!
You some kind of idiot?
VWISH
Be-sides,
who ever said I was alone?
?!

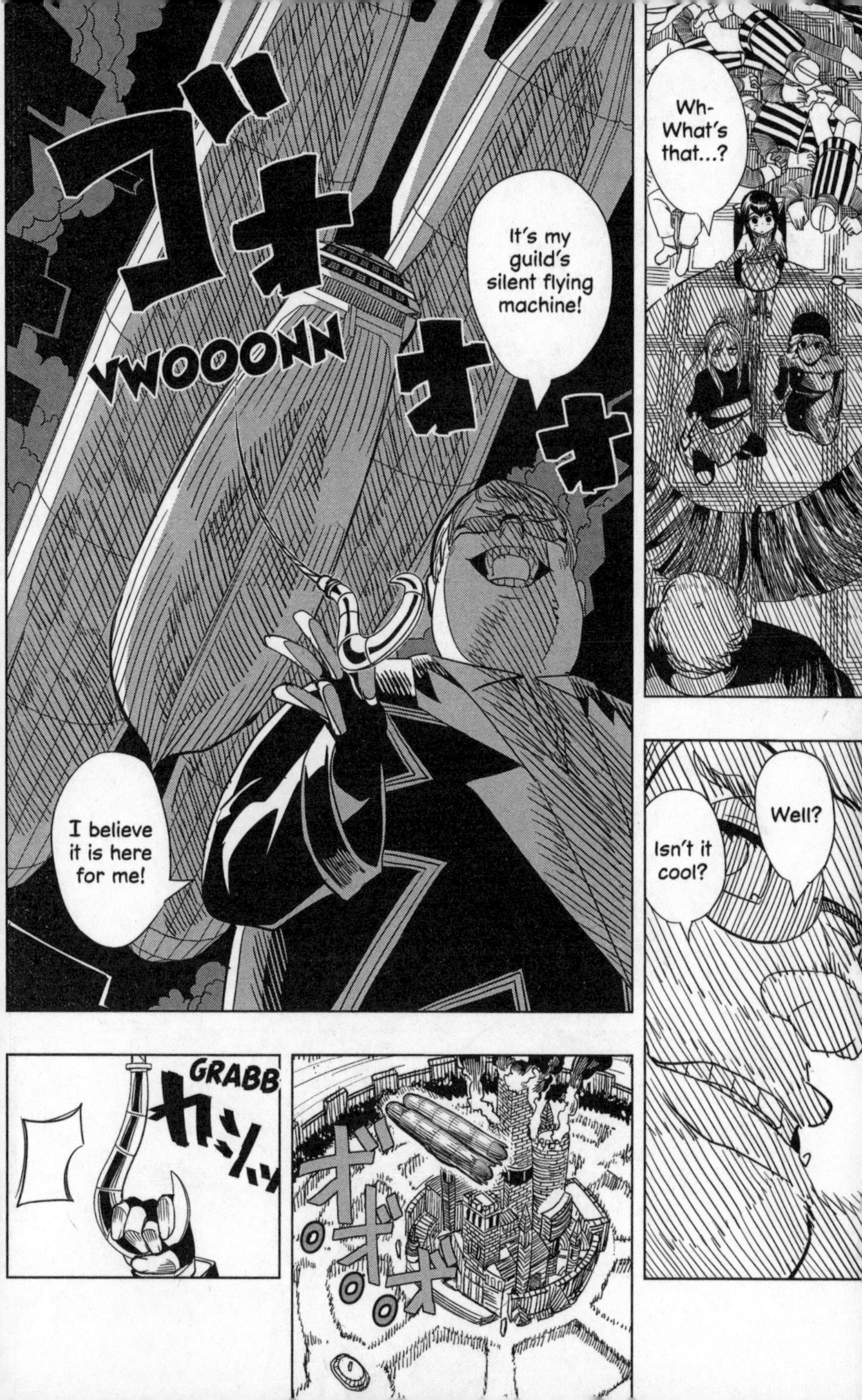
Wh- What's that...?
VWOOONN
It's my guild's silent flying machine!
I believe it is here for me!
Well?
Isn't it cool?
GRABB

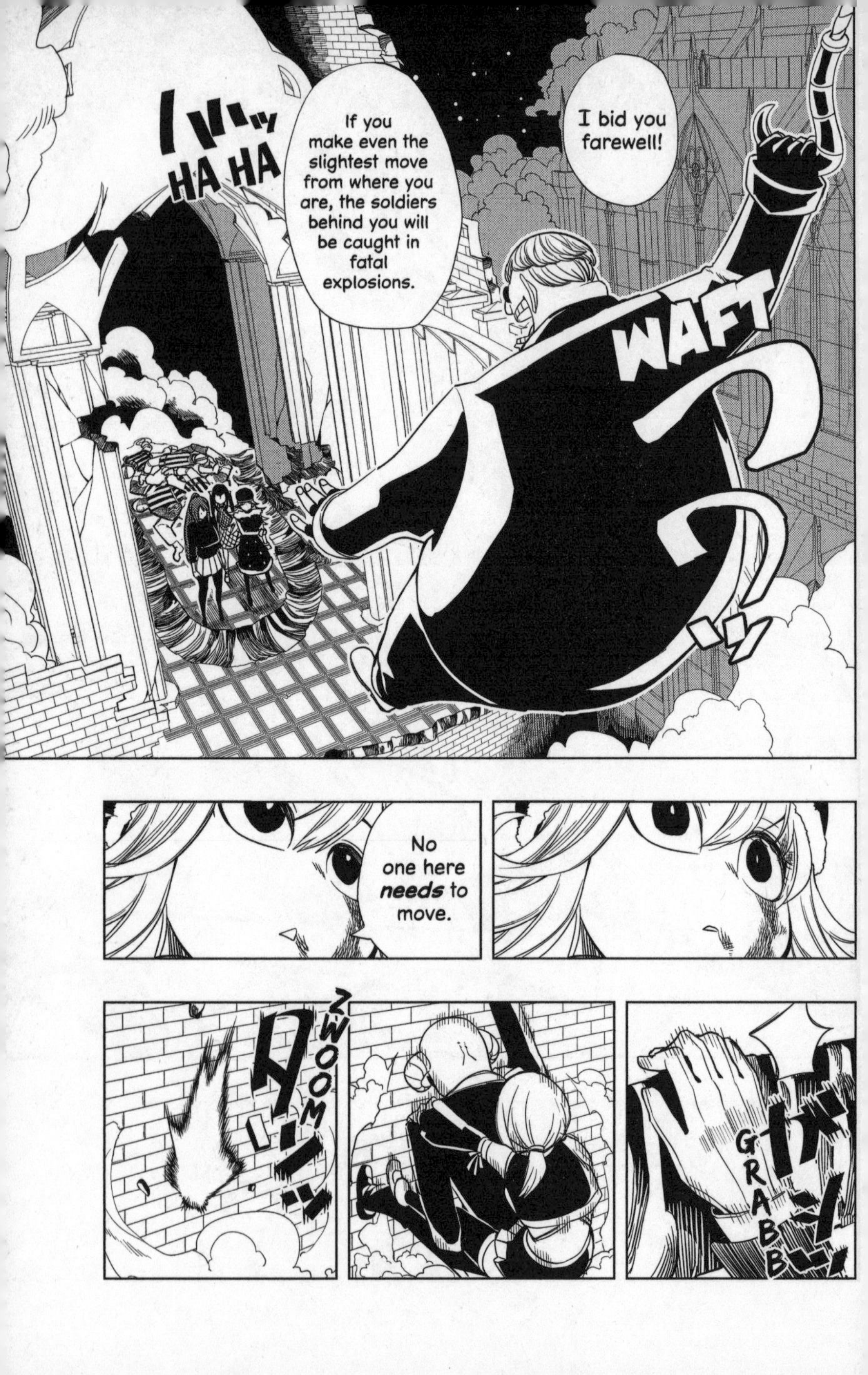
I bid you farewell!
WAFT
If you make even the slightest move from where you are, the soldiers behind you will be caught in fatal explosions.
HA HA
No one here *needs* to move.
GRABB
ZWOOM

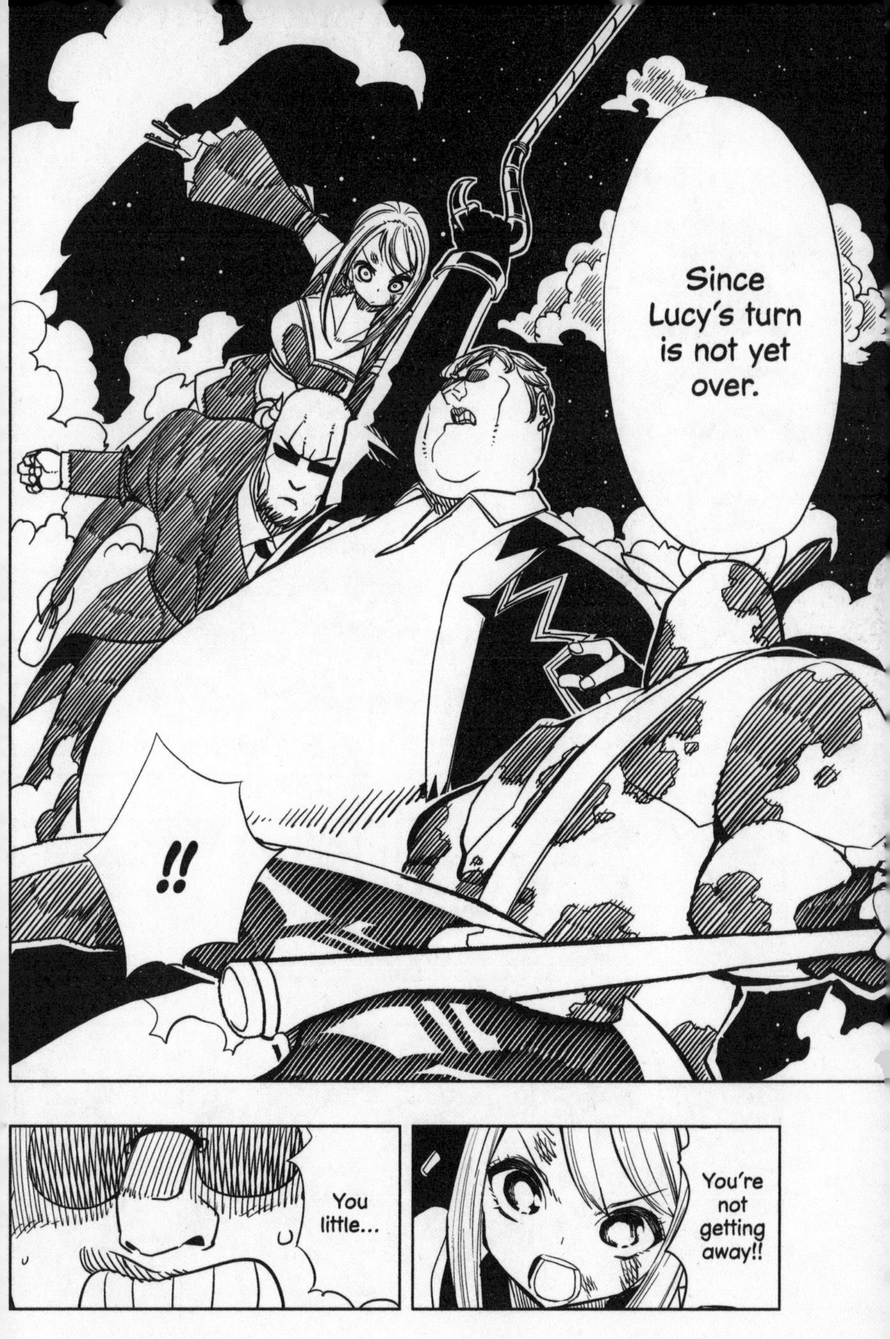
Since Lucy's turn is not yet over.
!!
You're not getting away!!
You little...

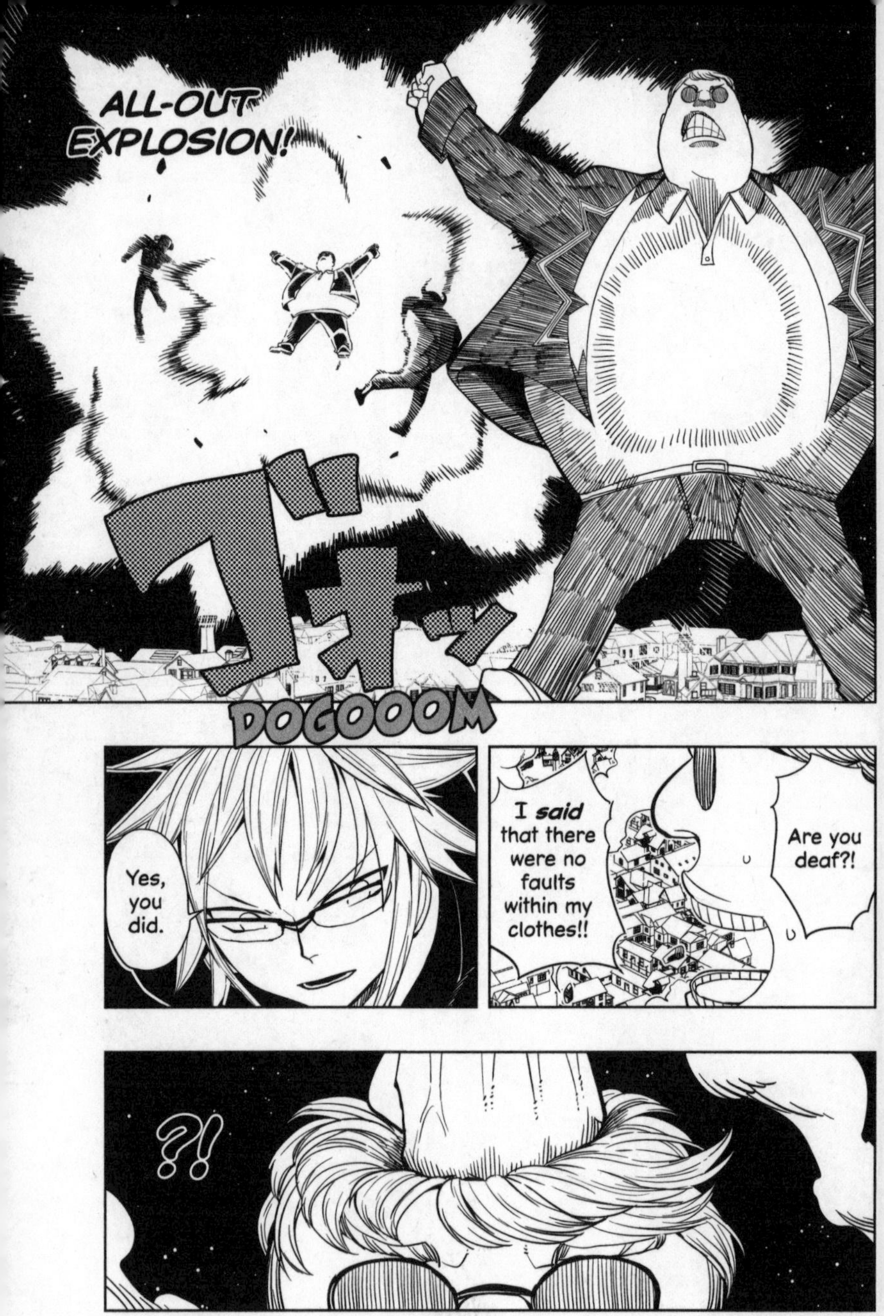
ALL-OUT EXPLOSION!
ゴオッ
DOGOOOM
I *said* that there were no faults within my clothes!!
Are you deaf?!
Yes, you did.
?!

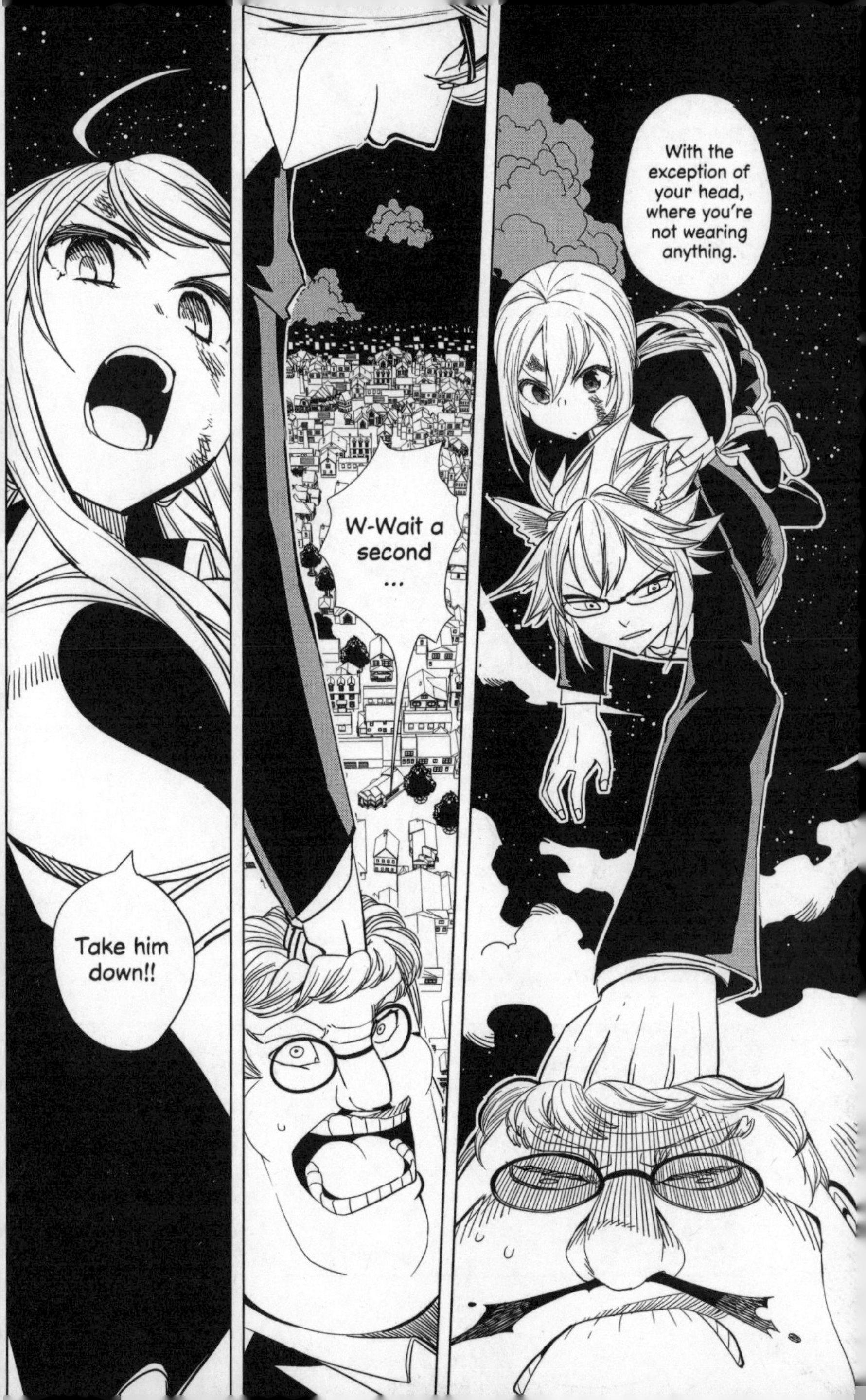
With the exception of your head, where you're not wearing anything.
W-Wait a second ...
Take him down!!

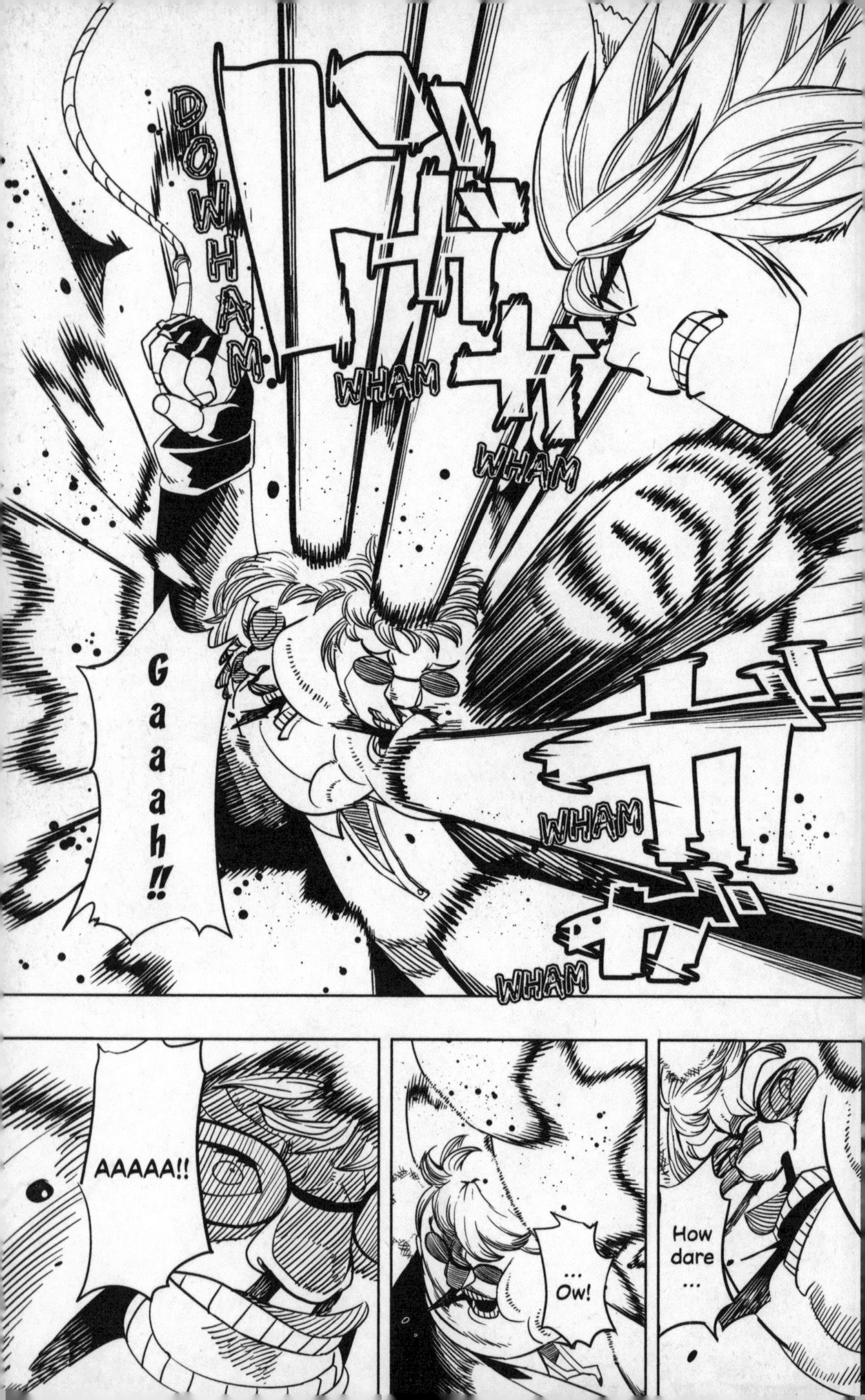
DOWHAM
WHAM
WHAM
WHAM
WHAM
Gaaah!!
How dare ...
... Ow!
AAAAA!!

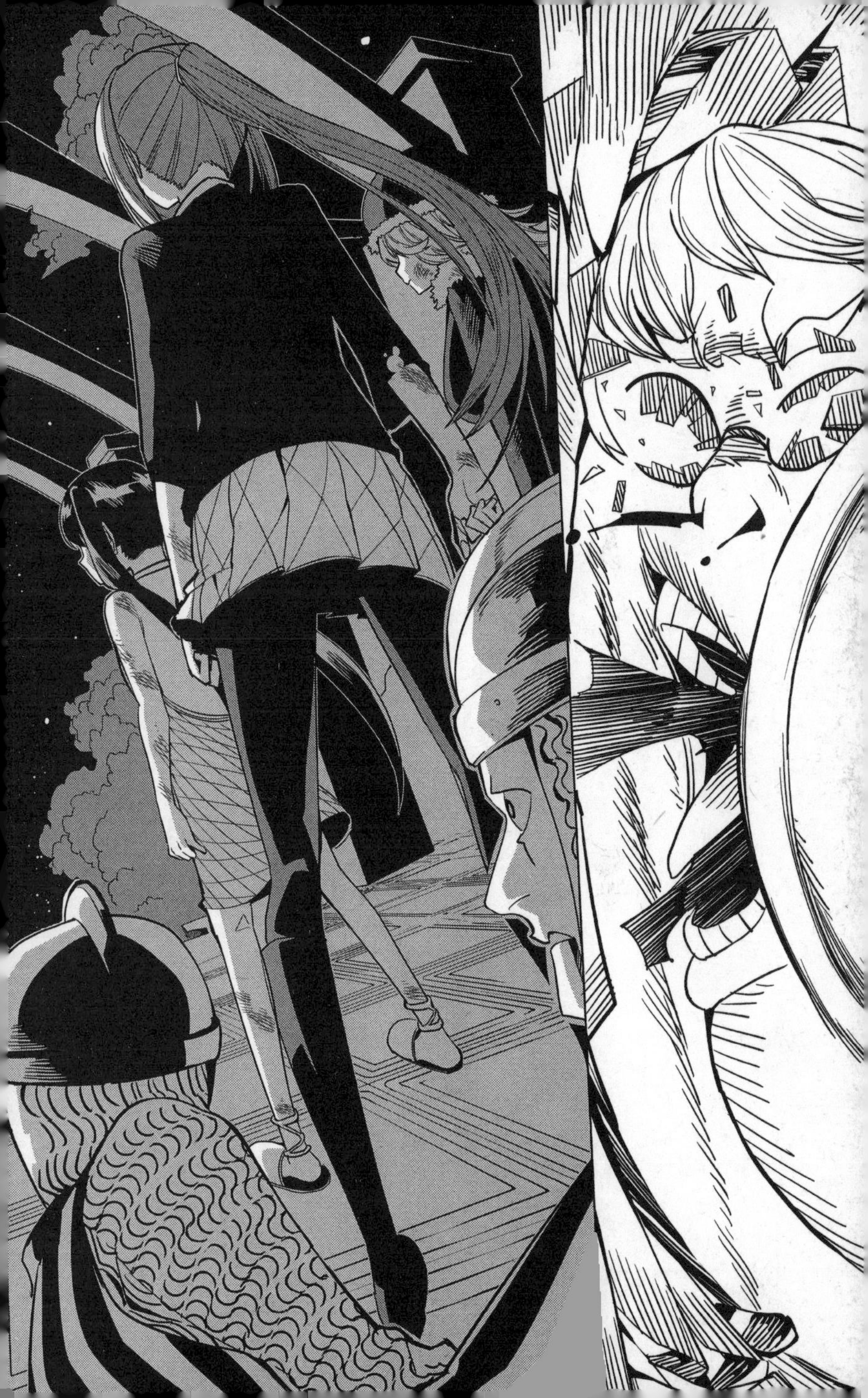

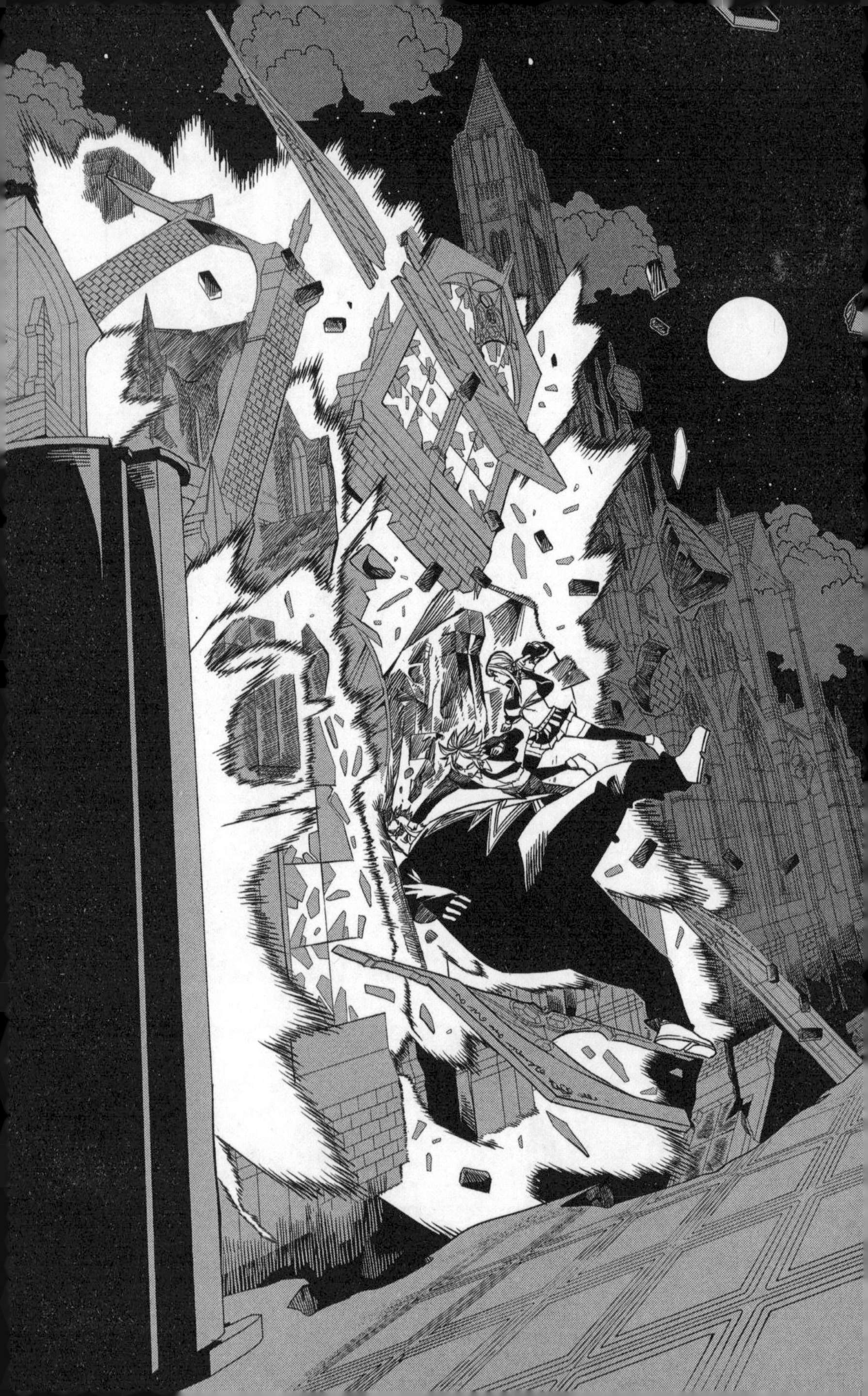

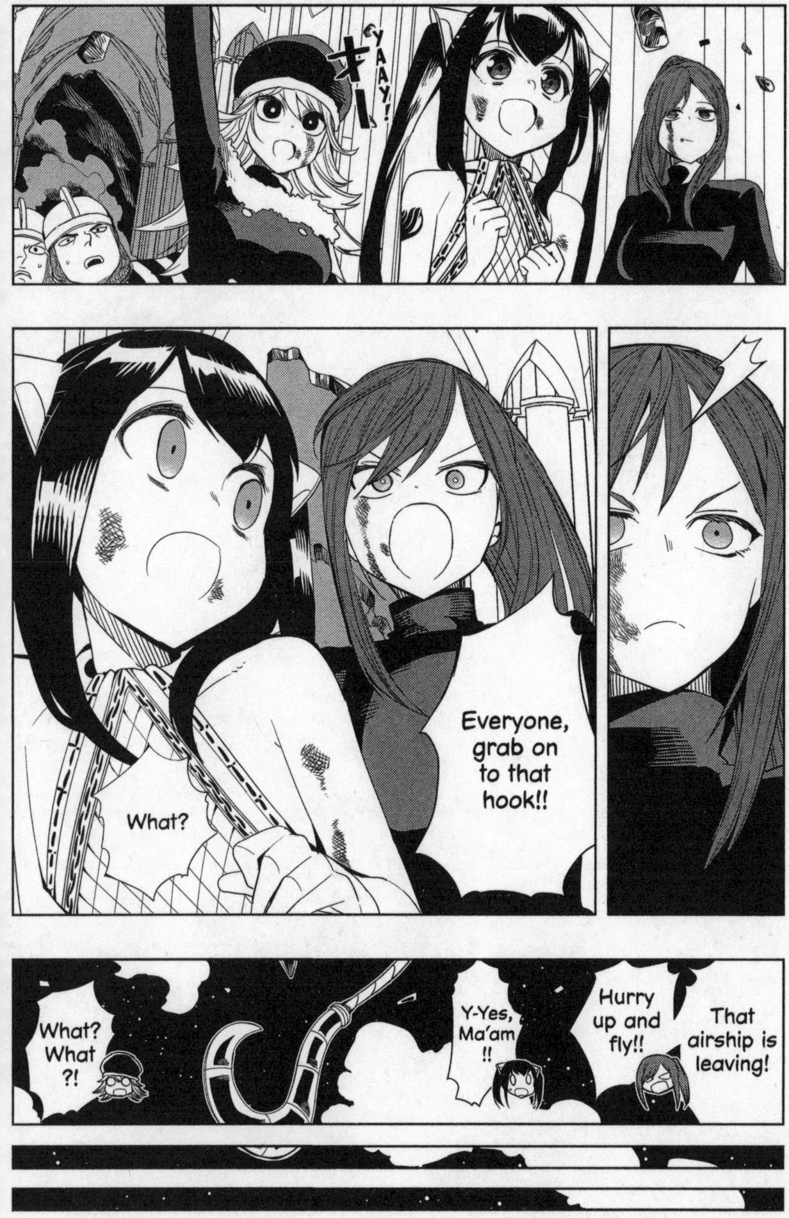
オー
YAAY!
Everyone, grab on to that hook!!
What?
That airship is leaving!
Hurry up and fly!!
Y-Yes, Ma'am !!
What? What ?!

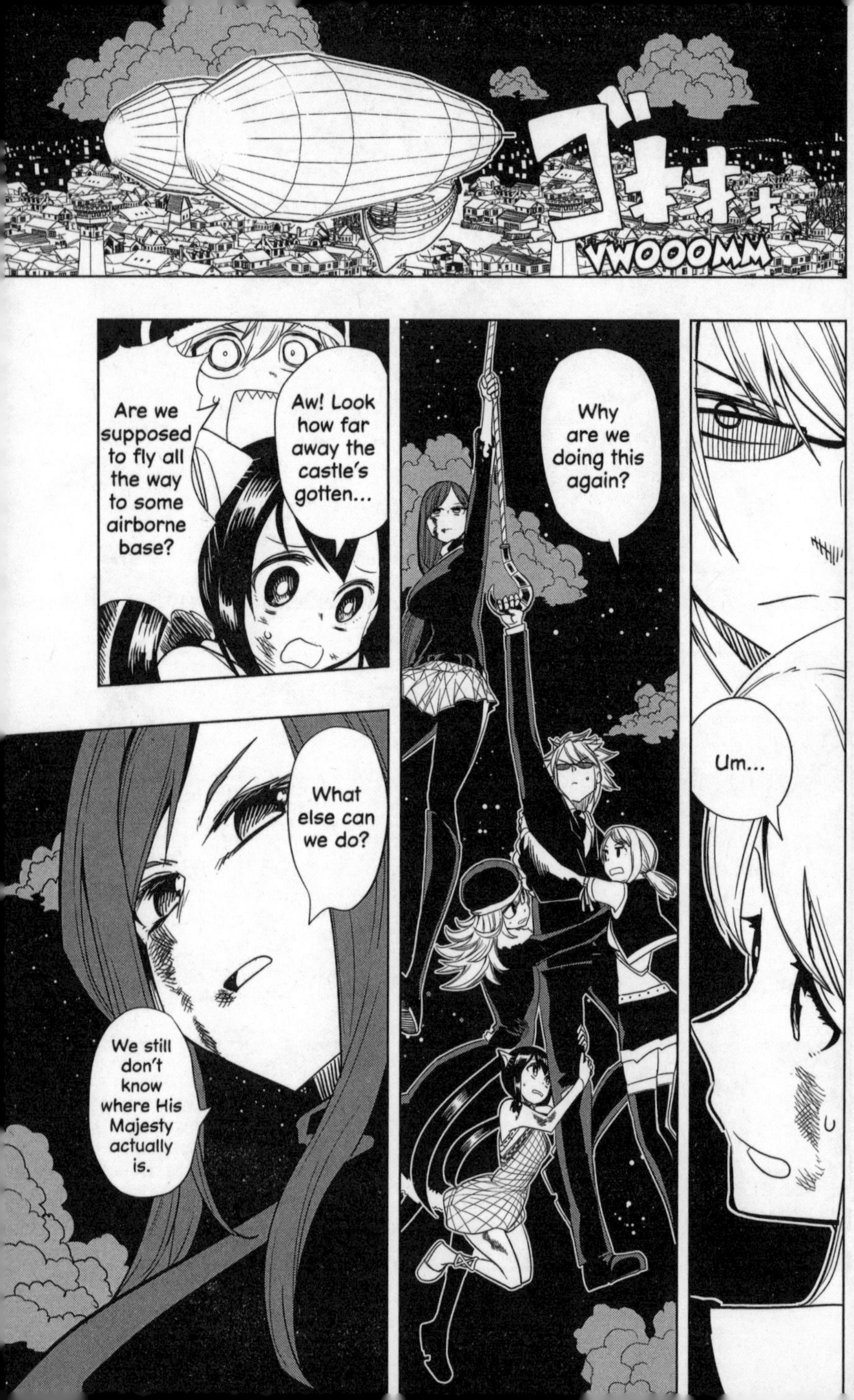
VWOOOMM
Um...
Why are we doing this again?
Aw! Look how far away the castle's gotten...
Are we supposed to fly all the way to some airborne base?
What else can we do?
We still don't know where His Majesty actually is.

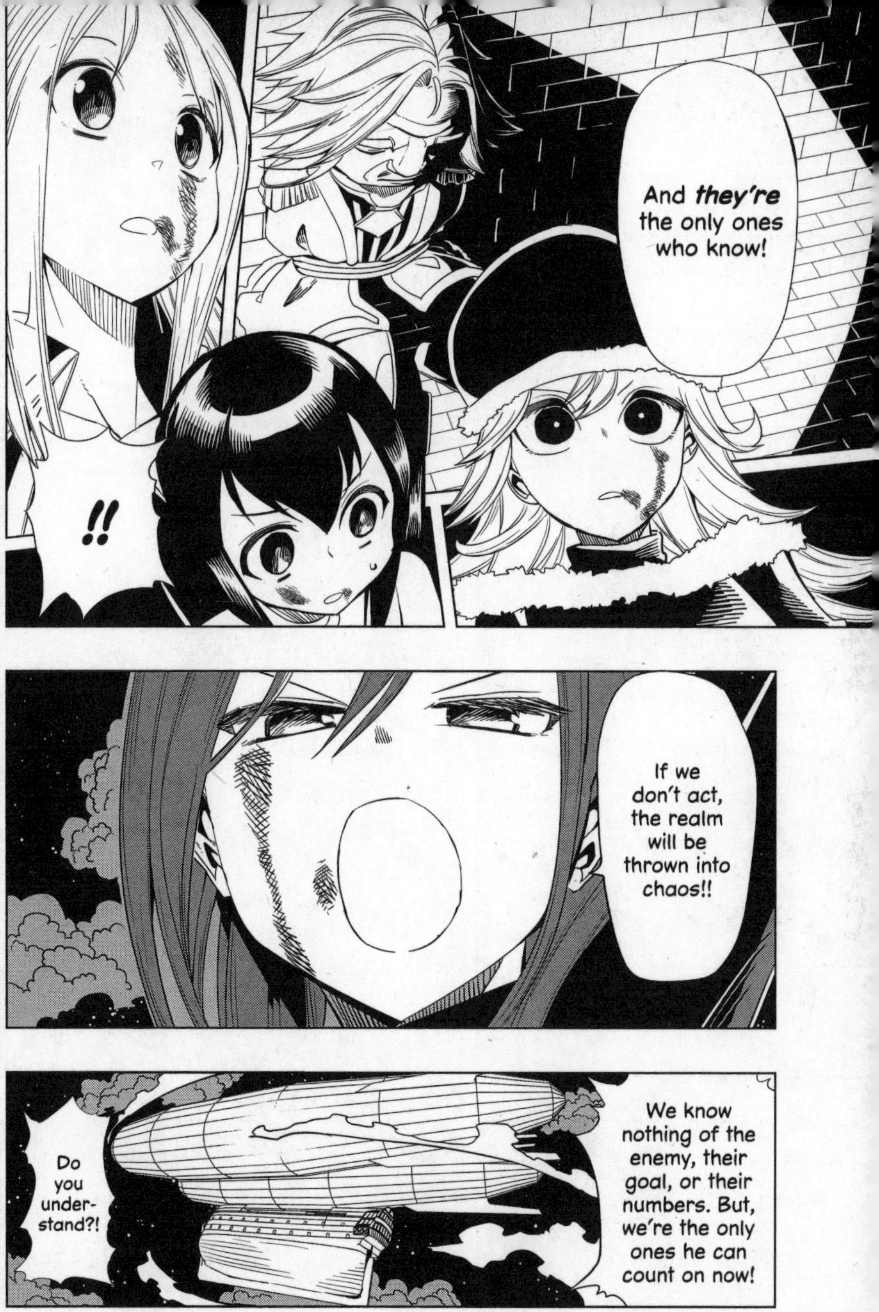
And they're the only ones who know!
!!
If we don't act, the realm will be thrown into chaos!!
We know nothing of the enemy, their goal, or their numbers. But, we're the only ones he can count on now!
Do you under-stand?!

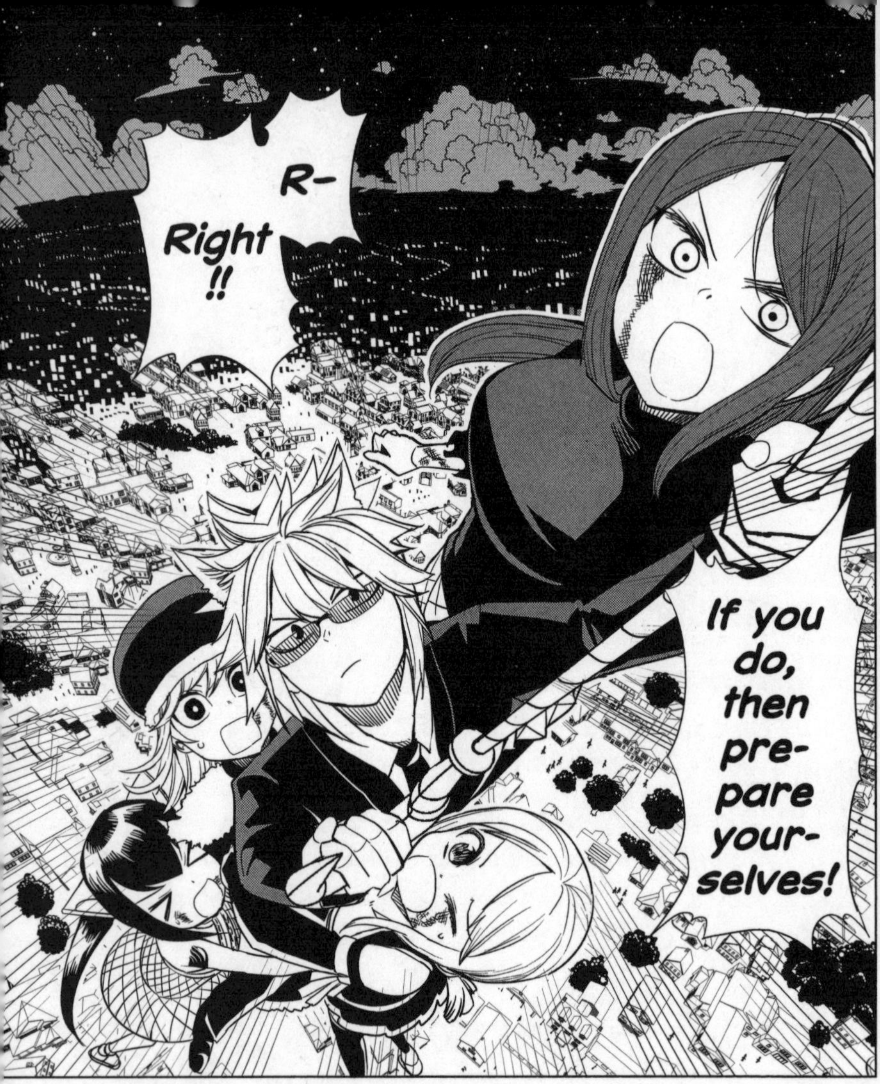
If you do, then prepare yourselves!
R- Right!!
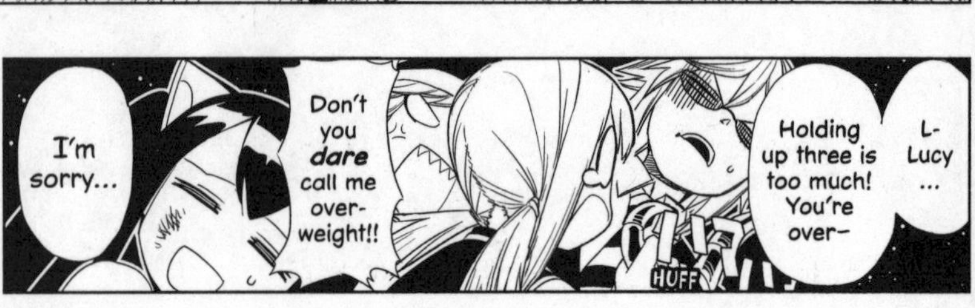
L- Lucy ...
Holding up three is too much! You're over-
HUFF
Don't you dare call me overweight!!
I'm sorry...

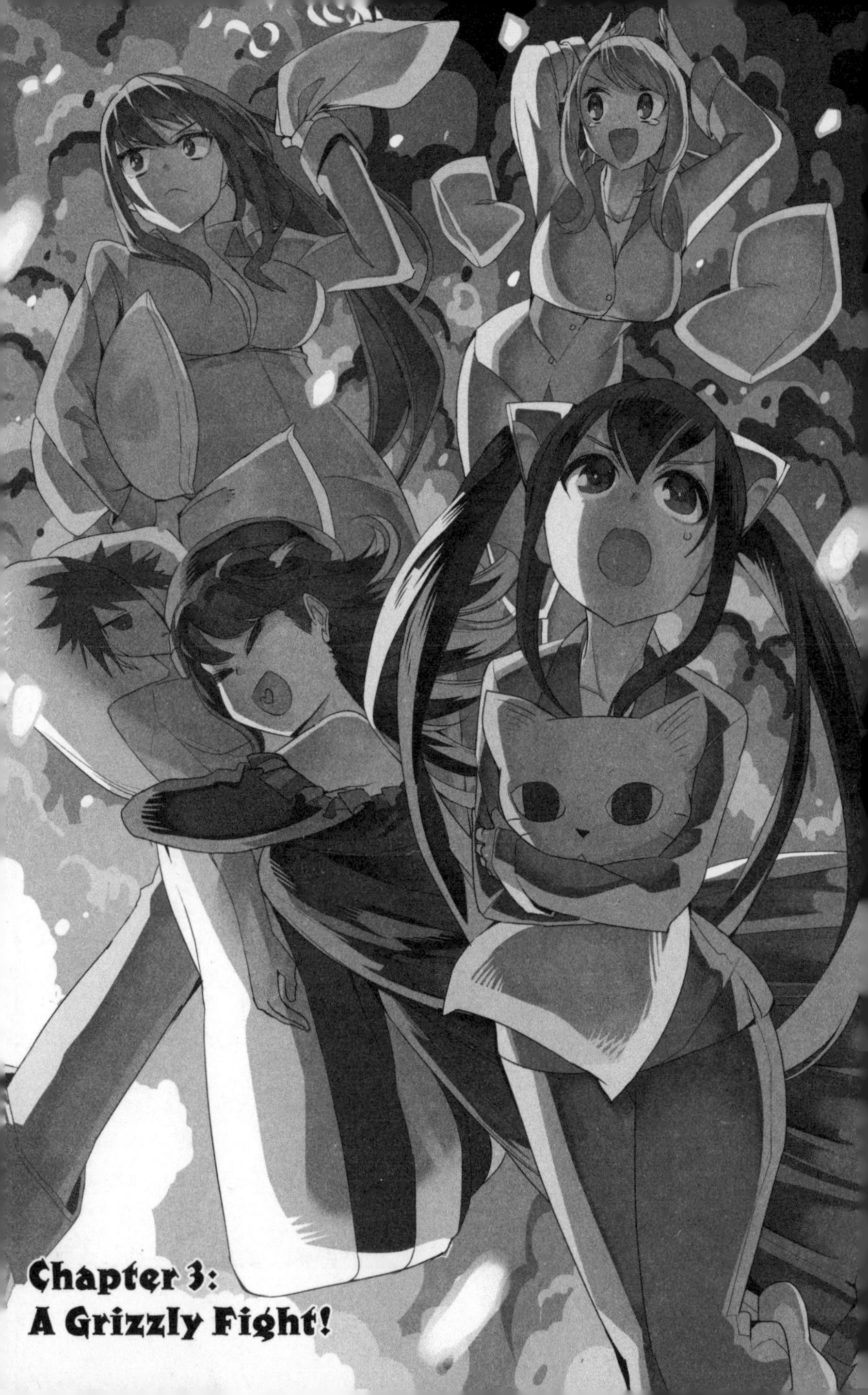
Chapter 3:
A Grizzly Fight!

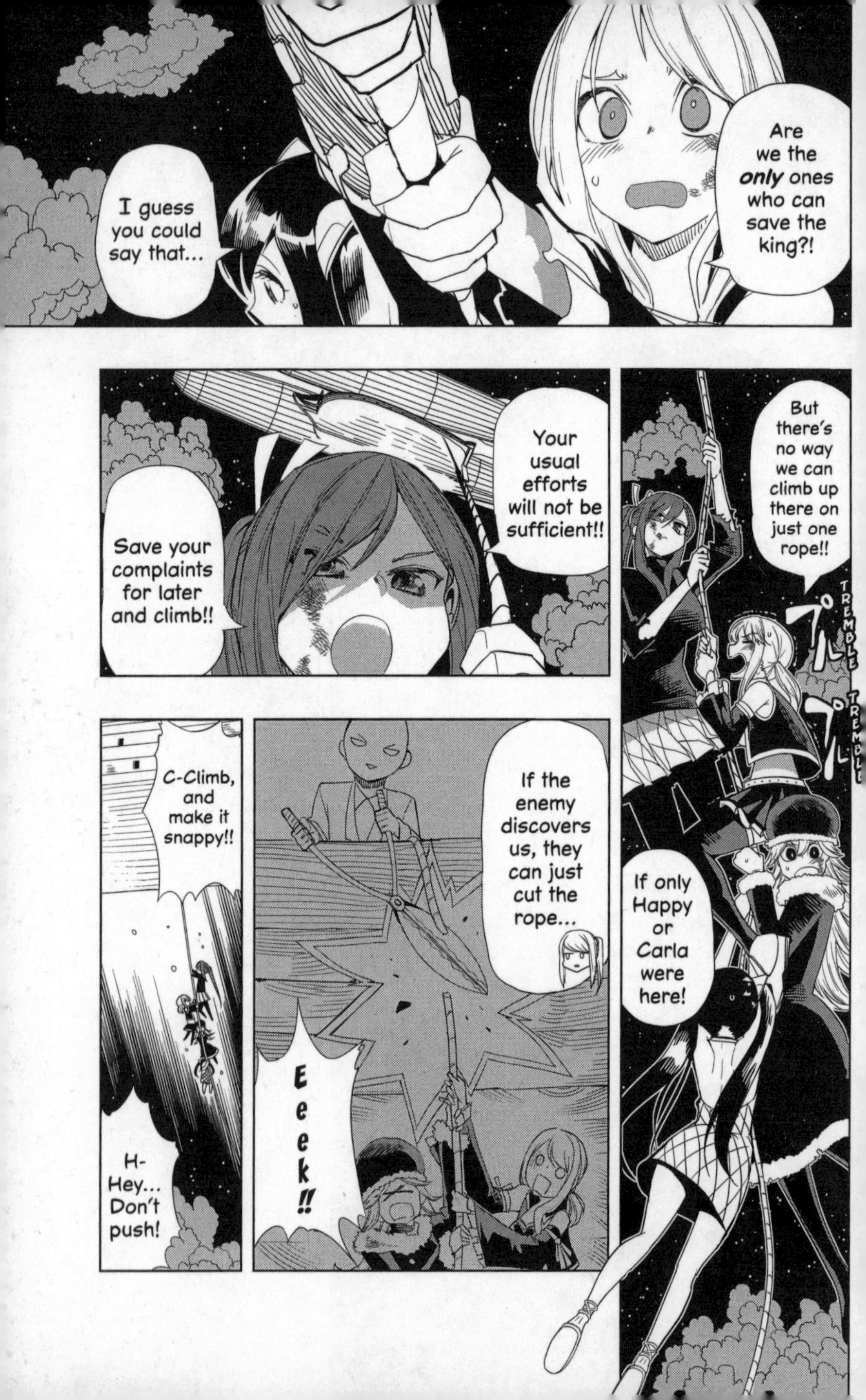

Are we the *only* ones who can save the king?!
I guess you could say that...
But there's no way we can climb up there on just one rope!!
TREMBLE
TREMBLE
If only Happy or Carla were here!
Your usual efforts will not be sufficient!!
Save your complaints for later and climb!!
If the enemy discovers us, they can just cut the rope...
Eeek!!
C-Climb, and make it snappy!!
H-Hey... Don't push!

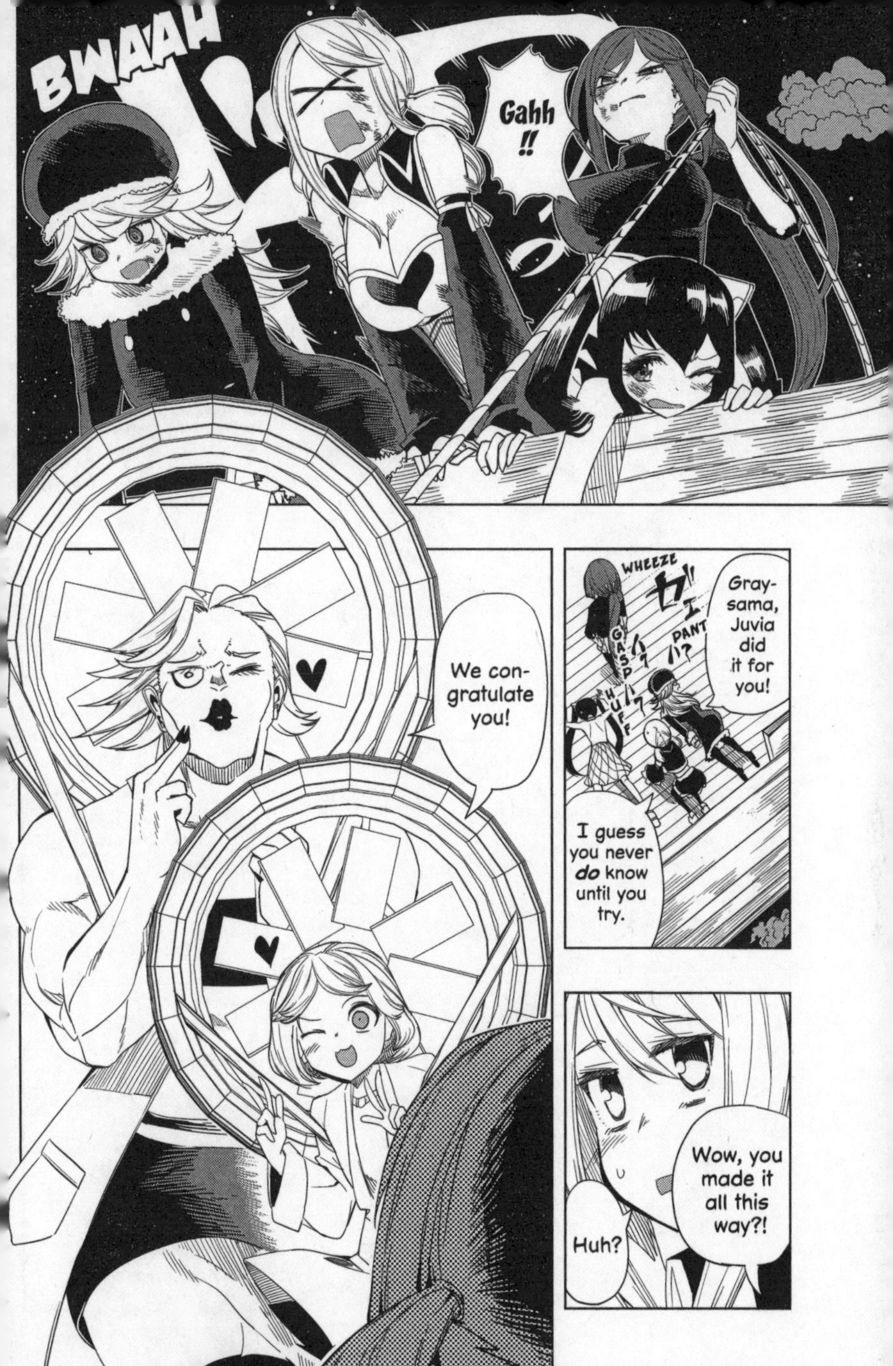
Gahh!!
BWAAH
Gray-sama, Juvia did it for you!
WHEEZE
PANT
GASP
HUFF
I guess you never *do* know until you try.
Wow, you made it all this way?!
Huh?
We congratulate you!

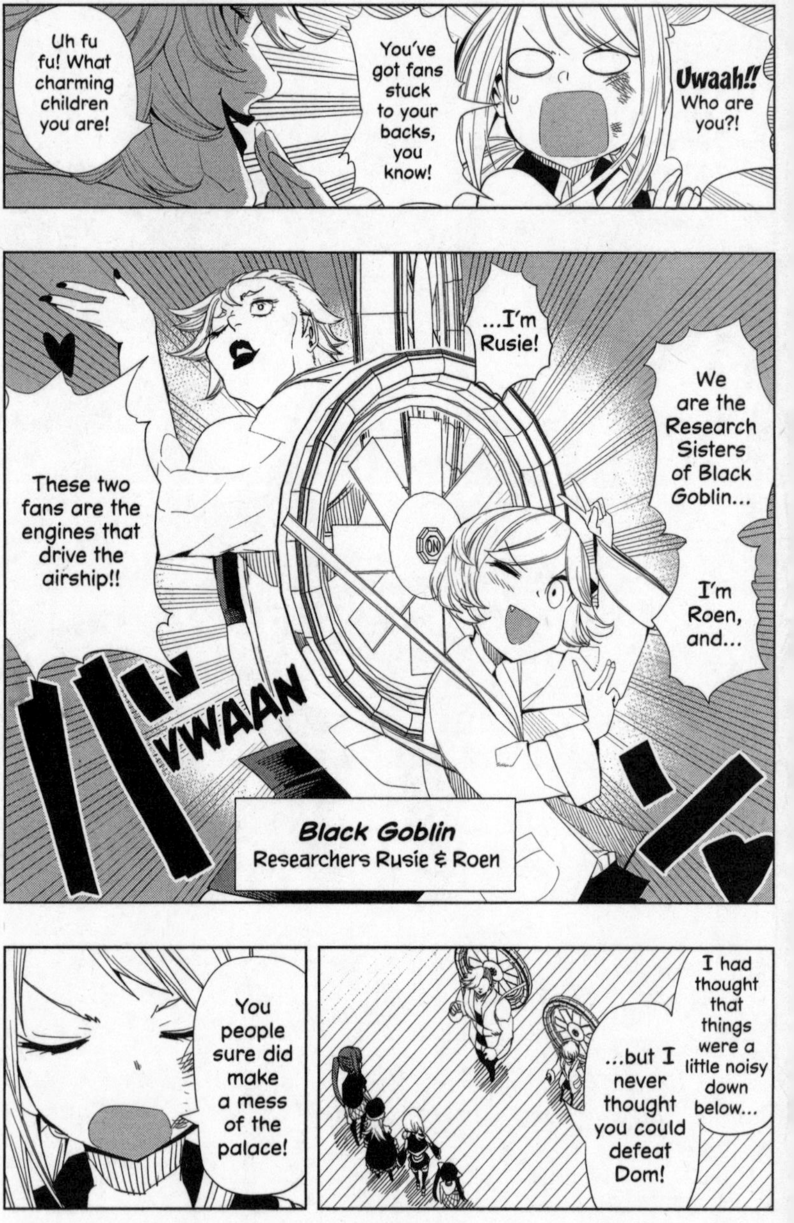
Uwaah!! Who are you?!
You've got fans stuck to your backs, you know!
Uh fu fu! What charming children you are!
We are the Research Sisters of Black Goblin...
I'm Roen, and...
...I'm Rusie!
These two fans are the engines that drive the airship!!
VWAAN
ON
Black Goblin
Researchers Rusie & Roen
I had thought that things were a little noisy down below...
...but I never thought you could defeat Dom!
You people sure did make a mess of the palace!

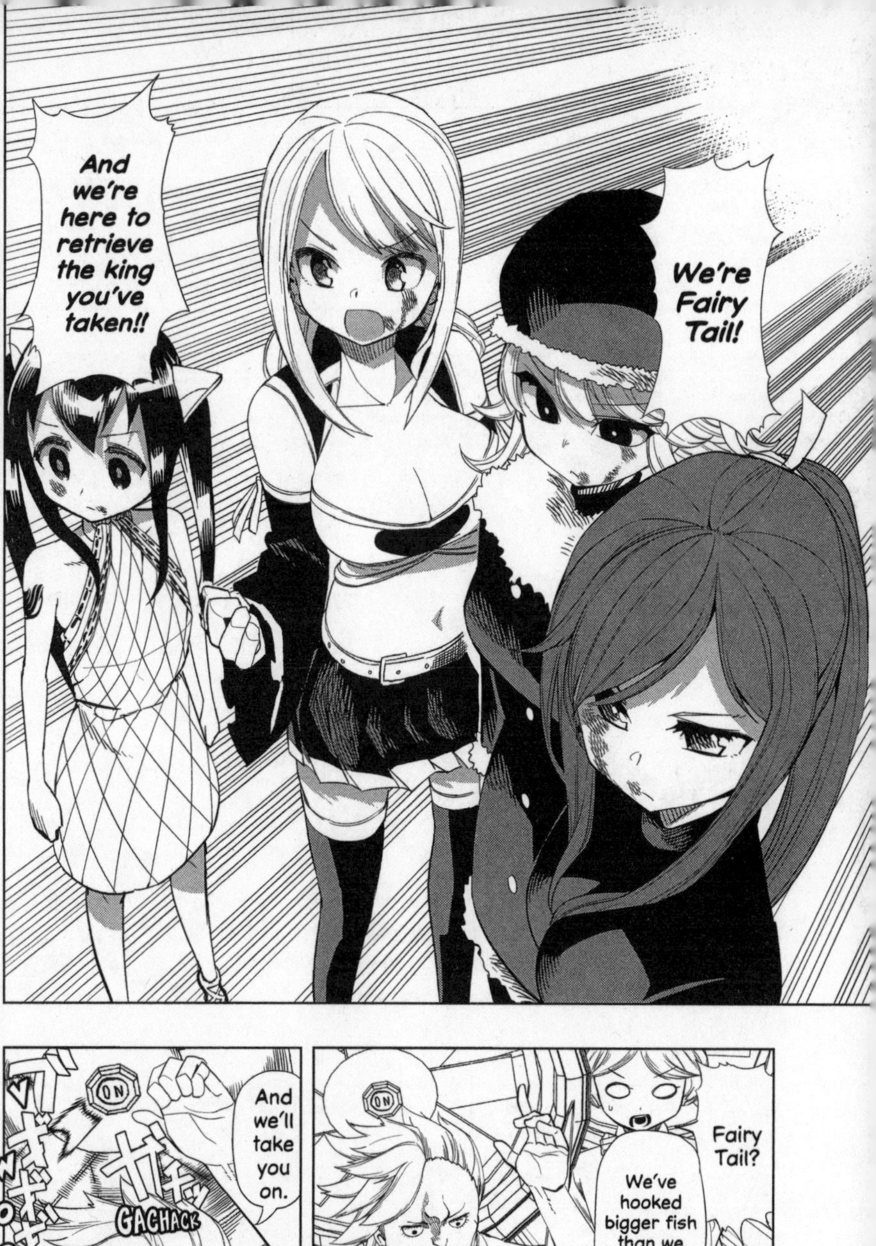
We're Fairy Tail!
And we're here to retrieve the king you've taken!!
Fairy Tail?
We've hooked bigger fish than we expected!
And we'll take you on.
GACHACK
WOOO

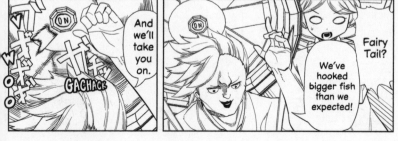

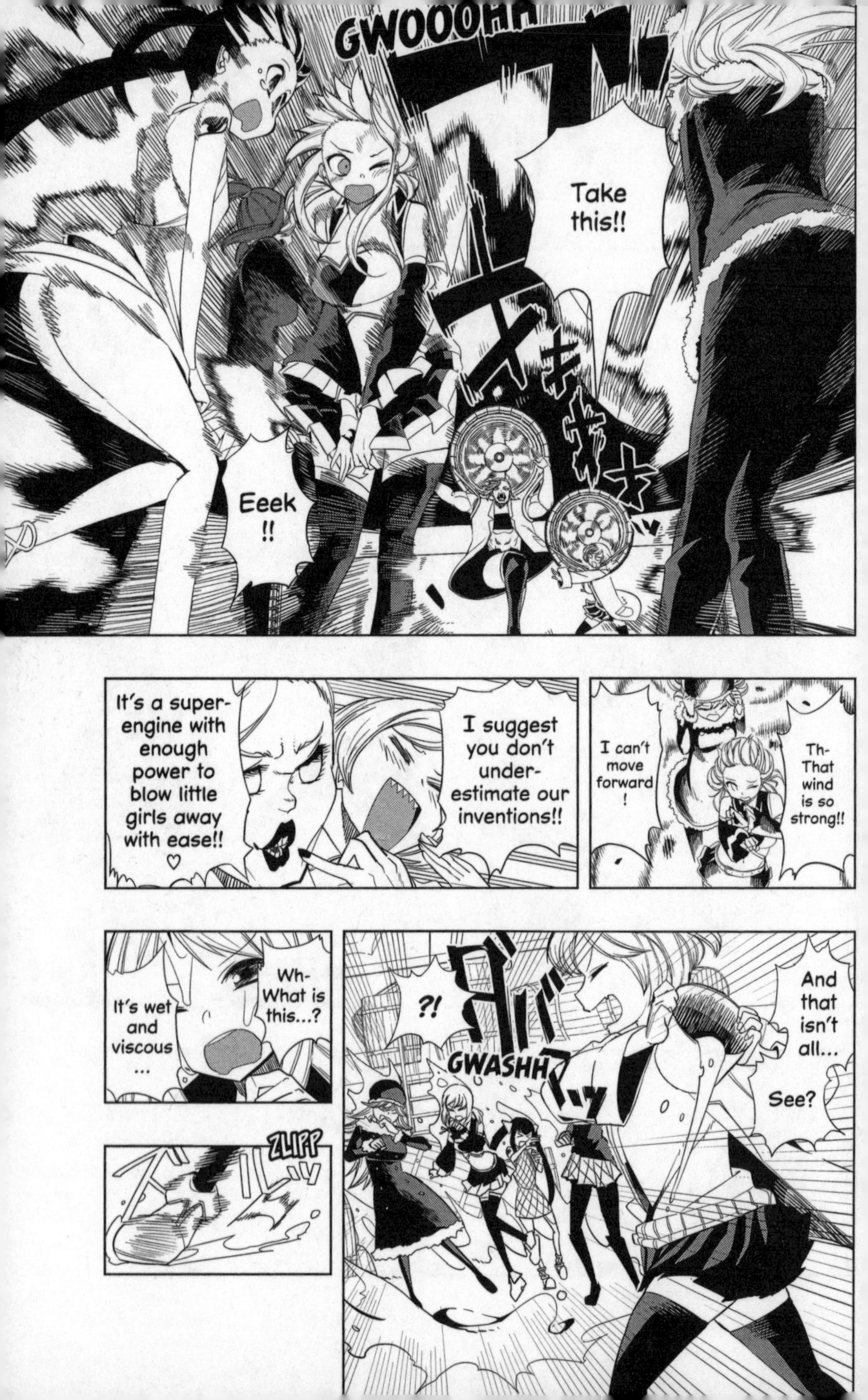
GWOOOHH
Take this!!
Eeek !!
Th- That wind is so strong!!
I can't move forward !
I suggest you don't under-estimate our inventions!!
It's a super-engine with enough power to blow little girls away with ease!! ♡
And that isn't all...
See?
?!
GWASHH
Wh- What is this...?
It's wet and viscous ...
ZLIPP

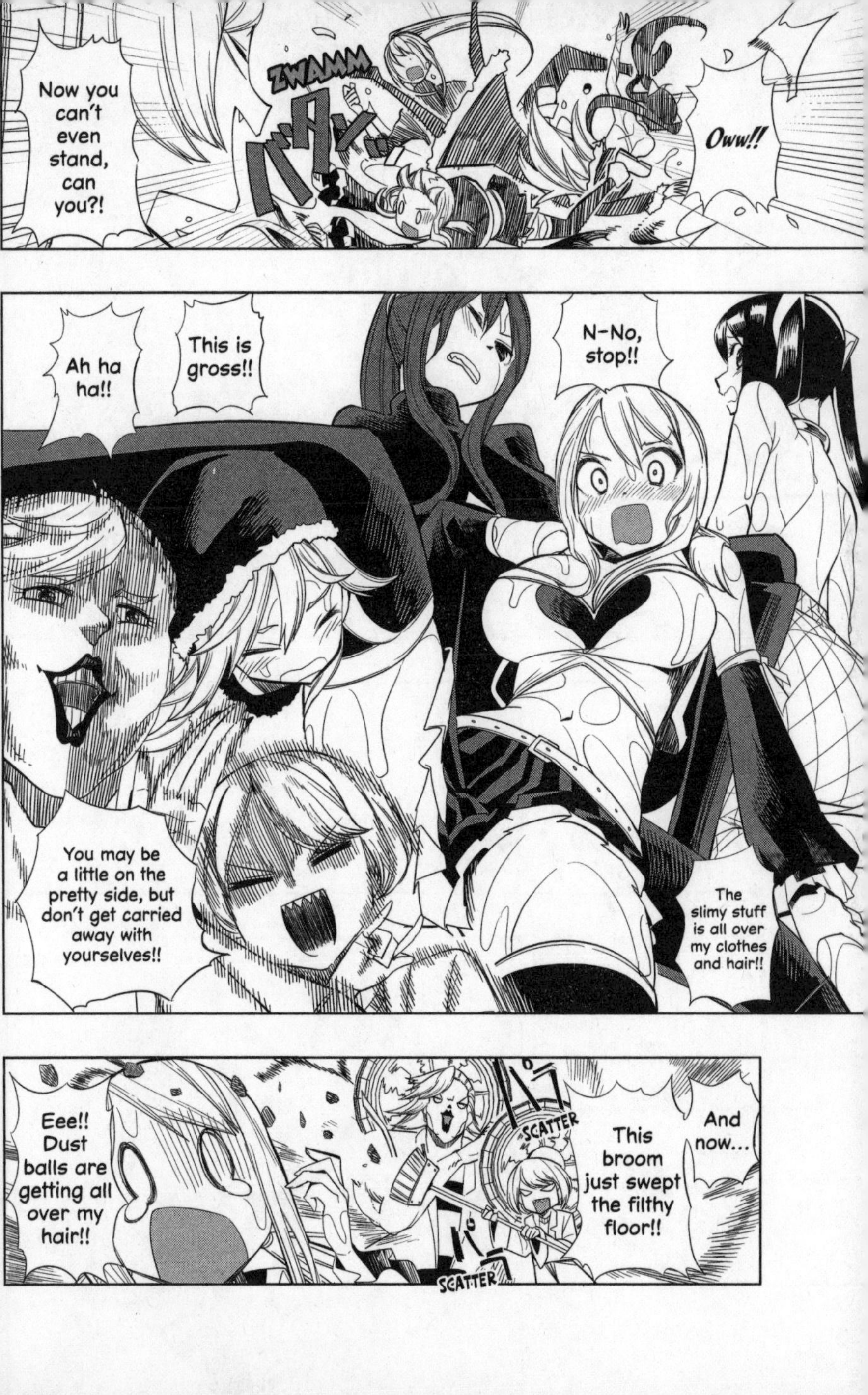
Oww!!
ZWAMM
Now you can't even stand, can you?!
N-No, stop!!
This is gross!!
Ah ha ha!!
The slimy stuff is all over my clothes and hair!!
You may be a little on the pretty side, but don't get carried away with yourselves!!
And now...
This broom just swept the filthy floor!!
SCATTER
SCATTER
Eee!! Dust balls are getting all over my hair!!

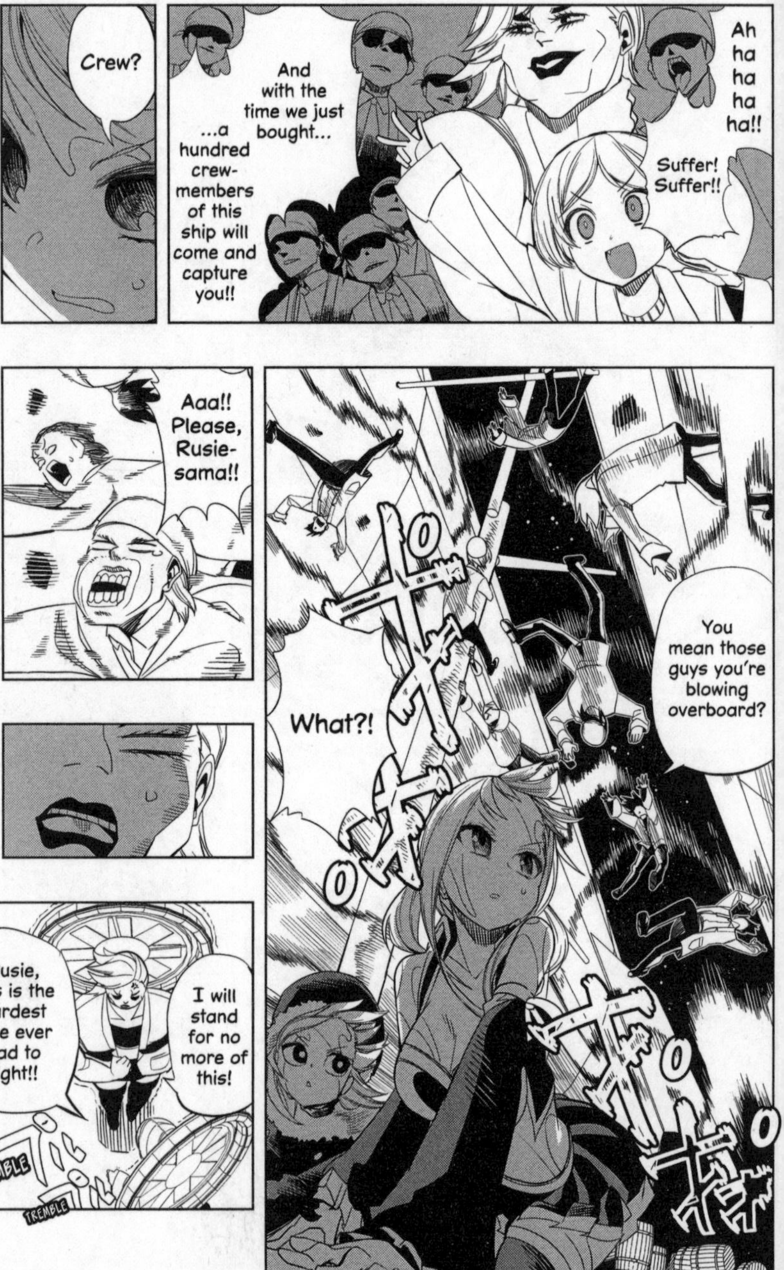
Ah ha ha ha ha!!
Suffer! Suffer!!
And with the time we just bought...
...a hundred crew-members of this ship will come and capture you!!
Crew?
You mean those guys you're blowing overboard?
What?!
Aaa!! Please, Rusie-sama!!
I will stand for no more of this!
Rusie, this is the hardest I've ever had to fight!!
TREMBLE
TREMBLE

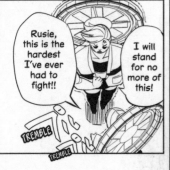

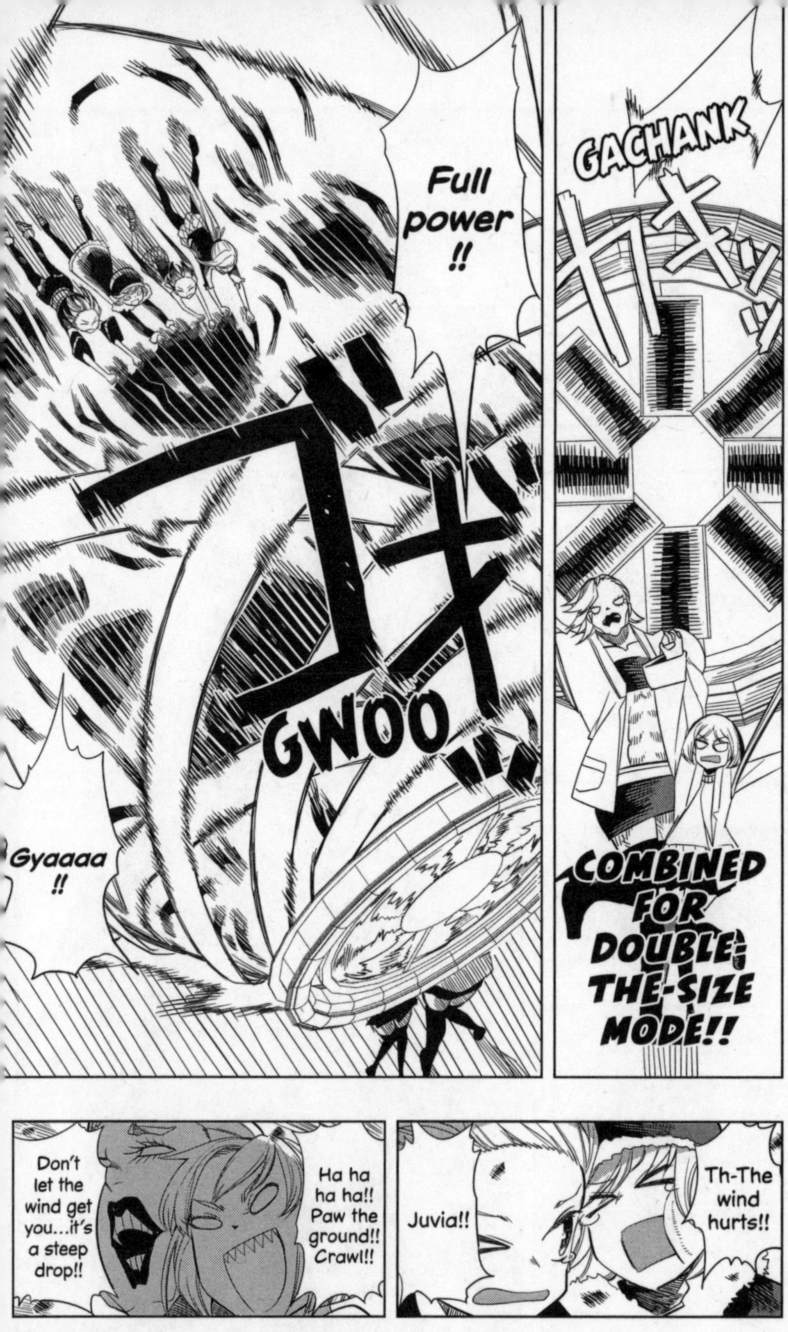
GACHANK
COMBINED FOR DOUBLE-THE-SIZE MODE!!
Full power!!
GWOO
Gyaaaa!!
Th-The wind hurts!!
Juvia!!
Ha ha ha!! Paw the ground!! Crawl!!
Don't let the wind get you…it's a steep drop!!

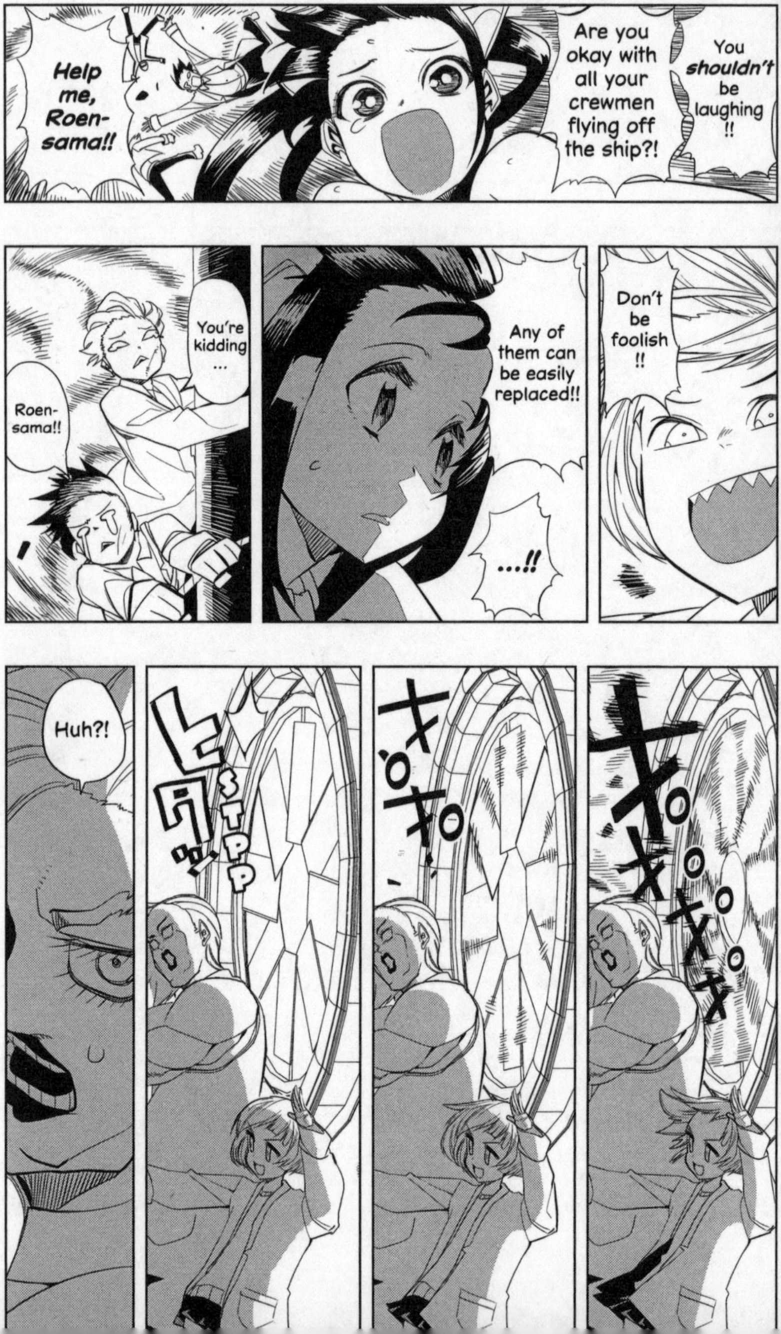
You *shouldn't* be laughing!!
Are you okay with all your crewmen flying off the ship?!
Help me, Roen-sama!!
Don't be foolish!!
Any of them can be easily replaced!!
...!!
You're kidding...
Roen-sama!!
STPP
Huh?!

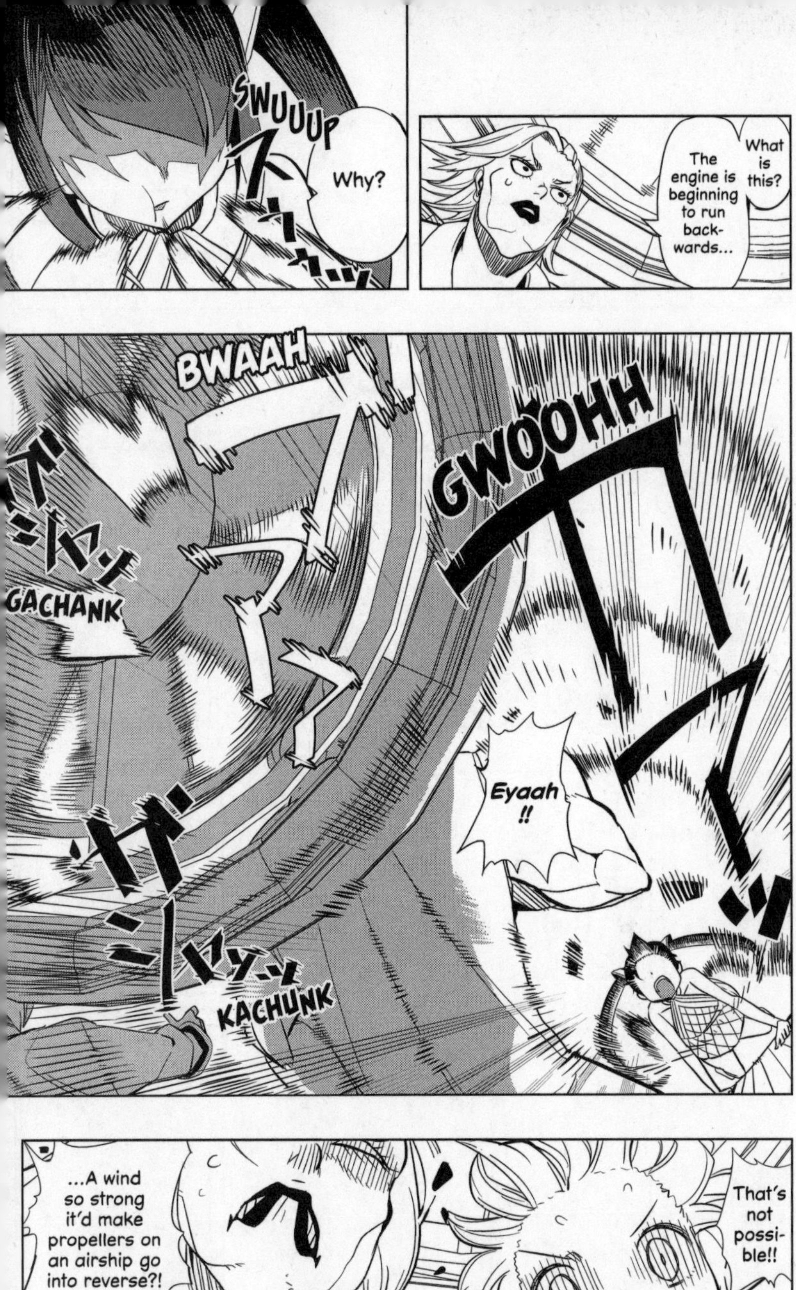
What is this?
The engine is beginning to run backwards...
SWUUUP
Why?
GWOOHH
Eyaah!!
BWAAH
GACHANK
KACHUNK
That's not possible!!
...A wind so strong it'd make propellers on an airship go into reverse?!

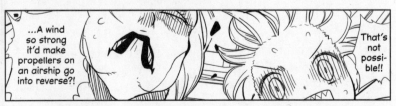

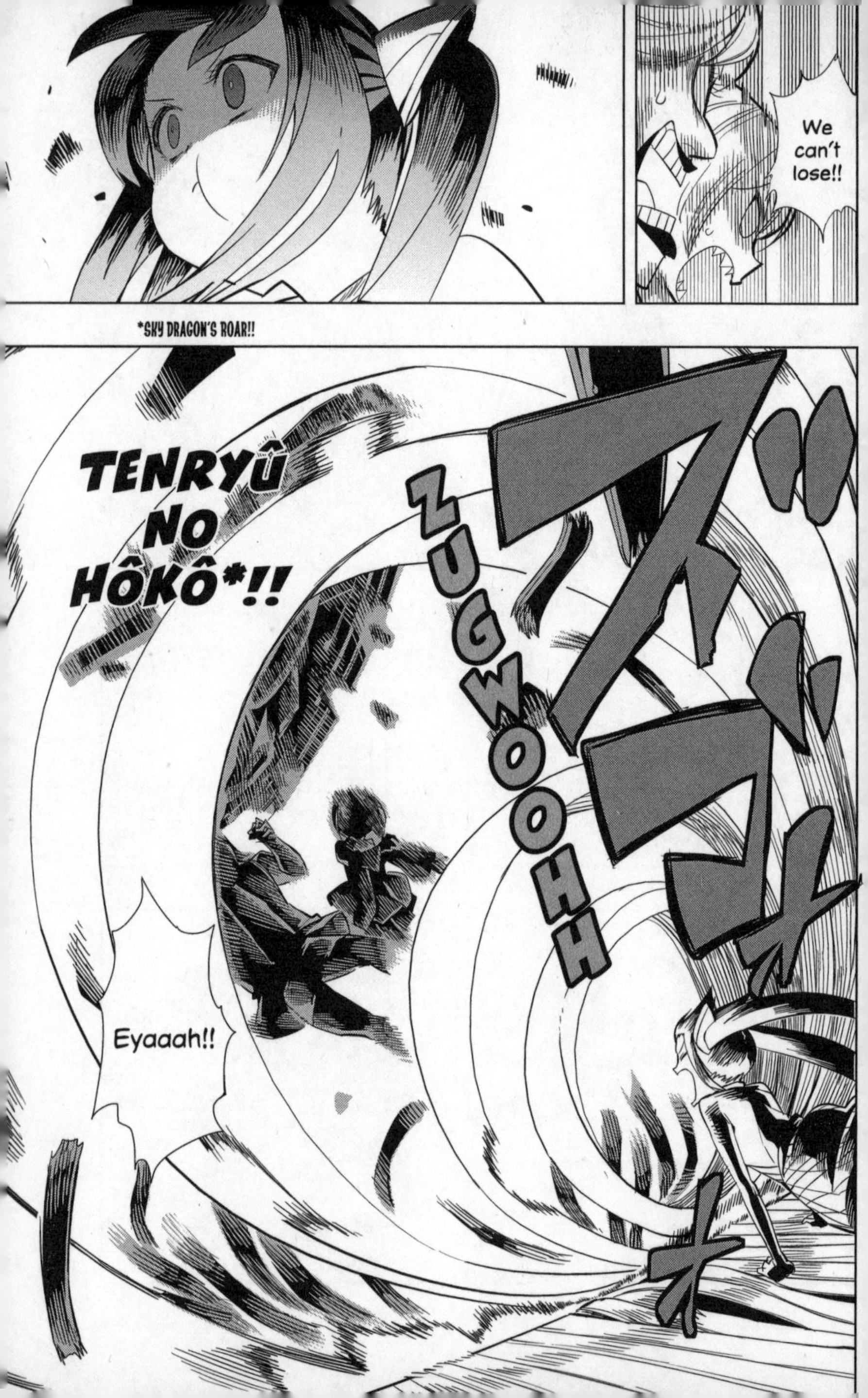
We can't lose!!
*SKY DRAGON'S ROAR!!
TENRYÛ NO HÔKÔ*!!
ZUGWOOHH
Eyaaah!!

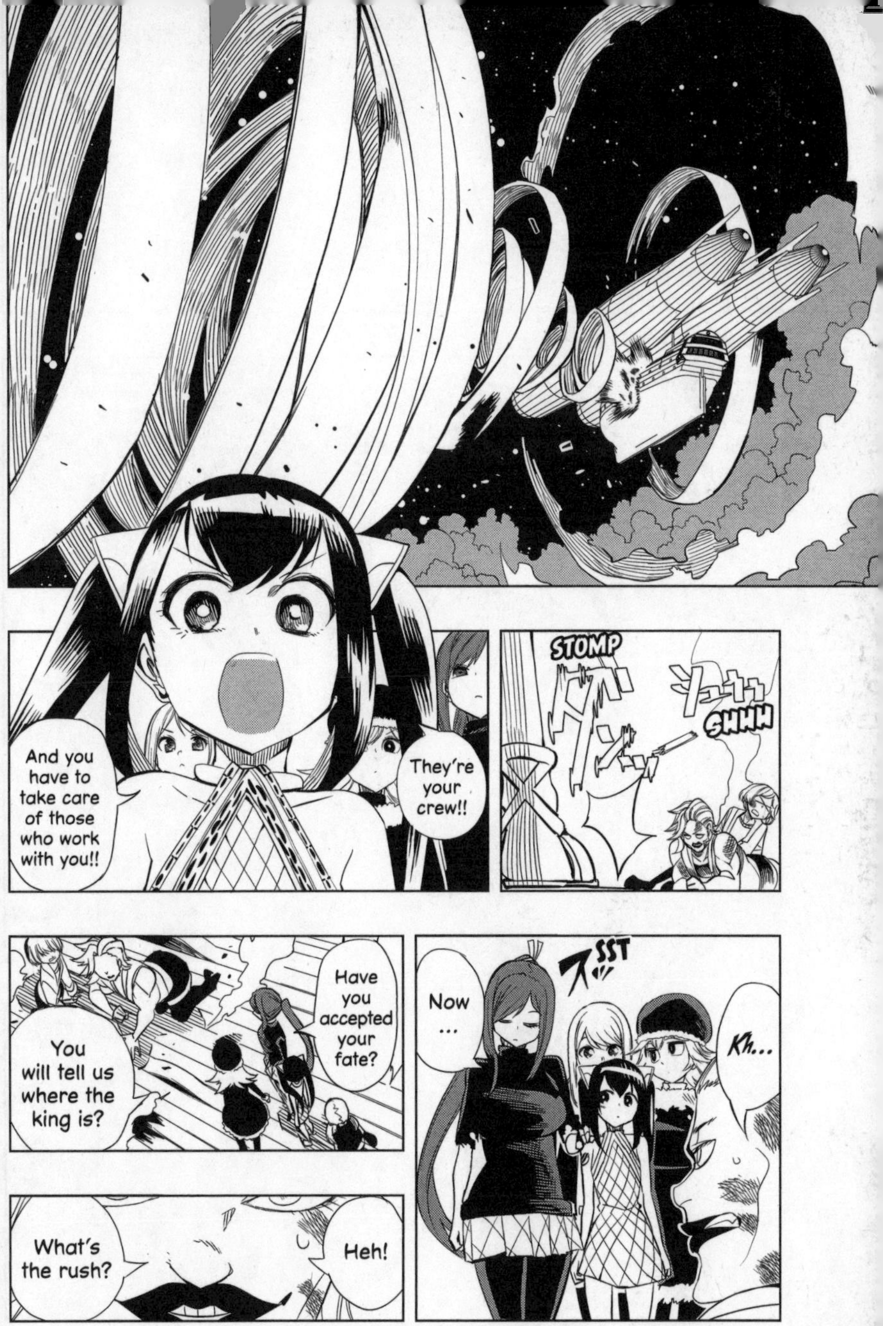
STOMP
SHHH
They're your crew!!
And you have to take care of those who work with you!!
SST
Kh...
Now ...
Have you accepted your fate?
You will tell us where the king is?
Heh!
What's the rush?

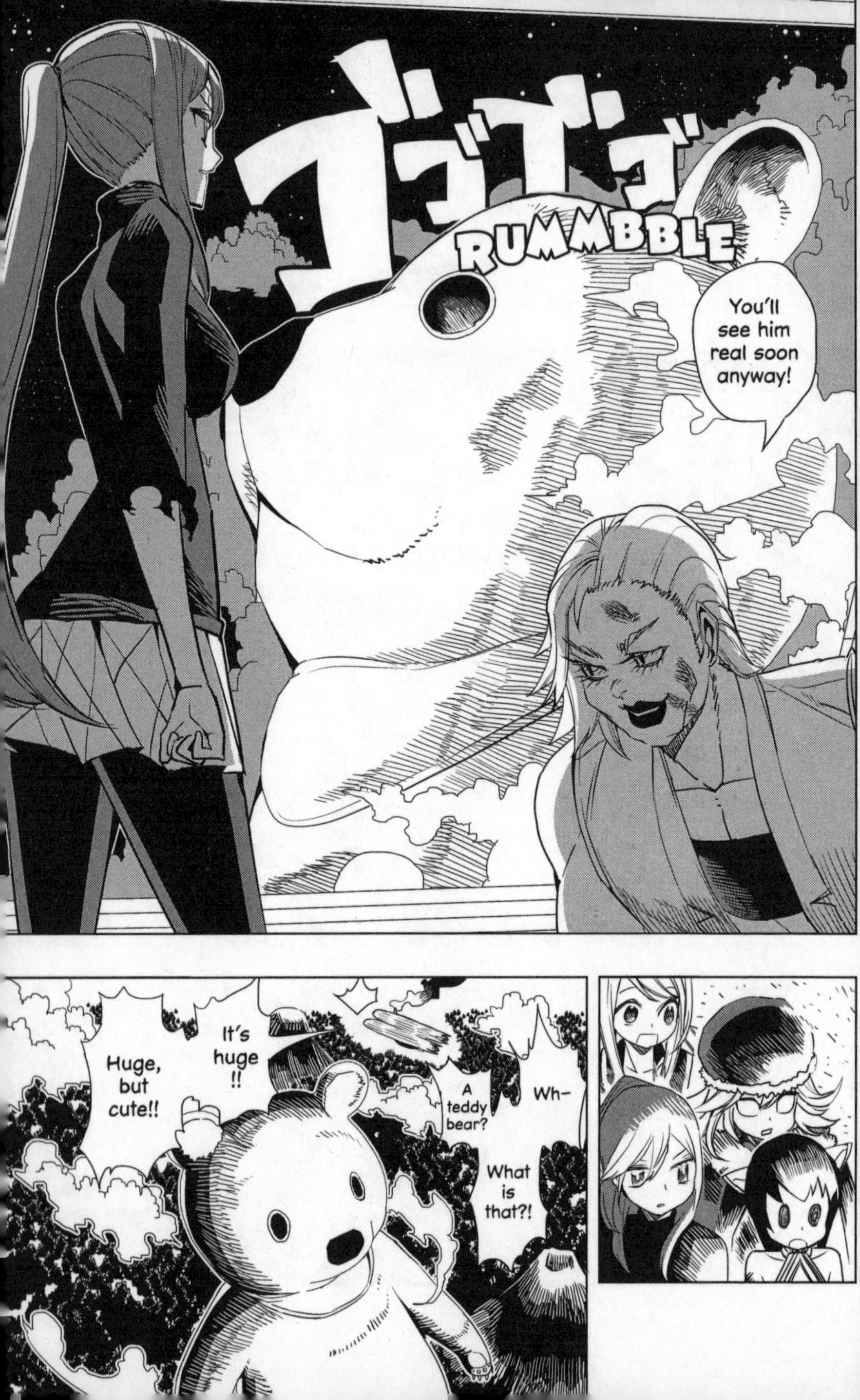
ゴゴゴ
RUMMBBLE
You'll see him real soon anyway!
Wh-
A teddy bear?
What is that?!
It's huge!!
Huge, but cute!!

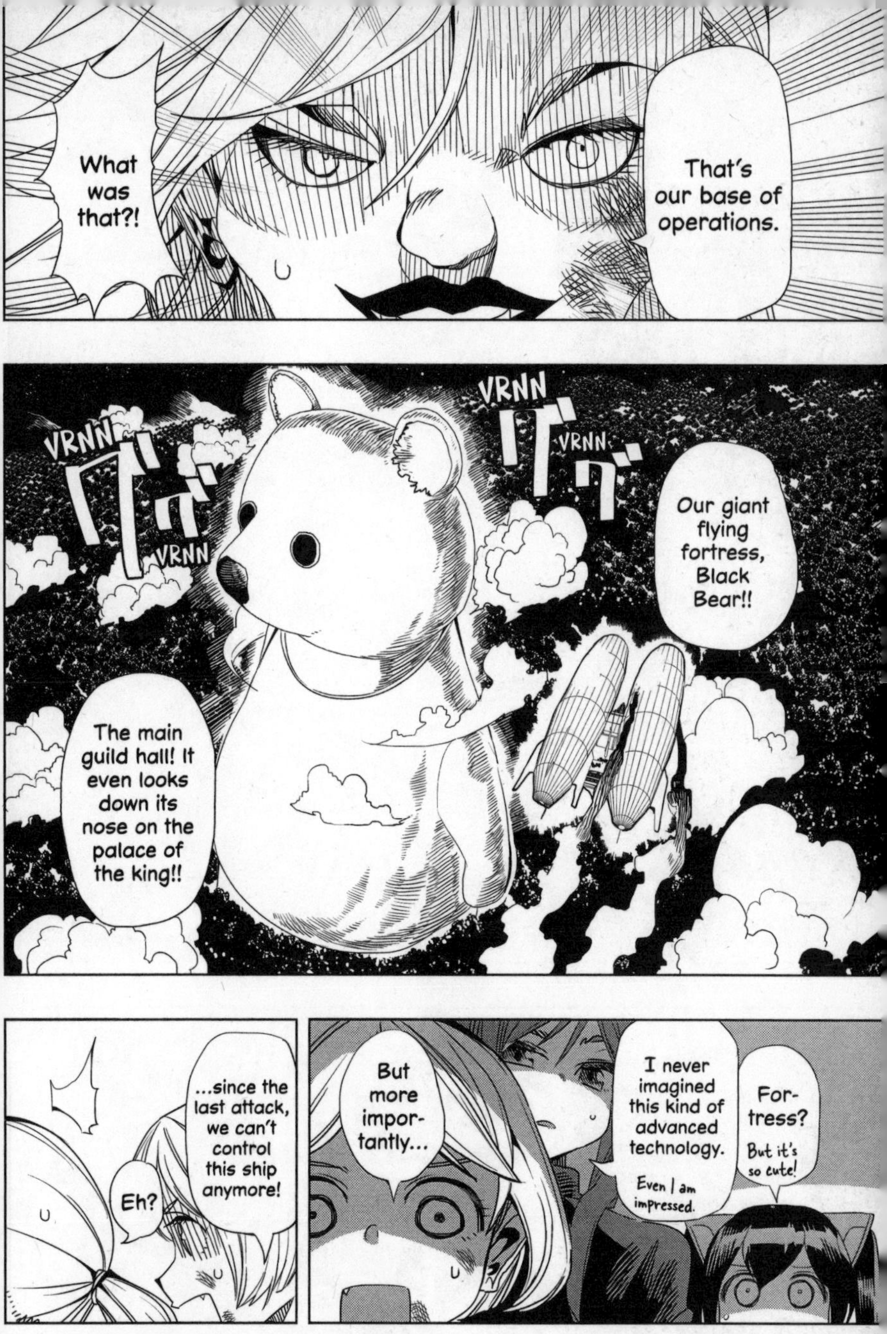
That's our base of operations.
What was that?!
VRNN
VRNN
Our giant flying fortress, Black Bear!!
VRNN
VRNN
The main guild hall! It even looks down its nose on the palace of the king!!
For-tress?
But it's so cute!
I never imagined this kind of advanced technology.
Even I am impressed.
But more impor-tantly...
...since the last attack, we can't control this ship anymore!
Eh?

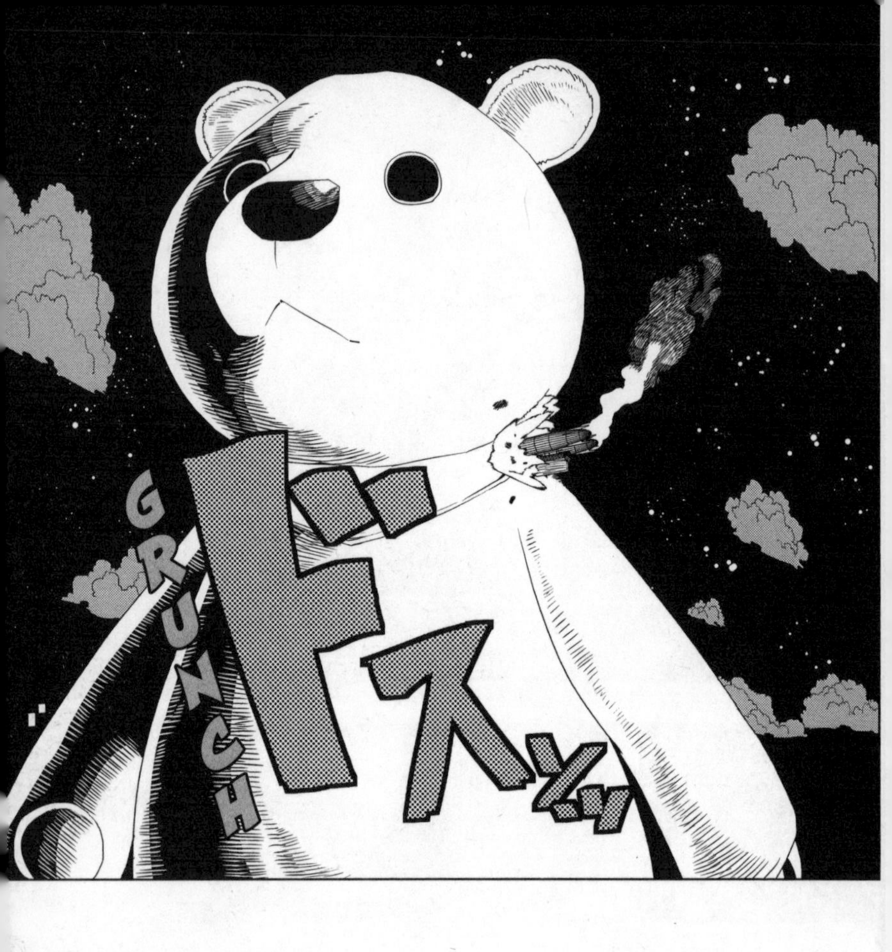
GRUNCH
ドスッ
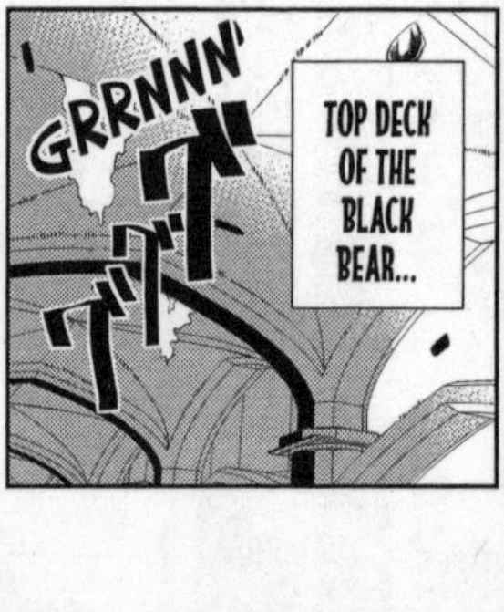
GRRNNN'
TOP DECK OF THE BLACK BEAR...
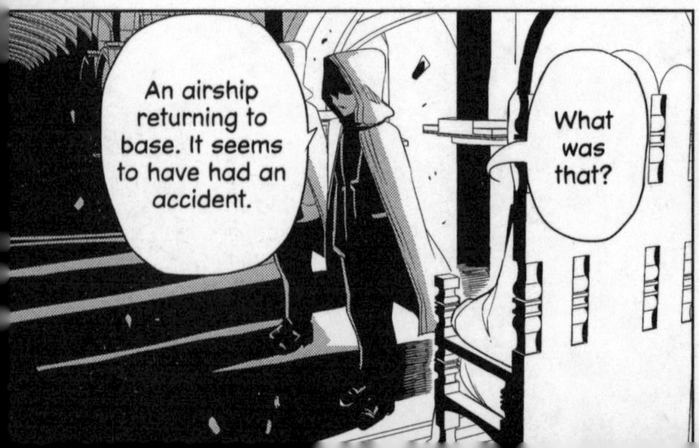
What was that?
An airship returning to base. It seems to have had an accident.

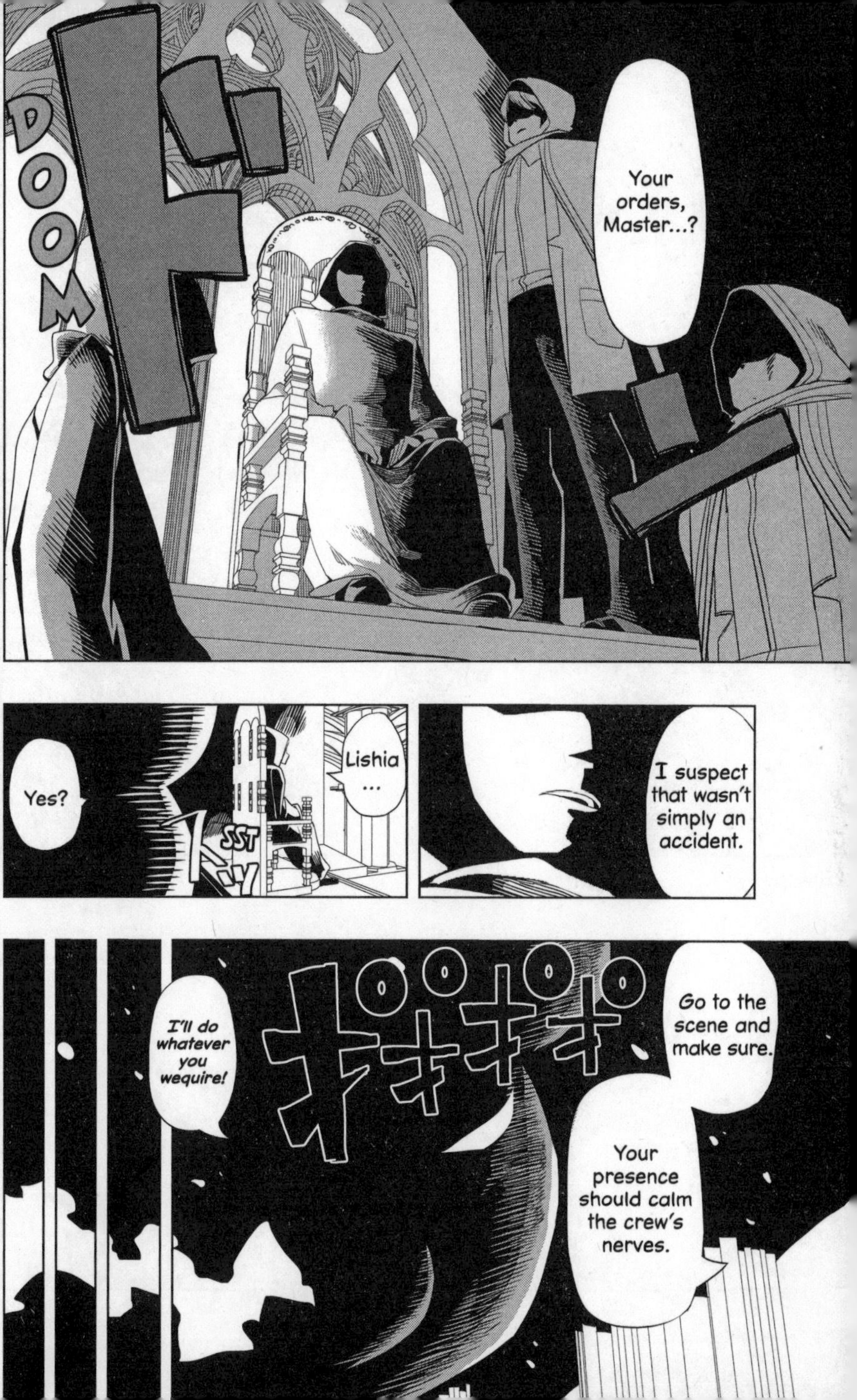
Your orders, Master...?
DOOM
I suspect that wasn't simply an accident.
Lishia ...
SST
Yes?
Go to the scene and make sure.
Your presence should calm the crew's nerves.
I'll do whatever you wequire!

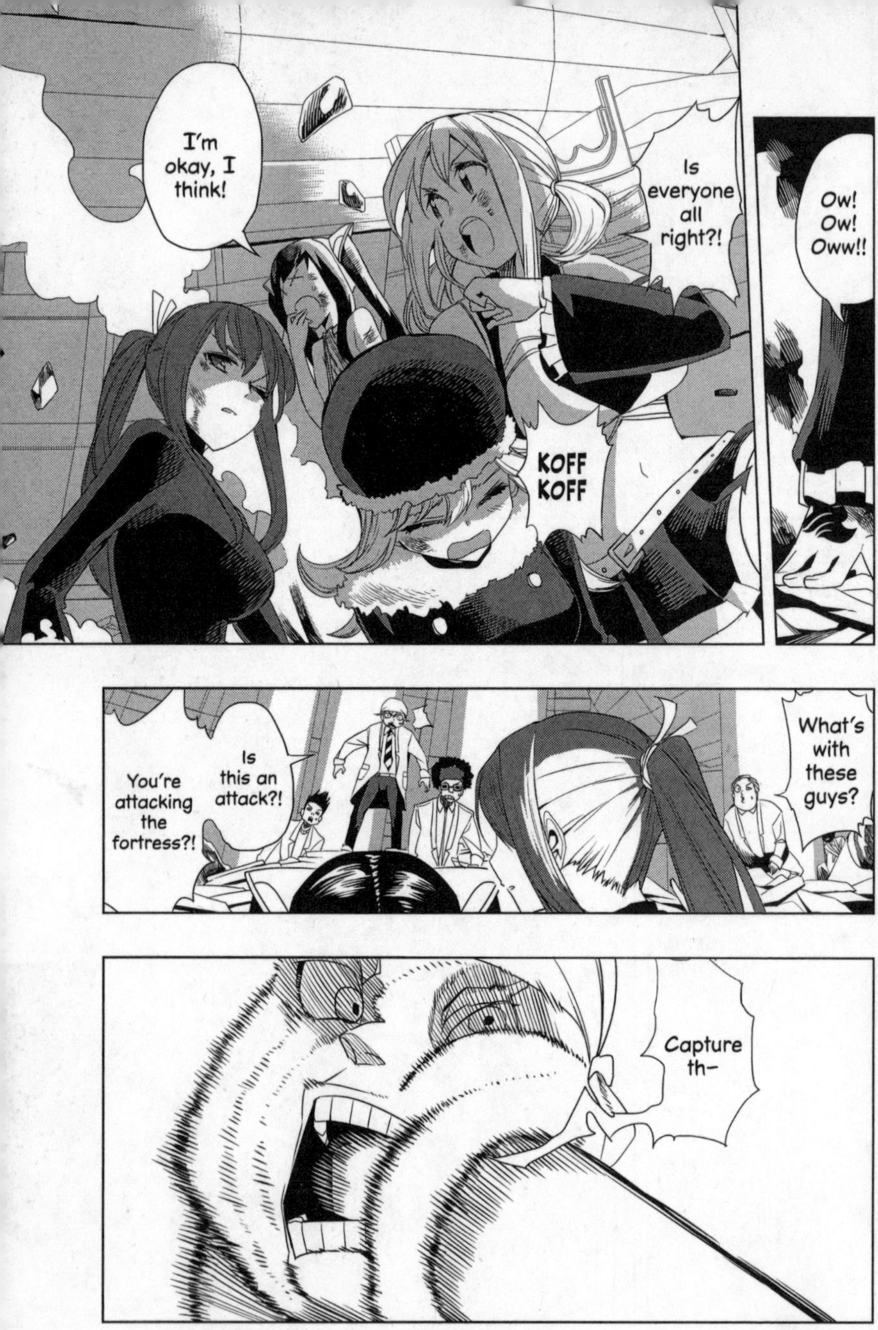
Ow! Ow! Oww!!
Is everyone all right?!
I'm okay, I think!
KOFF KOFF
What's with these guys?
Is this an attack?!
You're attacking the fortress?!
Capture th-

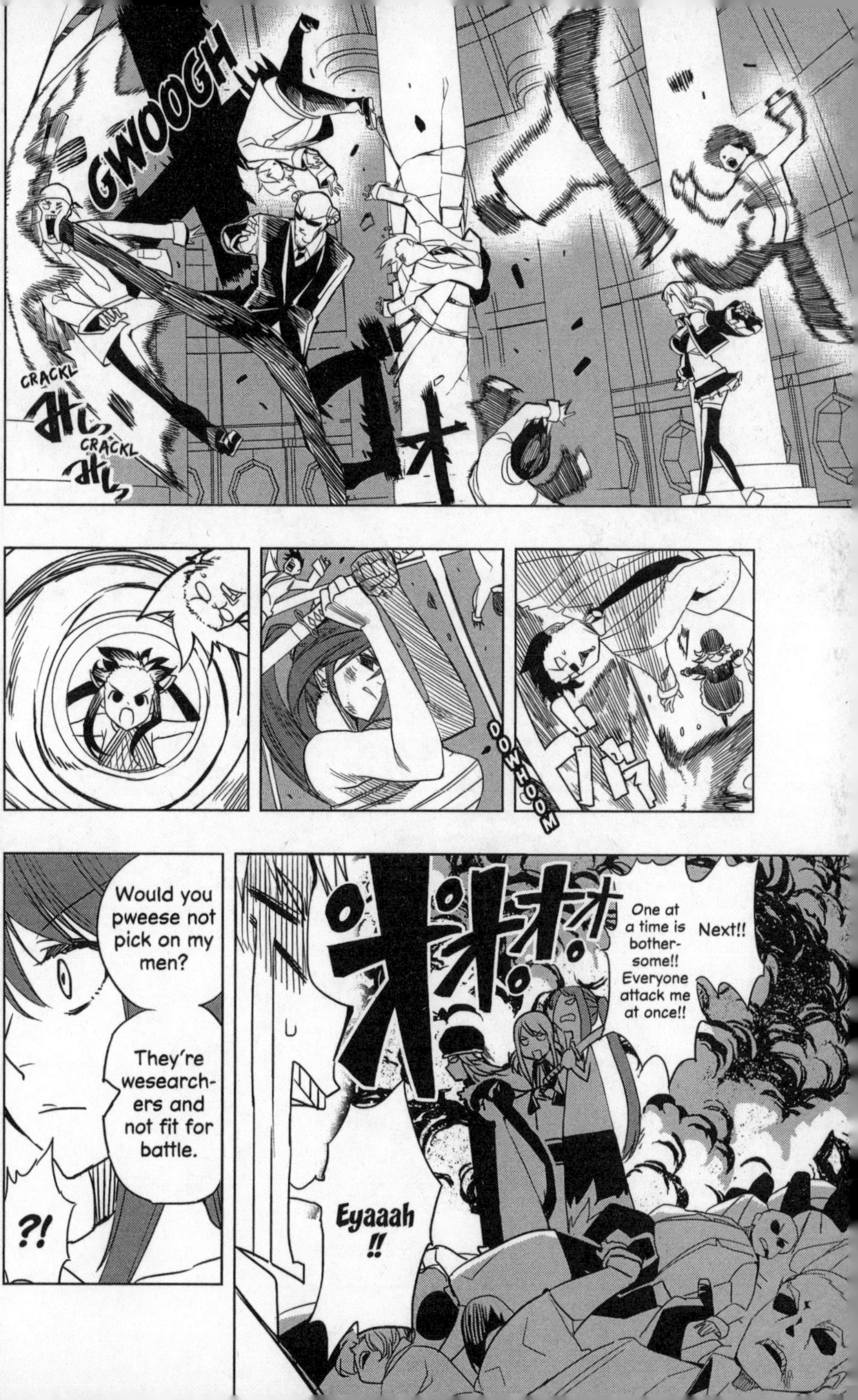
GWOOGH
CRACKL
CRACKL
DOWHOOM
Next!!
One at a time is bothersome!! Everyone attack me at once!!
Eyaaah!!
Would you pweese not pick on my men?
They're wesearchers and not fit for battle.
?!

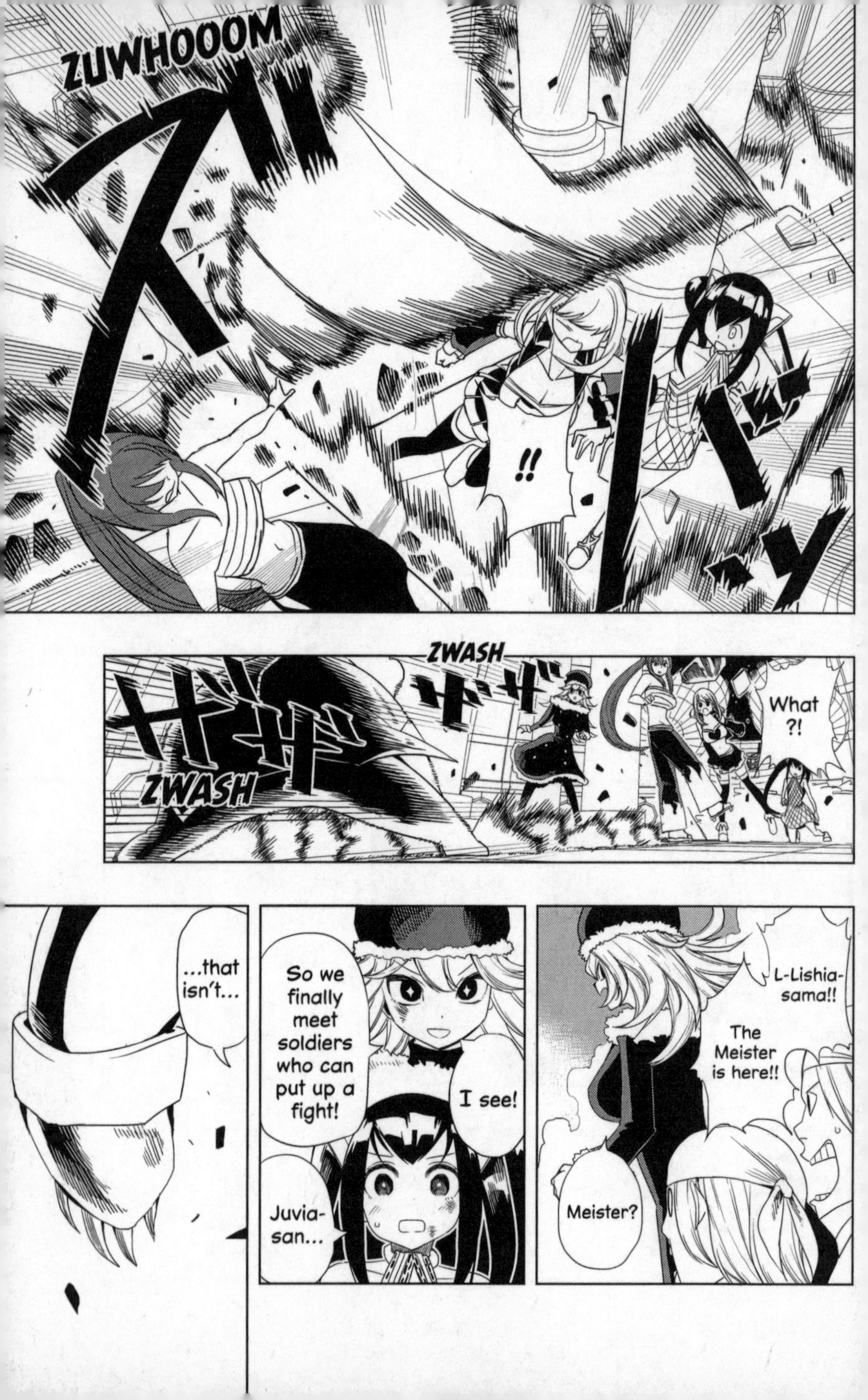
ZUWHOOOM
!!
What?!
ZWASH
ZWASH
L-Lishia-sama!!
The Meister is here!!
Meister?
So we finally meet soldiers who can put up a fight!
I see!
Juvia-san...
...that isn't...

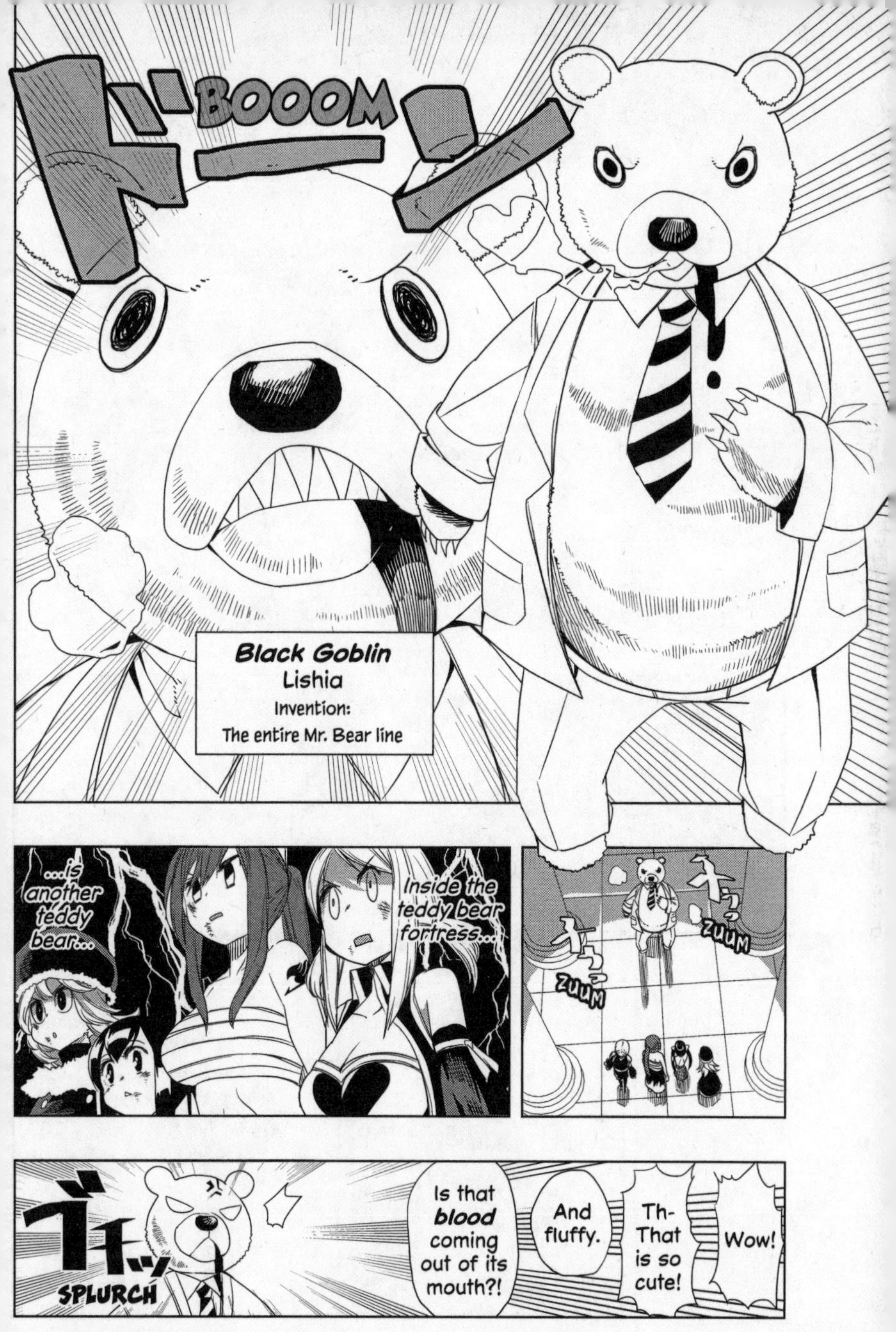
BOOOM
Black Goblin
Lishia
Invention:
The entire Mr. Bear line
ZUUM
ZUUM
Inside the teddy bear fortress...
...is another teddy bear...
Wow!
Th-That is so cute!
And fluffy.
Is that *blood* coming out of its mouth?!
SPLURCH

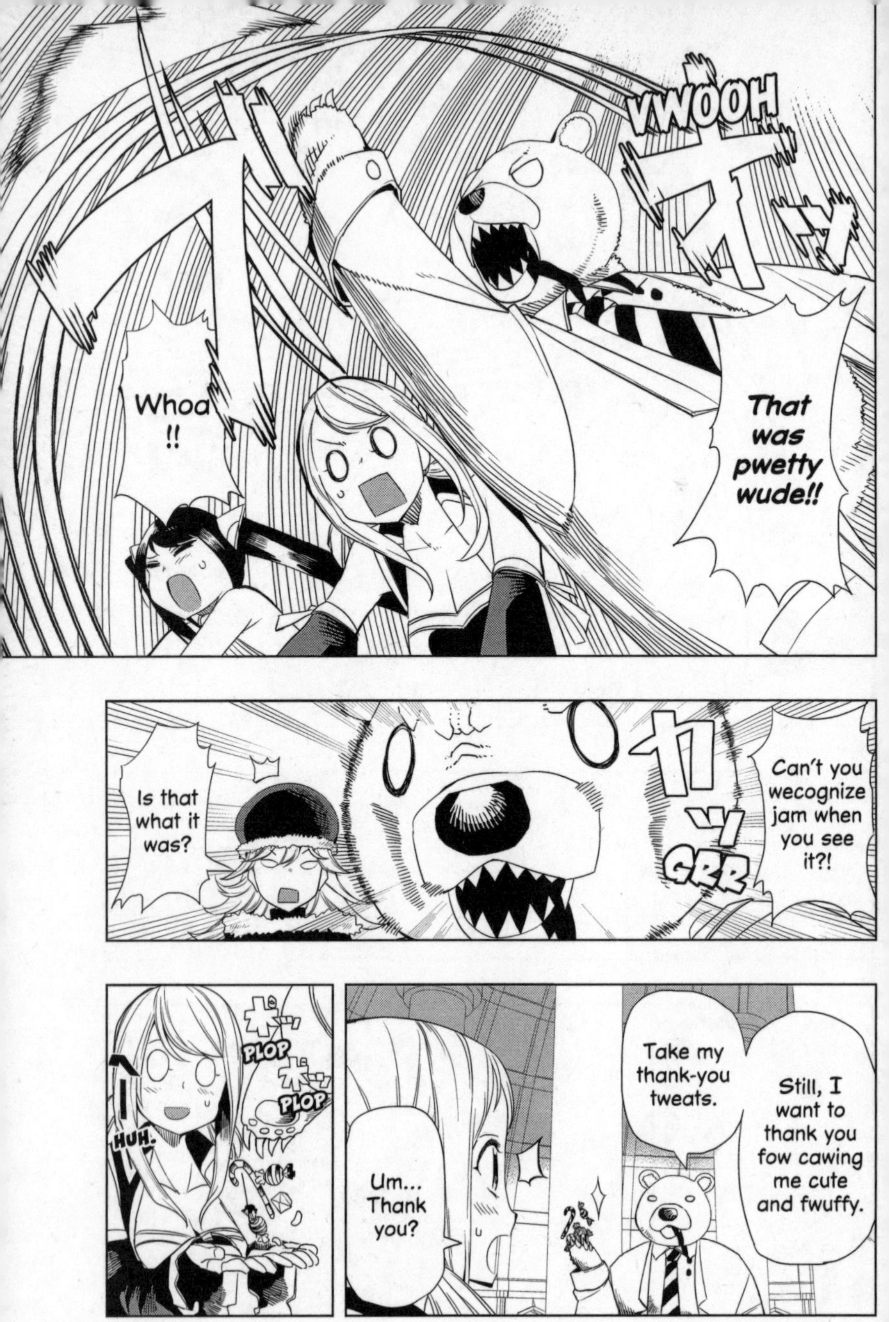
VWOOH
That was pwetty wude!!
Whoa !!
Can't you wecognize jam when you see it?!
GRR
Is that what it was?
Still, I want to thank you fow cawing me cute and fwuffy.
Take my thank-you tweats.
Um... Thank you?
PLOP
PLOP
HUH.

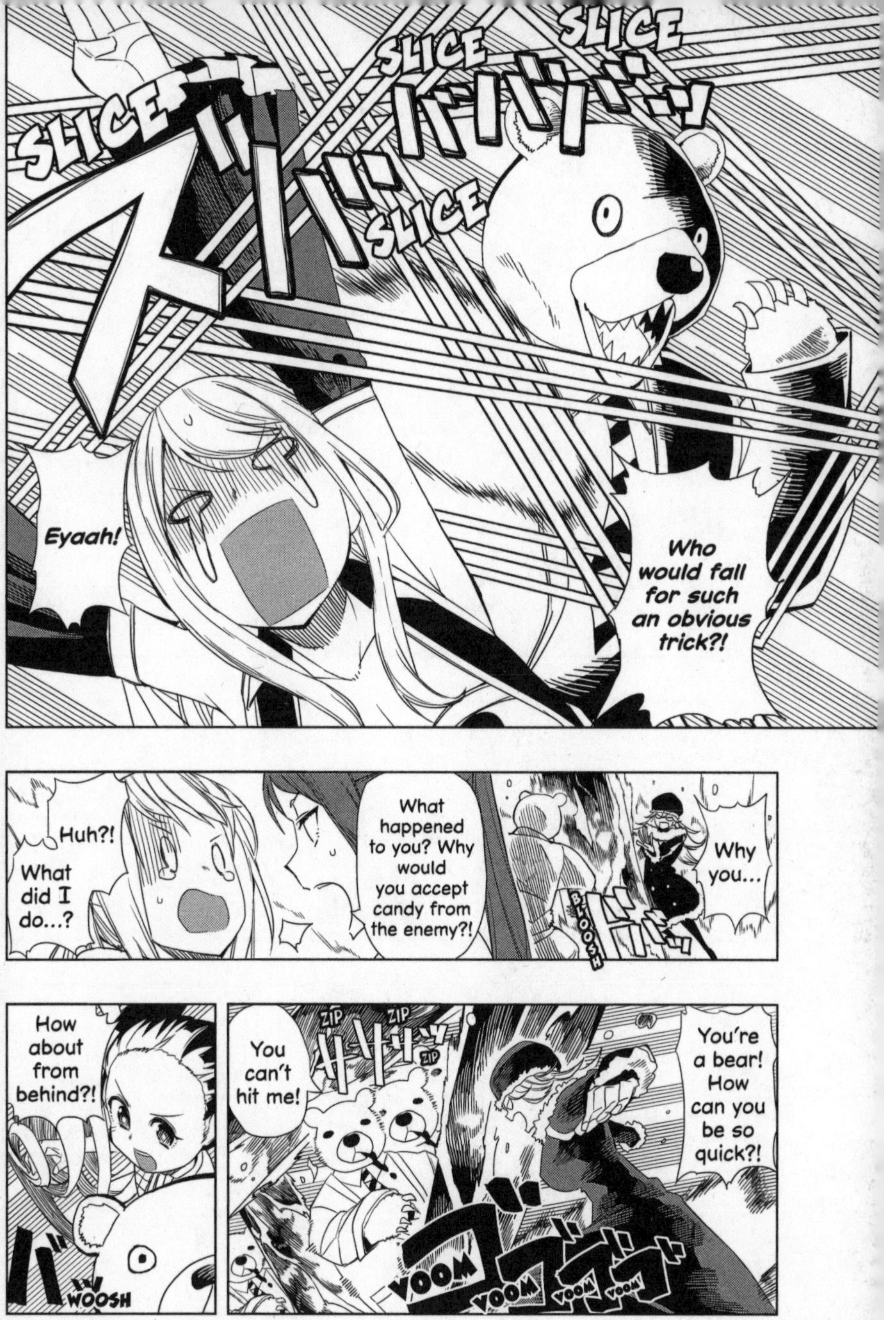
SLICE
SLICE
SLICE
SLICE
Who would fall for such an obvious trick?!
Eyaah!
Why you...
BLOOSH
What happened to you? Why would you accept candy from the enemy?!
Huh?!
What did I do...?
You're a bear! How can you be so quick?!
ZIP
ZIP
ZIP
You can't hit me!
VOOM
VOOM
VOOM
VOOM
How about from behind?!
WOOSH

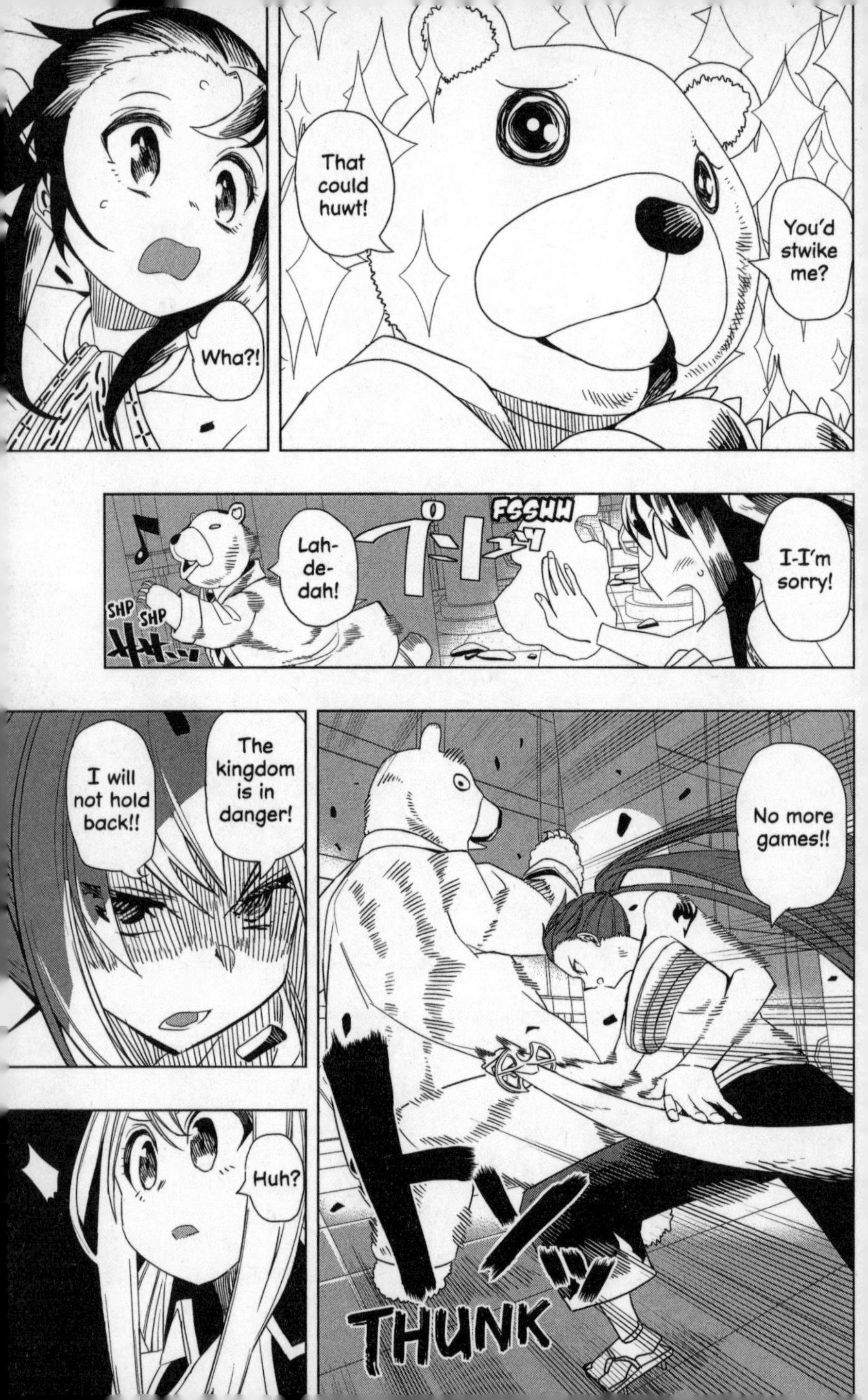

You'd stwike me?
That could huwt!
Wha?!
I-I'm sorry!
FSSHH
Lah-de-dah!
SHP SHP
No more games!!
THUNK
The kingdom is in danger!
I will not hold back!!
Huh?

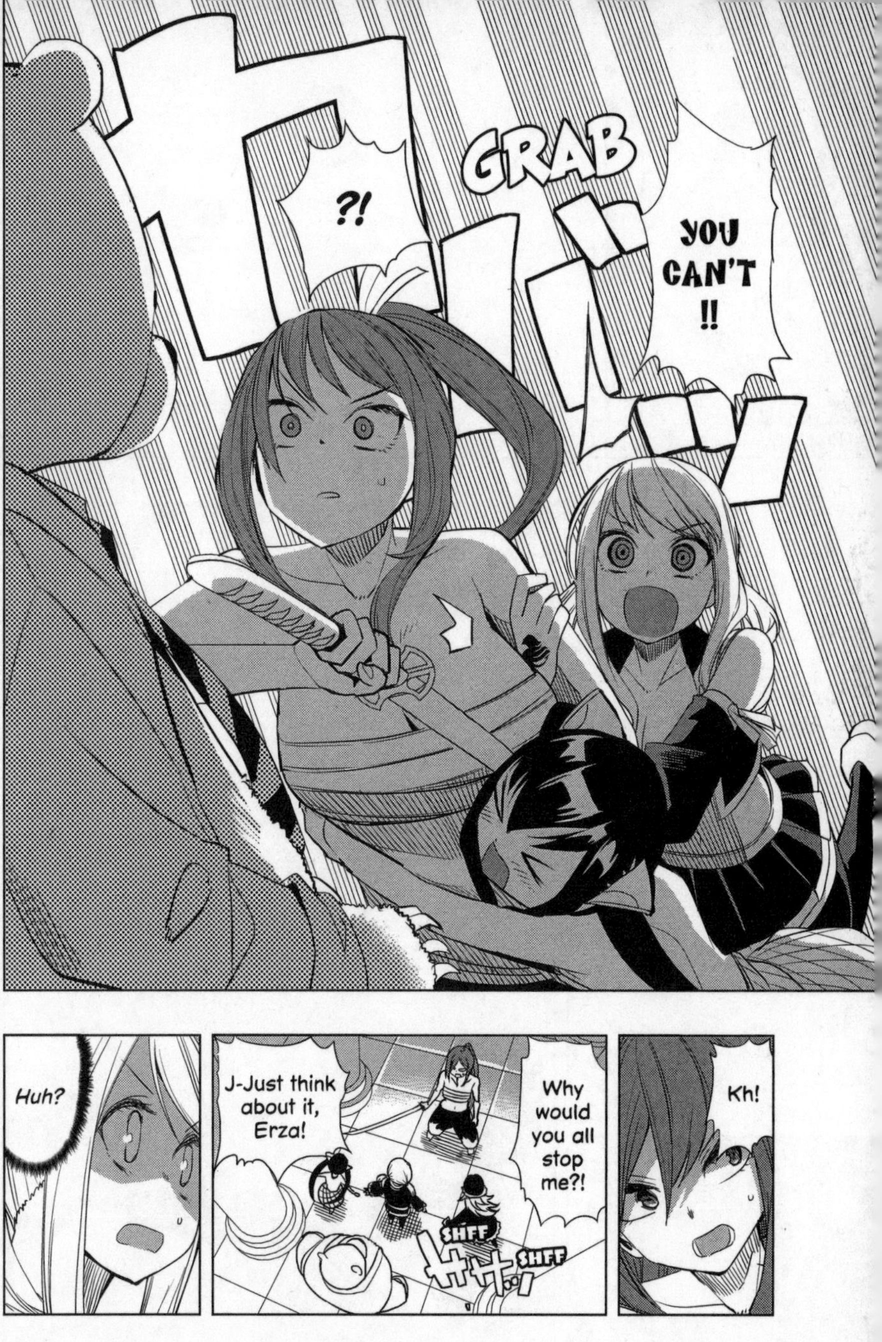
YOU CAN'T !!
GRAB
?!
Kh!
Why would you all stop me?!
J-Just think about it, Erza!
SHFF
SHFF
Huh?

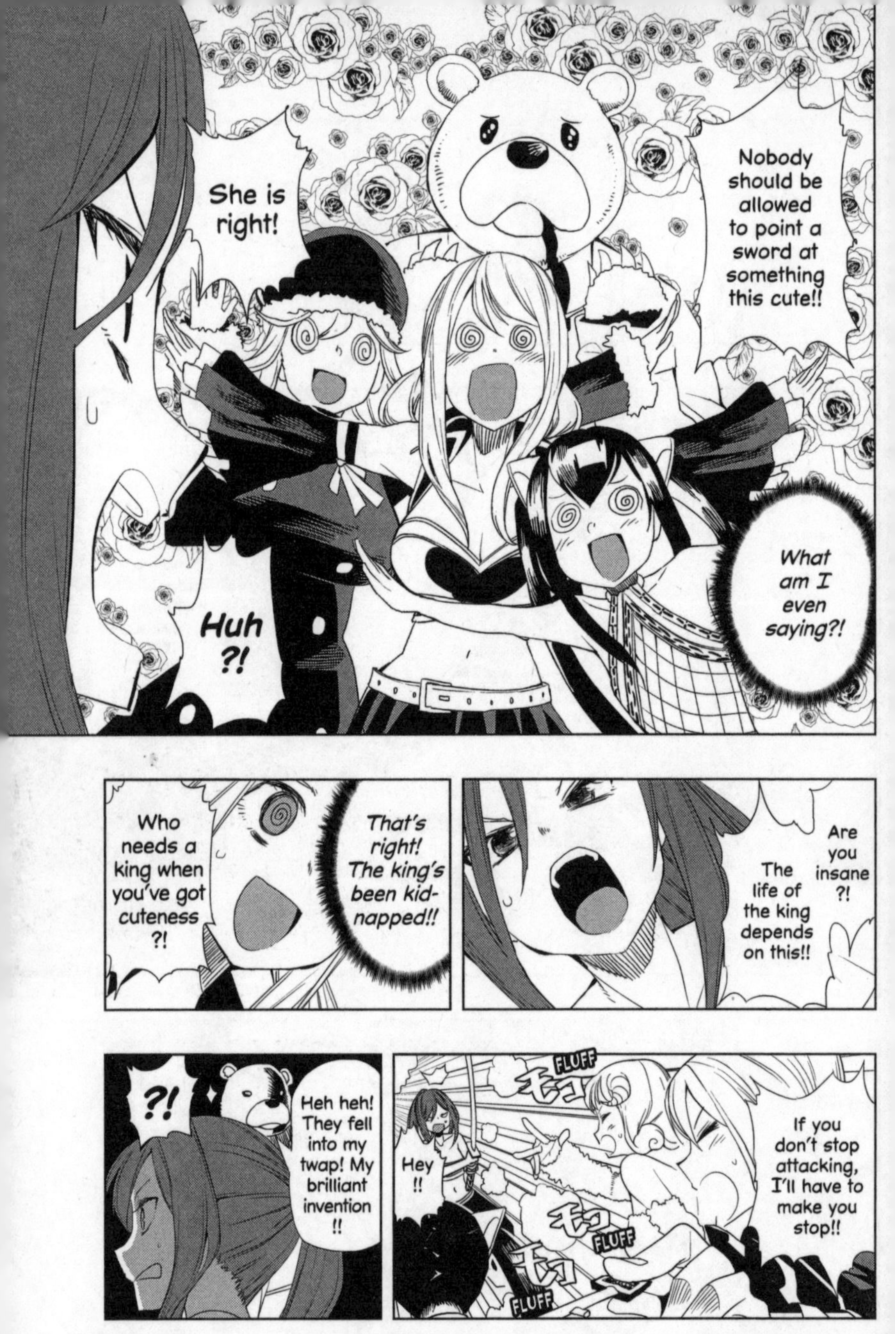
Nobody should be allowed to point a sword at something this cute!!
She is right!
What am I even saying?!
Huh ?!
Are you insane ?!
The life of the king depends on this!!
That's right! The king's been kid-napped!!
Who needs a king when you've got cuteness ?!
If you don't stop attacking, I'll have to make you stop!!
FLUFF
FLUFF
FLUFF
Hey !!
?!
Heh heh! They fell into my twap! My brilliant invention !!

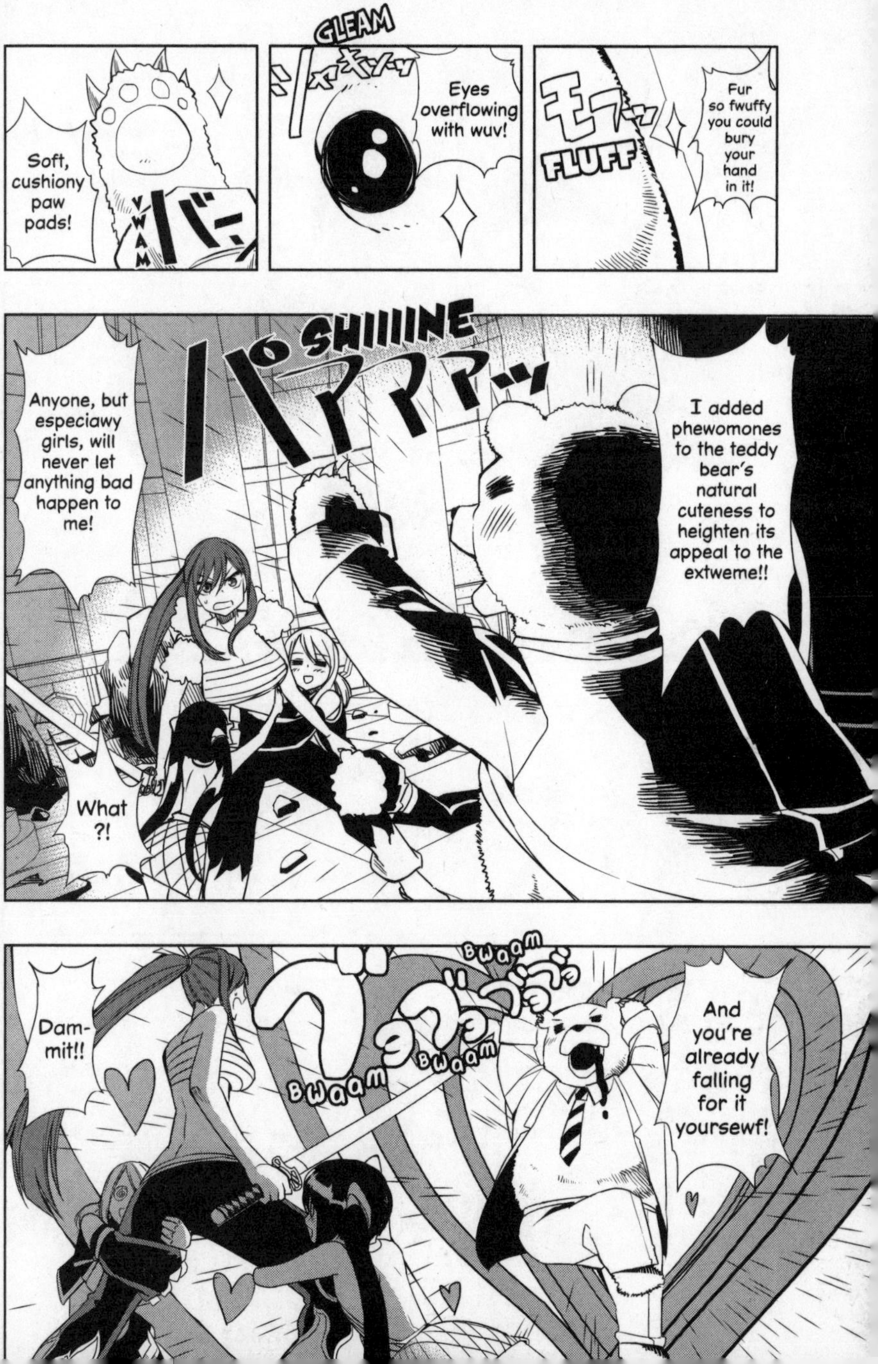
Fur so fwuffy you could bury your hand in it!
FLUFF
GLEAM
Eyes overflowing with wuv!
Soft, cushiony paw pads!
VWAM
SHIIIINE
I added phewomones to the teddy bear's natural cuteness to heighten its appeal to the extweme!!
Anyone, but especiawy girls, will never let anything bad happen to me!
What?!
And you're already falling for it yoursewf!
BWaam
BWaam
BWaam
Dam-mit!!

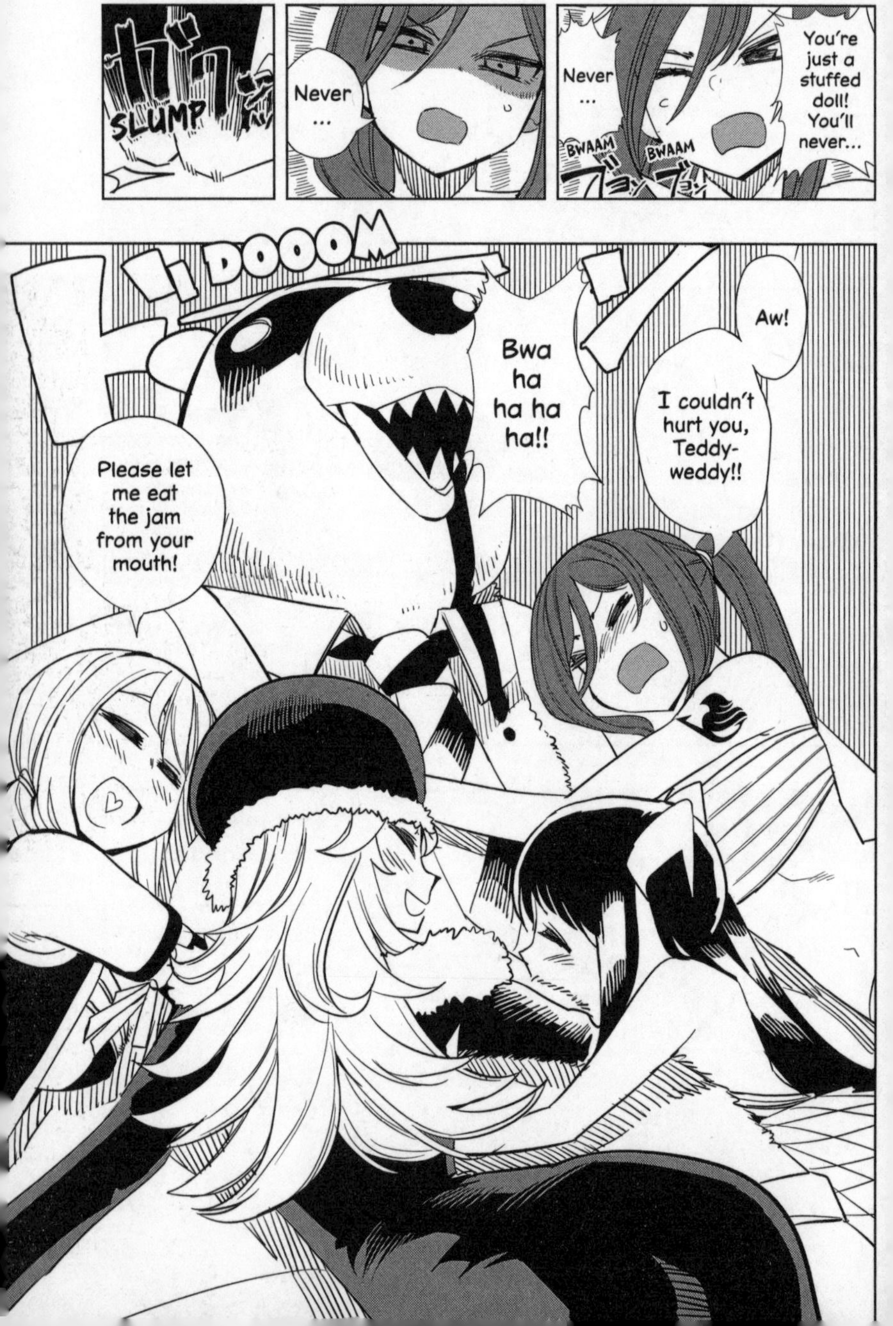
You're just a stuffed doll! You'll never...
Never ...
BWAAM BWAAM
Never ...
SLUMP
Aw!
DOOOM
I couldn't hurt you, Teddy-weddy!!
Bwa ha ha ha ha!!
Please let me eat the jam from your mouth!

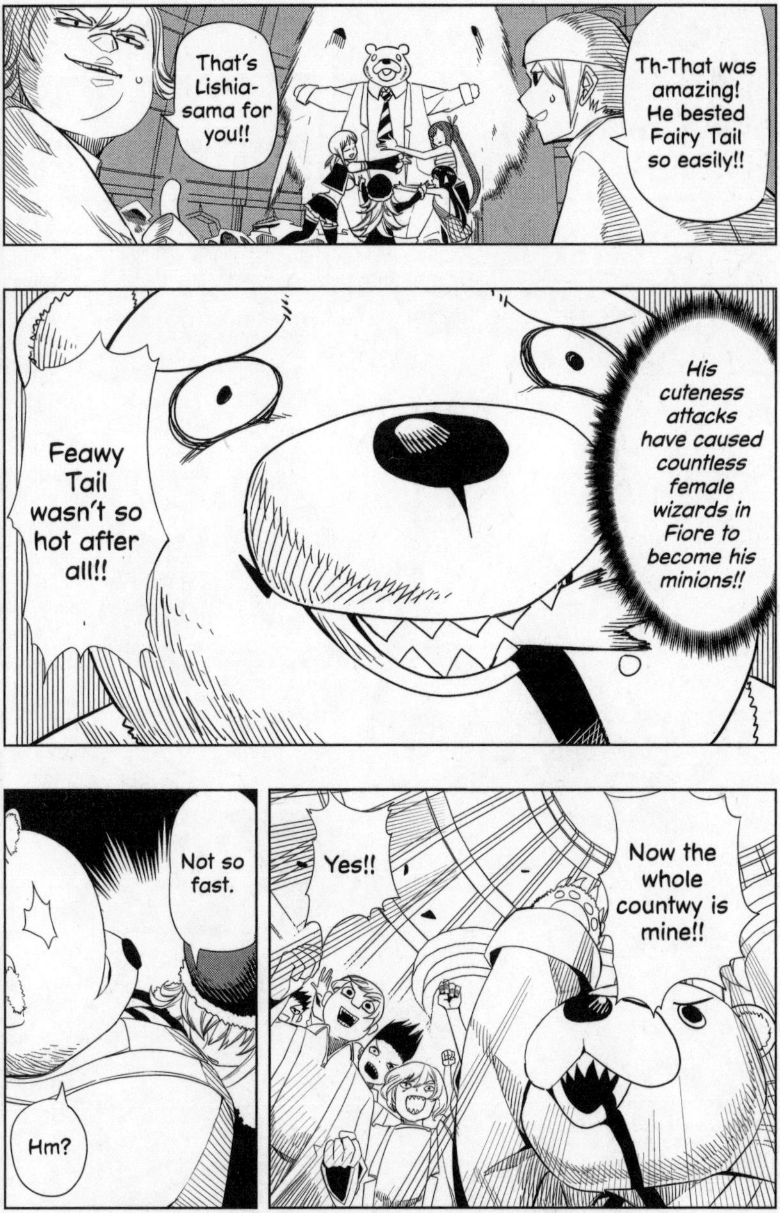
Th-That was amazing! He bested Fairy Tail so easily!!
That's Lishia-sama for you!!
His cuteness attacks have caused countless female wizards in Fiore to become his minions!!
Feawy Tail wasn't so hot after all!!
Now the whole countwy is mine!!
Yes!!
Not so fast.
Hm?

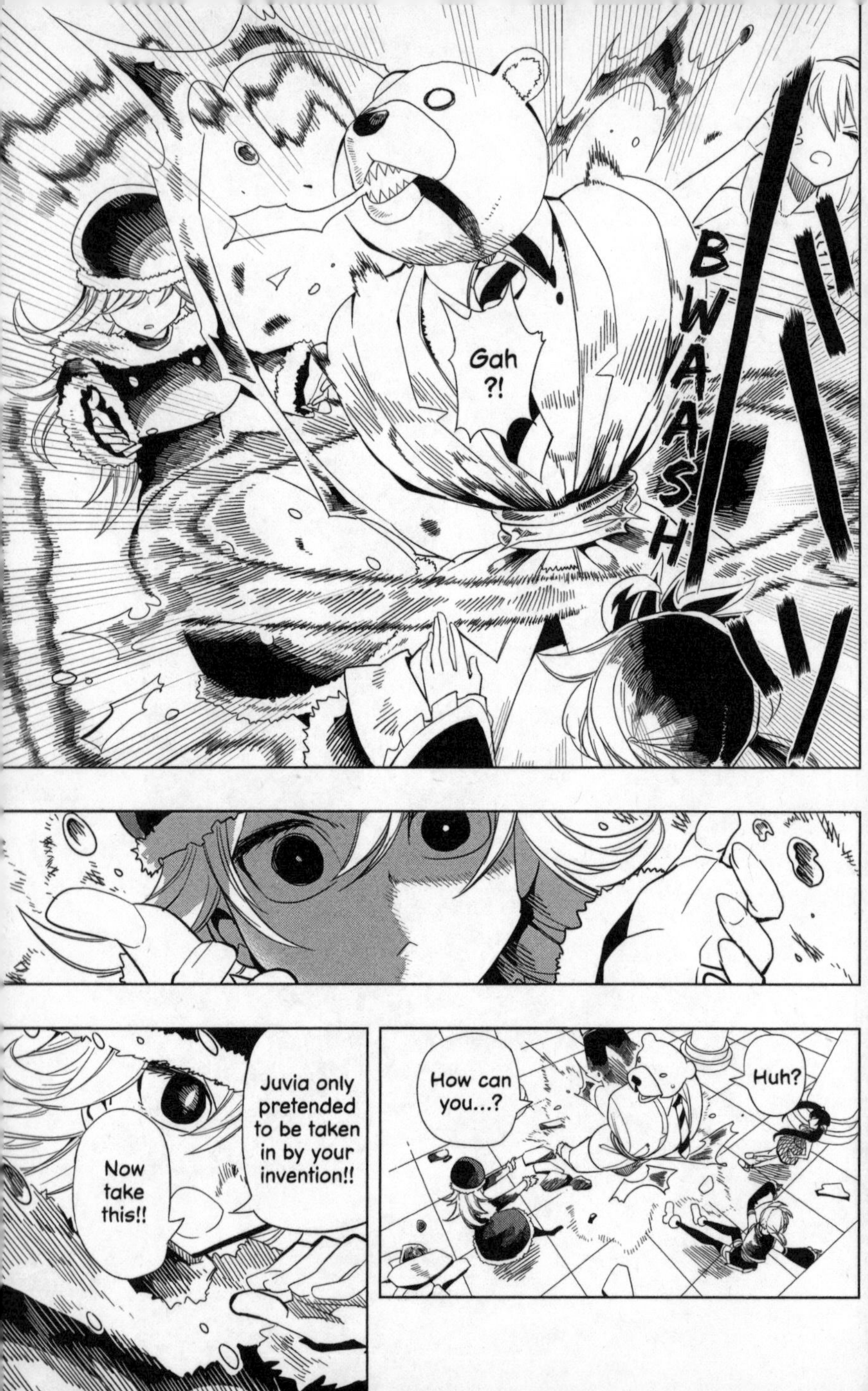
Gah ?!
BWAASH
Huh?
How can you...?
Juvia only pretended to be taken in by your invention!!
Now take this!!

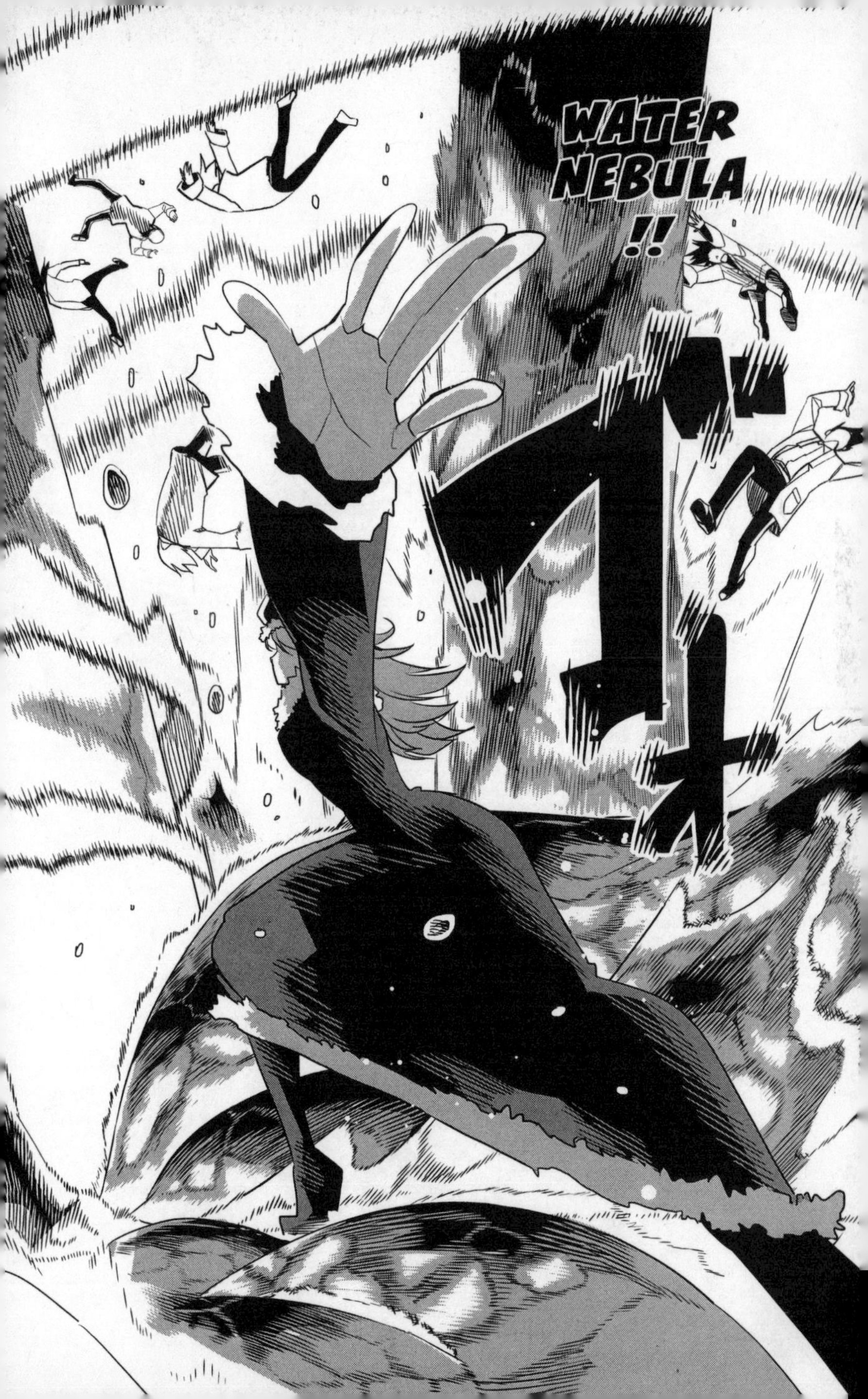
WATER NEBULA !!

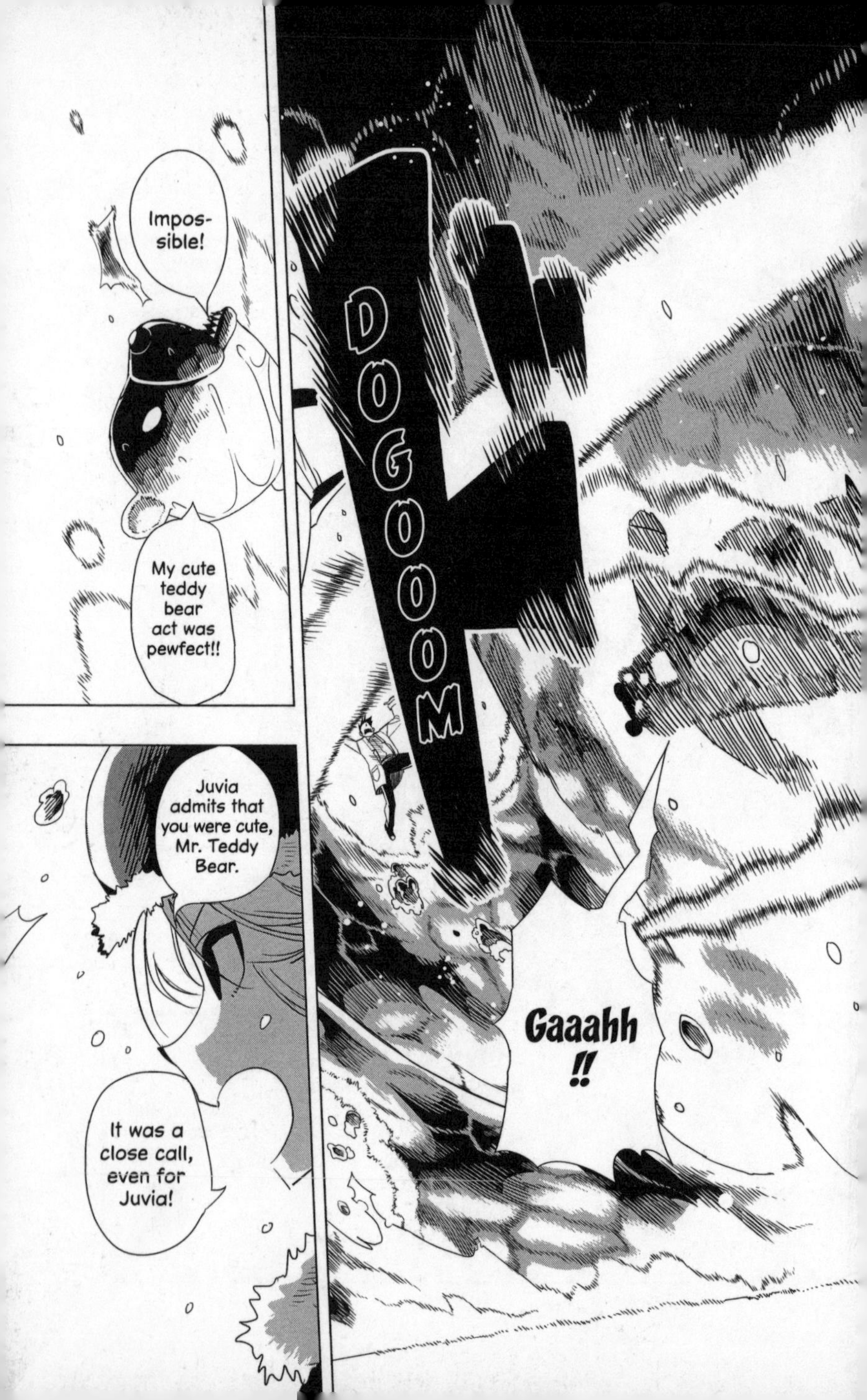
DOGOOOM
Gaaahh!!
Impos-sible!
My cute teddy bear act was pewfect!!
Juvia admits that you were cute, Mr. Teddy Bear.
It was a close call, even for Juvia!

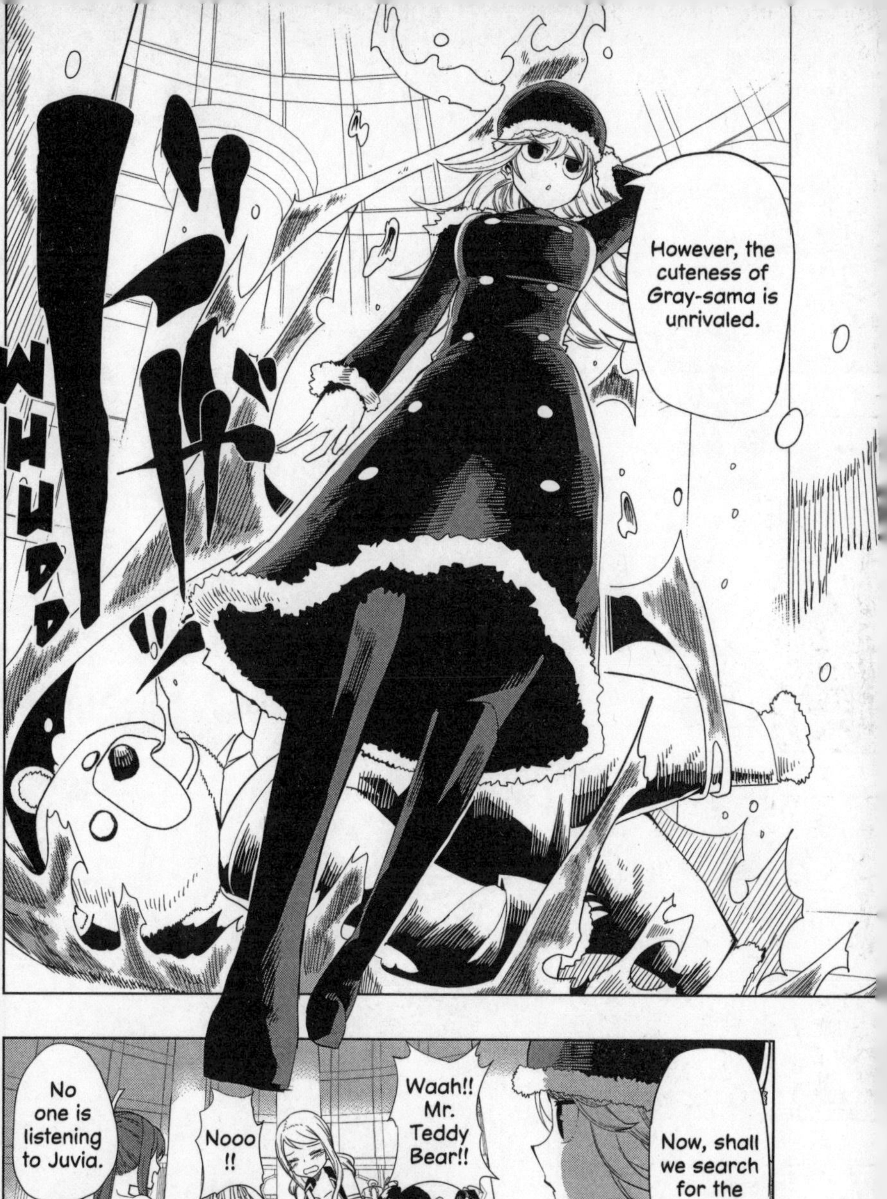
However, the cuteness of Gray-sama is unrivaled.
WHUDDD
Now, shall we search for the king?
Or...
Waah!! Mr. Teddy Bear!!
Nooo !!
No one is listening to Juvia.

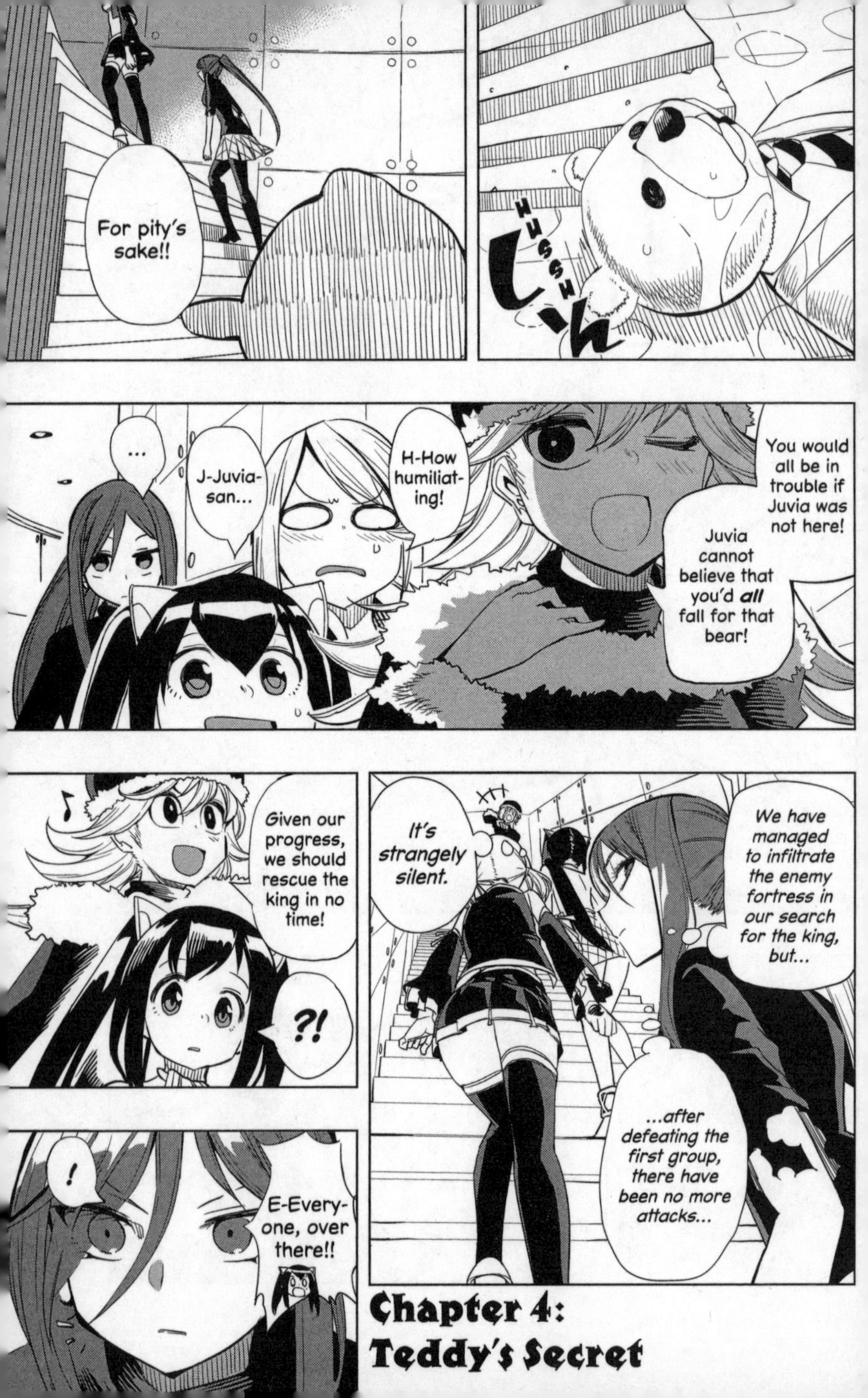
HUSSH
For pity's sake!!
You would all be in trouble if Juvia was not here!
Juvia cannot believe that you'd *all* fall for that bear!
H-How humiliating!
J-Juvia-san...
...
We have managed to infiltrate the enemy fortress in our search for the king, but...
It's strangely silent.
...after defeating the first group, there have been no more attacks...
Given our progress, we should rescue the king in no time!
?!
!
E-Everyone, over there!!

Chapter 4: Teddy's Secret

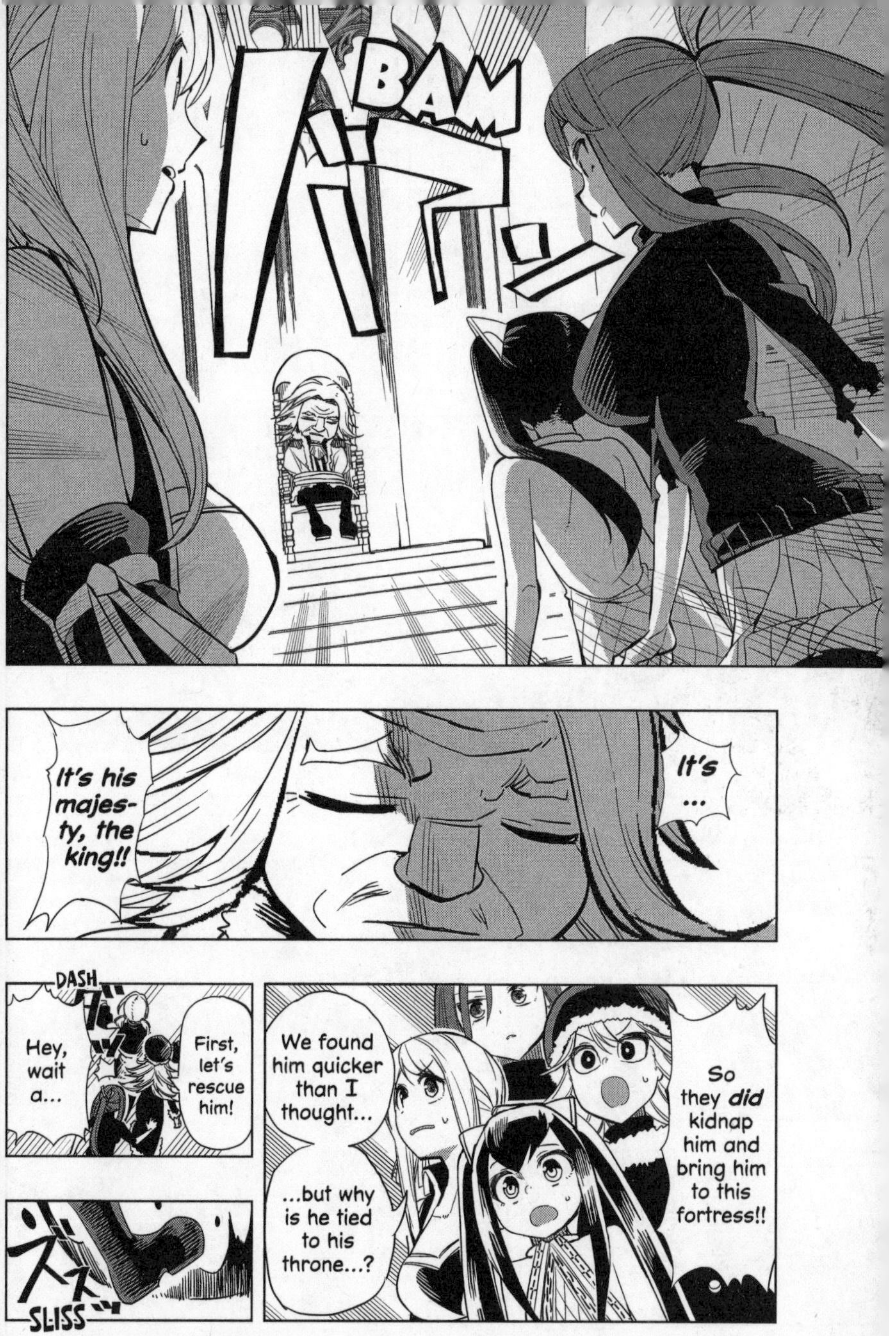
BAM
It's ...
It's his majesty, the king!!
So they *did* kidnap him and bring him to this fortress!!
We found him quicker than I thought...
...but why is he tied to his throne...?
DASH
First, let's rescue him!
Hey, wait a...
SLISS

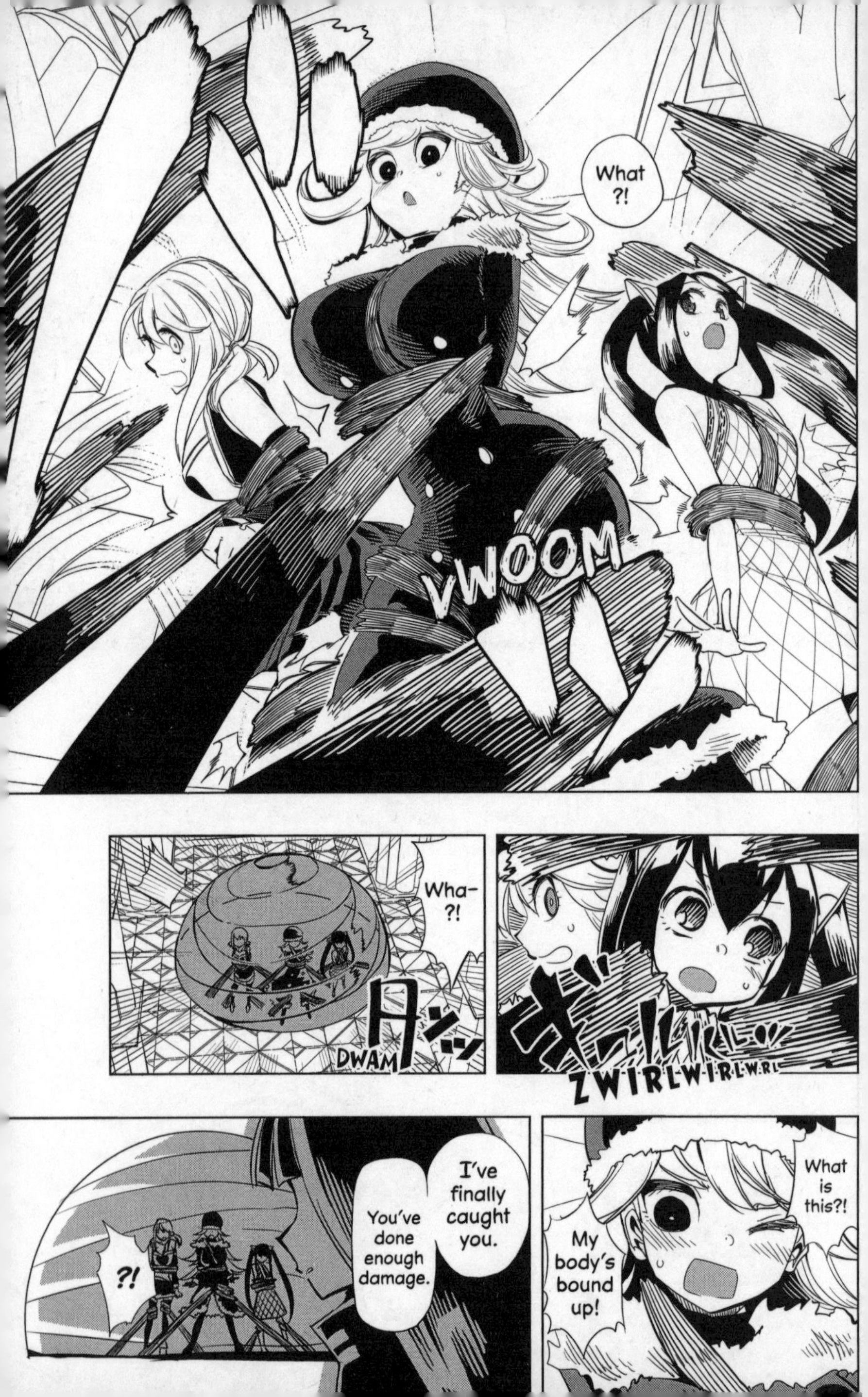
What ?!
VWOOM
ZWIRLWIRLWRL
Wha- ?!
DWAM
What is this?!
My body's bound up!
I've finally caught you.
You've done enough damage.
?!

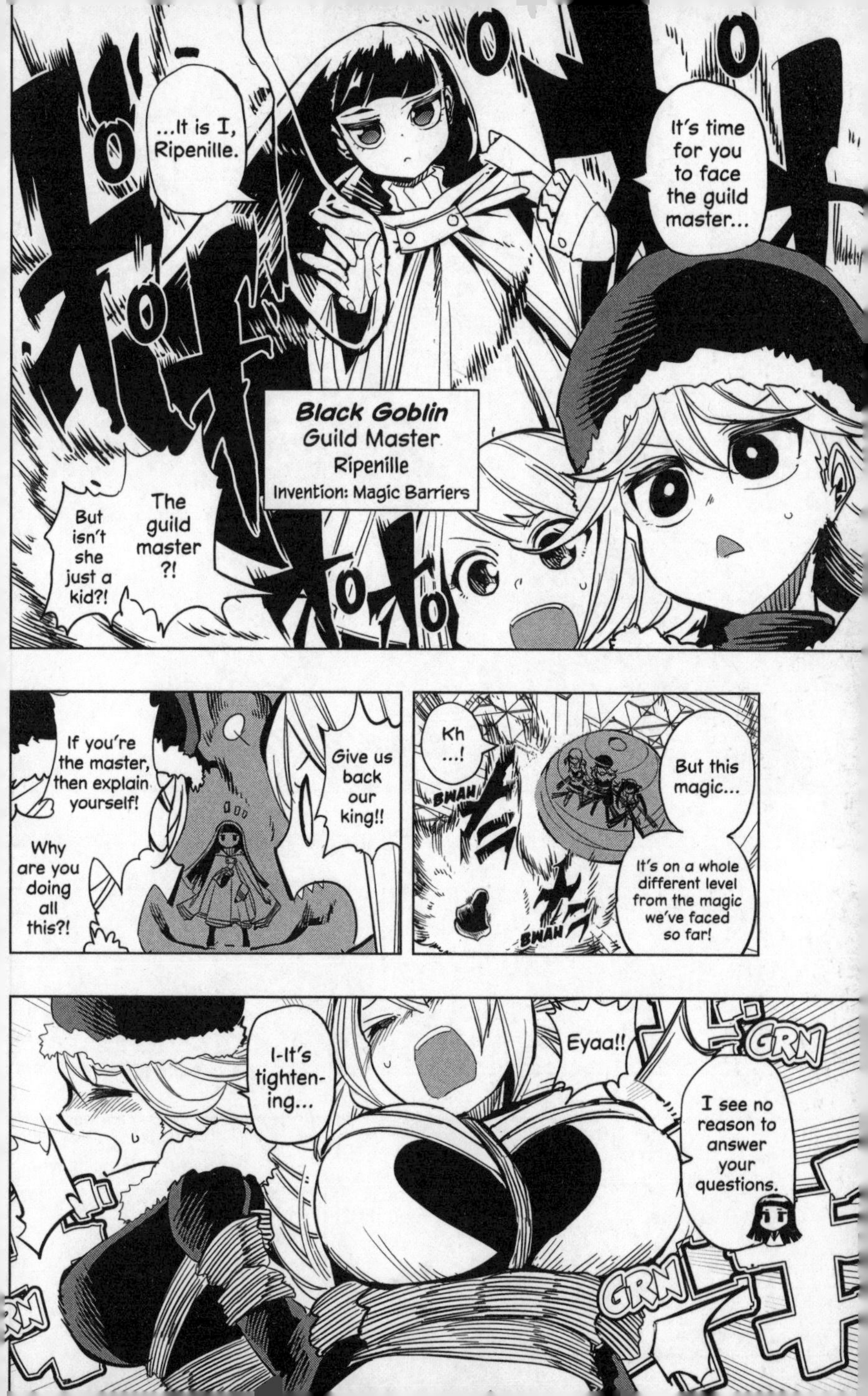
It's time for you to face the guild master...
...It is I, Ripenille.
Black Goblin
Guild Master
Ripenille
Invention: Magic Barriers
The guild master?!
But isn't she just a kid?!
But this magic...
Kh ...!
BWAH
It's on a whole different level from the magic we've faced so far!
BWAH
Give us back our king!!
If you're the master, then explain yourself!
Why are you doing all this?!
GRN
Eyaa!!
I see no reason to answer your questions.
I-It's tighten-ing...
GRN

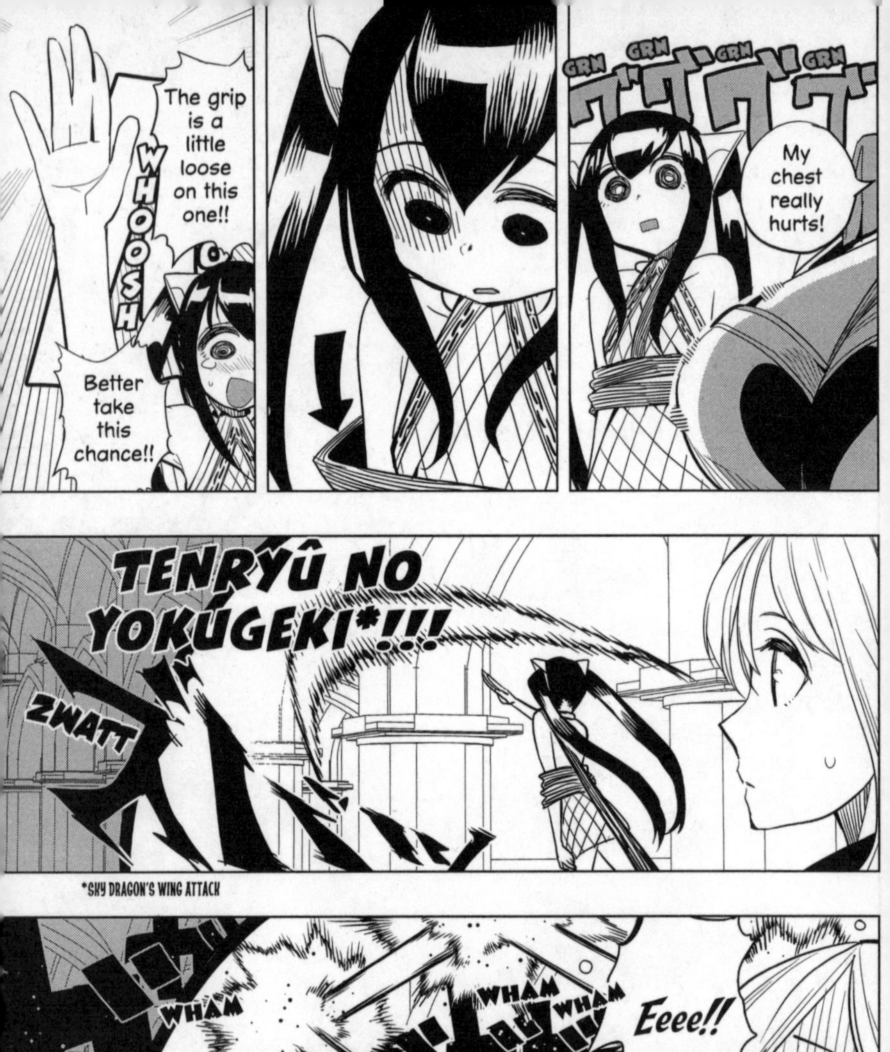
GRN GRN GRN GRN
My chest really hurts!
The grip is a little loose on this one!!
WHOOSH
Better take this chance!!
TENRYÛ NO YOKUGEKI*!!!
ZWATT

*SKY DRAGON'S WING ATTACK

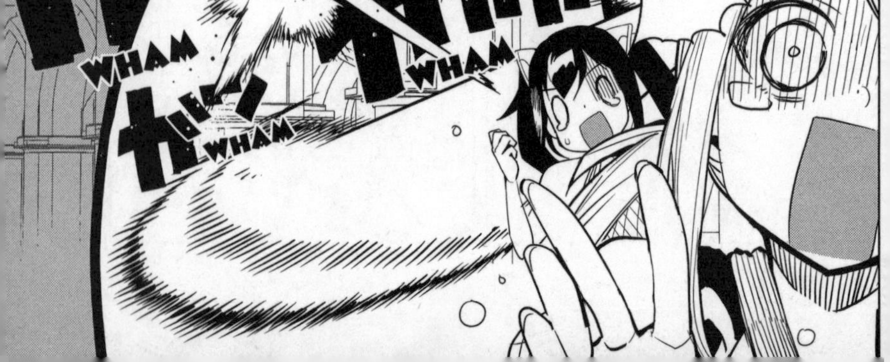
Eeee!!
WHAM
WHAM
WHAM
WHAM
WHAM
WHAM

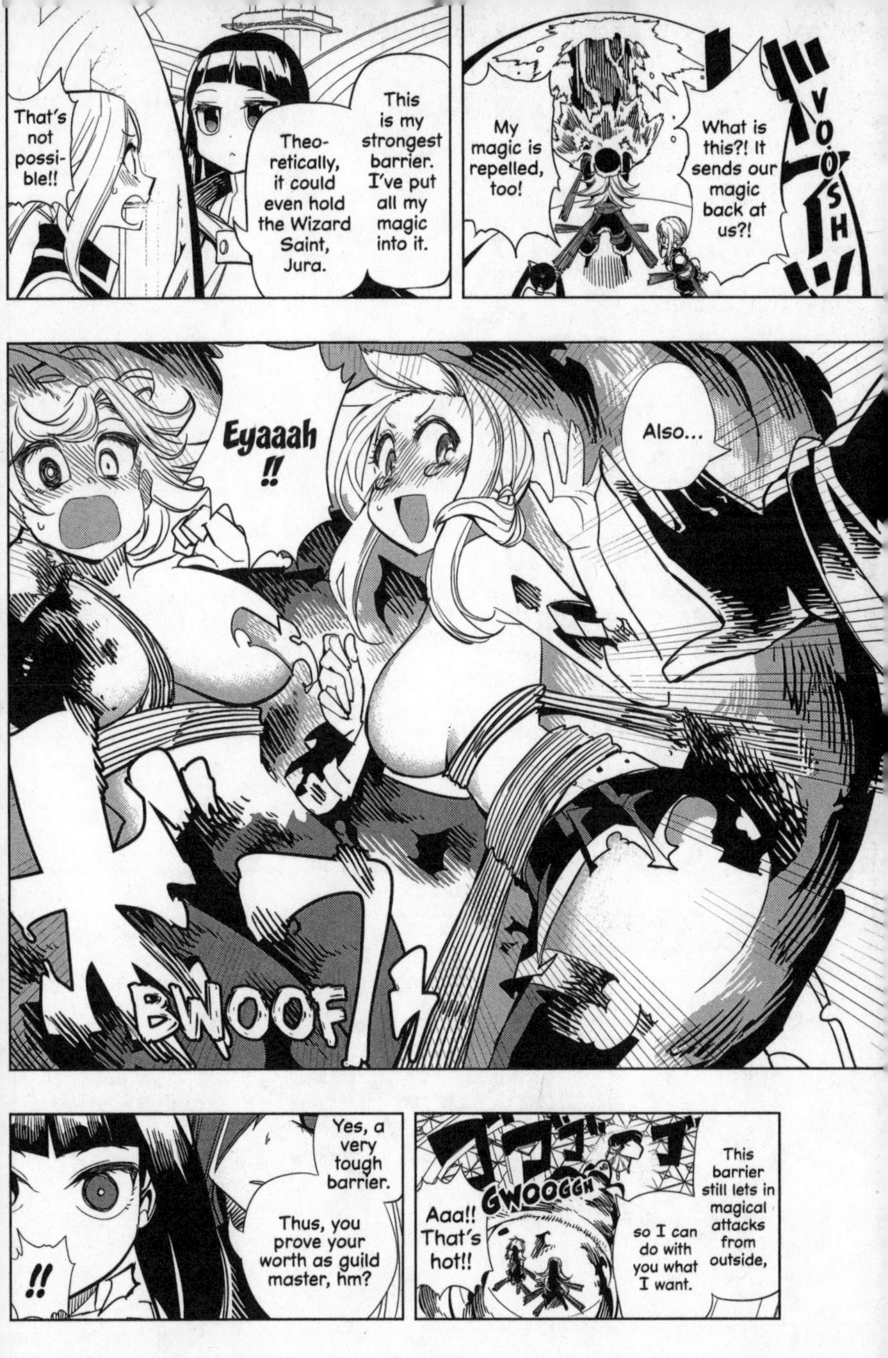
VOÖSH
What is this?! It sends our magic back at us?!
My magic is repelled, too!
This is my strongest barrier. I've put all my magic into it.
Theo-retically, it could even hold the Wizard Saint, Jura.
That's not possi-ble!!
Also...
Eyaaah!!
BWOOF
This barrier still lets in magical attacks from outside,
so I can do with you what I want.
GWOOGGH
Aaa!! That's hot!!
Yes, a very tough barrier.
Thus, you prove your worth as guild master, hm?
!!

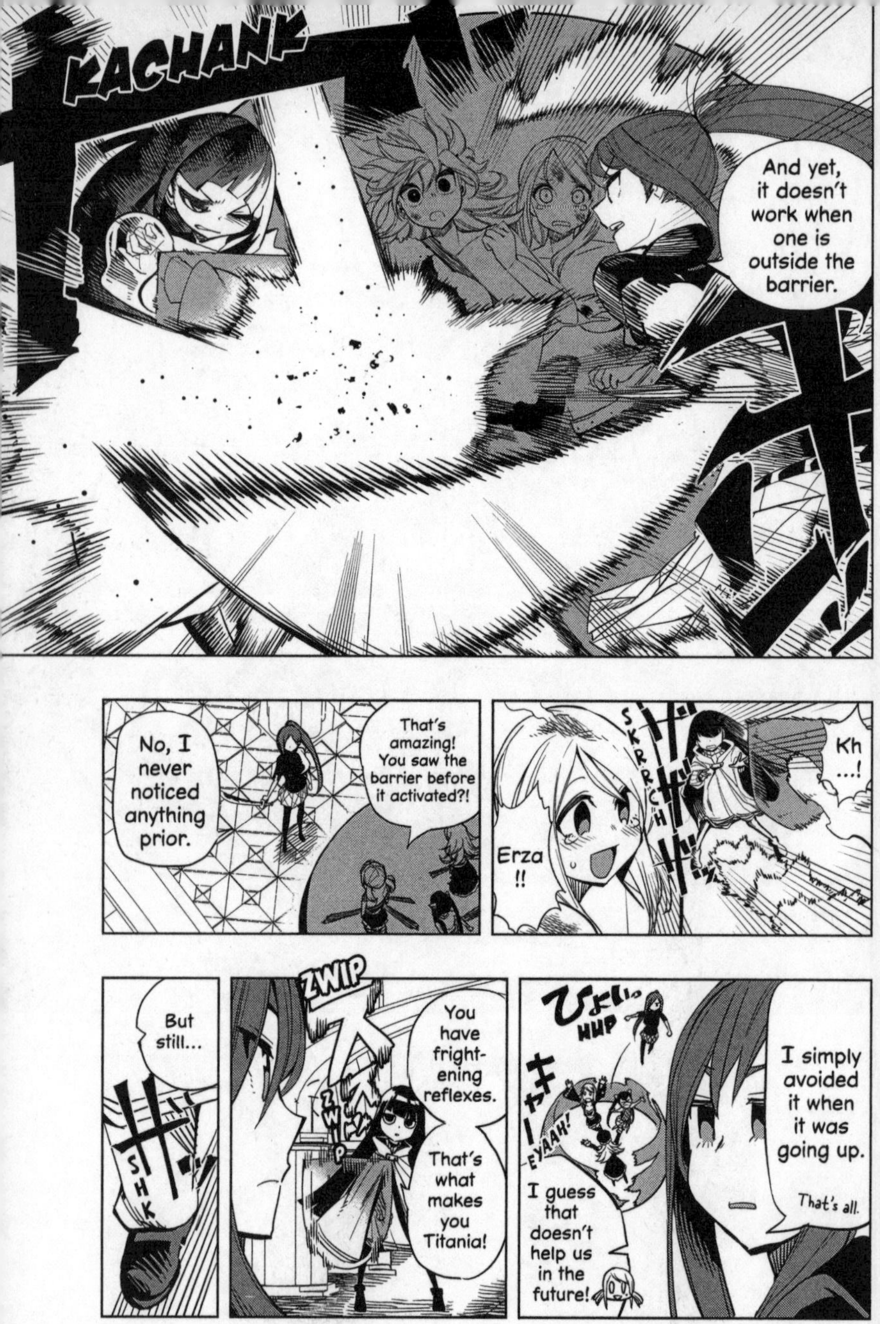
KACHANK
And yet, it doesn't work when one is outside the barrier.
SKRRCH
Kh ...!
Erza !!
That's amazing! You saw the barrier before it activated?!
No, I never noticed anything prior.
I simply avoided it when it was going up.
That's all.
HUP
EYAAH!
I guess that doesn't help us in the future!
ZWIP
You have frightening reflexes.
That's what makes you Titania!
ZWIP
But still...
SHK

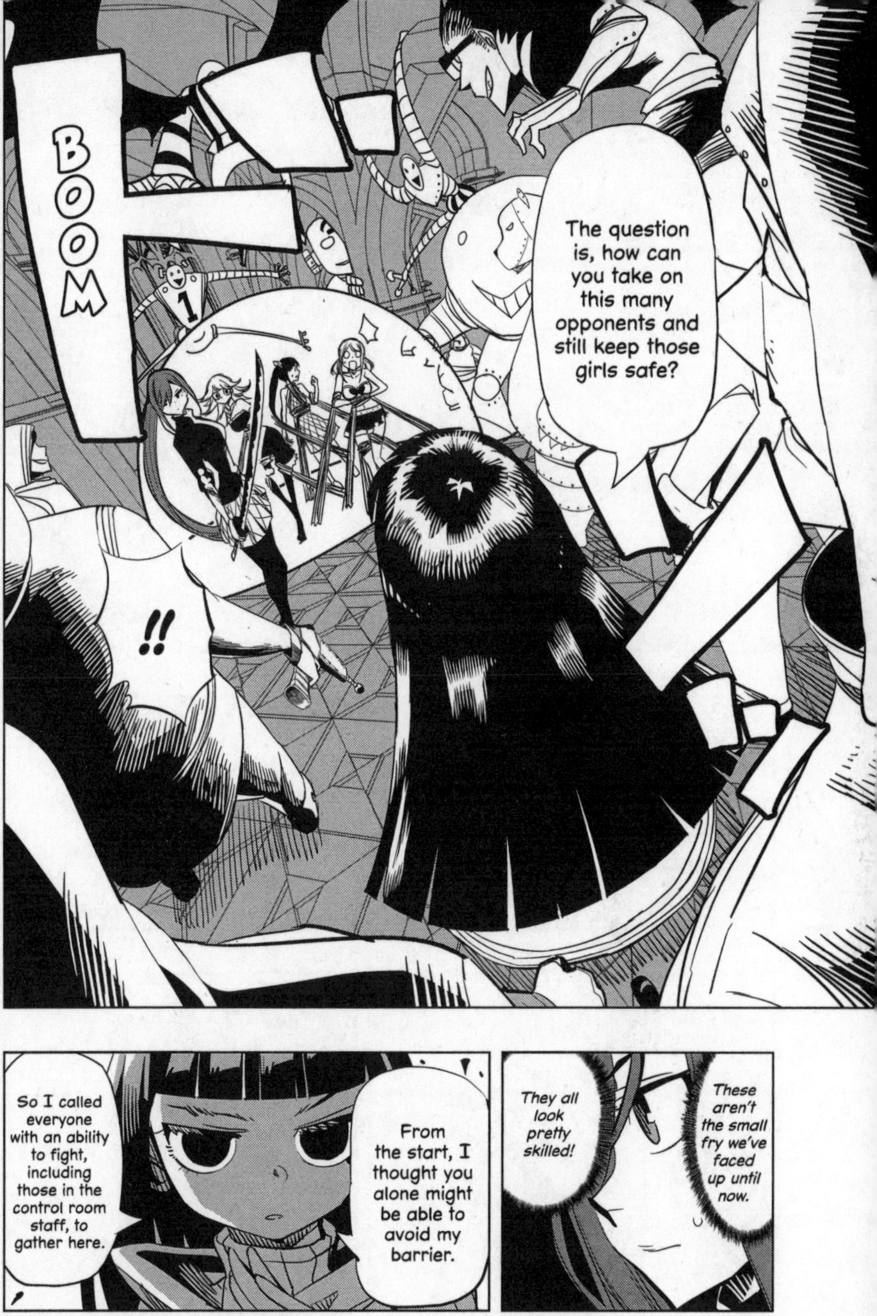
The question is, how can you take on this many opponents and still keep those girls safe?
BOOM
!!
These aren't the small fry we've faced up until now.
They all look pretty skilled!
From the start, I thought you alone might be able to avoid my barrier.
So I called everyone with an ability to fight, including those in the control room staff, to gather here.

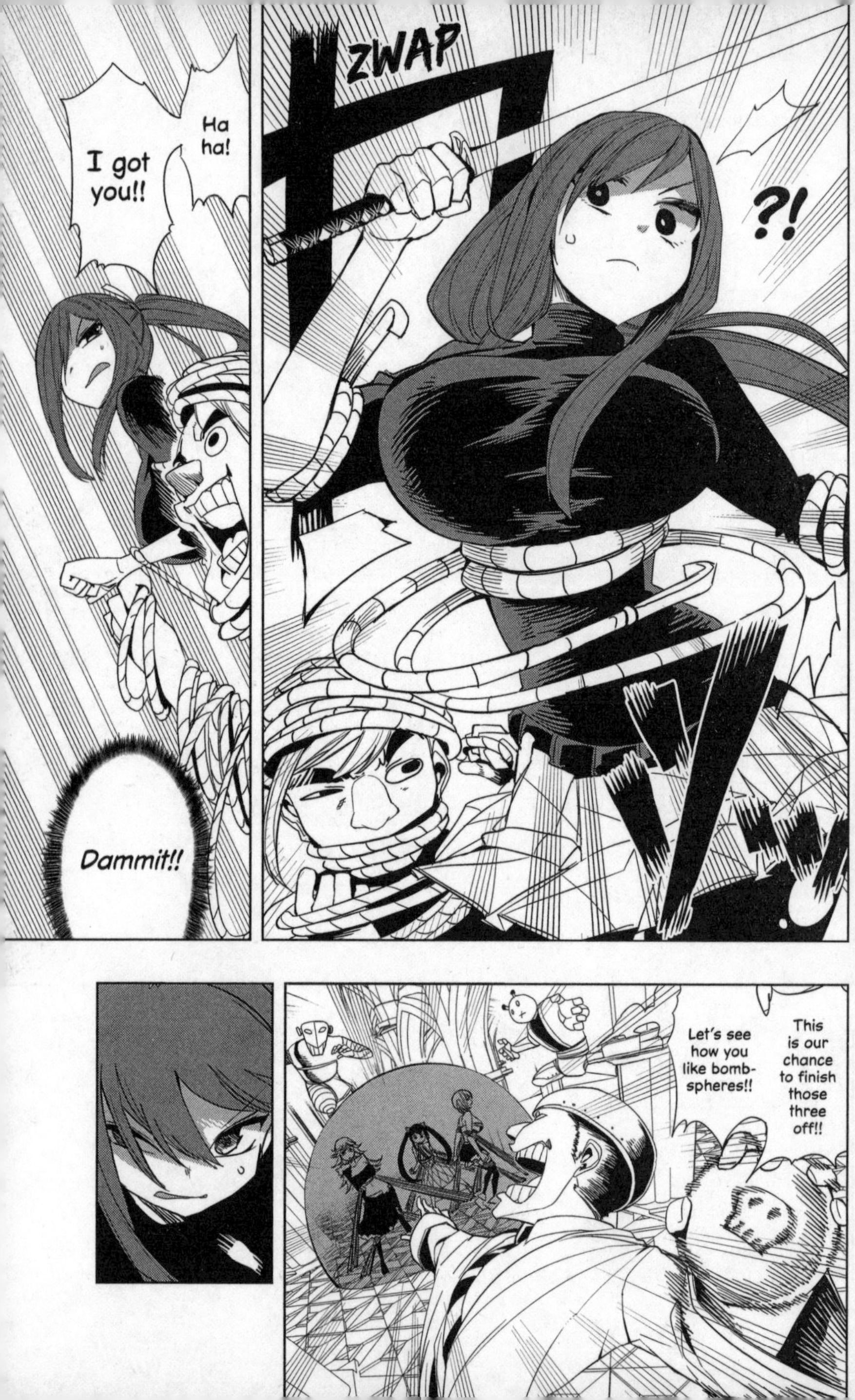
ZWAP
?!
Ha ha!
I got you!!
Dammit!!
This is our chance to finish those three off!!
Let's see how you like bomb-spheres!!

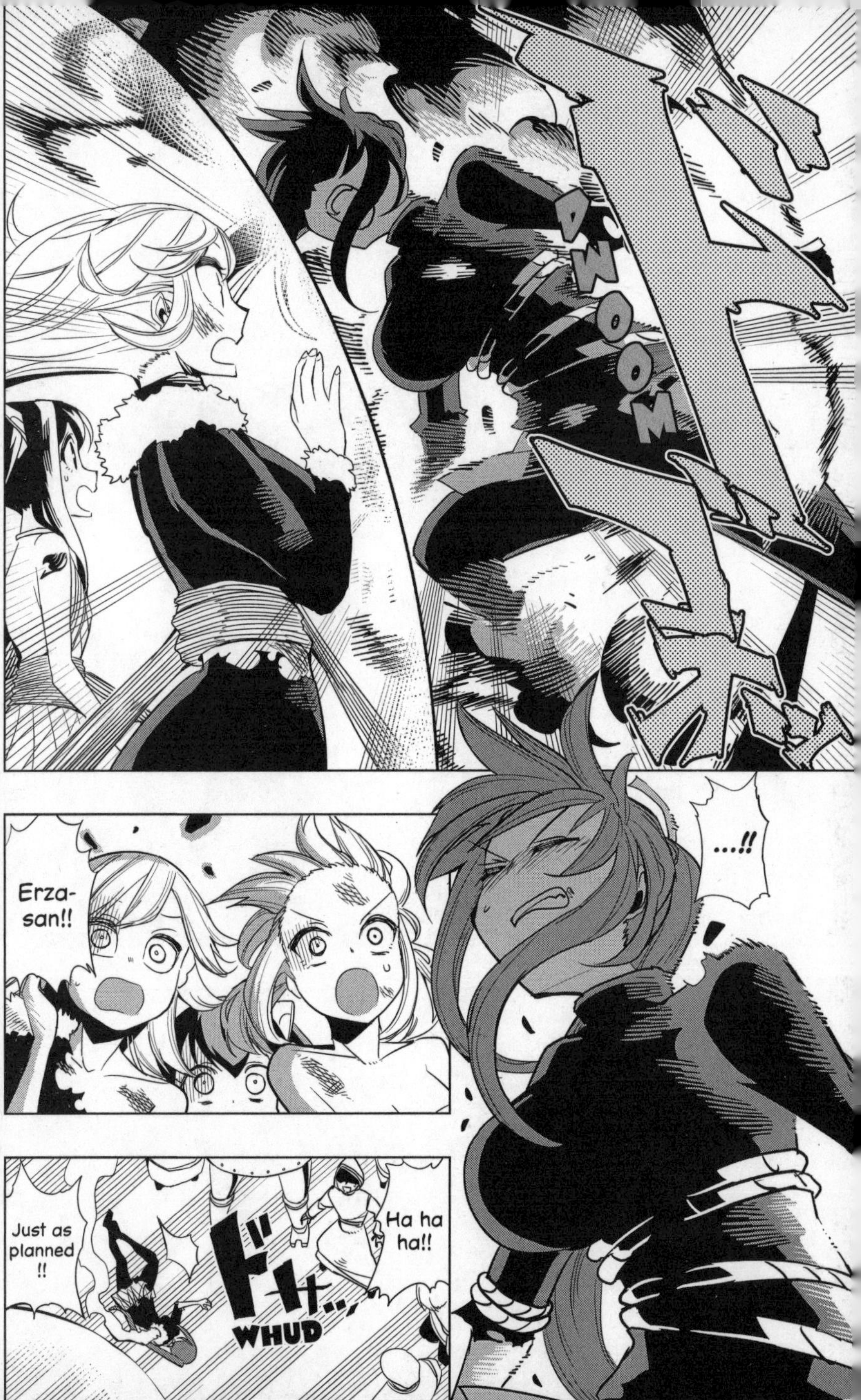
DWOOM
...!!
Erza-san!!
Ha ha ha!!
Just as planned !!
WHUD

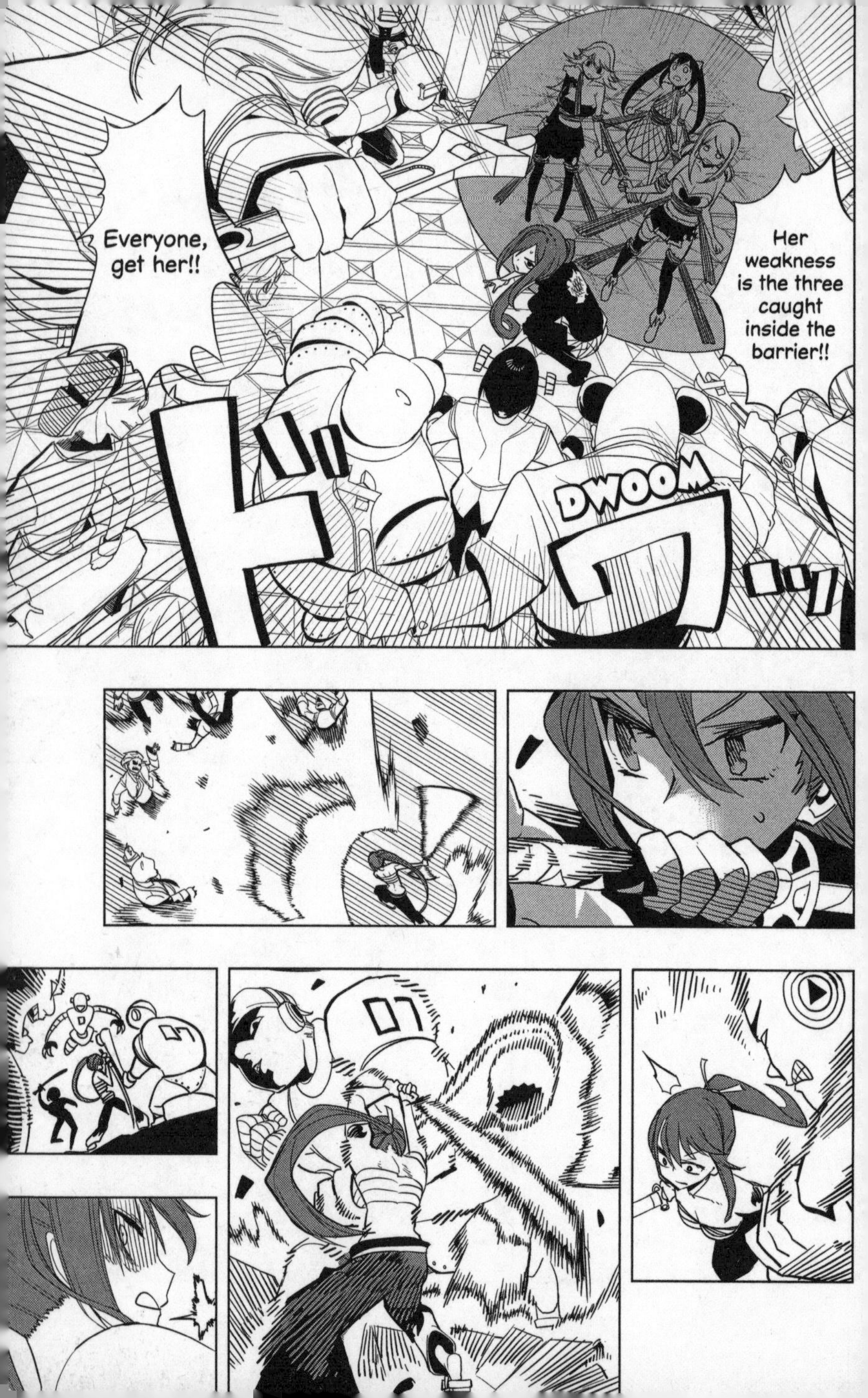
Her weakness is the three caught inside the barrier!!
Everyone, get her!!
DWOOM

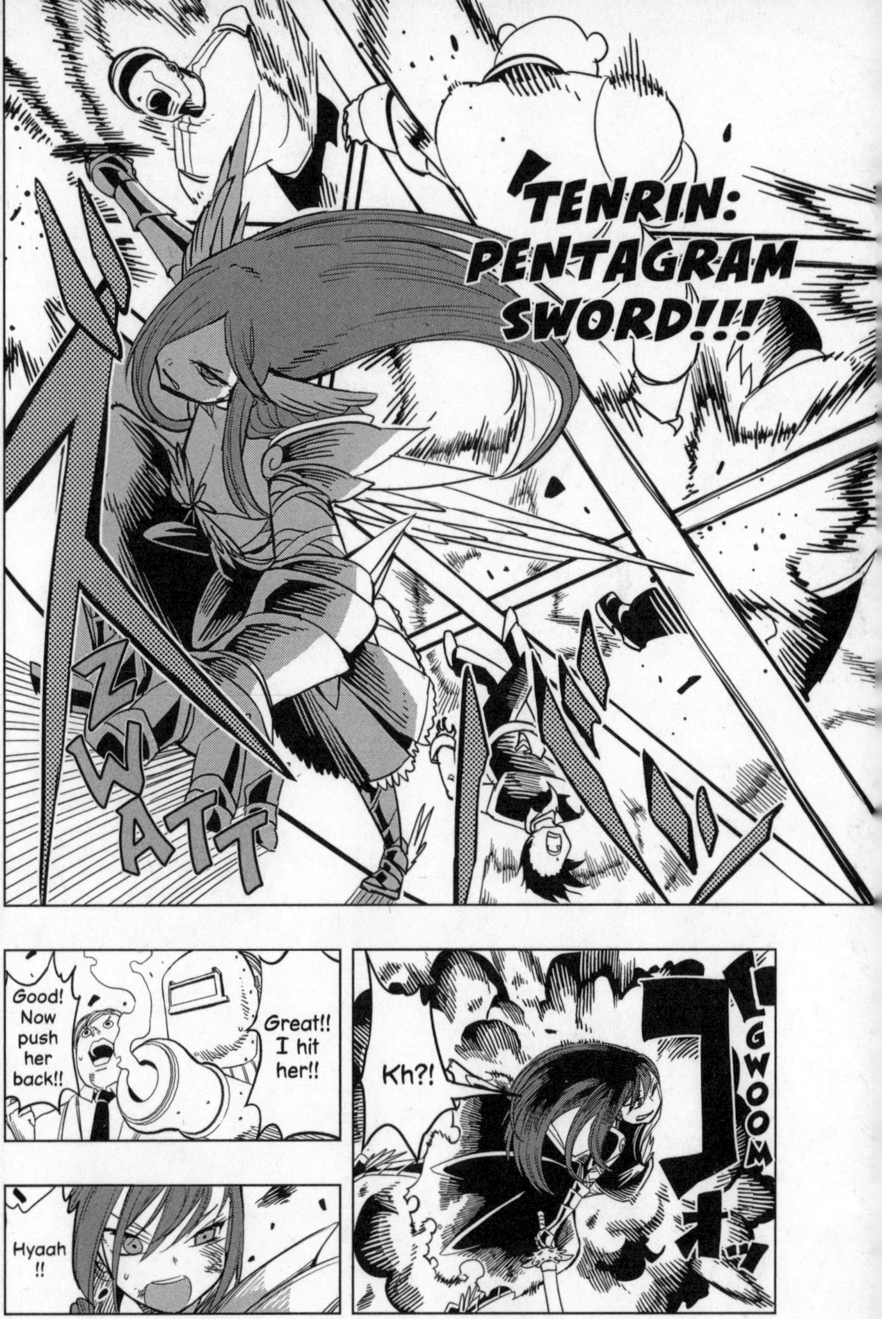
TENRIN: PENTAGRAM SWORD!!!
ZWATT
GWOOM
Kh?!
Great!! I hit her!!
Good! Now push her back!!
Hyaah !!

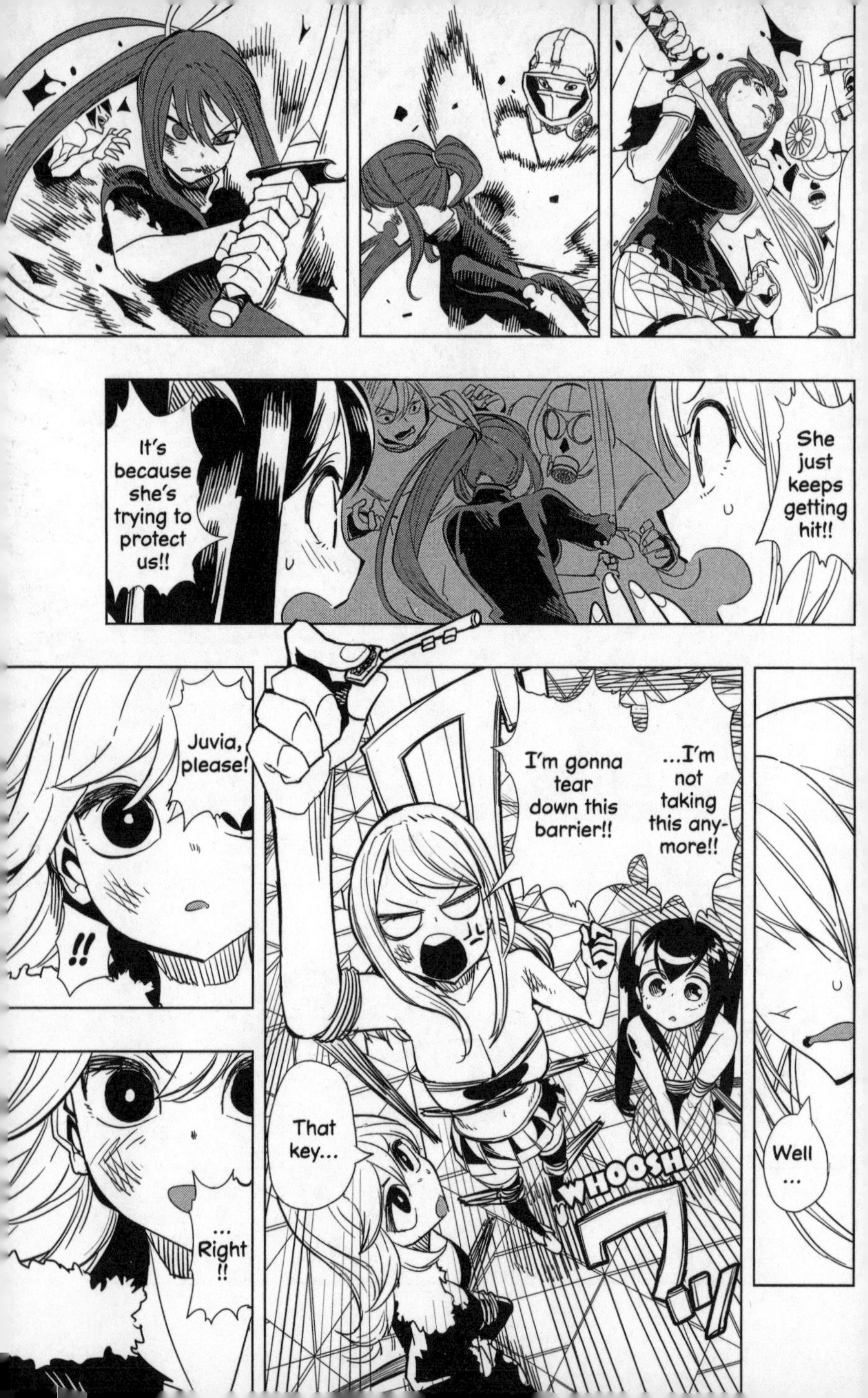
She just keeps getting hit!!
It's because she's trying to protect us!!
Well ...
...I'm not taking this any-more!!
I'm gonna tear down this barrier!!
WHOOSH
That key...
Juvia, please!
!!
... Right !!

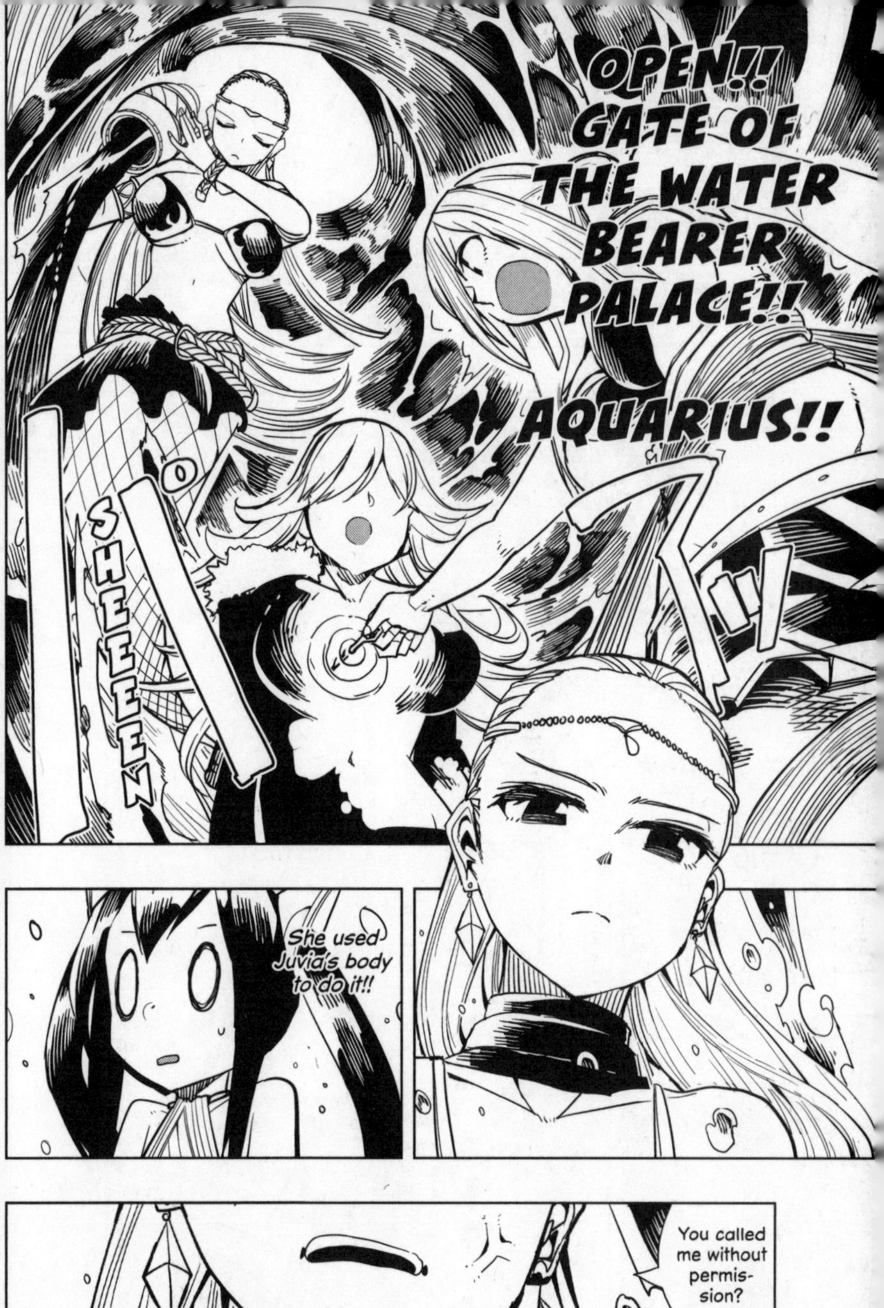
OPEN!! GATE OF THE WATER BEARER PALACE!!
AQUARIUS!!
SHEEEEEN
She used Juvia's body to do it!!
You called me without permis-sion?

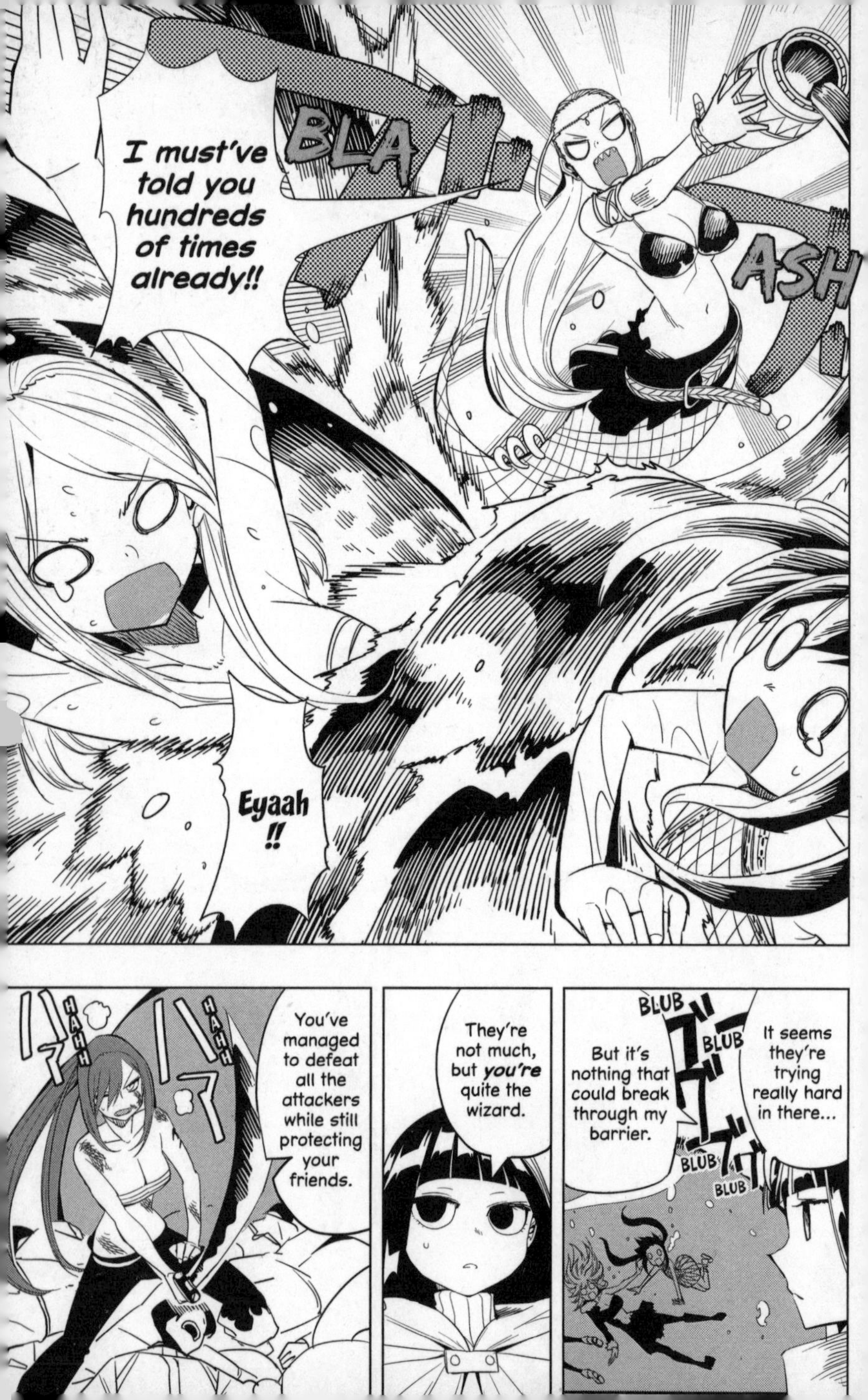
BLA
ASH
I must've told you hundreds of times already!!
Eyaah!!
BLUB
BLUB
It seems they're trying really hard in there...
But it's nothing that could break through my barrier.
BLUB
BLUB
They're not much, but *you're* quite the wizard.
You've managed to defeat all the attackers while still protecting your friends.
HAHH
HAHH

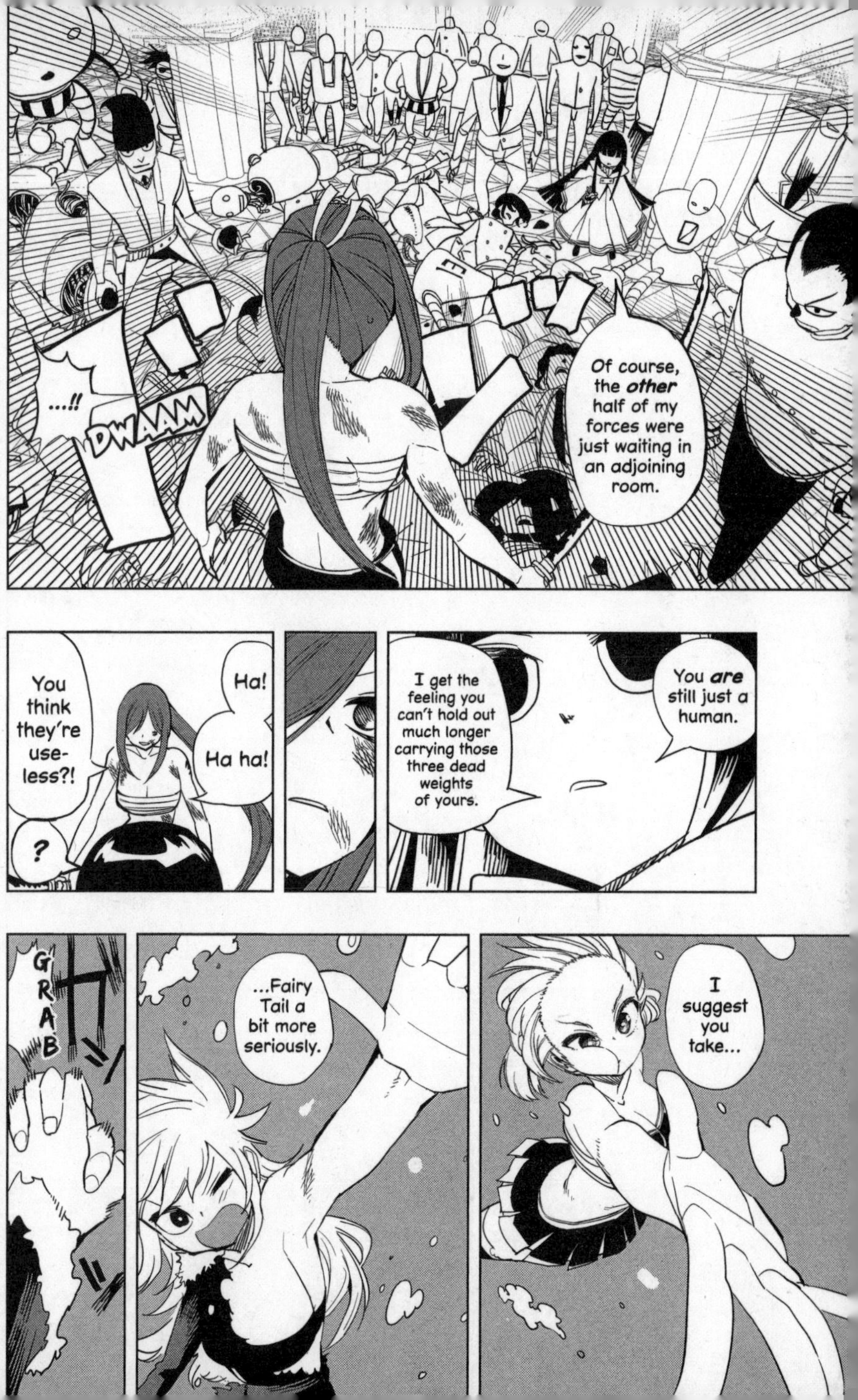
Of course, the *other* half of my forces were just waiting in an adjoining room.
DWAAM
...!!
You *are* still just a human.
I get the feeling you can't hold out much longer carrying those three dead weights of yours.
Ha!
Ha ha!
You think they're use-less?!
?
I suggest you take...
...Fairy Tail a bit more seriously.
GRAB

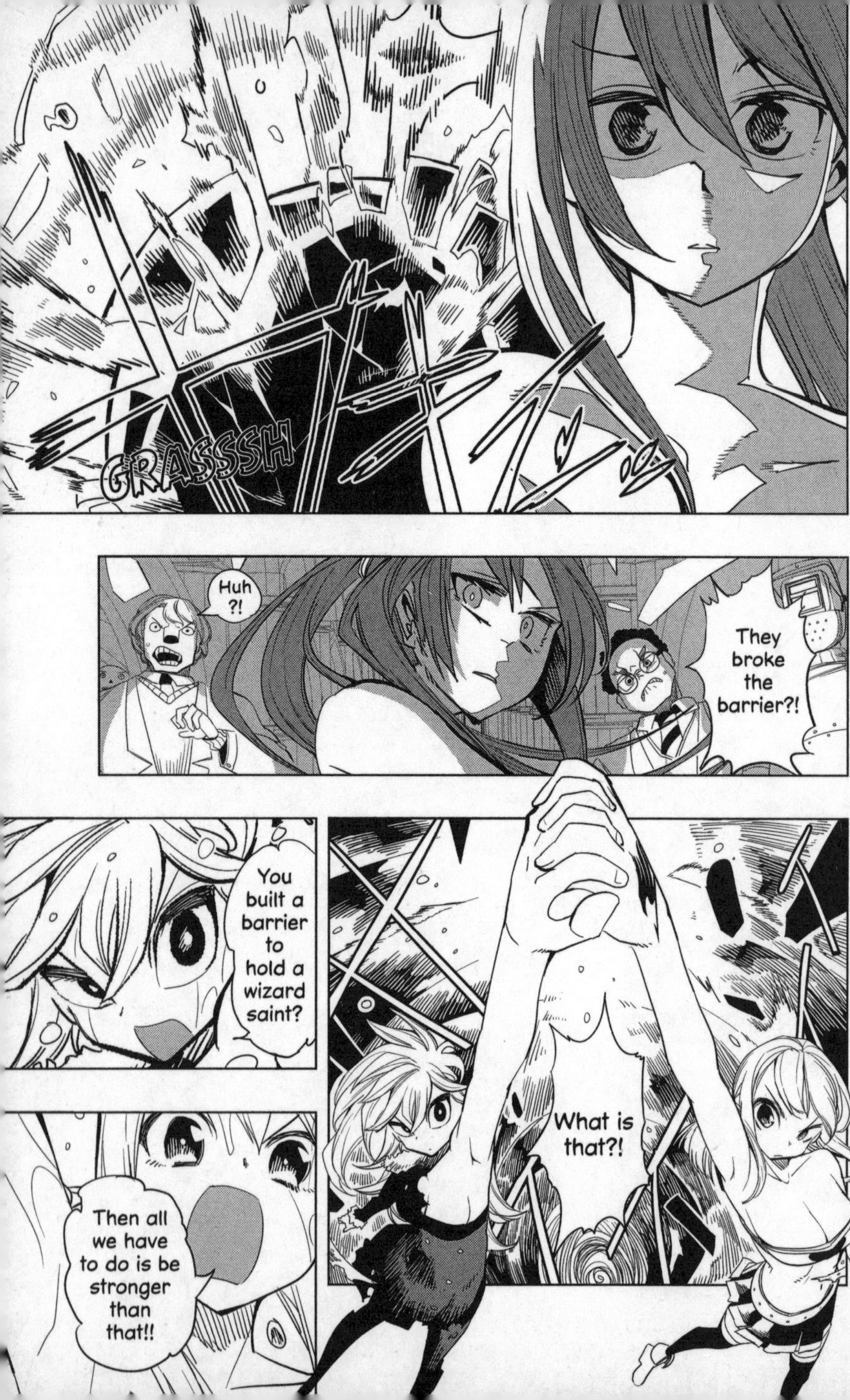
GRASSSH
They broke the barrier?!
Huh ?!
What is that?!
You built a barrier to hold a wizard saint?
Then all we have to do is be stronger than that!!

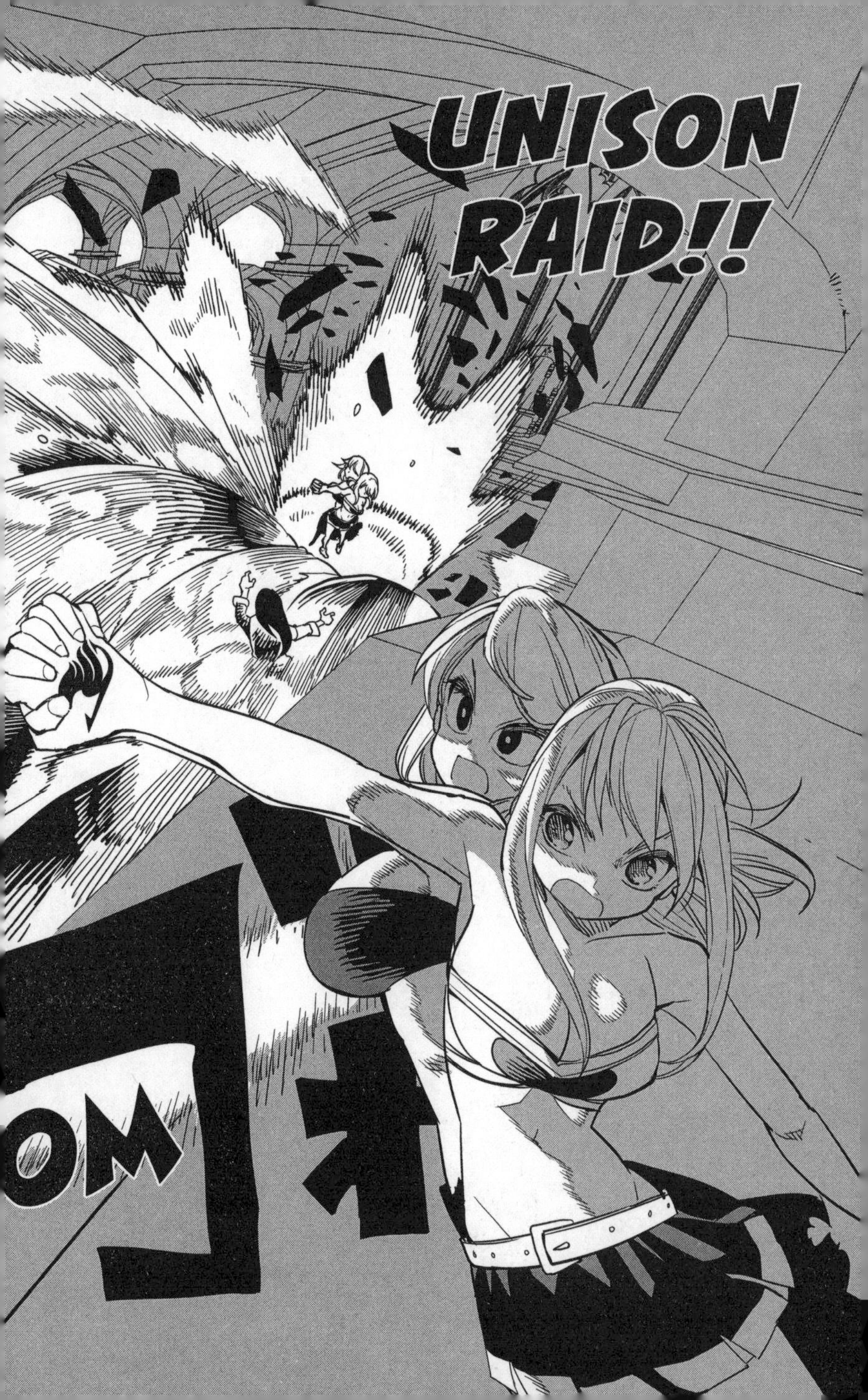
UNISON RAID!!
OM

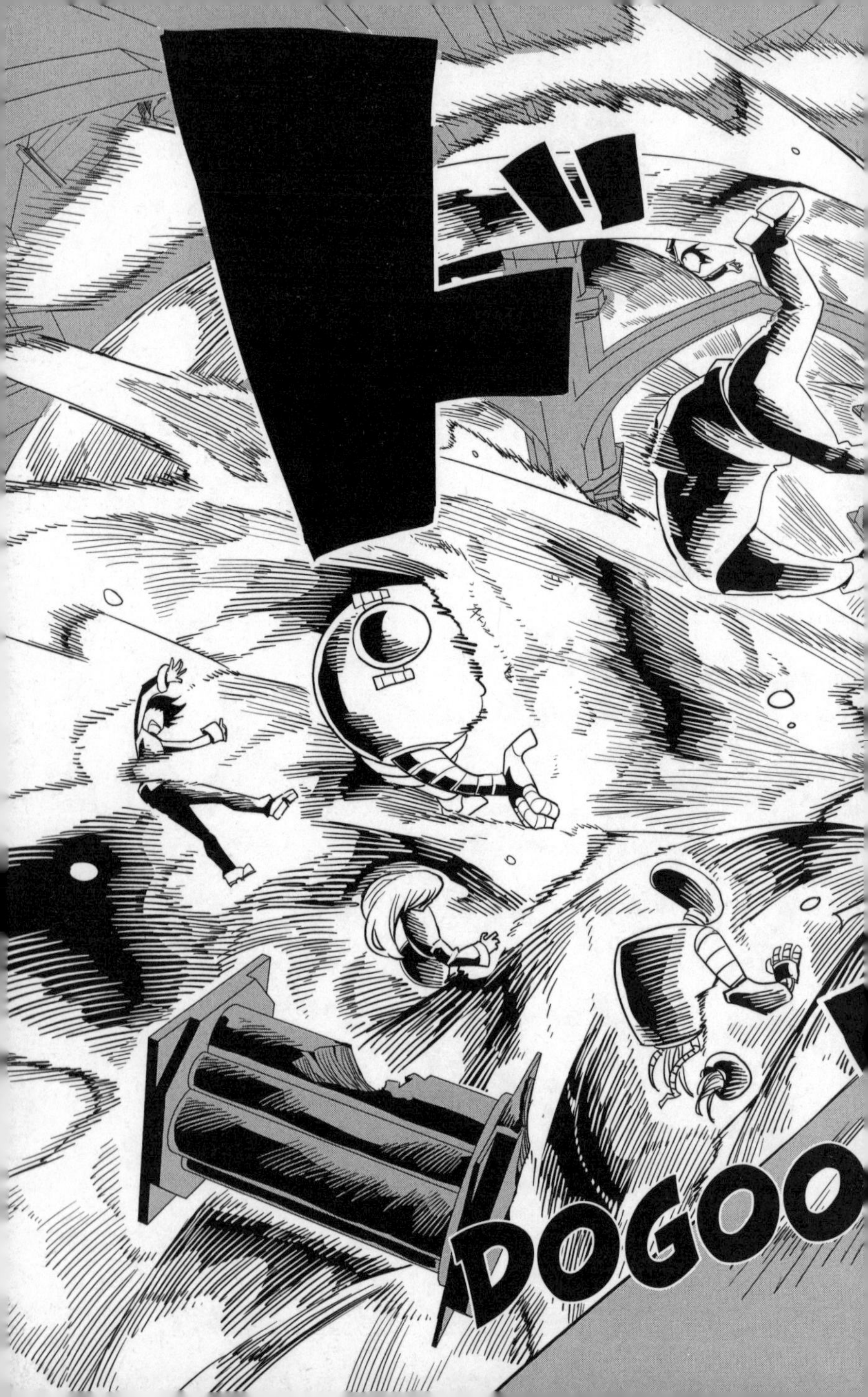
DOGOO

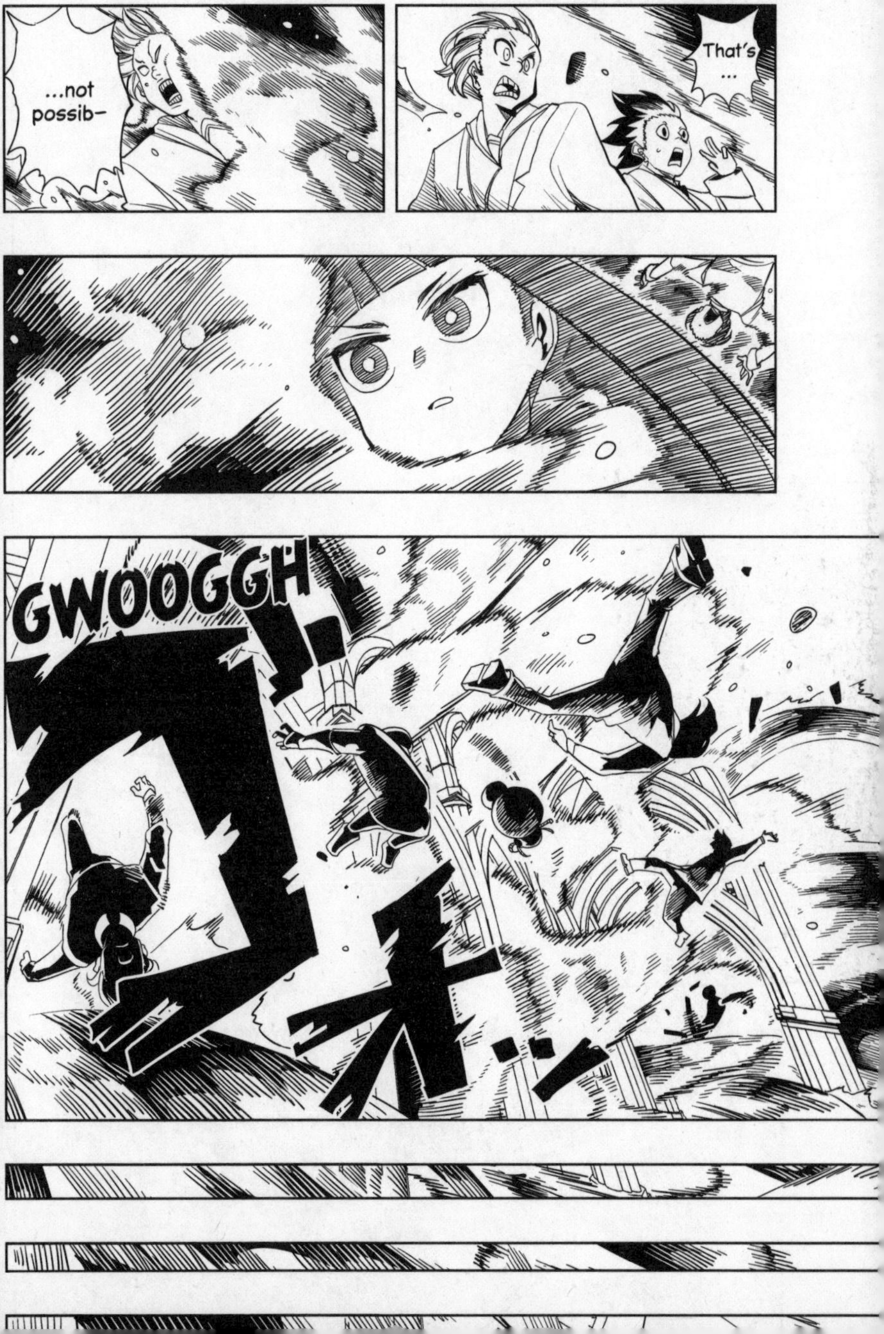
That's
...
...not
possib–
GWOOGGH

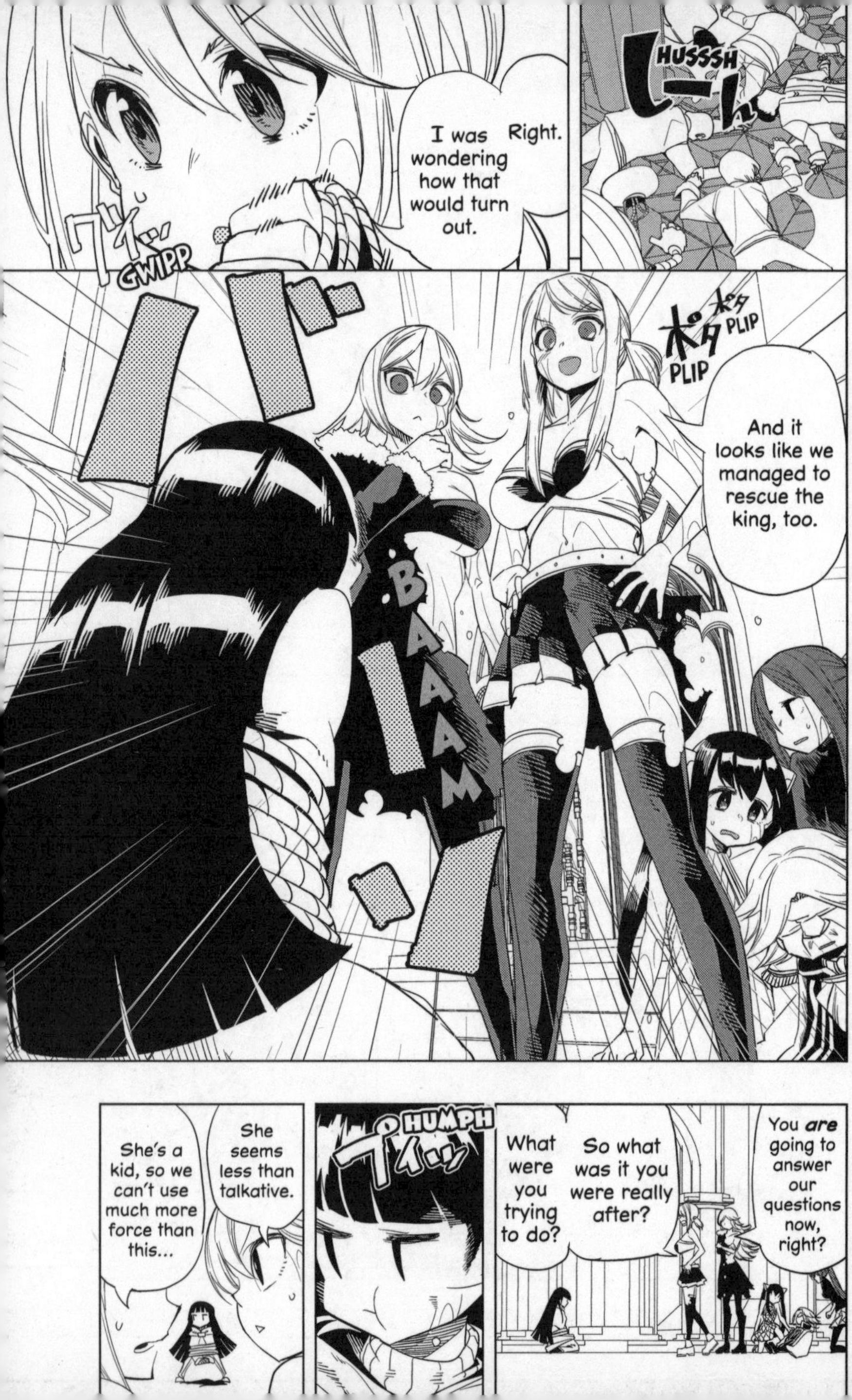
HUSSSH
Right.
I was wondering how that would turn out.
GWIPP
PLIP PLIP
And it looks like we managed to rescue the king, too.
BAAAAM
You *are* going to answer our questions now, right?
So what was it you were really after?
What were you trying to do?
HUMPH
She seems less than talkative.
She's a kid, so we can't use much more force than this...

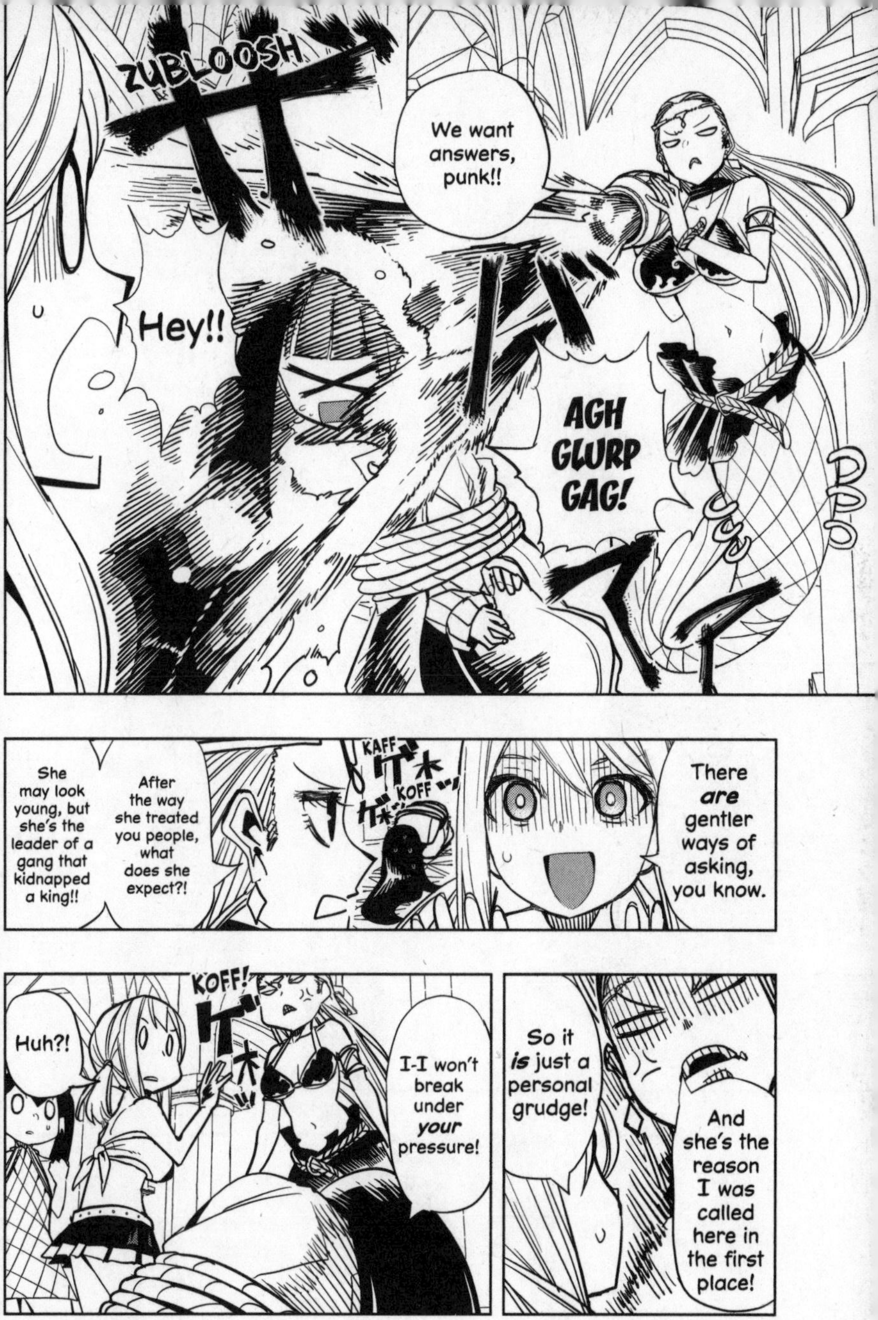
We want answers, punk!!
ZUBLOOSH
AGH GLURP GAG!
Hey!!
There *are* gentler ways of asking, you know.
KAFF
KOFF
After the way she treated you people, what does she expect?!
She may look young, but she's the leader of a gang that kidnapped a king!!
And she's the reason I was called here in the first place!
So it *is* just a personal grudge!
I-I won't break under *your* pressure!
KOFF!
Huh?!

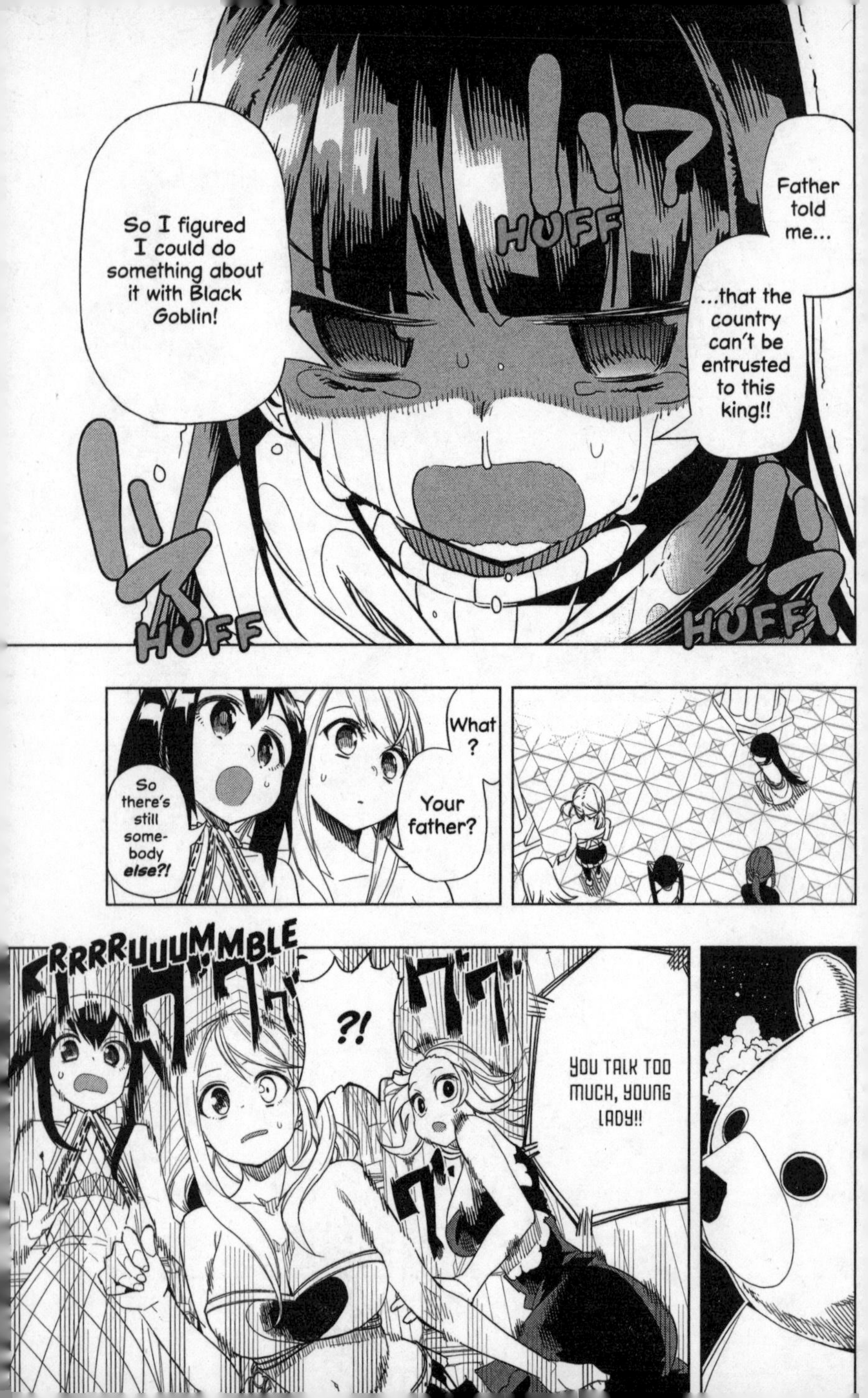
Father told me...
...that the country can't be entrusted to this king!!
HUFF
So I figured I could do something about it with Black Goblin!
HUFF
HUFF
What? Your father?
So there's still somebody *else?!*
YOU TALK TOO MUCH, YOUNG LADY!!
?!
FRRRUUUMMBLE

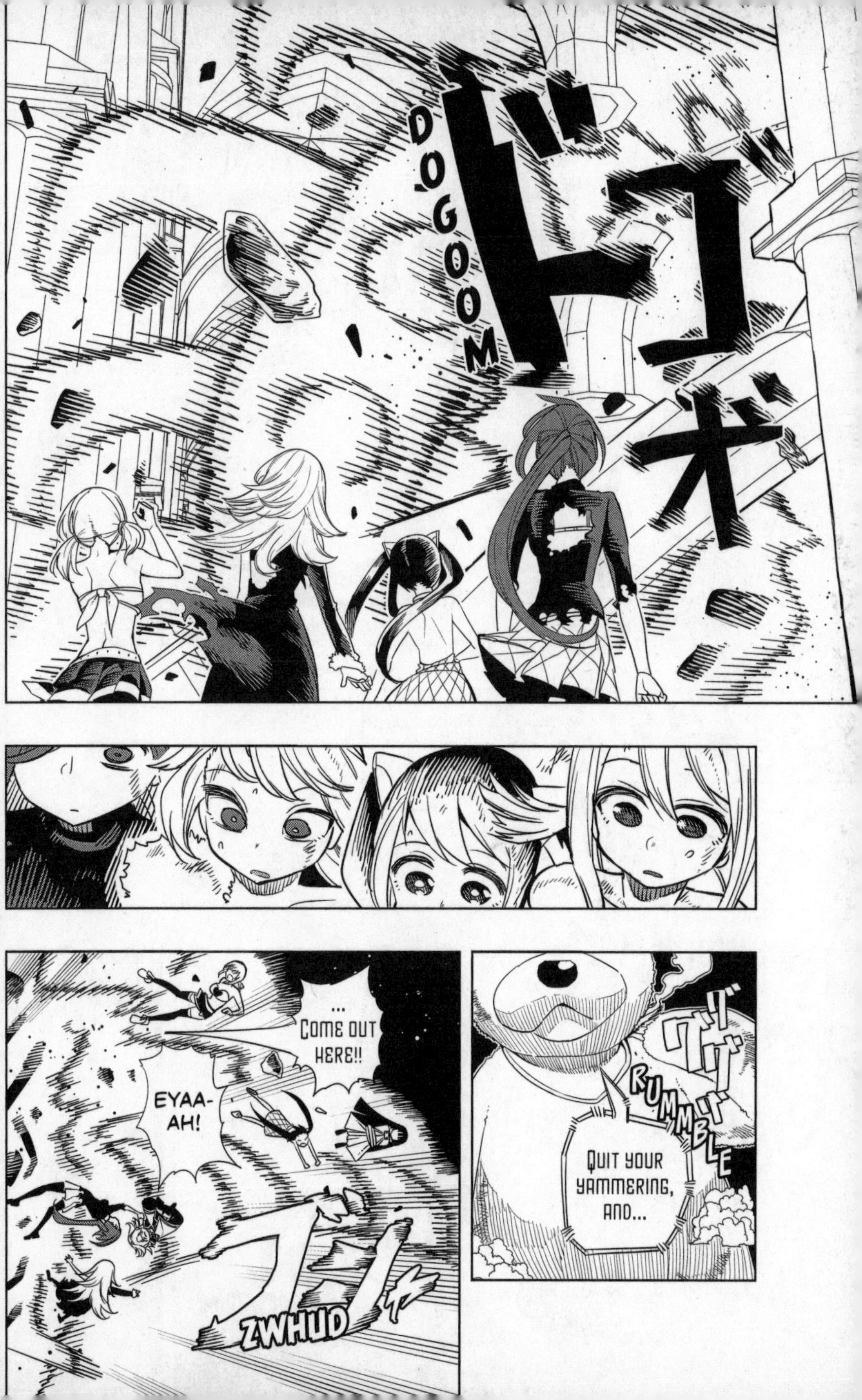
DOGOOM
ドゴォ
Quit your yammering, and...
RUMMBLE
... Come out here!!
EYAA-AH!
ZWHUD

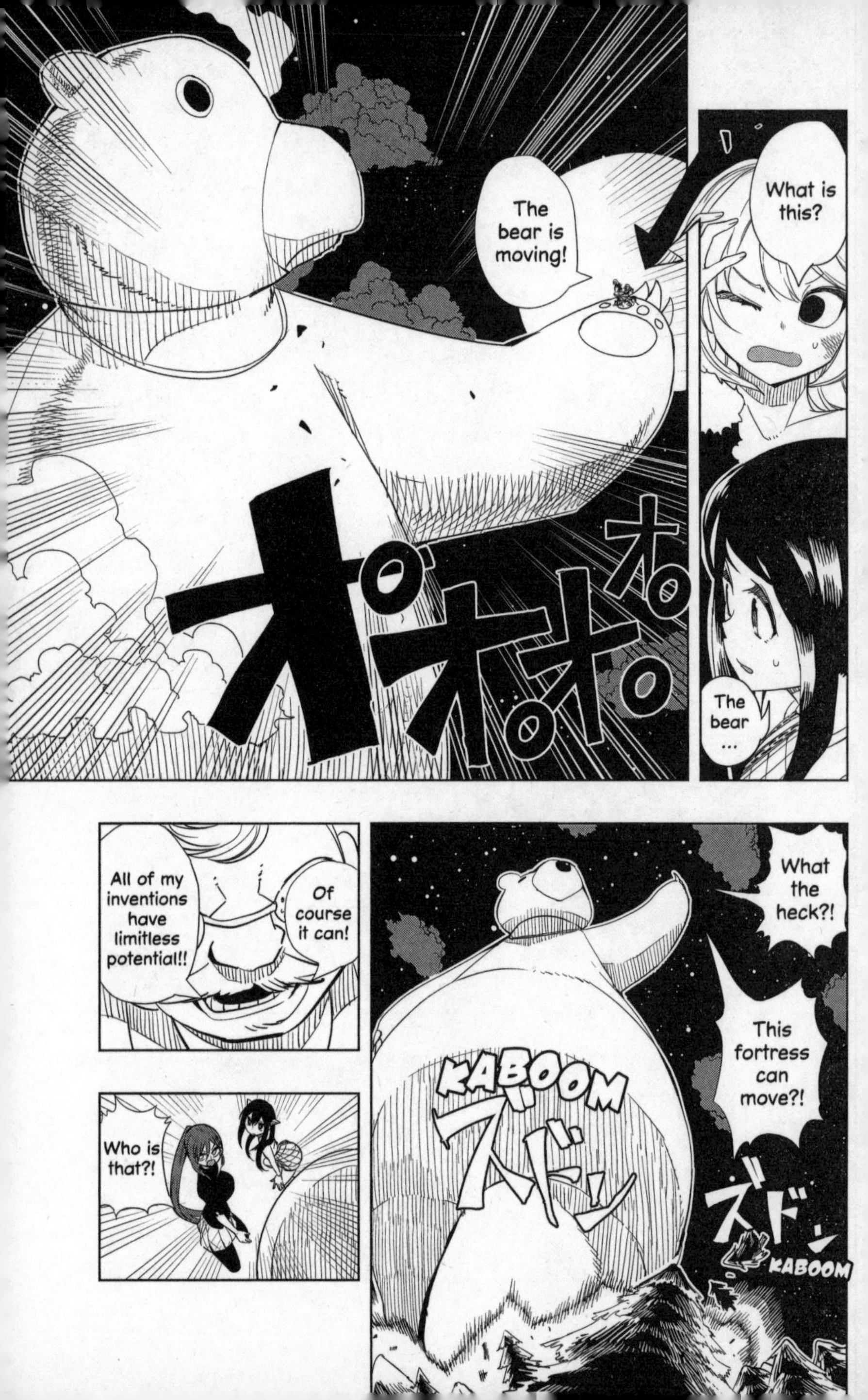
What is this?
The bear ...
The bear is moving!
What the heck?!
This fortress can move?!
KABOOM
KABOOM
Of course it can!
All of my inventions have limitless potential!!
Who is that?!

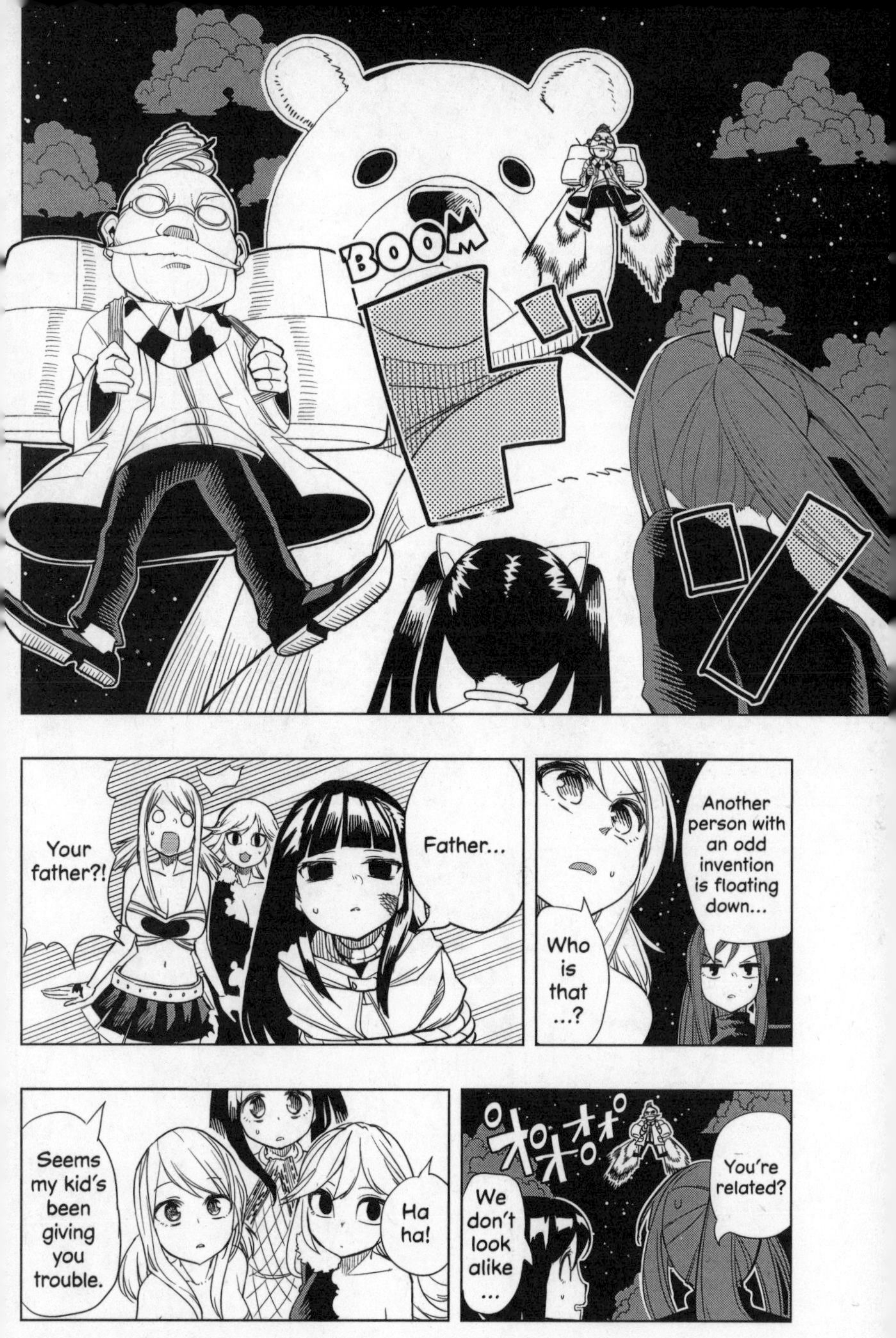
BOOM
Another person with an odd invention is floating down...
Who is that ...?
Father...
Your father?!
You're related?
We don't look alike ...
Ha ha!
Seems my kid's been giving you trouble.

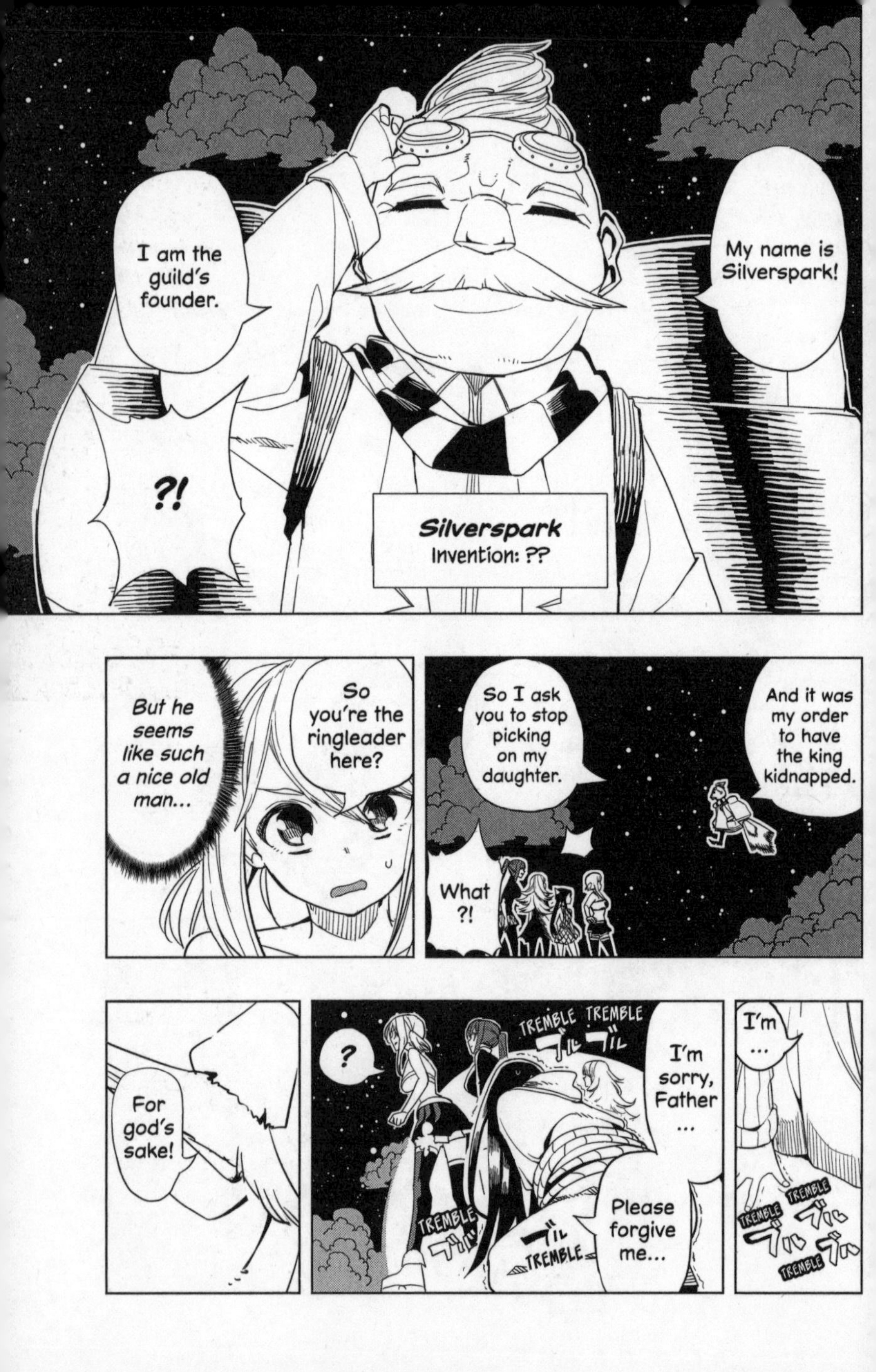
My name is Silverspark!
I am the guild's founder.
?!
Silverspark
Invention: ??
And it was my order to have the king kidnapped.
So I ask you to stop picking on my daughter.
What ?!
So you're the ringleader here?
But he seems like such a nice old man...
I'm ...
TREMBLE
TREMBLE
TREMBLE
TREMBLE TREMBLE
I'm sorry, Father ...
?
Please forgive me...
TREMBLE
TREMBLE
For god's sake!

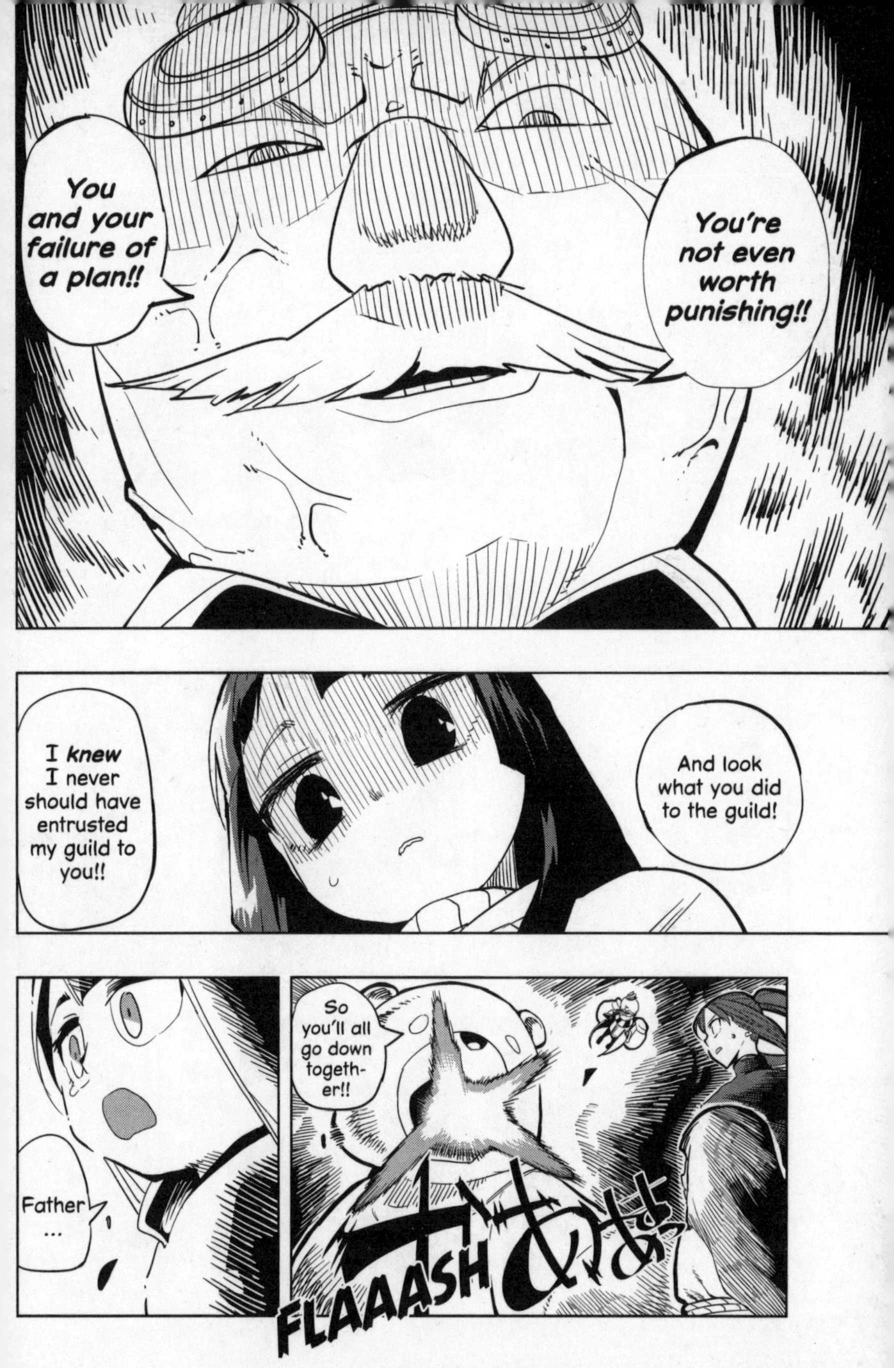
You're not even worth punishing!!
You and your failure of a plan!!
And look what you did to the guild!
I *knew* I never should have entrusted my guild to you!!
So you'll all go down togeth-er!!
FLAAASH
Father ...

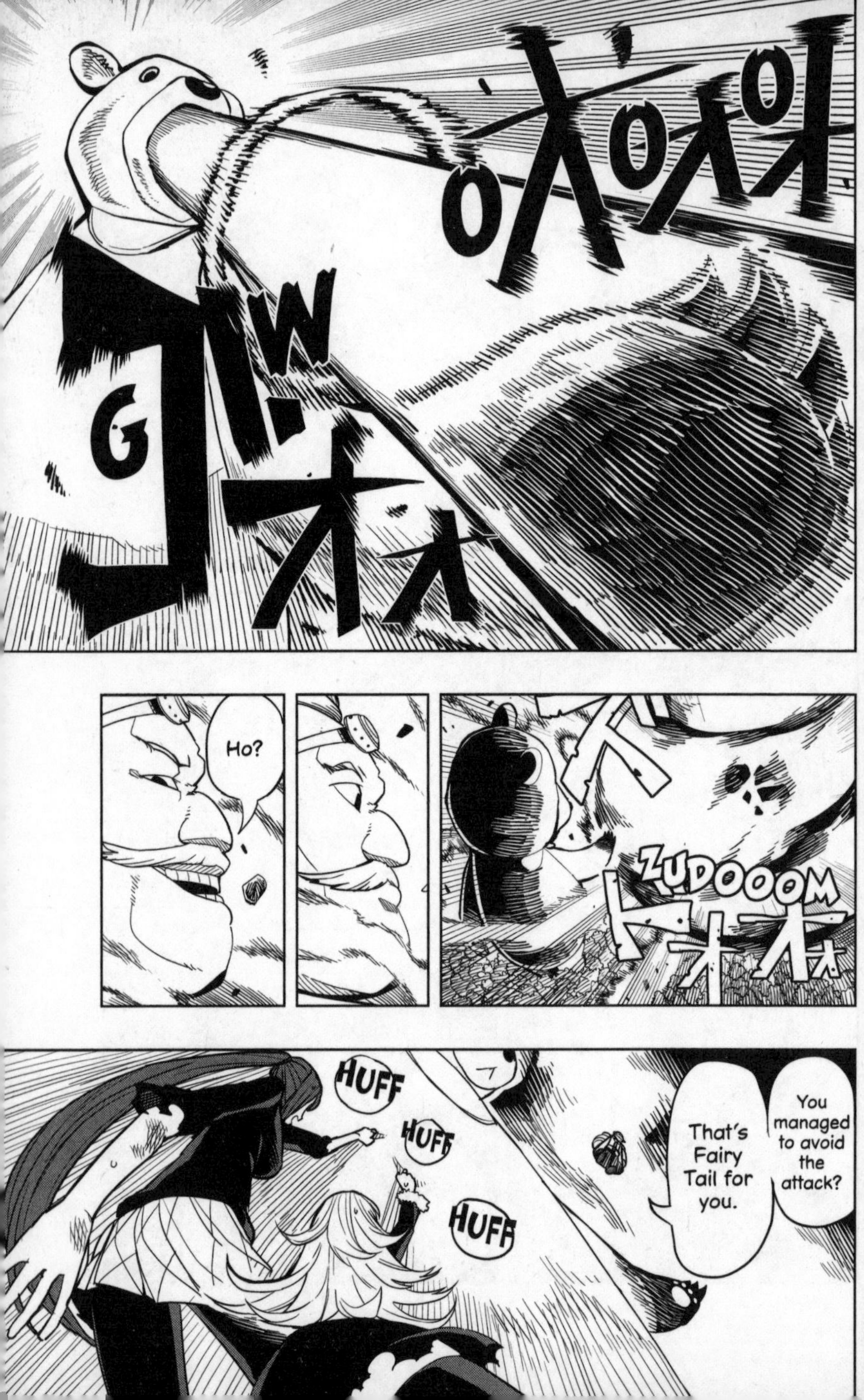
ZUDOOOM
Ho?
You managed to avoid the attack?
That's Fairy Tail for you.
HUFF
HUFF
HUFF

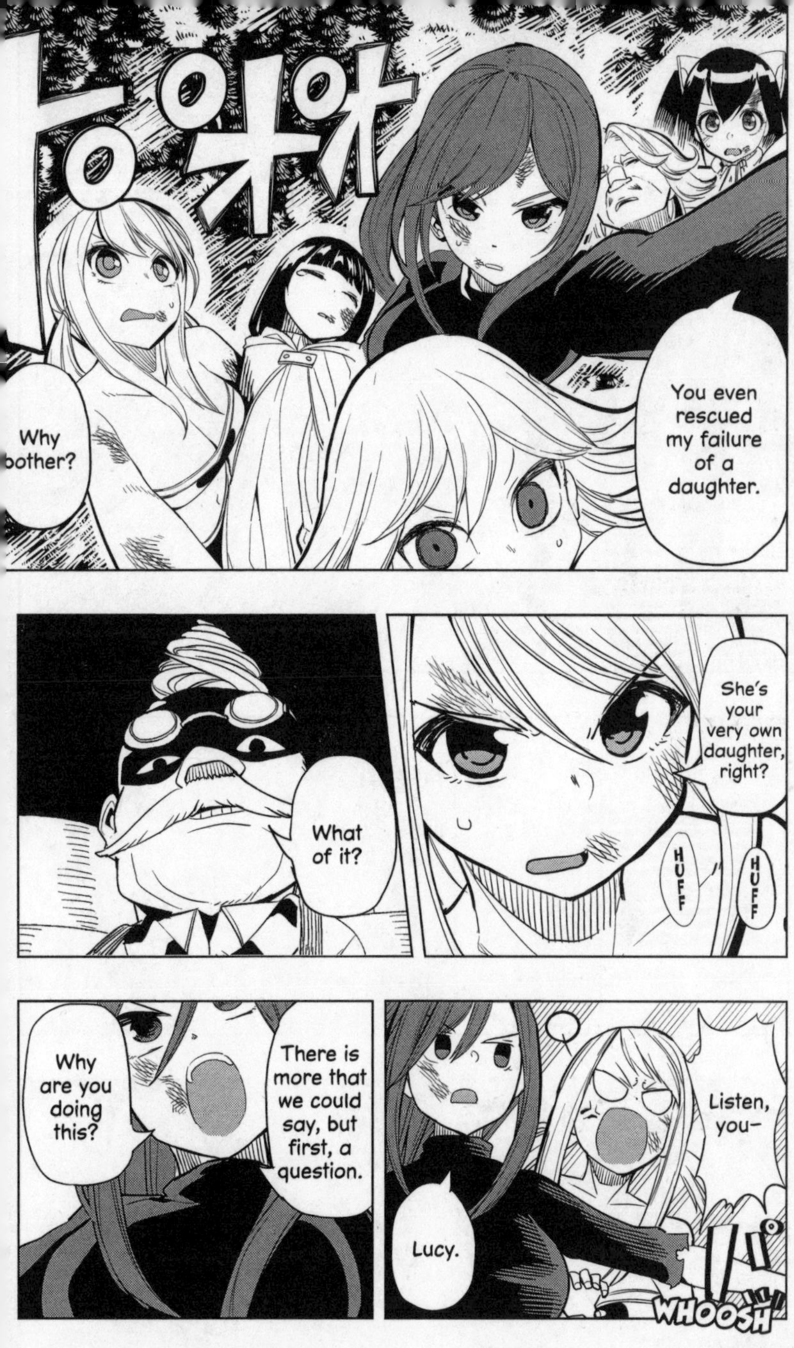
You even rescued my failure of a daughter.
Why bother?
She's your very own daughter, right?
HUFF
HUFF
What of it?
Listen, you–
Lucy.
WHOOSH
There is more that we could say, but first, a question.
Why are you doing this?

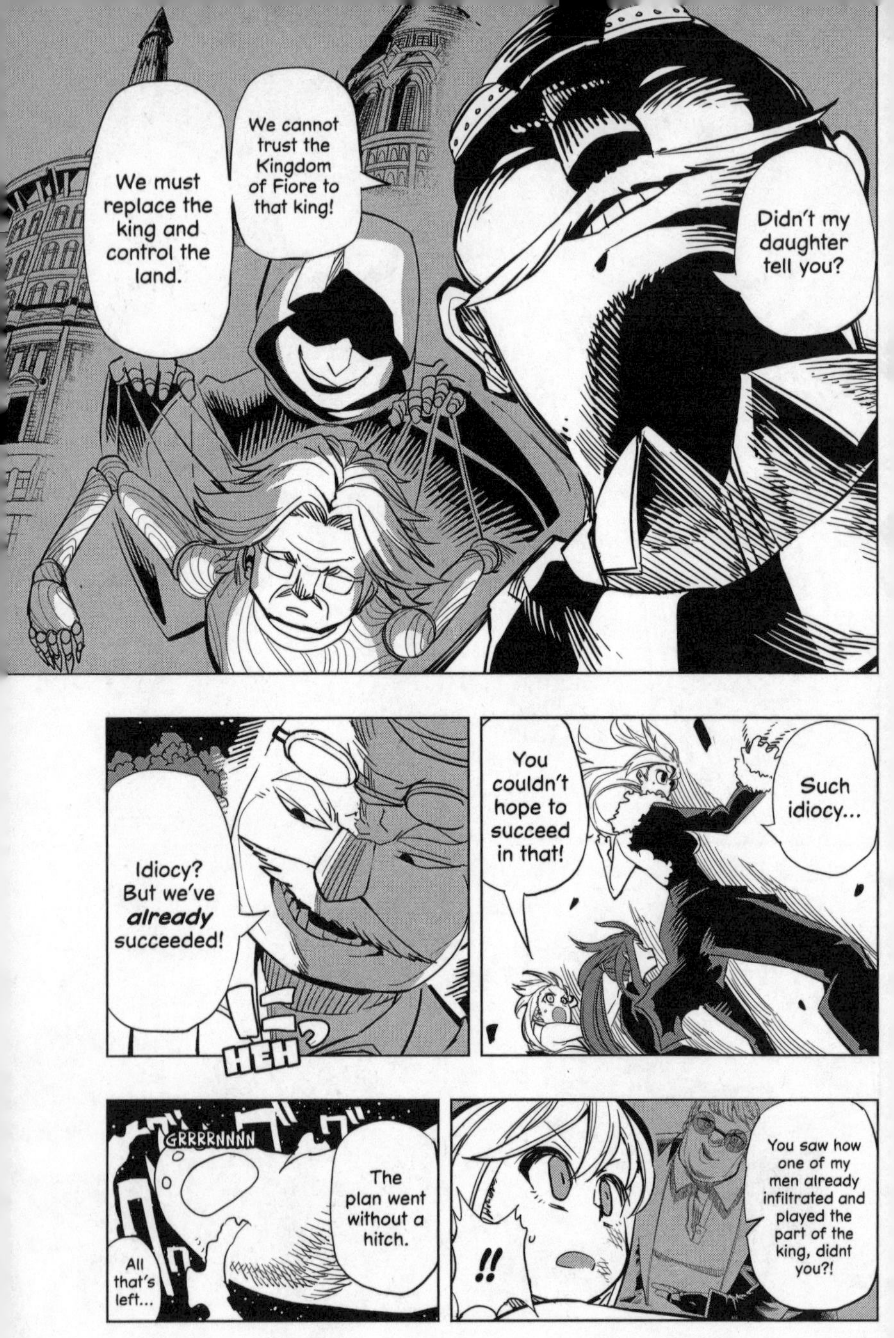
Didn't my daughter tell you?
We cannot trust the Kingdom of Fiore to that king!
We must replace the king and control the land.
Such idiocy...
You couldn't hope to succeed in that!
Idiocy? But we've *already* succeeded!
HEH
You saw how one of my men already infiltrated and played the part of the king, didnt you?!
!!
GRRRRNNNN
The plan went without a hitch.
All that's left...

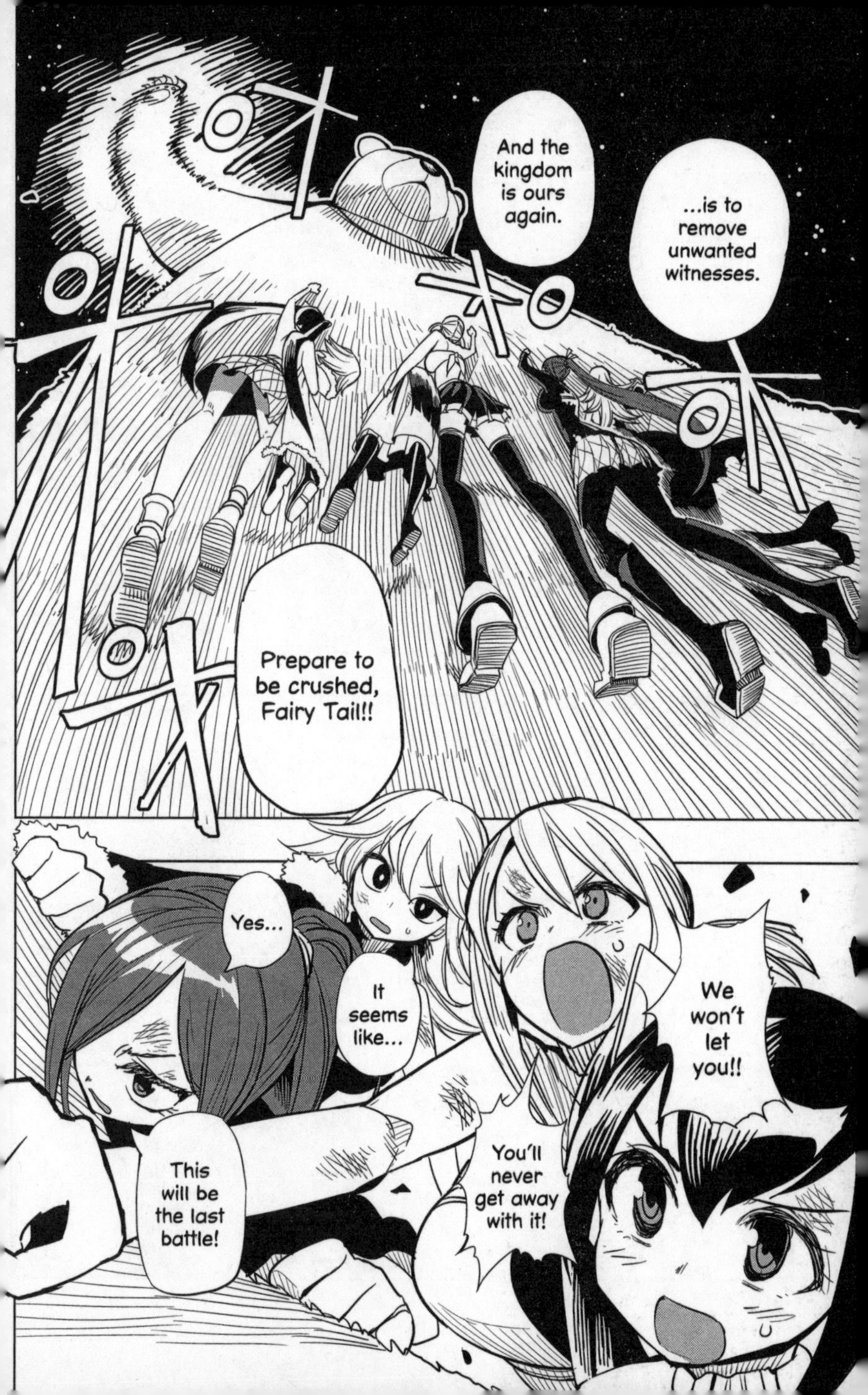
...is to remove unwanted witnesses.
And the kingdom is ours again.
Prepare to be crushed, Fairy Tail!!
We won't let you!!
You'll never get away with it!
Yes...
It seems like...
This will be the last battle!

Chapter 5: What a Wizard Is Prepared For

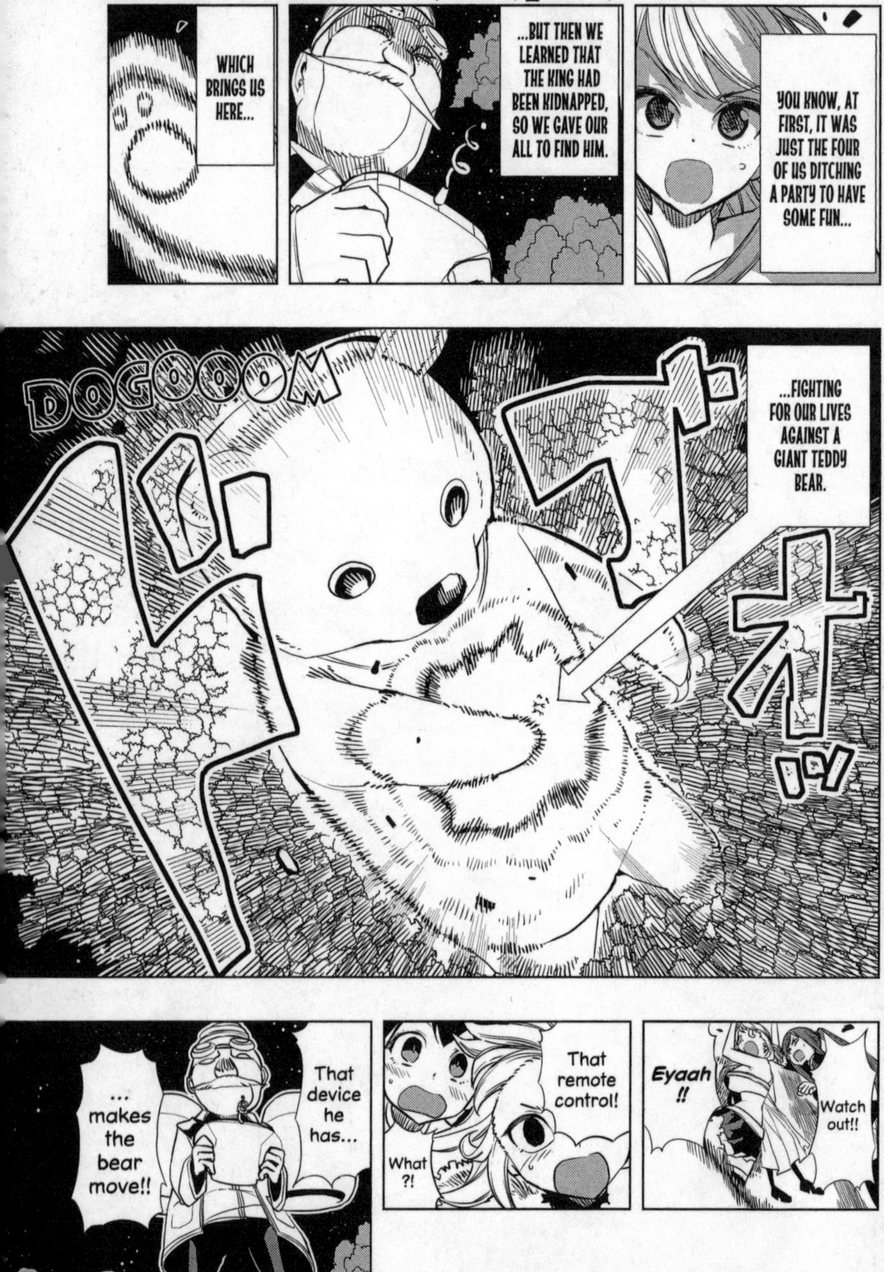
YOU KNOW, AT FIRST, IT WAS JUST THE FOUR OF US DITCHING A PARTY TO HAVE SOME FUN...
...BUT THEN WE LEARNED THAT THE KING HAD BEEN KIDNAPPED, SO WE GAVE OUR ALL TO FIND HIM.
WHICH BRINGS US HERE...
...FIGHTING FOR OUR LIVES AGAINST A GIANT TEDDY BEAR.
DOGOOOM
Eyaah!!
Watch out!!
That remote control!
What?!
That device he has...
...makes the bear move!!

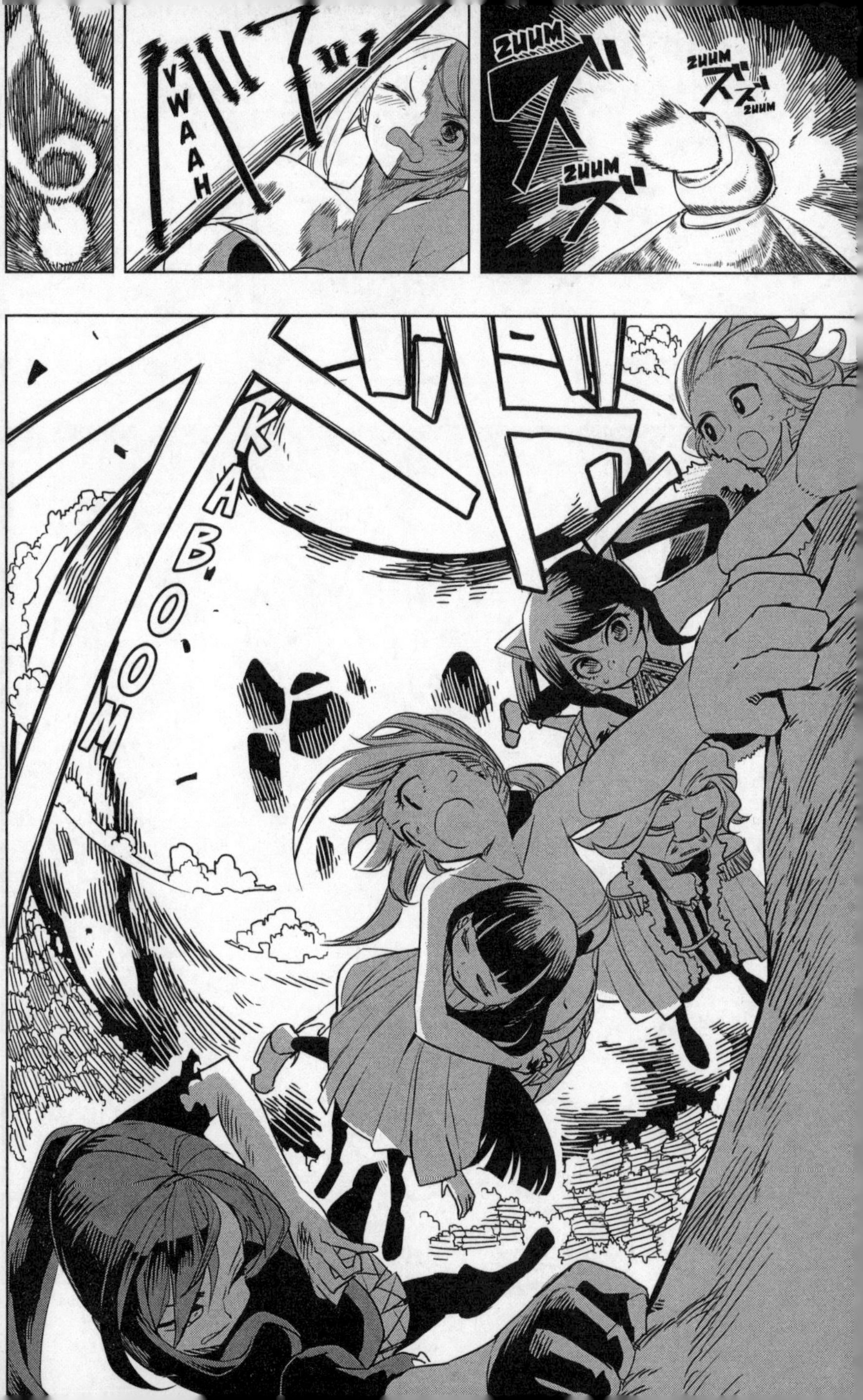
ZUUM
ZUUM
ZUUM
ZUUM
VWAAH
KABOOOM

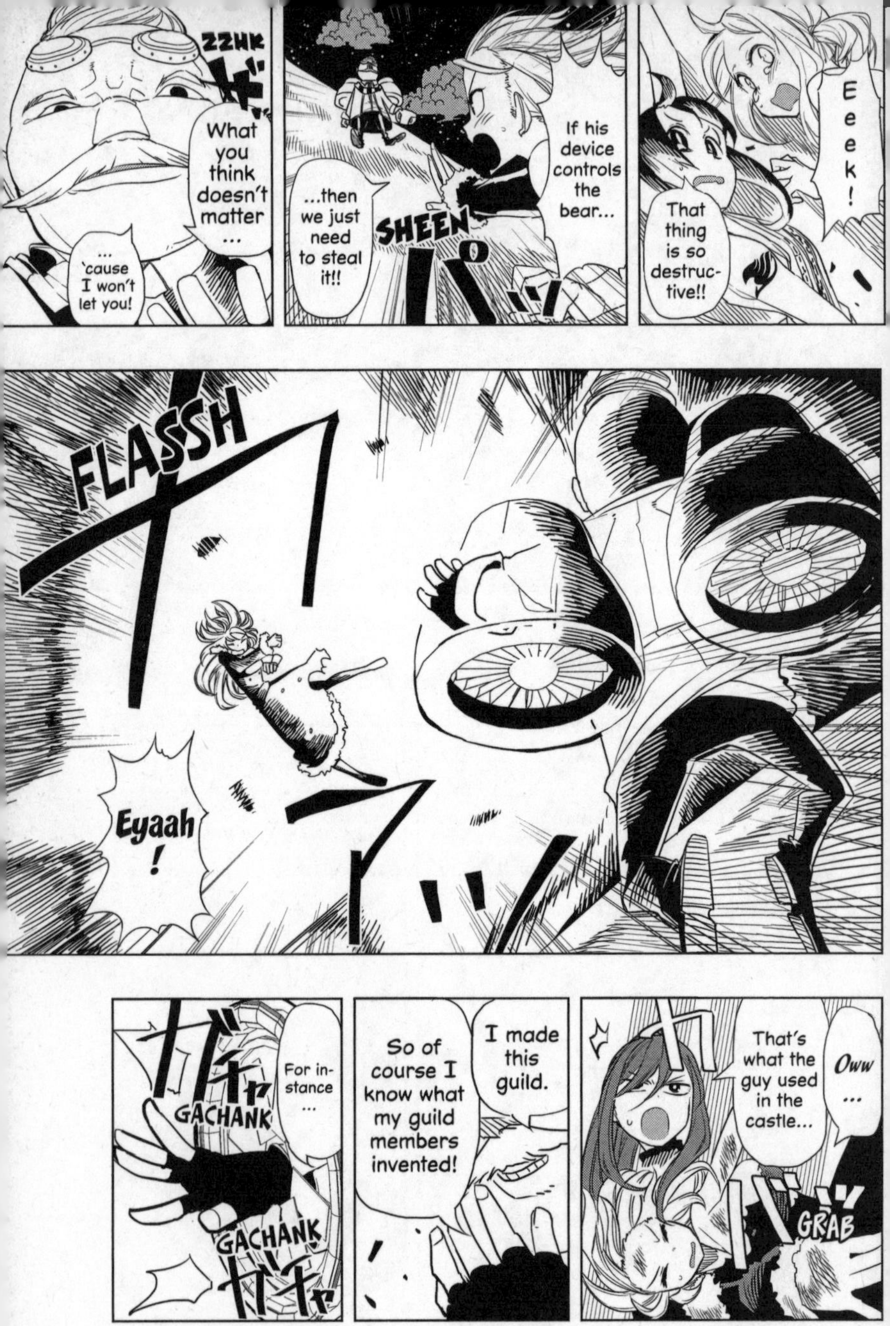
Eeek!
That thing is so destructive!!
If his device controls the bear...
...then we just need to steal it!!
SHEEN
ZZHK
What you think doesn't matter ...
... 'cause I won't let you!
FLASSH
Eyaah!
Oww ...
That's what the guy used in the castle...
GRAB
I made this guild.
So of course I know what my guild members invented!
For instance ...
GACHANK
GACHANK

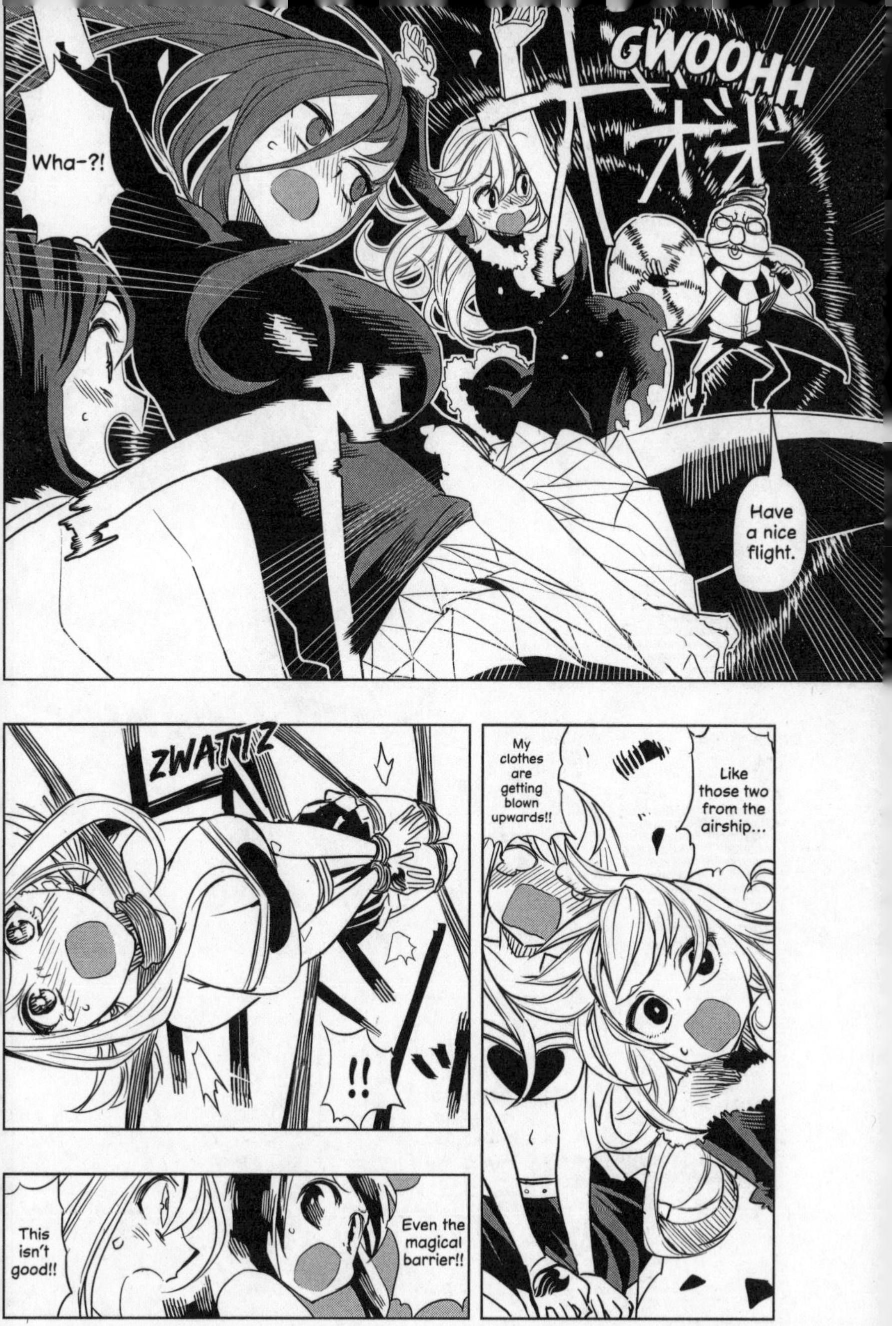
GWOOHH
Have a nice flight.
Wha-?!
Like those two from the airship...
My clothes are getting blown upwards!!
ZWATTZ
!!
Even the magical barrier!!
This isn't good!!

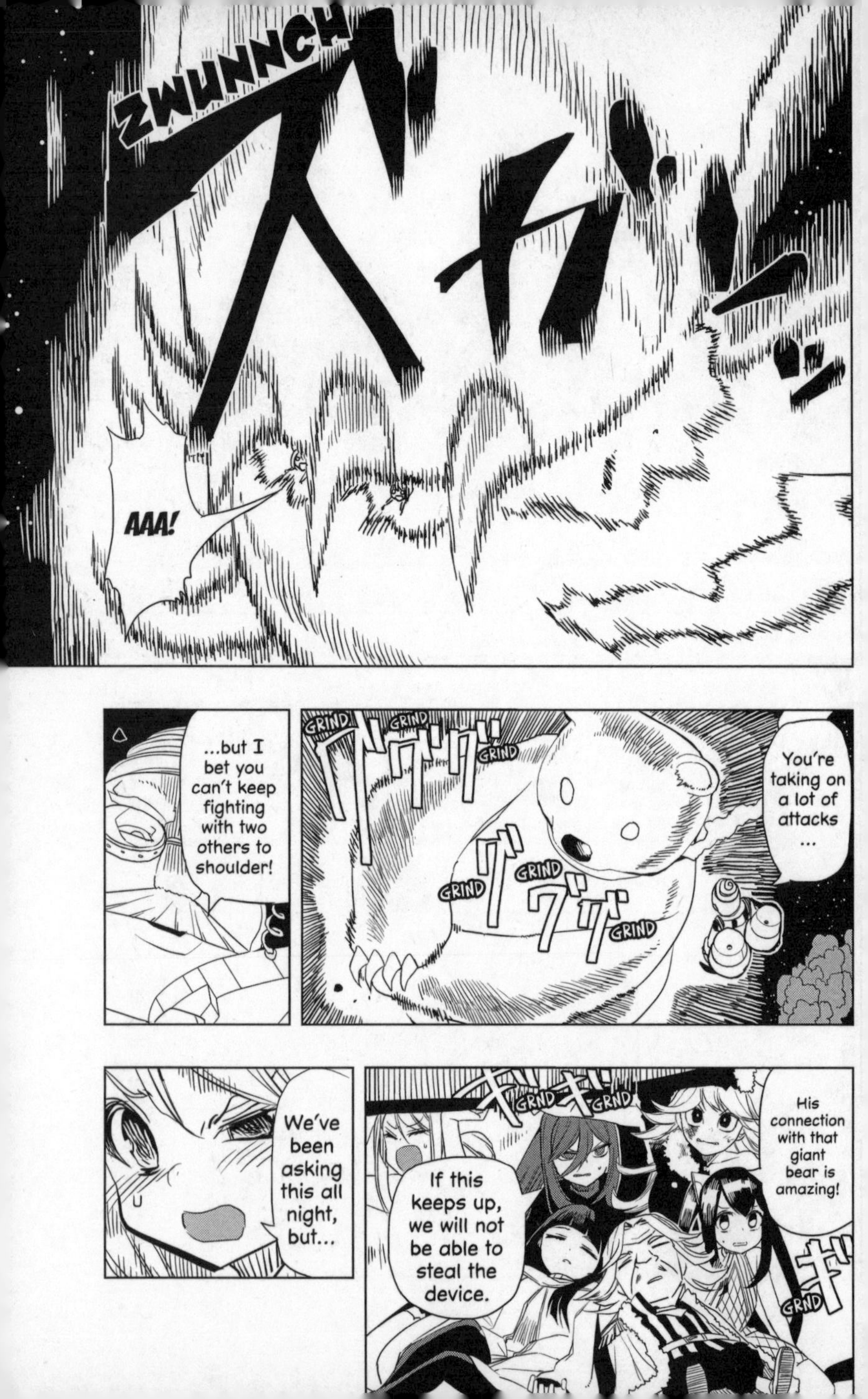
ZWUNNCH
AAA!
GRIND GRIND GRIND
GRIND GRIND GRIND
You're taking on a lot of attacks ...
...but I bet you can't keep fighting with two others to shoulder!
GRND GRND
His connection with that giant bear is amazing!
If this keeps up, we will not be able to steal the device.
GRND
We've been asking this all night, but...

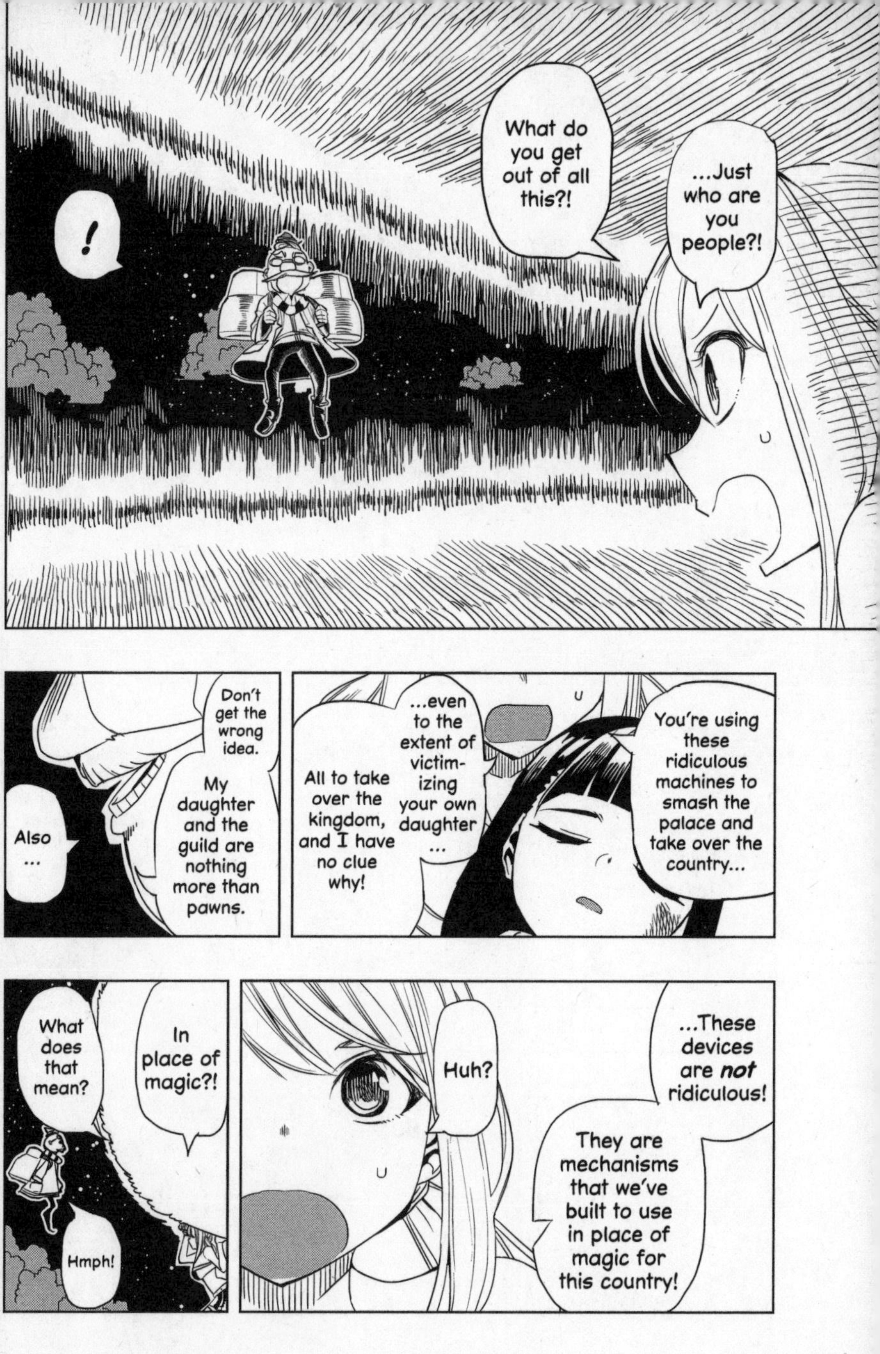
...Just who are you people?!
What do you get out of all this?!
!
You're using these ridiculous machines to smash the palace and take over the country...
...even to the extent of victimizing your own daughter...
All to take over the kingdom, and I have no clue why!
Don't get the wrong idea.
My daughter and the guild are nothing more than pawns.
Also...
...These devices are *not* ridiculous!
They are mechanisms that we've built to use in place of magic for this country!
Huh?
In place of magic?!
What does that mean?
Hmph!

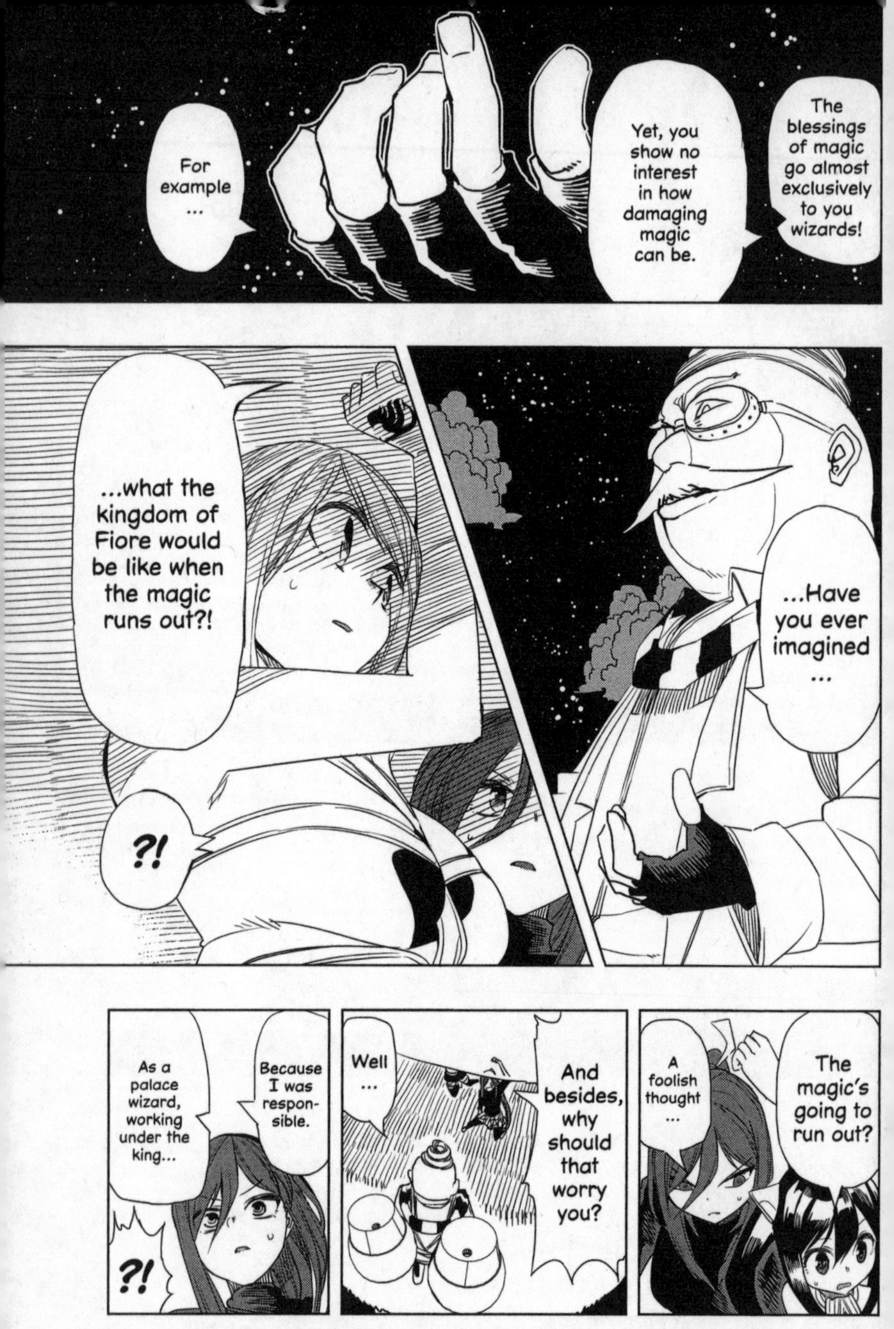
The blessings of magic go almost exclusively to you wizards!
Yet, you show no interest in how damaging magic can be.
For example ...
...Have you ever imagined ...
...what the kingdom of Fiore would be like when the magic runs out?!
?!
The magic's going to run out?
A foolish thought ...
And besides, why should that worry you?
Well ...
Because I was respon-sible.
As a palace wizard, working under the king...
?!

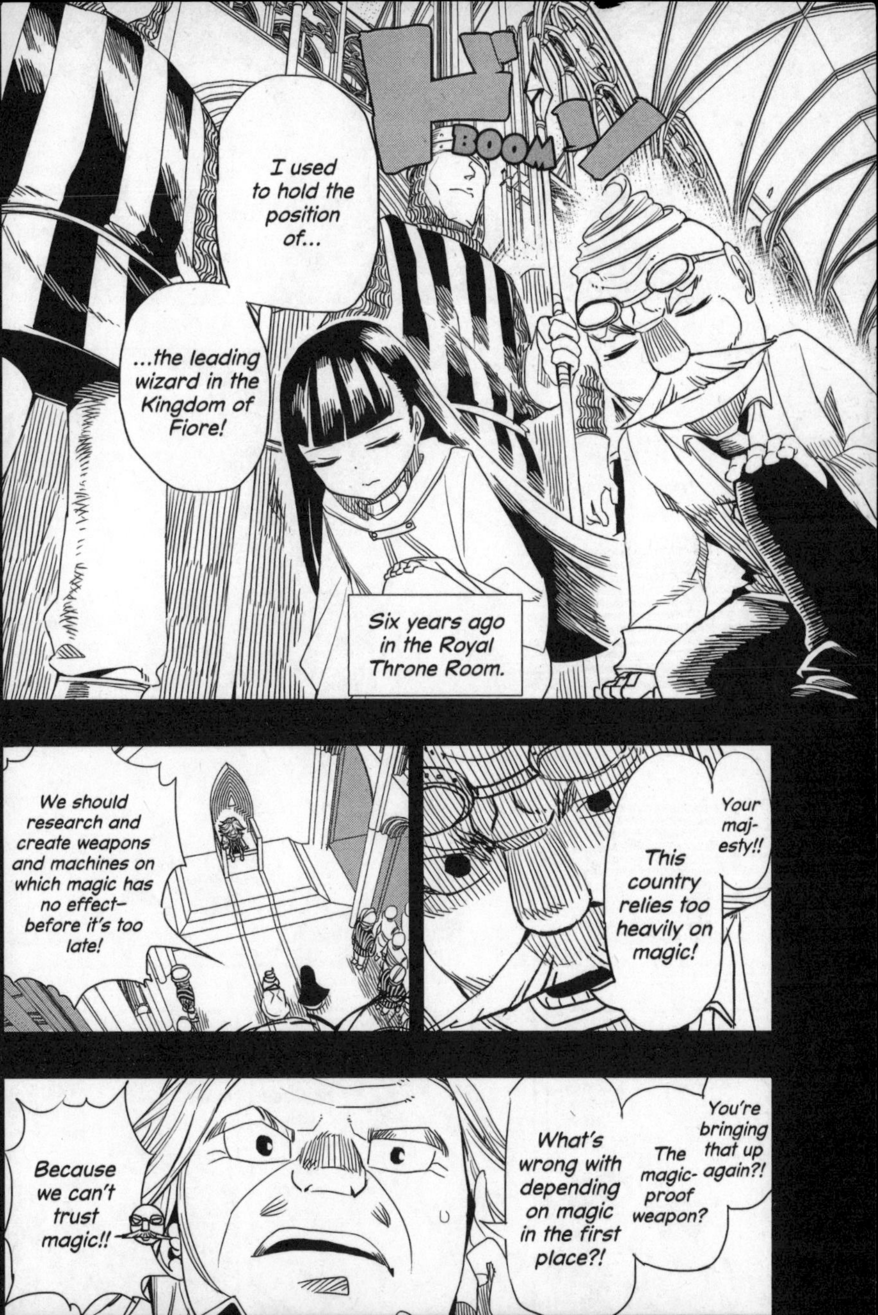
BOOM
I used to hold the position of...
...the leading wizard in the Kingdom of Fiore!
Six years ago in the Royal Throne Room.
Your majesty!!
This country relies too heavily on magic!
We should research and create weapons and machines on which magic has no effect—before it's too late!
You're bringing that up again?!
The magic-proof weapon?
What's wrong with depending on magic in the first place?!
Because we can't trust magic!!

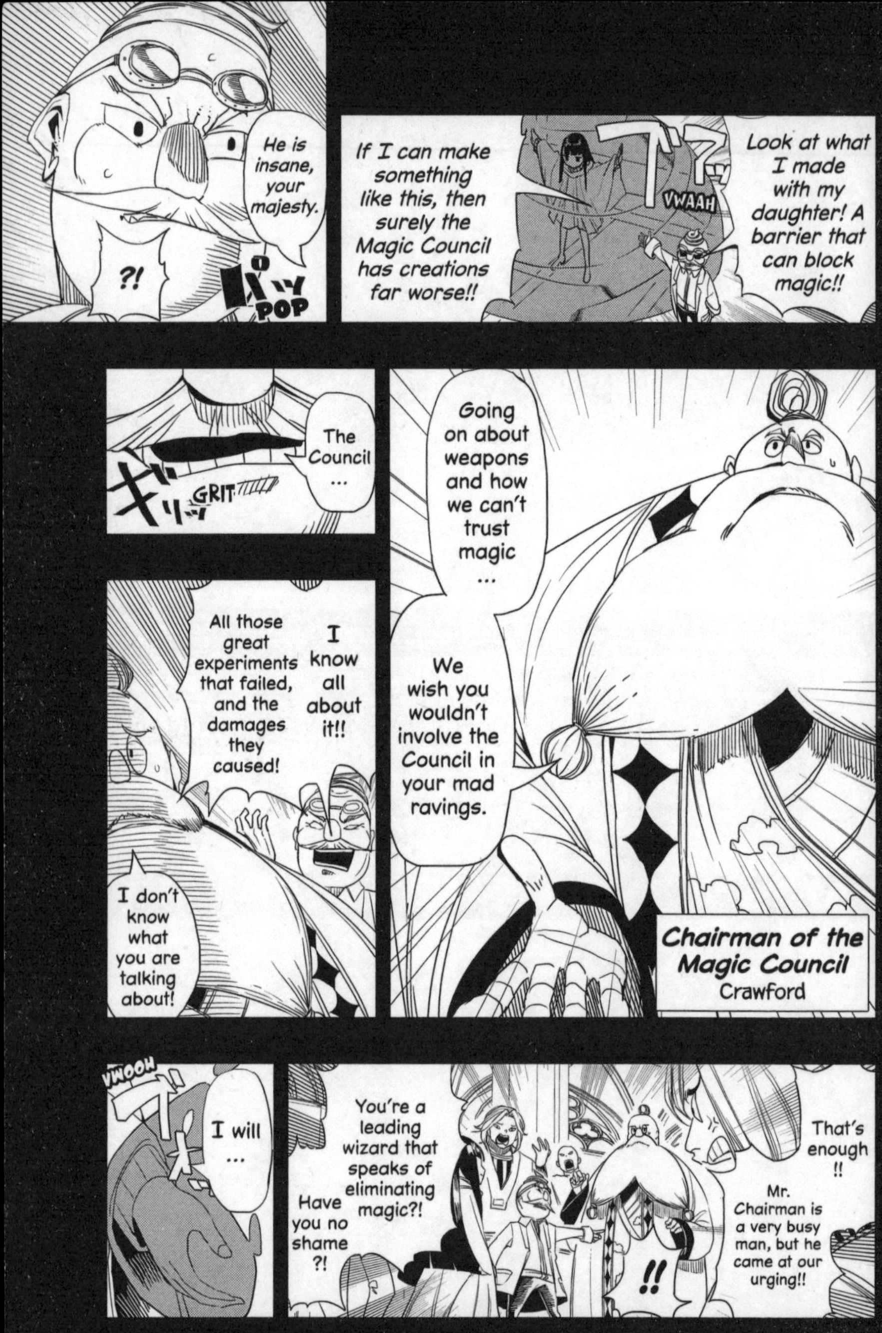
Look at what I made with my daughter! A barrier that can block magic!!
VWAAH
If I can make something like this, then surely the Magic Council has creations far worse!!
He is insane, your majesty.
?!
POP
Going on about weapons and how we can't trust magic ...
We wish you wouldn't involve the Council in your mad ravings.
Chairman of the Magic Council
Crawford
GRIT
The Council ...
I know all about it!!
All those great experiments that failed, and the damages they caused!
I don't know what you are talking about!
That's enough !!
Mr. Chairman is a very busy man, but he came at our urging!!
You're a leading wizard that speaks of eliminating magic?!
Have you no shame ?!
!!
VWOOH
I will ...

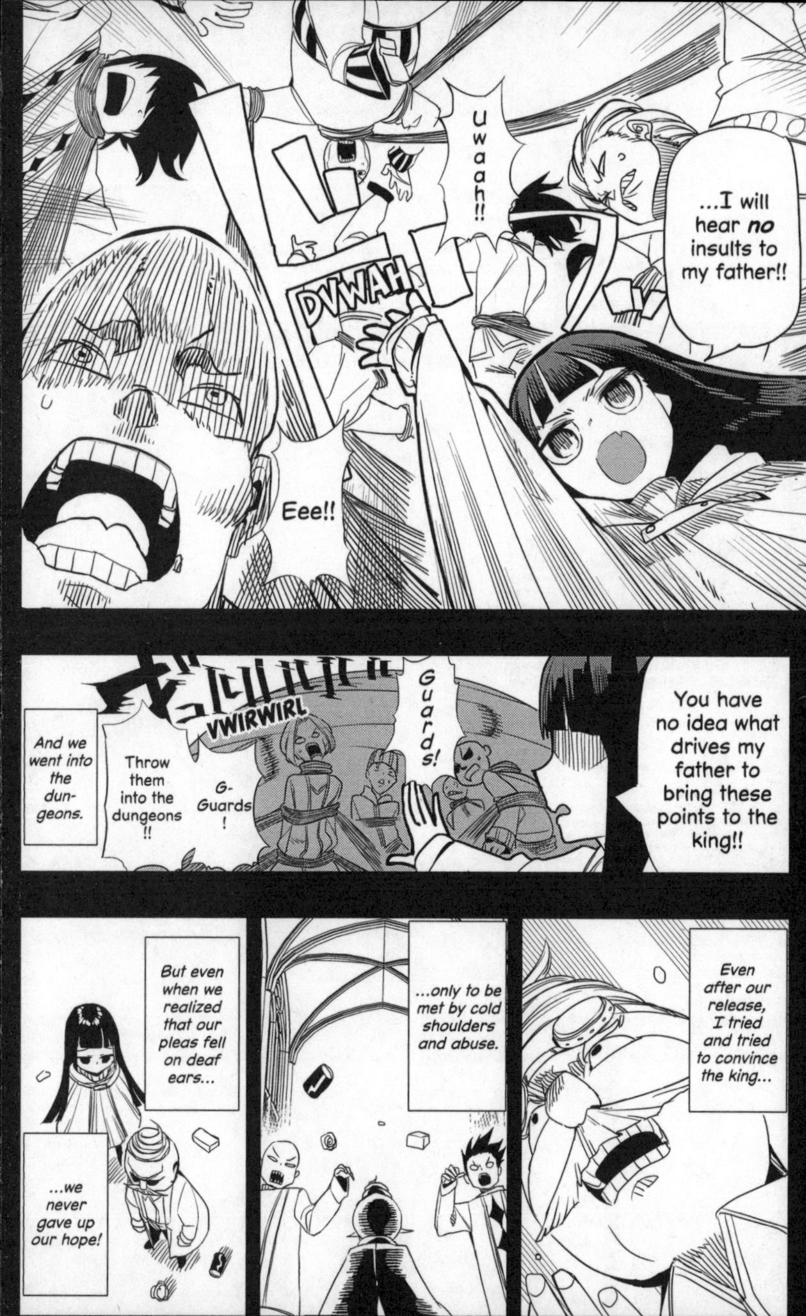
...I will hear **no** insults to my father!!
Uwaaah!!
DVWAH
Eee!!
You have no idea what drives my father to bring these points to the king!!
Guards!
VWIRWIRL
G-Guards!
Throw them into the dungeons!!
And we went into the dungeons.
Even after our release, I tried and tried to convince the king...
...only to be met by cold shoulders and abuse.
But even when we realized that our pleas fell on deaf ears...
...we never gave up our hope!

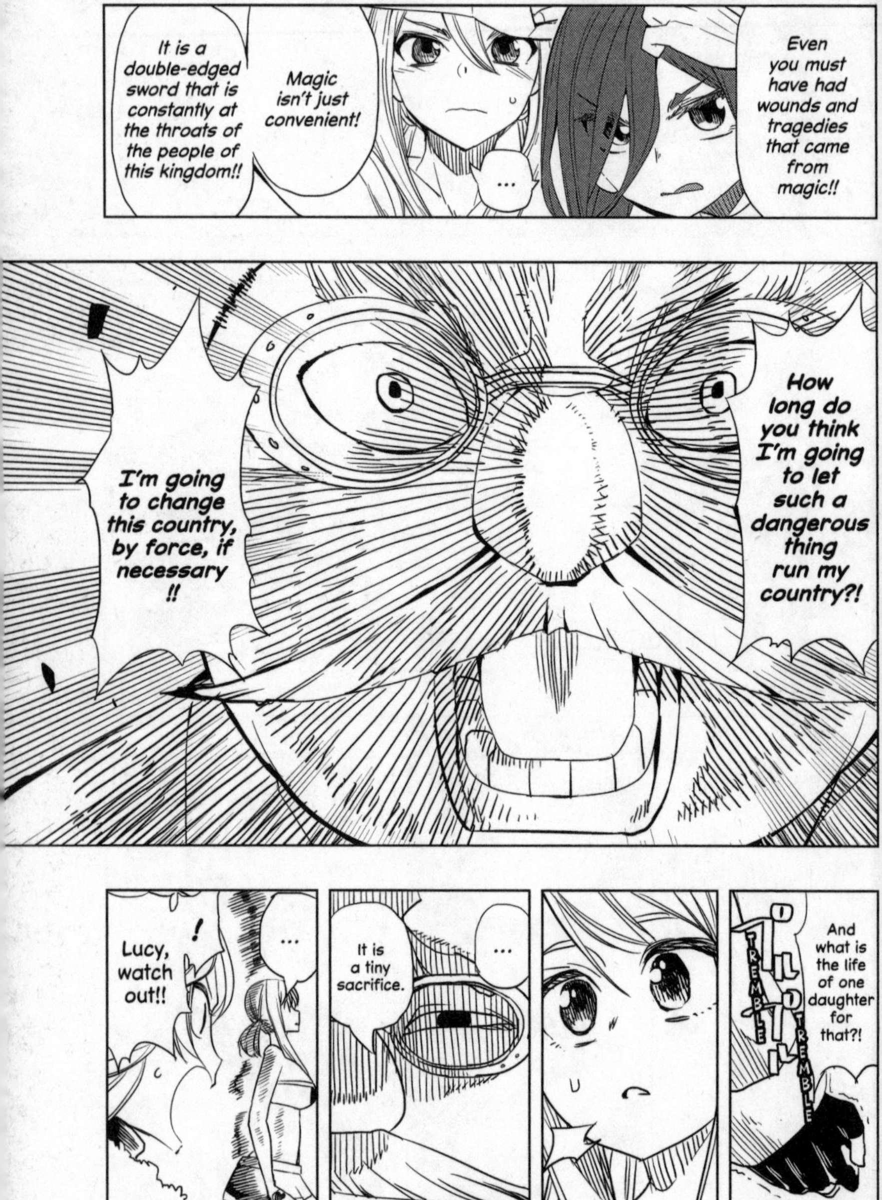

Even you must have had wounds and tragedies that came from magic!!
...
Magic isn't just convenient!
It is a double-edged sword that is constantly at the throats of the people of this kingdom!!
How long do you think I'm going to let such a dangerous thing run my country?!
I'm going to change this country, by force, if necessary!!
TREMBLE TREMBLE
And what is the life of one daughter for that?!
...
It is a tiny sacrifice.
...
!
Lucy, watch out!!

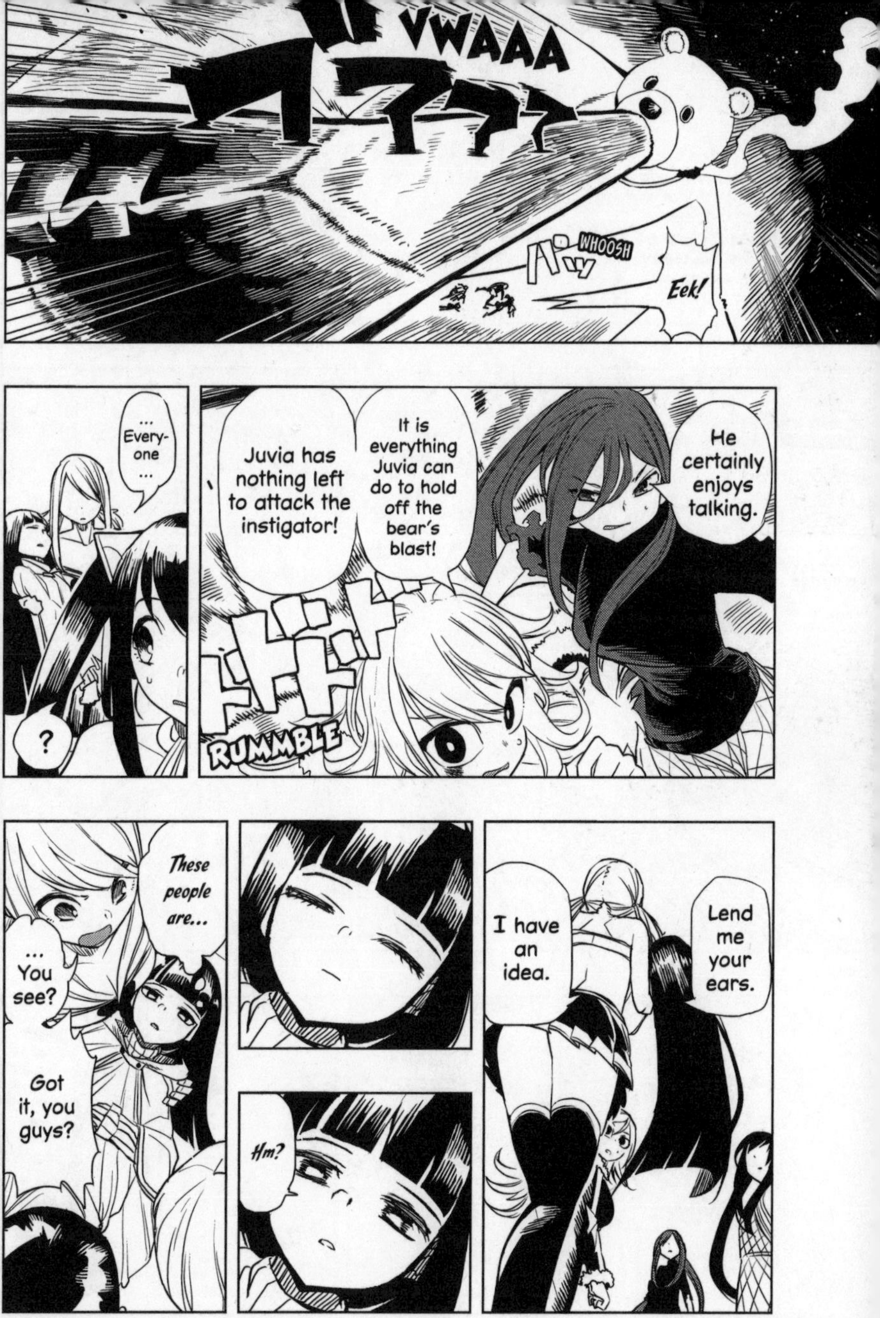
VWAAA
WHOOSH
Eek!
He certainly enjoys talking.
It is everything Juvia can do to hold off the bear's blast!
Juvia has nothing left to attack the instigator!
RUMMBLE
... Every-one ...
?
Lend me your ears.
I have an idea.
Hm?
These people are...
... You see?
Got it, you guys?

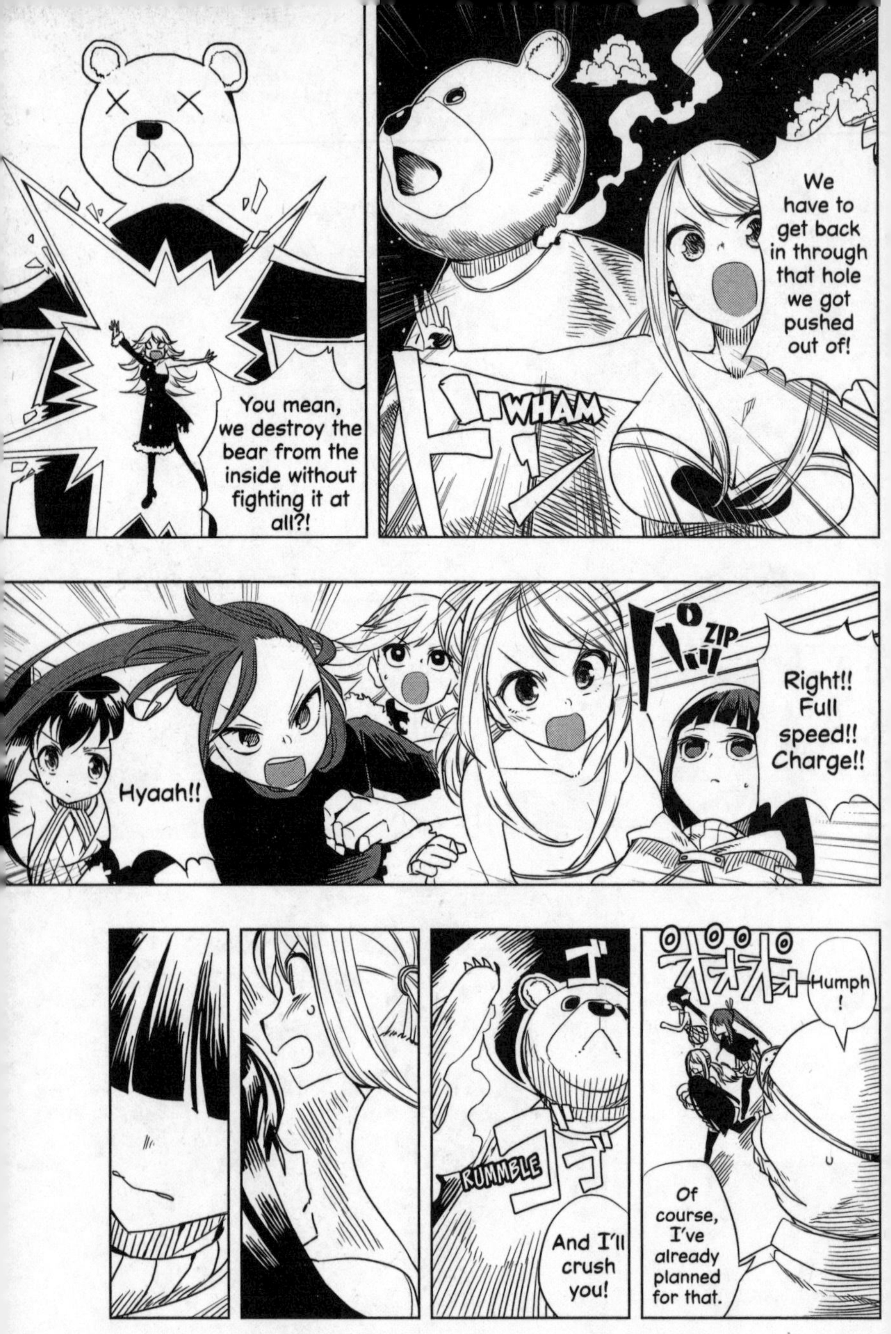
We have to get back in through that hole we got pushed out of!
WHAM
You mean, we destroy the bear from the inside without fighting it at all?!
Right!! Full speed!! Charge!!
ZIP
Hyaah!!
Humph!
Of course, I've already planned for that.
RUMMBLE
And I'll crush you!

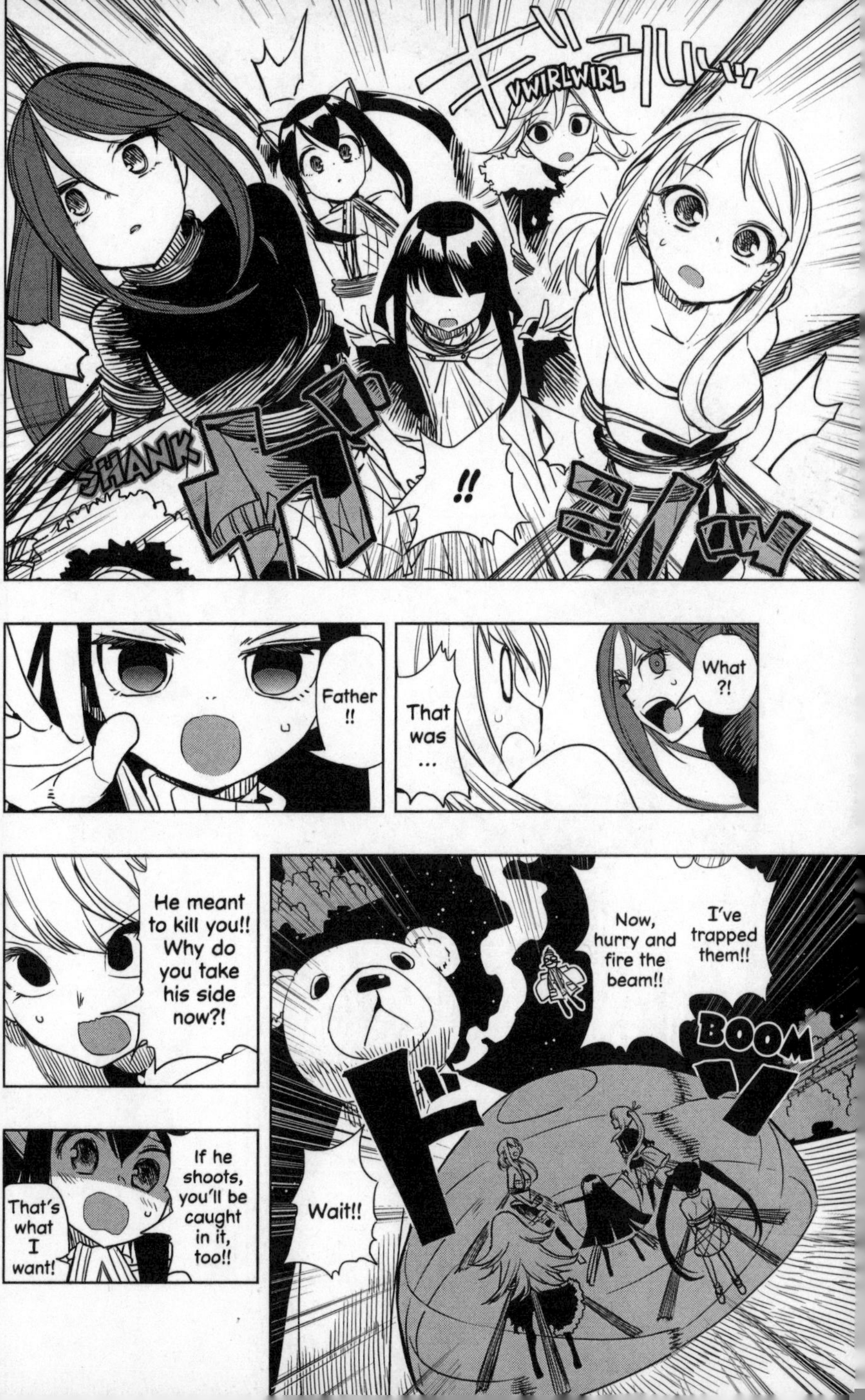
VWIRLWIRL
!!
SHANK
What ?!
That was ...
Father !!
I've trapped them!!
Now, hurry and fire the beam!!
BOOM
Wait!!
He meant to kill you!! Why do you take his side now?!
If he shoots, you'll be caught in it, too!!
That's what I want!

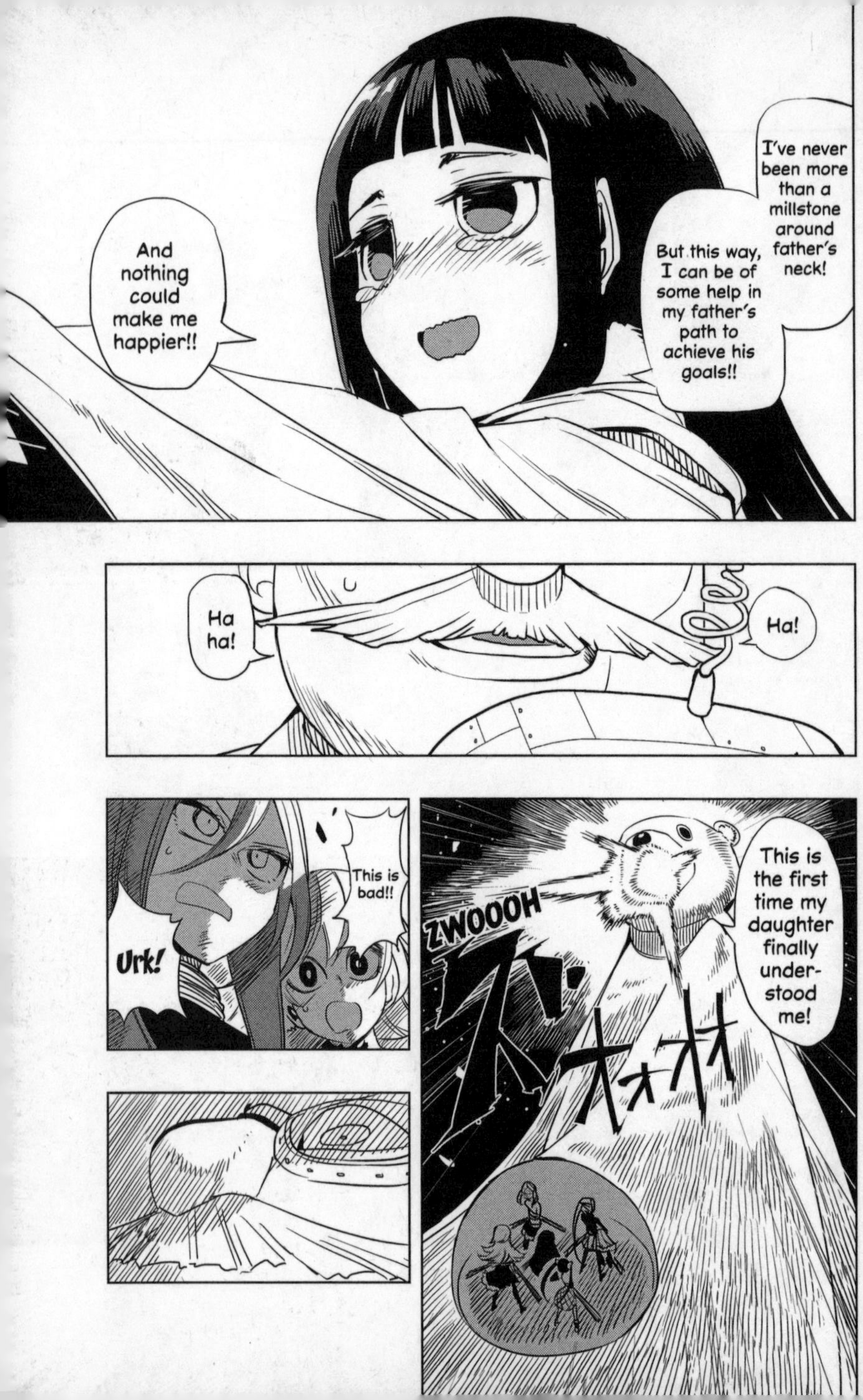
I've never been more than a millstone around father's neck!
But this way, I can be of some help in my father's path to achieve his goals!!
And nothing could make me happier!!
Ha!
Ha ha!
This is the first time my daughter finally understood me!
ZWOOOH
This is bad!!
Urk!

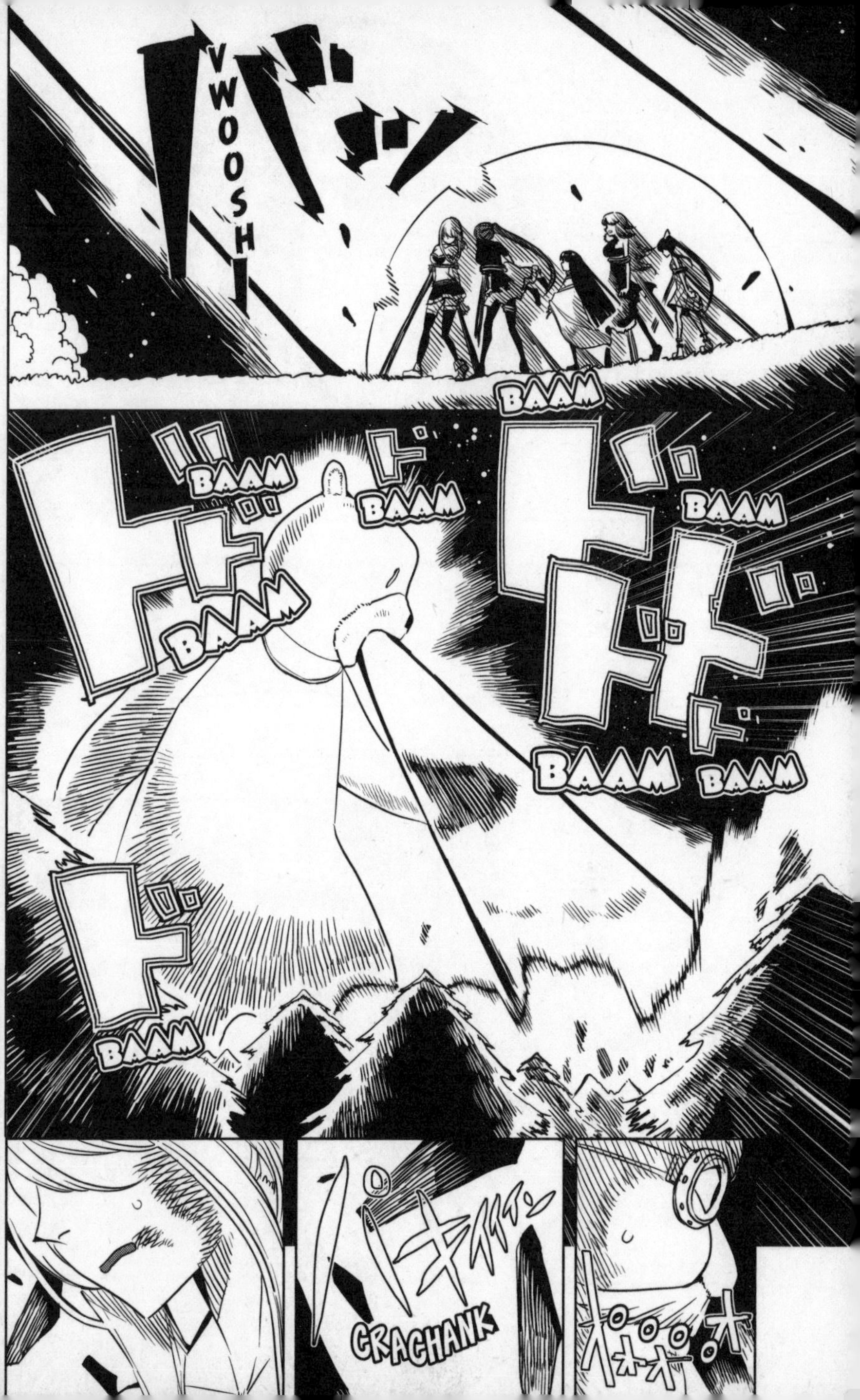
VWOOSH
BAAM
BAAM
BAAM
BAAM
BAAM
BAAM
BAAM
BAAM
BAAM
CRACHANK

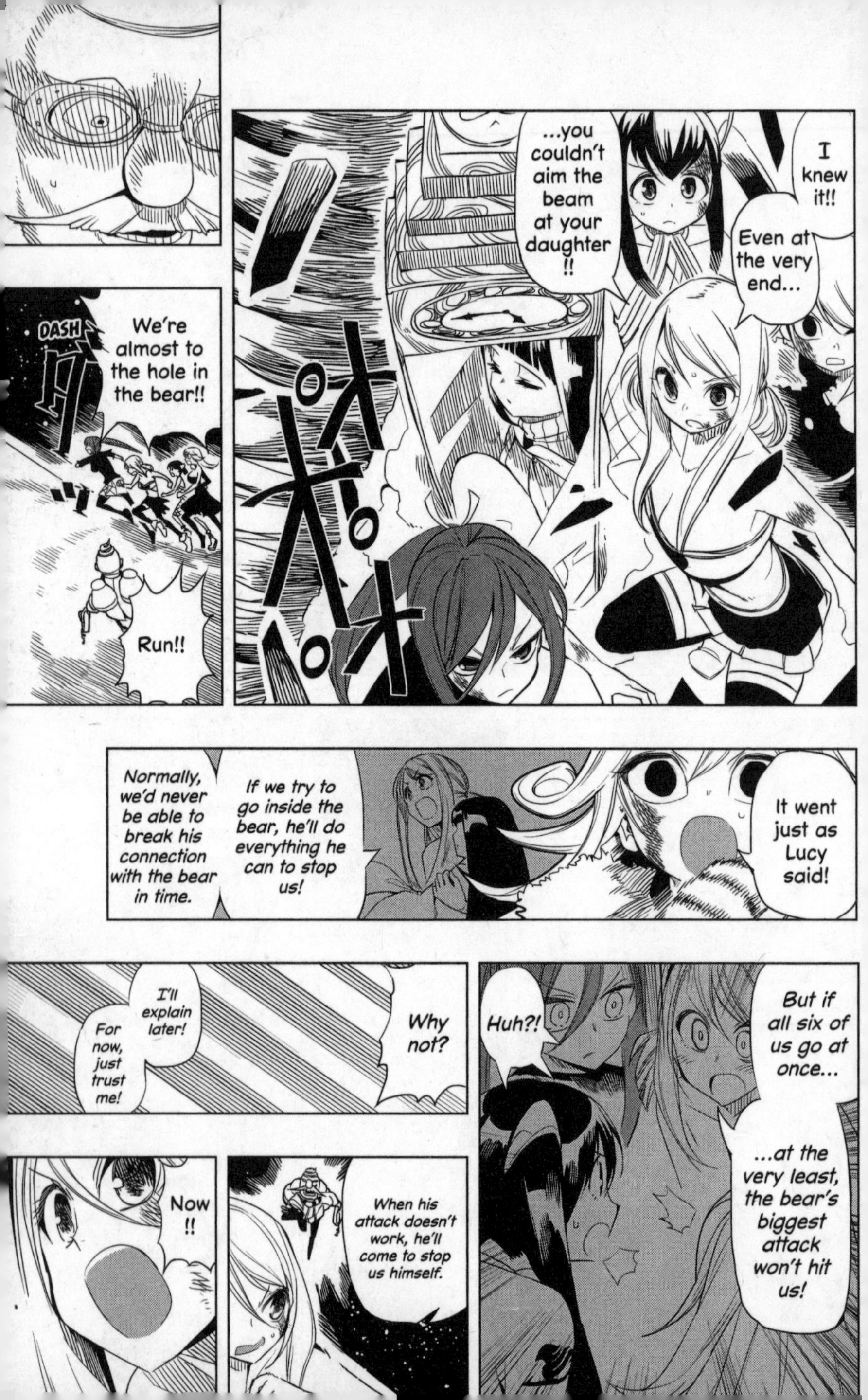
I knew it!!
Even at the very end...
...you couldn't aim the beam at your daughter !!
We're almost to the hole in the bear!!
DASH
Run!!
It went just as Lucy said!
If we try to go inside the bear, he'll do everything he can to stop us!
Normally, we'd never be able to break his connection with the bear in time.
But if all six of us go at once...
Huh?!
...at the very least, the bear's biggest attack won't hit us!
Why not?
I'll explain later!
For now, just trust me!
When his attack doesn't work, he'll come to stop us himself.
Now !!

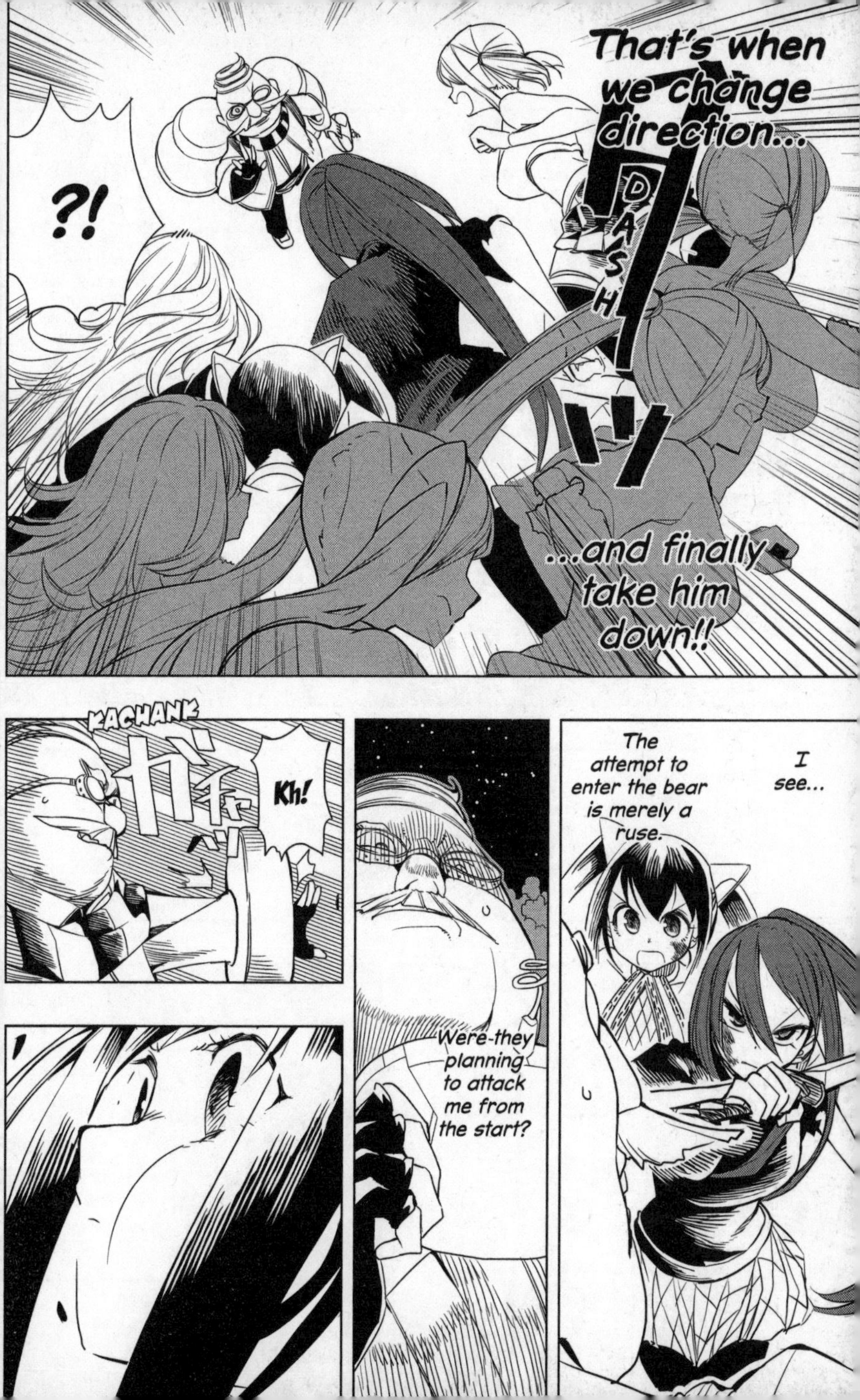
That's when we change direction...
DASH
?!
...and finally take him down!!
I see...
The attempt to enter the bear is merely a ruse.
Were-they planning to attack me from the start?
KACHANK
Kh!

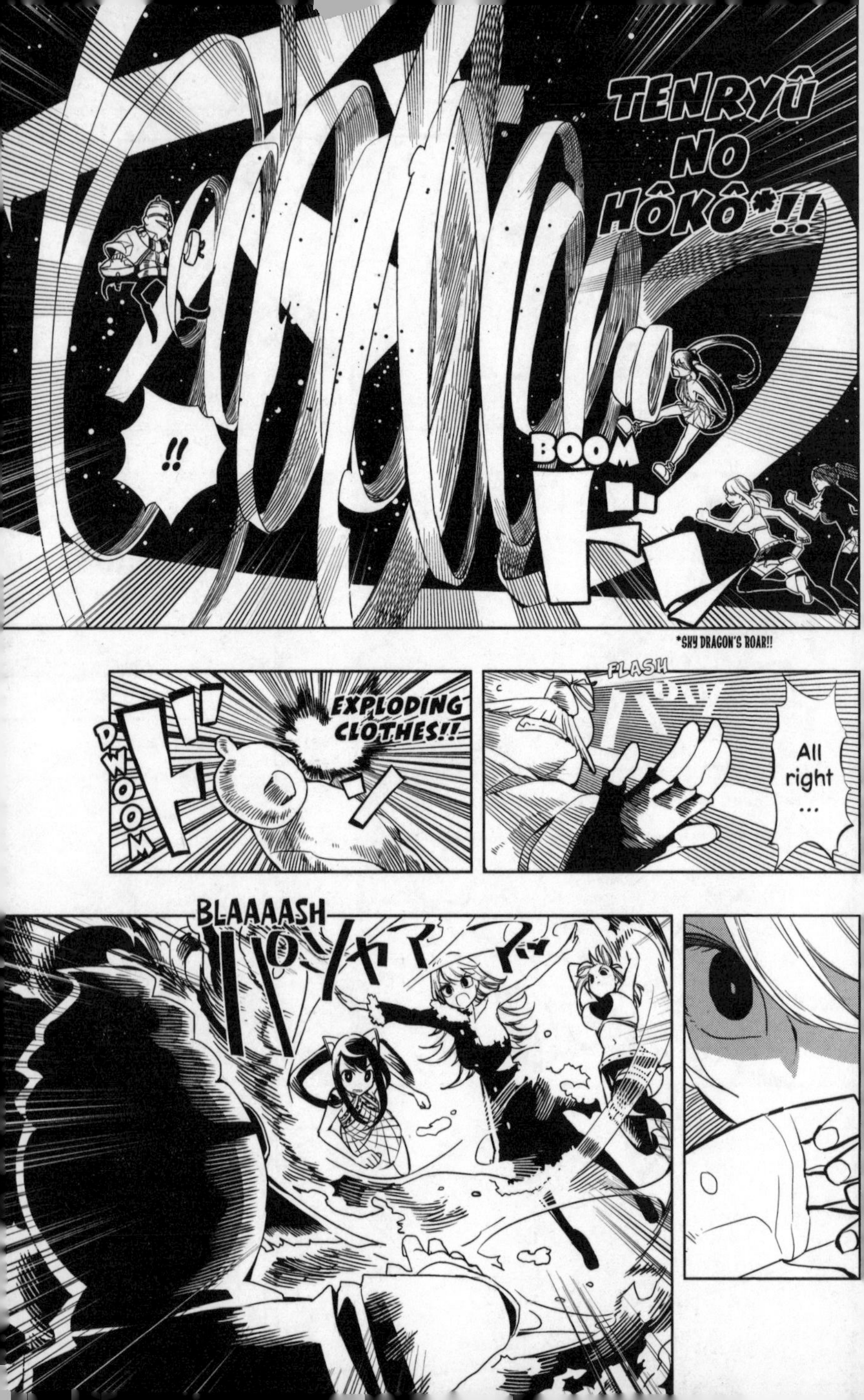
TENRYÛ NO HÔKÔ*!!
BOOM
!!
*SKY DRAGON'S ROAR!!
FLASH
All right ...
EXPLODING CLOTHES!!
DWOOM
BLAAAASH

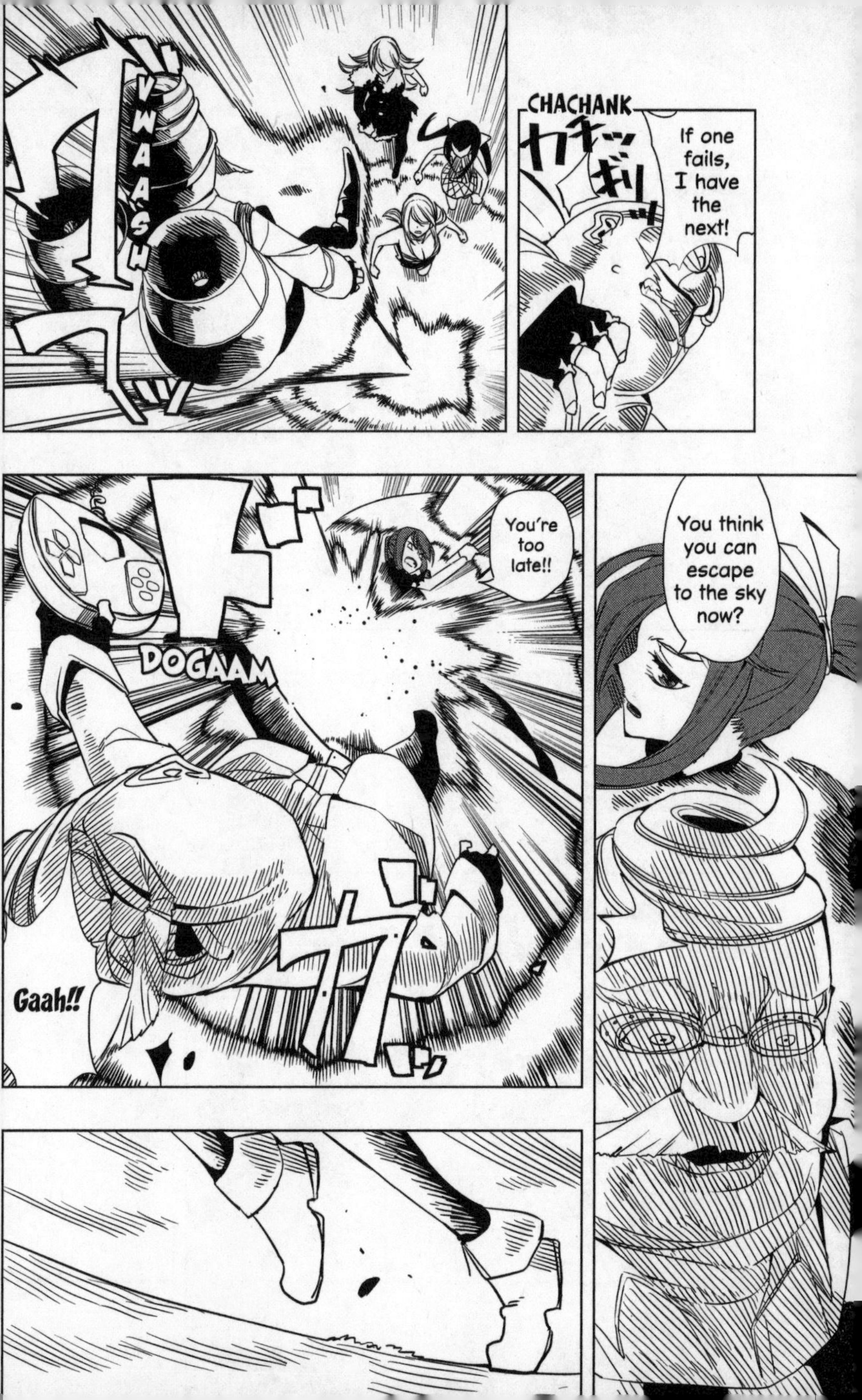
CHACHANK
カチーッ ギリッ
If one fails, I have the next!
VWAASH
You think you can escape to the sky now?
You're too late!!
DOGAAM
Gaah!!

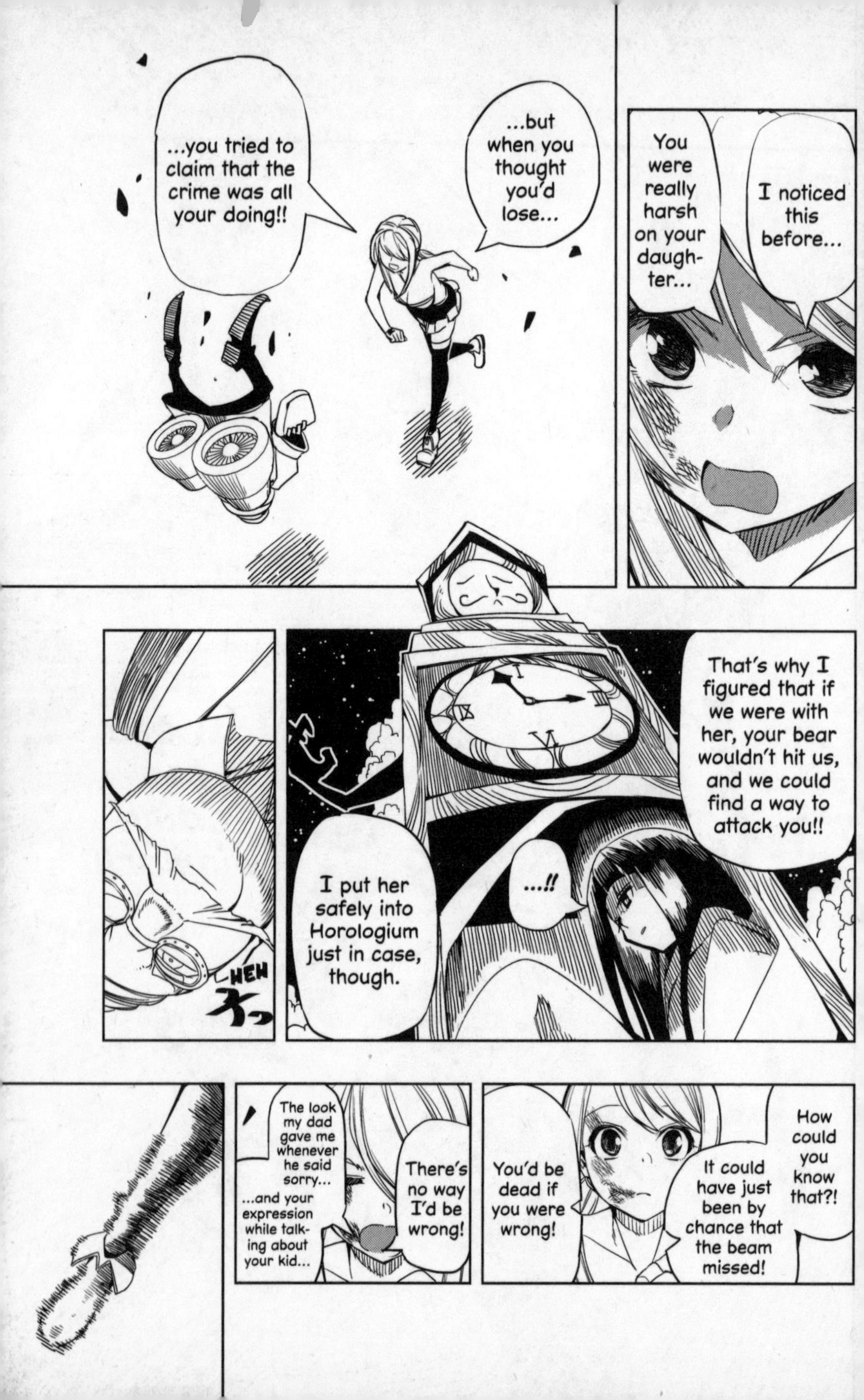
I noticed this before...
You were really harsh on your daughter...
...but when you thought you'd lose...
...you tried to claim that the crime was all your doing!!
That's why I figured that if we were with her, your bear wouldn't hit us, and we could find a way to attack you!!
...!!
I put her safely into Horologium just in case, though.
HEH
How could you know that?!
It could have just been by chance that the beam missed!
You'd be dead if you were wrong!
There's no way I'd be wrong!
The look my dad gave me whenever he said sorry...
...and your expression while talking about your kid...

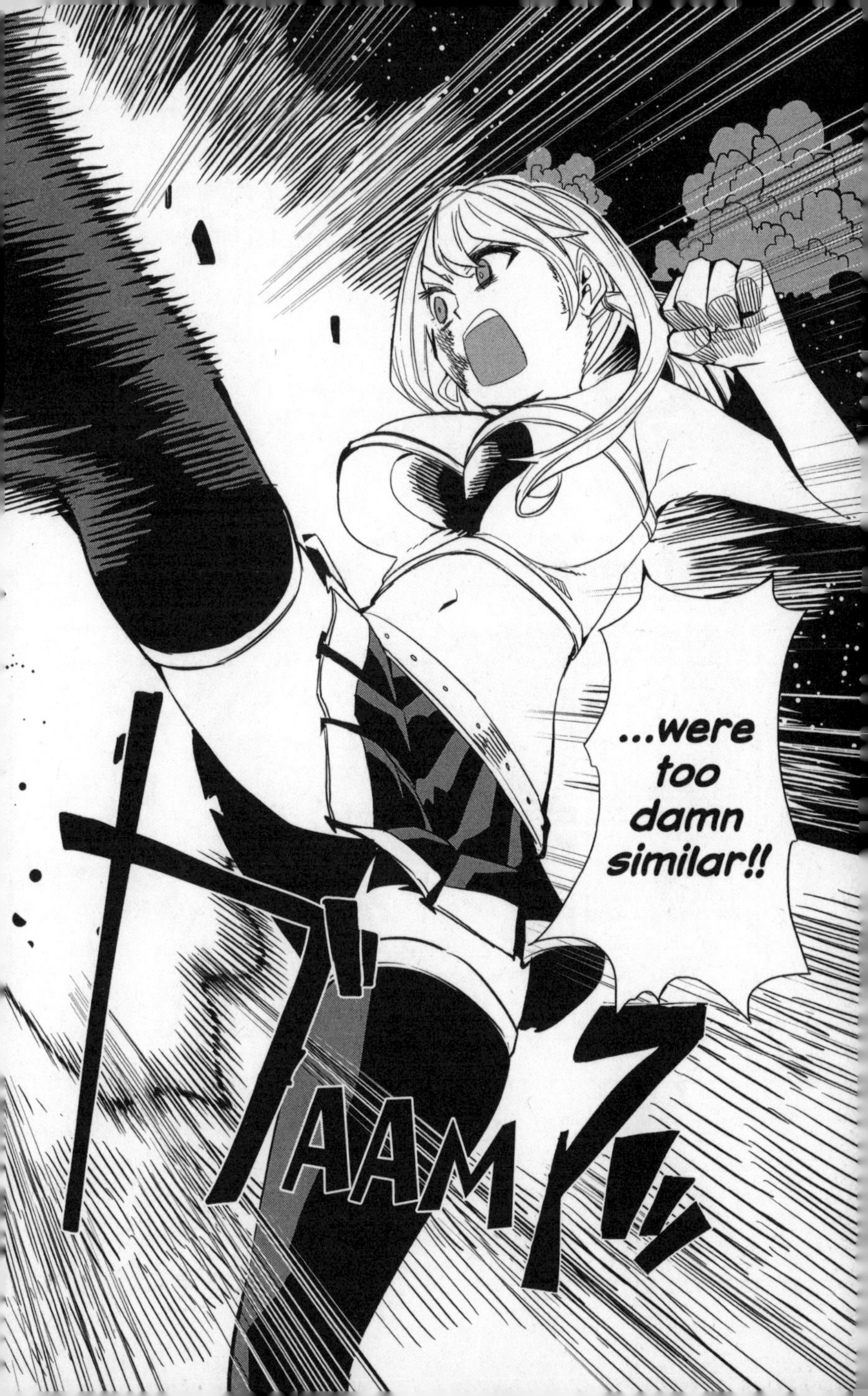
...were too damn similar!!
AAM

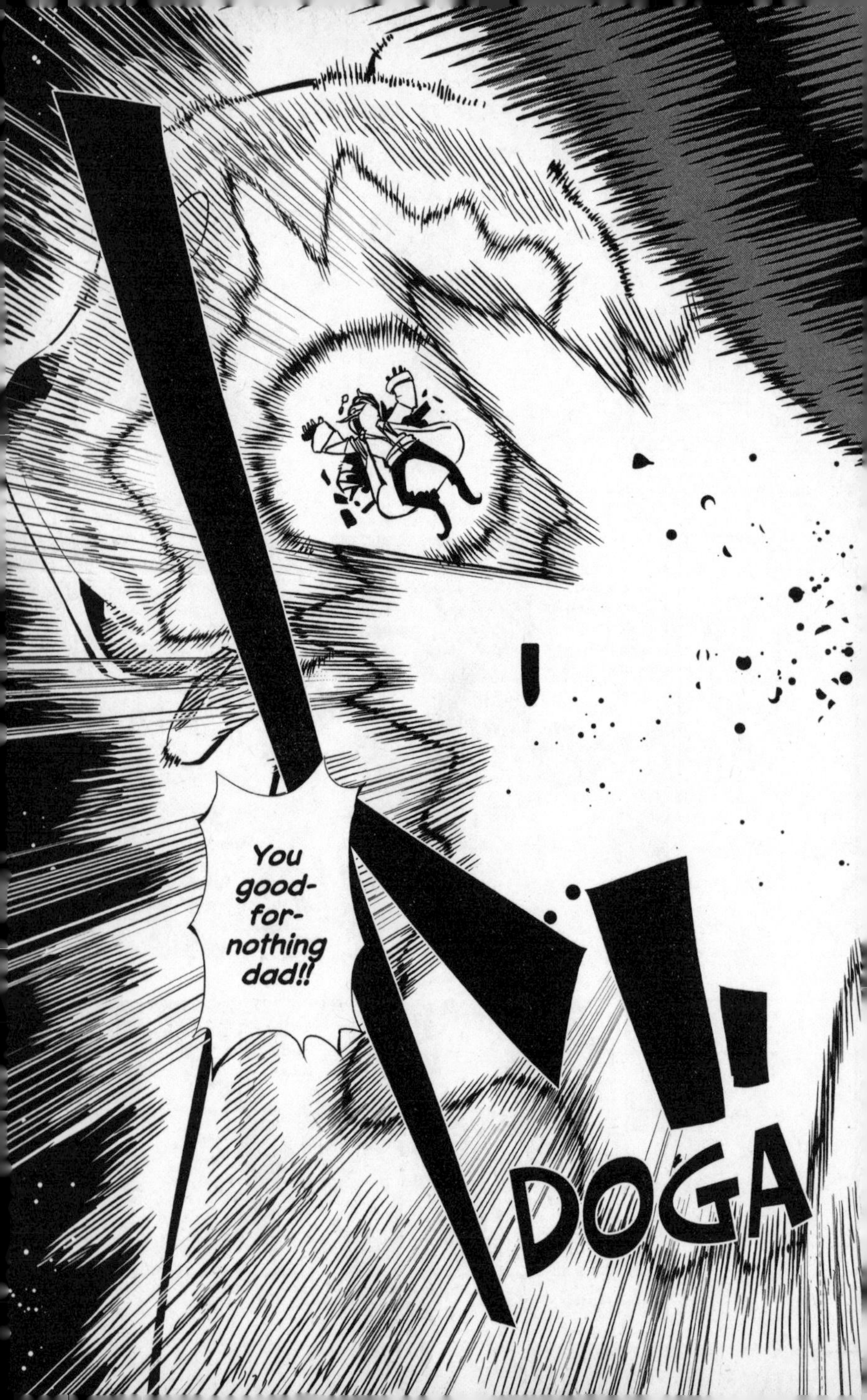
You good-for-nothing dad!!
DOGA

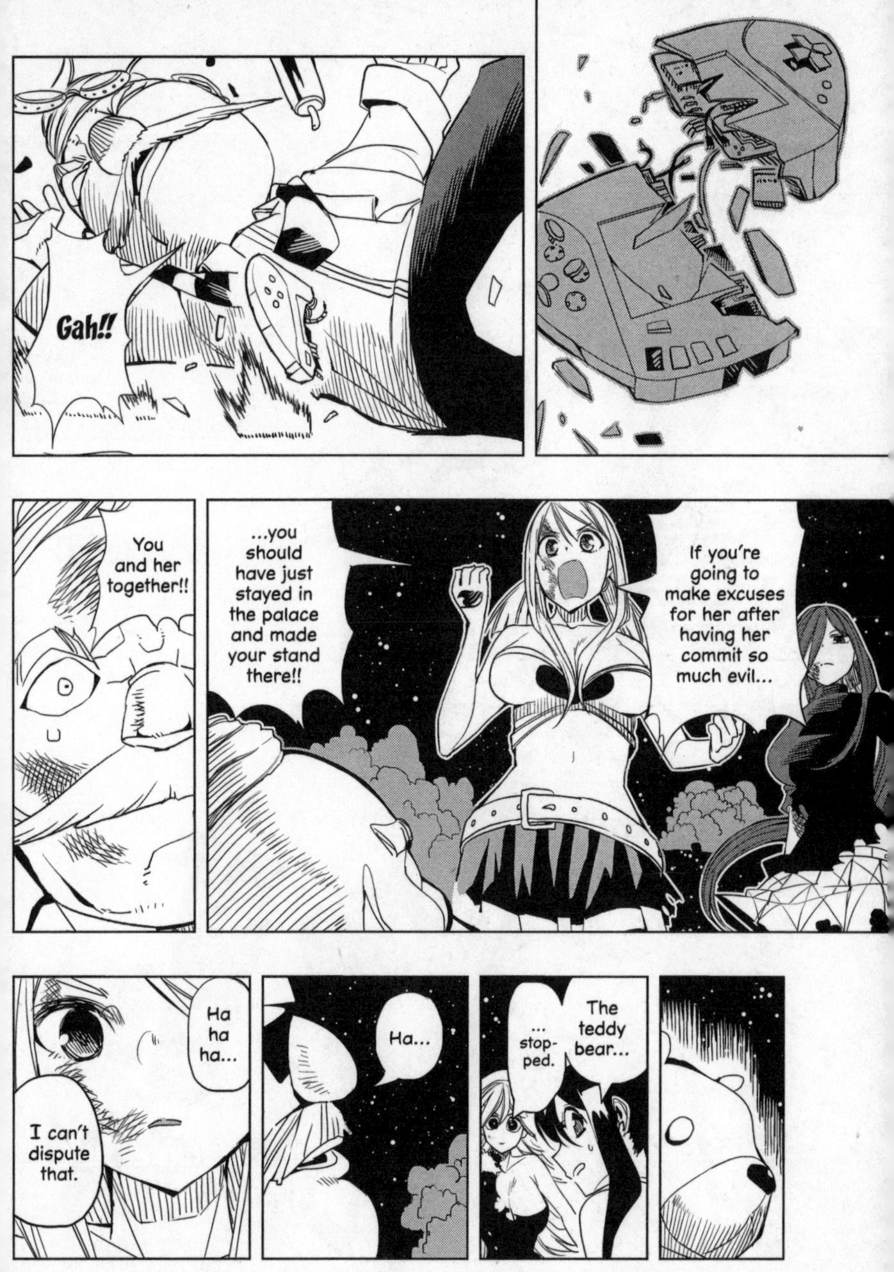
Gah!!
If you're going to make excuses for her after having her commit so much evil...
...you should have just stayed in the palace and made your stand there!!
You and her together!!
The teddy bear...
...stop-ped.
Ha...
Ha ha ha...
I can't dispute that.

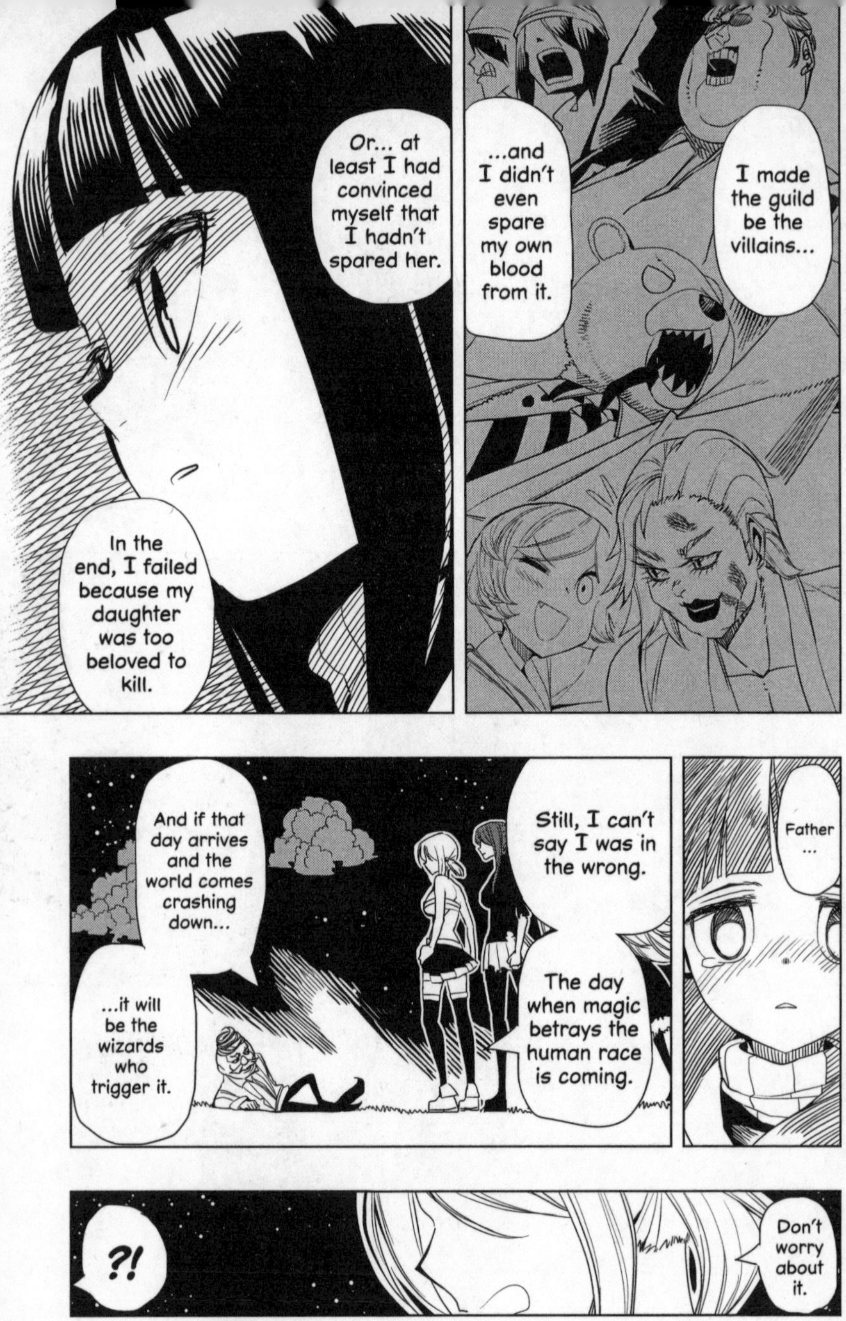
I made the guild be the villains...
...and I didn't even spare my own blood from it.
Or... at least I had convinced myself that I hadn't spared her.
In the end, I failed because my daughter was too beloved to kill.
Father ...
Still, I can't say I was in the wrong.
The day when magic betrays the human race is coming.
And if that day arrives and the world comes crashing down...
...it will be the wizards who trigger it.
Don't worry about it.
?!

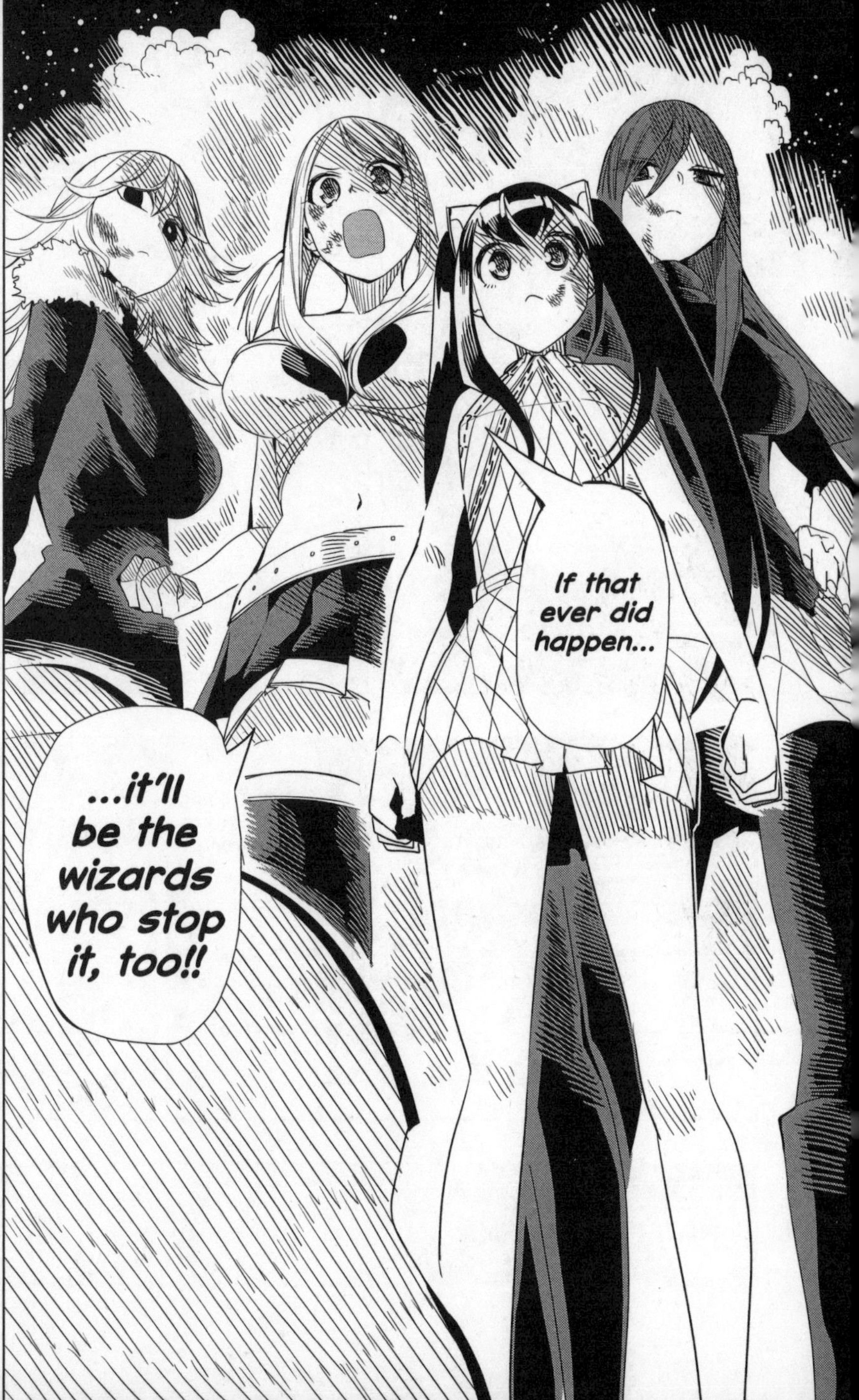
If that ever did happen...
...it'll be the wizards who stop it, too!!

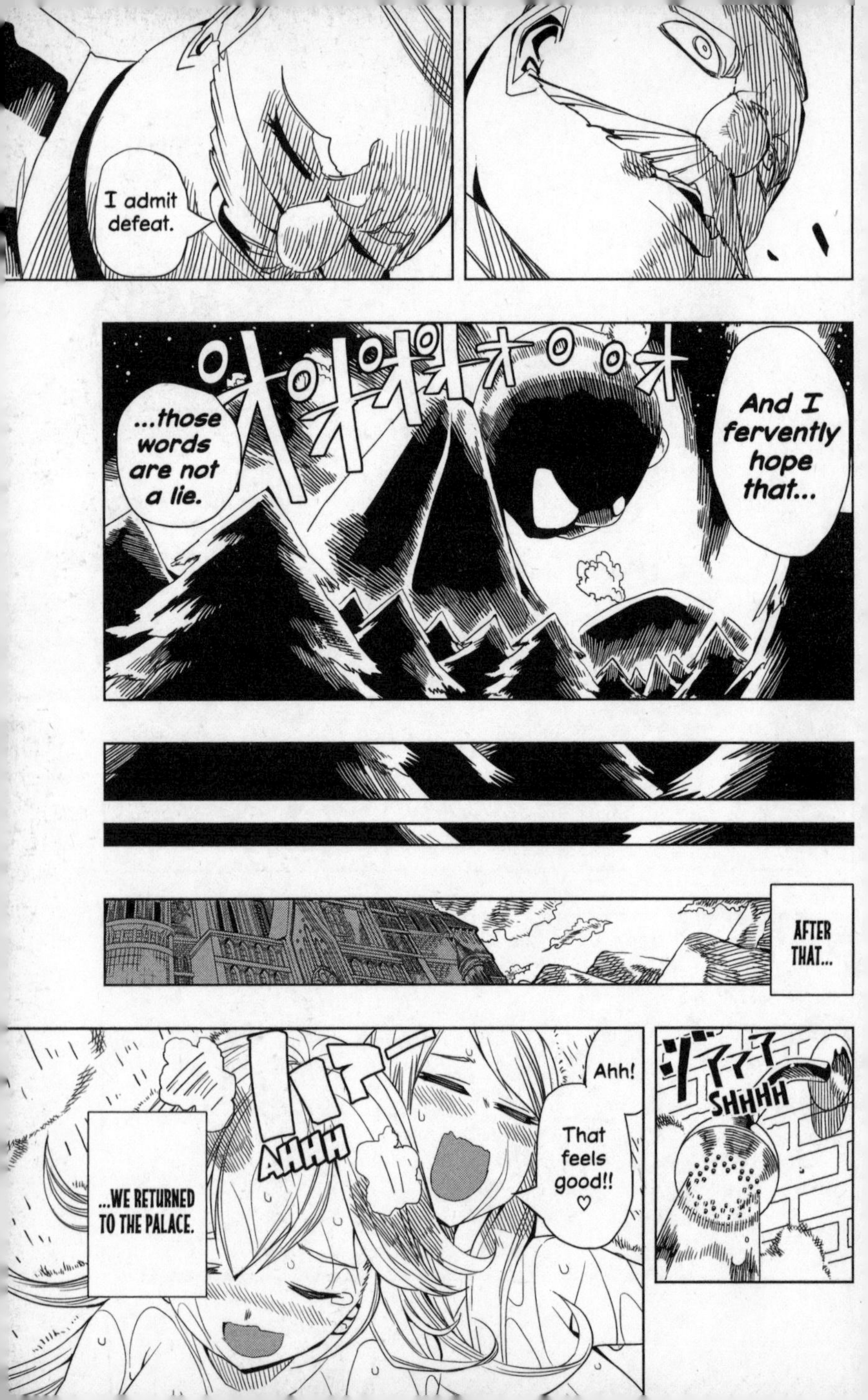
I admit defeat.
And I fervently hope that...
...those words are not a lie.
AFTER THAT...
SHHHH
Ahh! That feels good!! ♡
AHHH
...WE RETURNED TO THE PALACE.

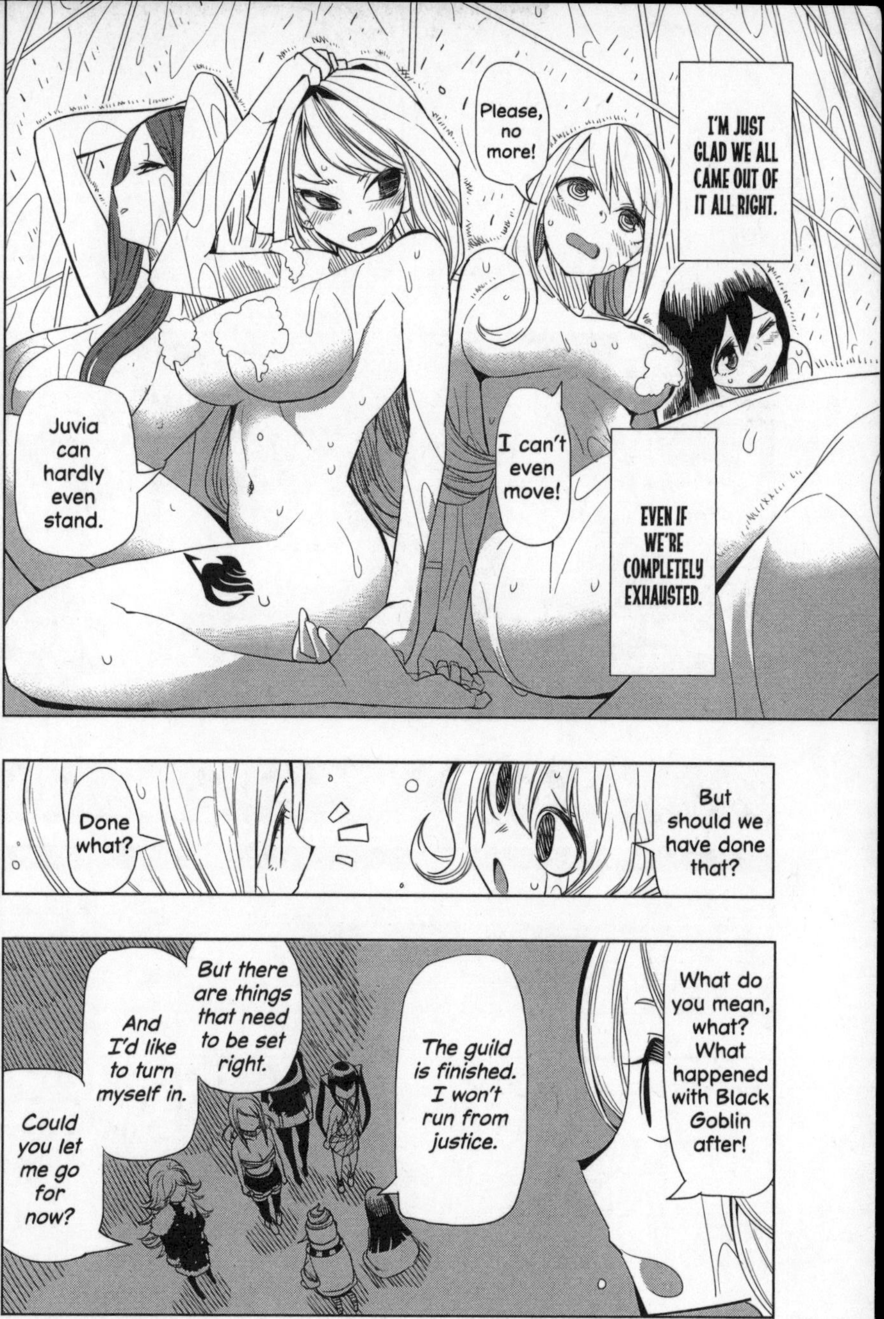
I'M JUST GLAD WE ALL CAME OUT OF IT ALL RIGHT.
Please, no more!
EVEN IF WE'RE COMPLETELY EXHAUSTED.
I can't even move!
Juvia can hardly even stand.
But should we have done that?
Done what?
What do you mean, what? What happened with Black Goblin after!
The guild is finished. I won't run from justice.
But there are things that need to be set right.
And I'd like to turn myself in.
Could you let me go for now?

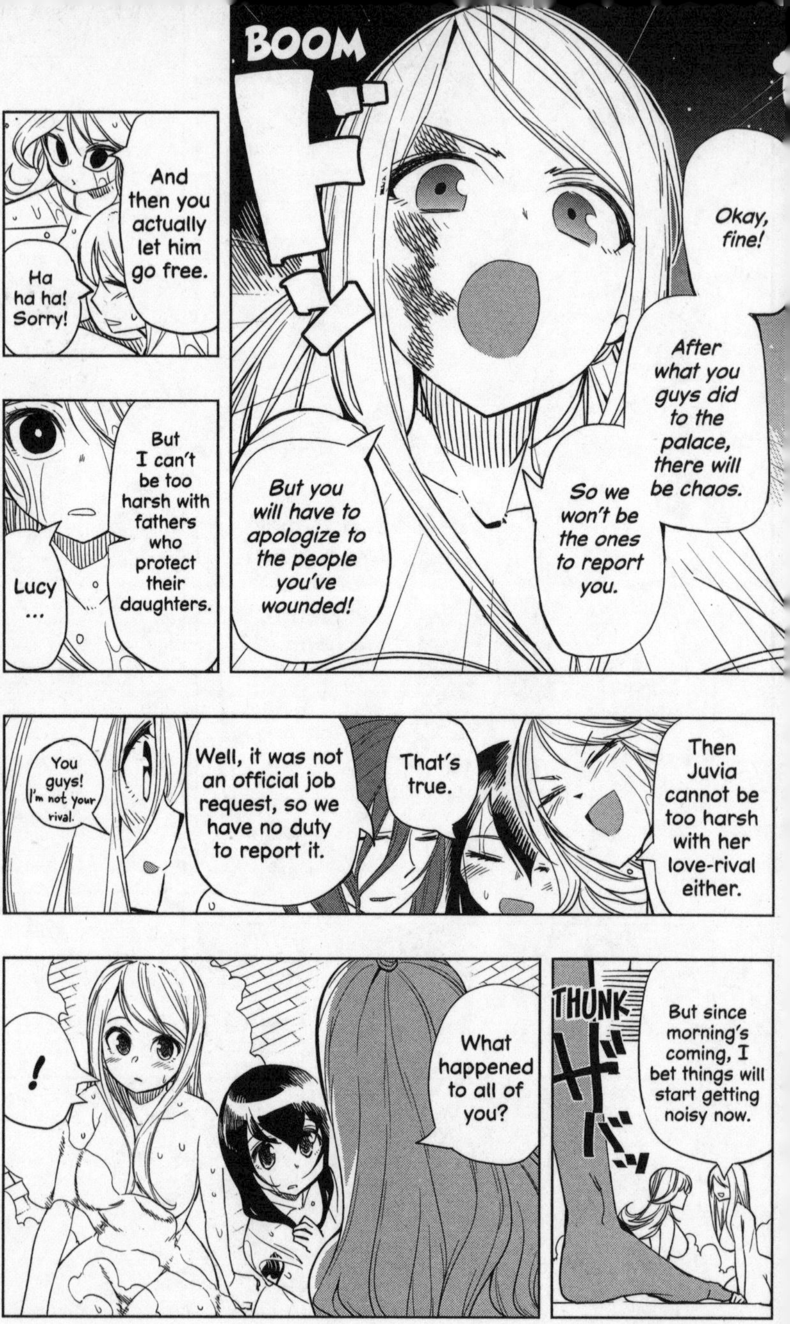
BOOM
Okay, fine!
After what you guys did to the palace, there will be chaos.
So we won't be the ones to report you.
But you will have to apologize to the people you've wounded!
And then you actually let him go free.
Ha ha ha! Sorry!
But I can't be too harsh with fathers who protect their daughters.
Lucy ...
Then Juvia cannot be too harsh with her love-rival either.
That's true.
Well, it was not an official job request, so we have no duty to report it.
You guys! I'm not your rival.
THUNK
But since morning's coming, I bet things will start getting noisy now.
What happened to all of you?
!

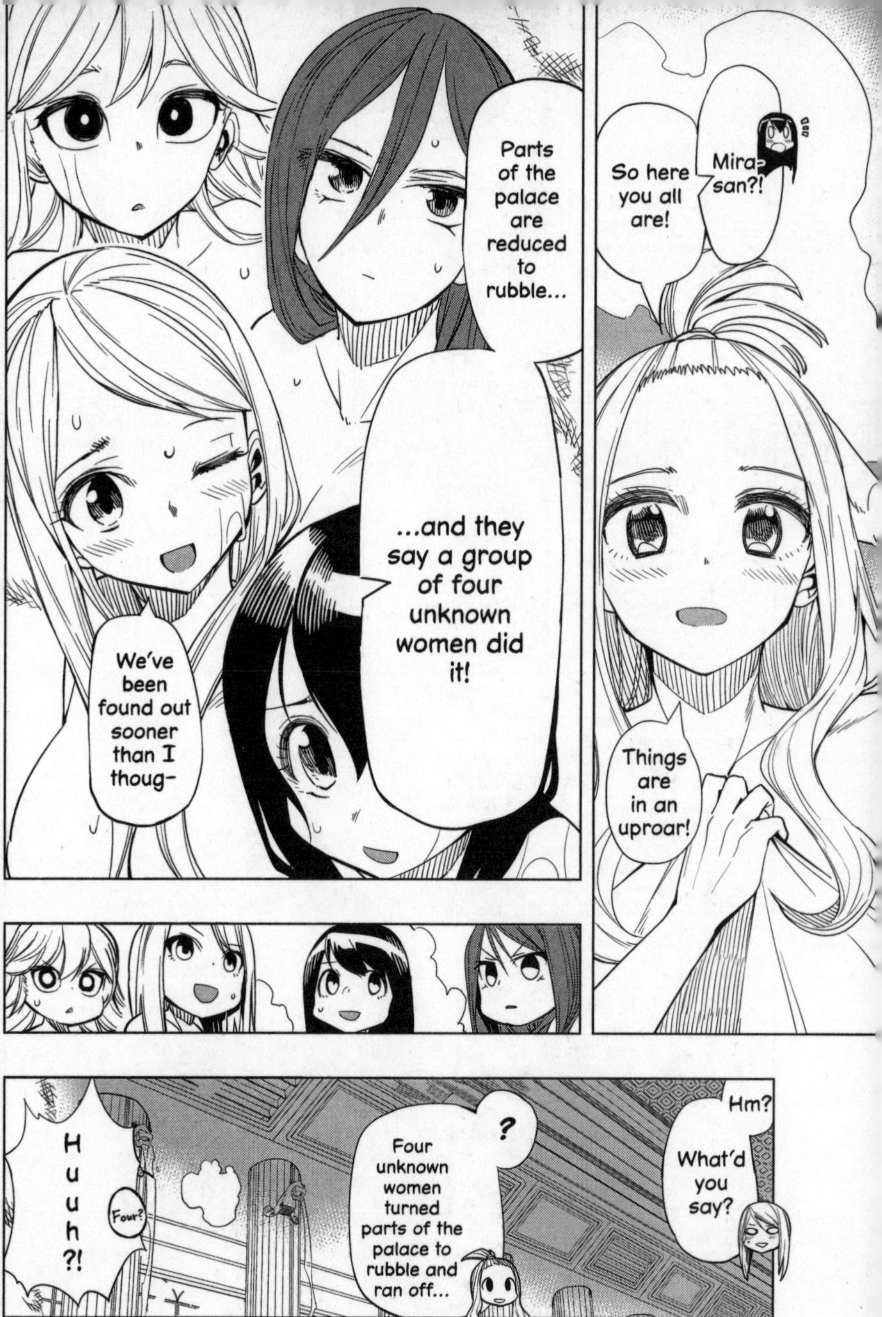
Mira-san?!
So here you all are!
Things are in an uproar!
Parts of the palace are reduced to rubble...
...and they say a group of four unknown women did it!
We've been found out sooner than I thoug-
Hm?
What'd you say?
?
Four unknown women turned parts of the palace to rubble and ran off...
Four?
Huuh?!

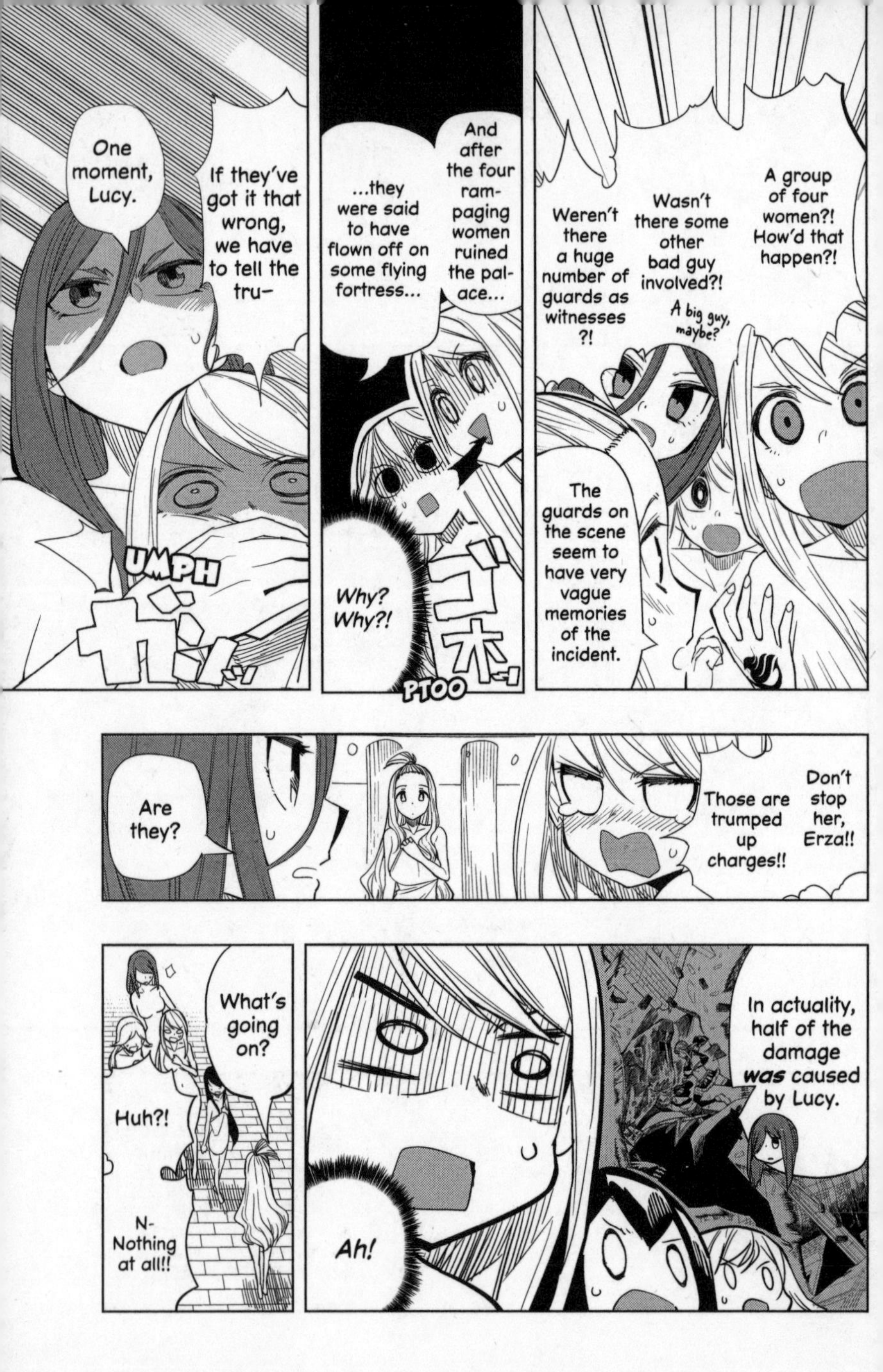
A group of four women?! How'd that happen?!
Wasn't there some other bad guy involved?!
A big guy, maybe?
Weren't there a huge number of guards as witnesses?!
The guards on the scene seem to have very vague memories of the incident.
And after the four ram-paging women ruined the pal-ace...
...they were said to have flown off on some flying fortress...
Why? Why?!
PTOO
If they've got it that wrong, we have to tell the tru–
One moment, Lucy.
UMPH
Don't stop her, Erza!!
Those are trumped up charges!!
Are they?
In actuality, half of the damage *was* caused by Lucy.
Ah!
What's going on?
Huh?!
N- Nothing at all!!

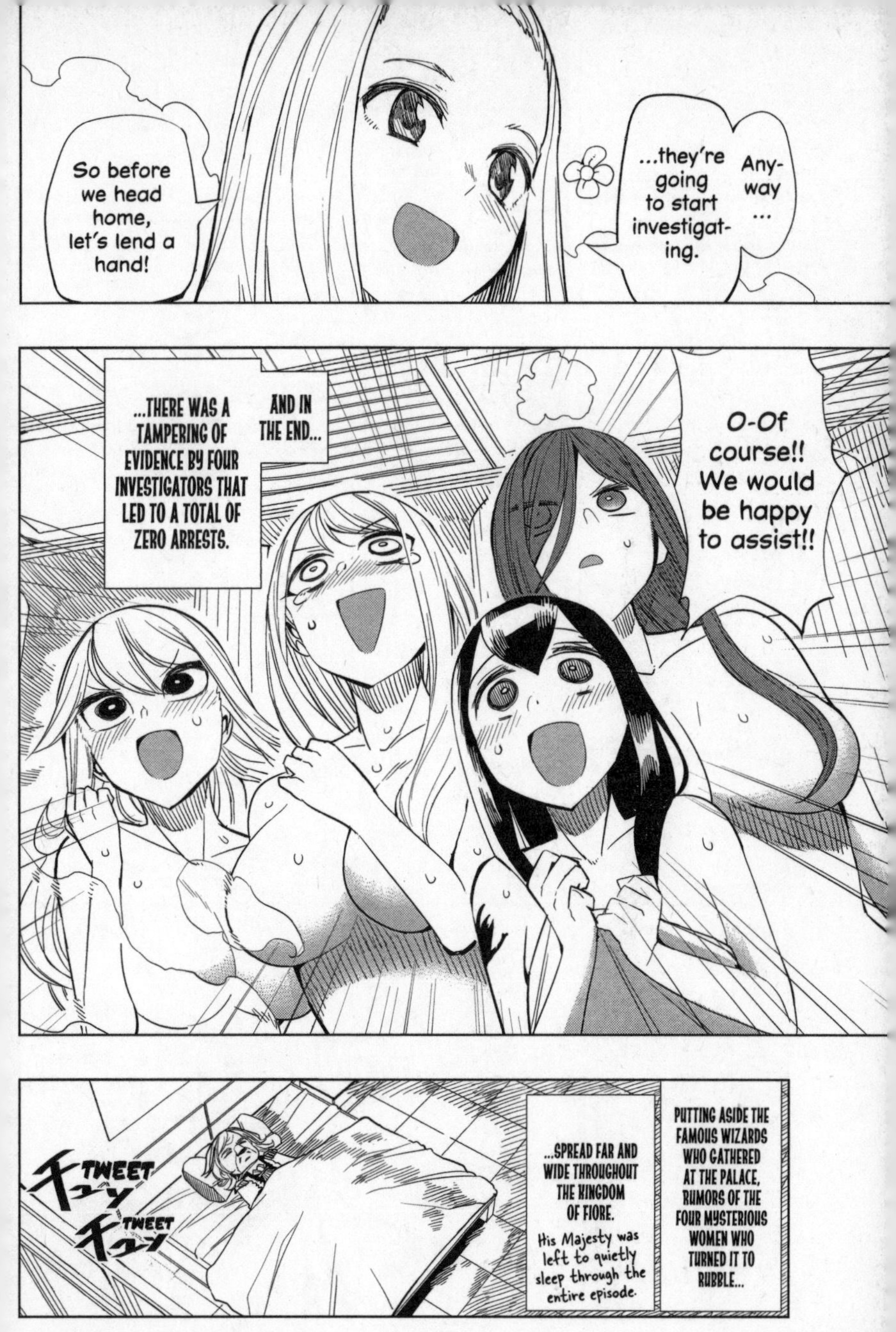
Any-way ...
...they're going to start investigat-ing.
So before we head home, let's lend a hand!
O-Of course!! We would be happy to assist!!
AND IN THE END...
...THERE WAS A TAMPERING OF EVIDENCE BY FOUR INVESTIGATORS THAT LED TO A TOTAL OF ZERO ARRESTS.
PUTTING ASIDE THE FAMOUS WIZARDS WHO GATHERED AT THE PALACE, RUMORS OF THE FOUR MYSTERIOUS WOMEN WHO TURNED IT TO RUBBLE...
...SPREAD FAR AND WIDE THROUGHOUT THE KINGDOM OF FIORE.
His Majesty was left to quietly sleep through the entire episode.
チュン TWEET
チュン TWEET

FAIRY GIRLS

vol.1 ········ END

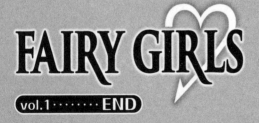

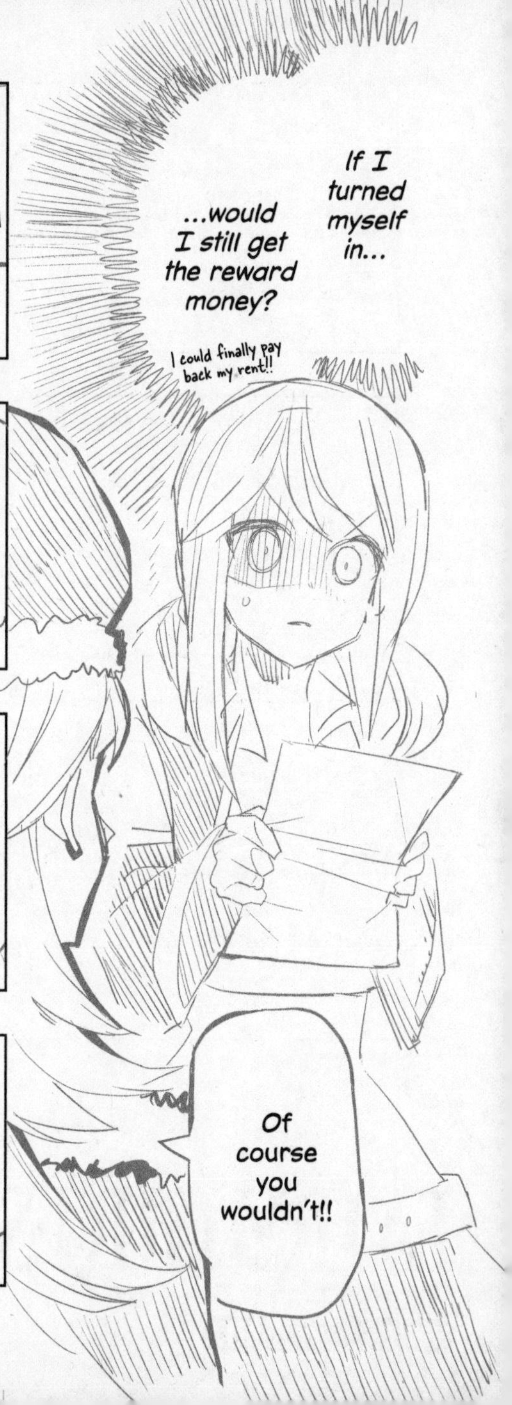
If I turned myself in...
...would I still get the reward money?
I could finally pay back my rent!!
Of course you wouldn't!!

★BONUS★

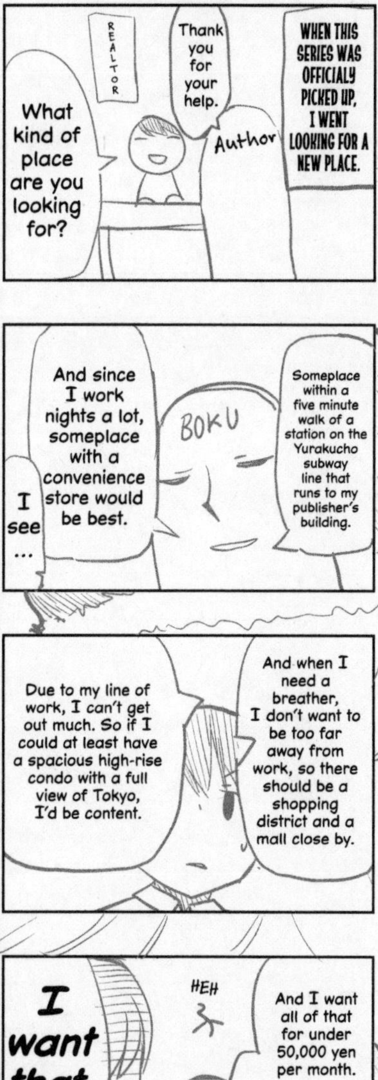
WHEN THIS SERIES WAS OFFICIALY PICKED UP, I WENT LOOKING FOR A NEW PLACE.
Author
Thank you for your help.
REALTOR
What kind of place are you looking for?
Someplace within a five minute walk of a station on the Yurakucho subway line that runs to my publisher's building.
BOKU
And since I work nights a lot, someplace with a convenience store would be best.
I see...
And when I need a breather, I don't want to be too far away from work, so there should be a shopping district and a mall close by.
Due to my line of work, I can't get out much. So if I could at least have a spacious high-rise condo with a full view of Tokyo, I'd be content.
And I want all of that for under 50,000 yen per month.
That includes all fees!
HEH
I want that, too!!
It doesn't exist!
50,000 YEN = ABOUT $500

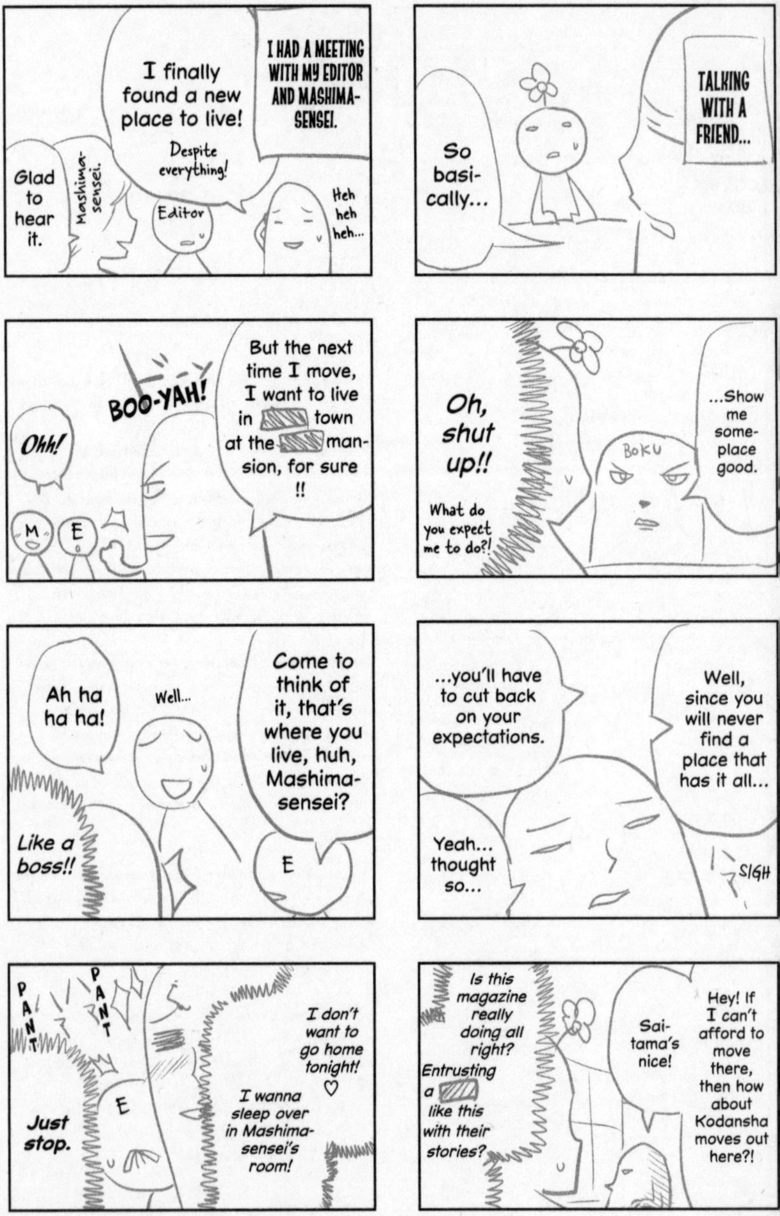
TALKING WITH A FRIEND...
So basically...
I HAD A MEETING WITH MY EDITOR AND MASHIMA-SENSEI.
I finally found a new place to live!
Despite everything!
Heh heh heh...
Editor
Mashima-sensei.
Glad to hear it.
...Show me someplace good.
BOKU
Oh, shut up!!
What do you expect me to do?!
But the next time I move, I want to live in town at the mansion, for sure!!
BOO-YAH!
Ohh!
M
E
Well, since you will never find a place that has it all...
SIGH
...you'll have to cut back on your expectations.
Yeah... thought so...
Come to think of it, that's where you live, huh, Mashima-sensei?
E
Well...
Ah ha ha ha!
Like a boss!!
Hey! If I can't afford to move there, then how about Kodansha moves out here?!
Saitama's nice!
Is this magazine really doing all right?
Entrusting a like this with their stories?
I don't want to go home tonight! ♡
I wanna sleep over in Mashima-sensei's room!
PANT
PANT
E
Just stop.

AFTERWORD

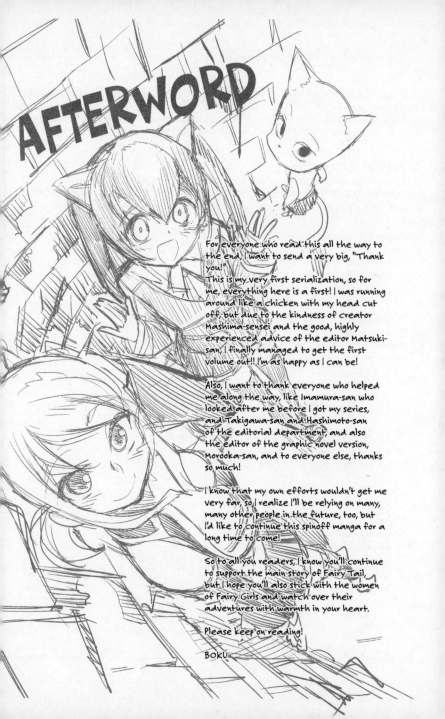

For everyone who read this all the way to the end, I want to send a very big, "Thank you!"
This is my very first serialization, so for me, everything here is a first! I was running around like a chicken with my head cut off, but due to the kindness of creator Mashima-sensei and the good, highly experienced advice of the editor Matsuki-san, I finally managed to get the first volume out!! I'm as happy as I can be!

Also, I want to thank everyone who helped me along the way, like Imamura-san who looked after me before I got my series, and Takigawa-san and Hashimoto-san of the editorial department, and also the editor of the graphic novel version, Morooka-san, and to everyone else, thanks so much!

I know that my own efforts wouldn't get me very far, so I realize I'll be relying on many, many other people in the future, too, but I'd like to continue this spinoff manga for a long time to come!

So to all you readers, I know you'll continue to support the main story of Fairy Tail, but I hope you'll also stick with the women of Fairy Girls and watch over their adventures with warmth in your heart.

Please keep on reading!

BOKU

Translation Notes:

Japanese is a tricky language for most Westerners, and translation is often more art than science. For your edification and reading pleasure, here are notes on some of the places where we could have gone in a different direction with our translation of the work, or where a Japanese cultural reference is used.

Page 12, After party
In Japan, breaking off from a main party or gathering for smaller parties is a very common custom, and each spot they go to is counted as another "party" after the main one, so they can go to third, fourth, and fifth after-parties (or even more).

Page 19, Sweets shops
Although there certainly are brand-name sweets shops in the West, Japan specializes in them with high-quality (and high-priced) sweets such as chocolates or cakes that are exquisitely decorated. Every large department store has several of these in a specialty-foods section; they can also be found in stand-alone shops.

Page 21, Meeting dates and getting picked up
In Japan's dating culture, there are certain locations that are commonly picked as places to meet up with one's date. Since most people use public transportation in urban areas, these meet-up spots are often near train and bus stations. Perhaps the most popular spot like this in Japan is by the famous statue of the dog Hachikō, outside Shibuya station in the Western part of central Tokyo. Bustling places like these are good for pick up artists and flirts. This is because some people go here specifically looking for girls who have been stood up by their date.

Page 56, Communal nighttime bathing
In Japan, it is common to take a bath at night before bed. The palace featured in this manga, like high-quality hot spring hotels, have places for communal bathing, separated by gender. Taking a hot bath in the evening is thought to relax and refresh a person after a long day.

Page 110, Lishia's (the teddy bear's) speech patterns
Like many cutesy Japanese "accents," Lishia's statements have an extra syllable tacked on at the end. This time, the syllable was, "-bu." So this translation substituted the sentence-ending "-bu" with an affect that some English speakers use when attempting to sound cute: changing certain "r" or "l" sounds to "w" sounds.

Fairy Girls volume 1 is a work of fiction. Names, characters, places, and incidents are the products of the author's imagination or are used fictitiously. Any resemblance to actual events, locales, or persons, living or dead, is entirely coincidental.

A Kodansha Comics Trade Paperback Original.

Published in the United States by Kodansha Comics, an imprint of Kodansha USA Publishing, LLC, New York.

Publication rights for this English edition arranged through Kodansha Ltd., Tokyo.

First published in Japan in 2015 by Kodansha Ltd., Tokyo
ISBN 978-1-63236-184-4

Printed in the United States of America.

www.kodanshacomics.com

9 8 7 6 5 4 3 2 1

Translation: William Flanagan
Lettering: AndWorld Design
Editing: Haruko Hashimoto and Ben Applegate
Kodansha Comics edition cover design by Phil Balsman